BEYOND
PHILADELPHIA

BEYOND PHILADELPHIA

The
American Revolution
in the
Pennsylvania Hinterland

Edited by
John B. Frantz and William Pencak

The Pennsylvania State University Press
University Park, Pennsylvania

Library of Congress Cataloging-in-Publication Data

Beyond Philadelphia : the American Revolution in the Pennsylvania Hinterland / edited by
John B. Frantz and William Pencak.
   p.   cm.
   Includes bibliographical references (p.   ) and index.
   ISBN 0-271-01766-X (cloth : alk. paper)
   ISBN 0-271-01767-8 (pbk. : alk. paper)
   1. Pennsylvania—History—Revolution, 1775–1783. I. Frantz, John B. II. Pencak,
William, 1951– .
   E263.P4B54   1998
   973.3'448—dc21   98-13554
                                                              CIP

Published by The Pennsylvania State University Press,
University Park, PA 16802–1003

It is the policy of The Pennsylvania State University Press to use acid-free paper for the
first printing of all clothbound books. Publications on uncoated stock satisfy the minimum
requirements of American National Standard for Information Sciences—Permanence of
Paper for Printed Library Materials, ANSI Z39.48–1992.

Contents

Preface

In 1990, at the annual convocation of the Penn State History Department, the editors of this volume were lamenting the paucity of accessible knowledge about the American Revolution in Pennsylvania apart from state or national politics and what happened in Philadelphia. At the same meeting, we realized that the unpublished work of our colleagues at several campuses in the Penn State system addressed the Revolution in different parts of the state. Using this material as a core, we commissioned others also to write chapters in order to cover as much of the state as possible. With the exception of Gregory Knouff's chapter on Revolutionary soldiers' perceptions of Indians, which serendipitously came our way, we asked all our authors to address specifically (1) the nature of the population and settlement in a particular county or region as of the 1760s; (2) what happened in the Revolution in that area—that is, the nature of the participation in the Revolution and who opposed and supported it; and (3) how the Revolution transformed social, economic, and political life. We hope that these chapters answer these questions for much of Pennsylvania far more thoroughly than before, although, as the Introduction points out, no single pattern describes the entire state's experiences.

We thank John M. Murrin and Robert M. Calhoon for careful, critical readings of the entire manuscript; Paul Douglas Newman and George Franz for astute comments on six chapters given as papers at the 1996 annual meeting of the Pennsylvania Historical Association; and Peter J. Potter and the staff at Penn

State Press for expert and courteous editorial support. David DiBiase and the staff of Deasy GeoGraphics at Penn State, especially Thaddeus Lenker, prepared the fine maps, which enable readers to locate obscure places. We also thank Peggy Hoover for her prompt, easy-to-follow, and thorough copyediting. And we thank Mary Mortensen for preparing the index. The Barra Foundation of Wyndmoor, Pennsylvania, Robert L. McNeil Jr., President, generously funded the production of the maps and the index.

We dedicate this volume to the memory of the late Robert G. Crist, former President of the Pennsylvania Historical Association, indefatigable publisher and promoter of the state's history, and a beloved teacher and colleague at Penn State's Harrisburg and York campuses. His was the first chapter finished, and we regret that he did not live to see the finished product.

Introduction: Pennsylvania and Its Three Revolutions

John B. Frantz   William Pencak

Much has been written about the Revolution in Pennsylvania, but not much of the literature deals with the hinterland. Instead, most historians have directed their attention to Philadelphia.[1] Perhaps this is understandable. The city was the largest in British North America, and the colony's capital. Its attorneys, merchants, and artisans were active in the protests that became the revolt against British rule. It was in Philadelphia that the Continental Congresses met, and there that the delegates declared independence. Nevertheless, only a fraction of the colony's inhabitants lived in the city.[2] The vast majority lived in the hinterland. If the story of the Revolution in Pennsylvania is to have any claim to comprehensiveness, it must include more about what happened outside Philadelphia than heretofore has been available.

From the time William Penn founded Pennsylvania in 1681, to the outbreak of hostilities in 1775, the colony had a lively history. Its location between older settlements to the north, specifically New York, and to the south, Maryland and Virginia, combined with a deepwater port on the Delaware Bay, made it a center of trade. West of the Delaware River, its eastern border, lay fertile soils that were heavily forested on the surface with limestone, iron ore, and other resources beneath, which could sustain agriculture and suggest manufacturing.

The area that became Pennsylvania was sparsely populated when William Penn Jr. first visited this land in 1682. The exact number of Native American

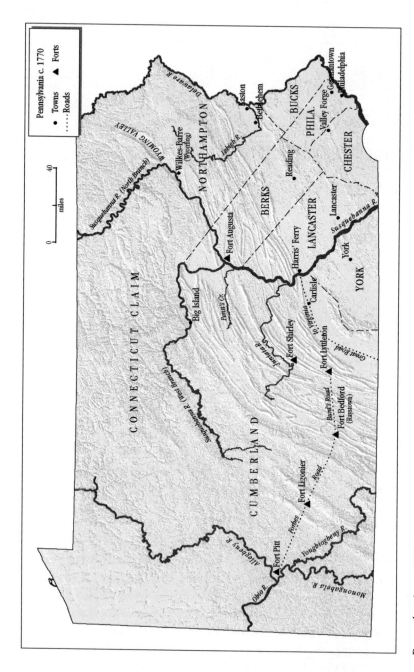

Pennsylvania c. 1770

inhabitants cannot be determined, but there may have been approximately 15,000.[3] Perhaps as many as 1,000 descendants of Dutch and Swedish settlers who had arrived a half-century or so earlier,[4] and English who had more recently spilled over from western New Jersey, also lived on the western bank of the Delaware River.[5]

Pennsylvania's population grew quickly, however. In contrast to the French and the Spanish, British officials placed few restrictions on immigration. Furthermore, Penn aggressively advertised his colony not only among the English but also among Welsh, Scots-Irish, and German-speaking Europeans.[6] His desire for diversity was not only a part of his large-scale real-estate venture but also a dimension of his religious faith as a Friend (Quaker). He wanted to develop what he called "an Holy Experiment" to demonstrate that people of different ethnic and religious backgrounds could live together harmoniously without repressive economic, political, and religious restrictions.[7] A multitude of Europeans responded to Penn's invitation—3,000 in the first few years. By 1700, Pennsylvania's population had increased to about 30,000, and by 1776 it may have been as large as 300,000, including about 11,000 African slaves, making it one of the largest British colonies in America.[8]

With few exceptions, Pennsylvania colonists settled in the southeastern quarter of the province, with the largest single concentration of more than 20,000 in Philadelphia, although there were other urban communities as well. Upland, on the Delaware, was an early Swedish town that became Chester under the English. Lancaster, due west of Philadelphia, emerged in the 1730s and became one of the largest inland towns in the colonies. Reading, on the Schuylkill, and York, west of the Susquehanna, also became significant after the mid-eighteenth century. Despite the importance of these cities and towns, approximately 90 percent of the inhabitants lived in rural areas, and many on farms that averaged not more than a few hundred acres.[9] They poured rapidly into the rich hinterland like beer spilled on a plastic tabletop.

Pennsylvania's farmers were essential to the colony's economic development. For example, they fed its commerce, providing especially grain products that made it the "breadbasket of America" by 1700, well before large numbers of German-speaking agriculturalists brought their productive methods into the interior. Farmers took their grain to mills that were powered by water from the numerous streams, and had it ground into flour, which was basic to the breads, rolls, and biscuits that Philadelphia's merchants shipped to the West Indies. In urban marketplaces, artisans bought the farmers' food products, enabling townsfolk to specialize more exclusively on their crafts. Even the iron "plantations" that proliferated in the eighteenth century, making the colony America's leading iron producer, had contingents of farmers to feed the miners, charcoal burners, and other workers.[10]

For some immigrants, Pennsylvania was a land of opportunity. One called it "the best poor man's country."[11] Except for slaves, the colony's society was mobile. Families could enter the colony with few resources and advance socioeconomically. Some arrived as indentured servants, worked for their "masters" for a short period of time, received "freedom dues" of land or tools of their trade, and moved up into the middle class.[12]

Cheap land and low provincial taxes, due in part to the lack of a military establishment in the pacifistic Quaker colony, also facilitated personal economic advancement. Penn's separation of the church from the civil government, which he wrote indelibly into his frames of government, meant that there could be no ecclesiastical taxes. Land prices were low for those who went through the formality of buying property, and nonexistent for "squatters," who simply resided temporarily on one tract after another, often moving farther and farther into the interior.[13] The abundance of land facilitated the geographic mobility of both purchasers and nonpurchasers. Lutheran pastor Henry Melchior Muhlenberg noted that half of his Providence (Trappe) congregation had either "died or moved away" within a decade of his 1742 arrival.[14]

Land ownership was the hallmark of prestige. As a result, some artisans abandoned their crafts and joined the ranks of farmers in the interior.[15] It was possible for urbanites also to advance while remaining in the city, as the Bostonian emigrant to Philadelphia Benjamin Franklin demonstrated.[16]

The ownership of property, 50 acres of land, or possession of other kinds of property worth 50 British pounds, qualified adult males to vote.[17] Liberal naturalization laws passed by the British Parliament and the provincial legislature enabled even non-Britishers to exercise the franchise. Before the French and Indian War, the bastion of support for the dominant Quaker party was German-speaking men who approved of light taxes and pacifism toward the Indians.[18] Although men with little property could vote, they usually elected to office well-to-do candidates. This was no modern democracy, but what J. R. Pole called a society of "deference."[19]

Whether politics in Pennsylvania were more "factious" than politics in other colonies is an open question.[20] It is certain, however, that from the beginning divisive issues abounded. Controversy over the proprietor's authority led Penn to give up, in his Second Frame of Government (1683), the three votes he held in the legislature's upper house according to his First Frame of Government (1682). Opposition to that body's legislative authority resulted in its elimination in the 1701 "Charter of Privileges." Pressed for funds, Penn claimed that the colony's legislature should assume its administrative costs and that settlers who bought land should pay a "quit rent," an annual charge that dated back to the Middle Ages, but neither paid regularly.[21] Some colonists urged the expansion of paper currency, while others objected, and it may not have been a class issue. The most prominent and pervasive issue throughout Pennsylvania's first seventy-five years was military defense, first against the Spaniards in the East and later against the French and the Indians in the North and the West. Should there be a military establishment at all? And if so, how much, and who should pay for it? In the middle decades of the eighteenth century, assemblymen argued about continuing the proprietorship; opponents claimed that a royal government would provide more effective protection.[22]

Philadelphians were more involved in most of these issues than hinterland residents, and that was natural. After all, the city was the colony's cultural center as well as its political capital. James Logan, secretary to the proprietary family, was prominent in both aspects, as were, later, Franklin and William Smith, provost of the College of Philadelphia. The names of Philadelphians Joseph Galloway and John Dickinson became household words in provincial politics. Of the interior's inhabitants, possibly only Conrad Weiser, the chief Indian negotiator, who lived west of Reading, achieved comparable fame.[23] News of world events usually reached the city first with traders and other travelers. Philadelphia newspapers then spread the word. In 1719, Andrew Bradford began to publish his newspaper, *The American Mercury*. Others, such as Samuel Keimer, Franklin, and David Hall, followed a few years later. The Christopher Sauers I, II, and III, as well as Henry Miller, printed German-language papers. Until the end of the eighteenth century, the interior had only one newspaper, and that was a biweekly that lasted only from 1751 until 1752.[24]

As the province's hub of politics, trade, and information, Philadelphia residents were the first Pennsylvanians to respond to the British officials' revision of colonial policy in 1763, after the French and Indian War. For the British, this conflict was a "Great War for the Empire" that they fought in Asia, Africa, and the Caribbean, as well as in North America. On this continent, the British did for their colonists what they could not or would not do for themselves—defend their frontiers. The Treaty of Paris that ended the war in 1763 required the French to surrender Canada, which the British hoped would secure the borders of British America from further attacks by Indians allegedly aroused by the French.

During the war, the British resented the colonists' failure to enlist insufficiently large numbers in their armies, to provide supplies, and to refrain from illegal shipments of food to the Dutch West Indies, which, they charged, eventually went to French troops. Consequently, they determined to forbid the colonists' expansion beyond the Appalachian Mountains and to station troops in the American colonies to prevent Indian wars. Britain also cracked down on illegal trade and determined to collect a colonial revenue to reduce the wartime indebtedness and to pay the costs of administering and defending their enlarged empire.[25]

Through the years, historians have written in detail about Philadelphians' reactions to these British innovations. Thomas P. Abernethy noted that the Proclamation of 1763 did not prevent restless adventurers like Daniel Boone, born in Berks County in 1734, from moving through the Cumberland Gap into the Kentucky country, although it did alarm land speculators like "Franklin and His Friends," who could not buy and sell western lands legally.[26] Marc Egnal attributed the revolt to the leadership of such urban "expansionists."[27]

Curtailment of western expansion was soon followed by other measures designed to bring the colonies into line. Parliament's Sugar Act (1764) provided for more vigorous enforcement of trade restrictions and established a three-penny-per-gallon tax on all molasses, which could not be evaded.

The Stamp Act of 1765, a more obvious measure that taxed legal transactions and publications, sparked even more widespread dissatisfaction in the city. It aroused Pennsylvania assemblymen to inform their agent in London that they and no one else would tax the colony's residents.[28] Edmund S. Morgan called it the "Prologue to the Revolution" and described how a mob of Philadelphians took to the streets, threatened to tear down the house of "Distributor of the Stamps" John Hughes, and prevented him from implementing the tax.[29] Repeal of the measure, and substitution of the Declaratory Act in 1766, in which Parliament claimed the right to "bind" the colonies but did nothing for the moment, quieted the controversy temporarily.

The Townshend Duties, which followed in 1767, taxed numerous goods that the colonists imported from Britain. Philadelphians protested once again with riots. The organization of boycotts against British imports—described in detail by Thomas Doerflinger[30]—and committees of artisans to enforce them, have been discussed best by Richard Ryerson.[31] The committees soon spurned their traditional upper-class leaders and increasingly expressed hostility to both the city's elite and the British officials.[32] Pennsylvania's most famous response to the Townshend Acts, however, came from an intellectual politician. John Dickinson's masterful "Letters from a Farmer in Pennsylvania," published first serially in almost all American newspapers in 1767–68, and then in pamphlet form, explained that taxation by Parliament was unprecedented and unconstitutional because it was passed without the colonists' consent. He advocated a return to the "federal" empire where Parliament controlled the external affairs of the colonies and the provincial legislatures handled internal matters, such as levying taxes.[33]

Elimination of the Townshend Duties in 1770, except for the tax on tea, restored a measure of quiet to Philadelphia. Had it not been for Parliament's attempt in 1773 to assist the ailing East India Company by lowering the duty on tea while giving the company a monopoly on tea sales in America, the city might have remained calm. Benjamin Labaree has described how Boston's "Sons of Liberty" unloaded the tea ships there by tossing the tea into the harbor. Parliament retaliated promptly in early 1774 by passing the Coercive Acts, labeled "intolerable" by the colonists, practically closing the port of Boston, restricting local government in Massachusetts, and allowing colonial resistance leaders to be taken to England for trial. Just as promptly, Paul Revere rode into Philadelphia to relate the Bostonians' plight.[34]

Thereafter, British Americans moved rapidly toward a full-scale revolt. The First Continental Congress gathered in the city's newly constructed Carpenters Hall in September of that year to protest British actions. The Second Continental Congress followed a year later, meeting in the provincial capitol building, just a few weeks after British regulars and Massachusetts Minutemen clashed at Lexington and Concord. A popular pamphlet, *Common Sense,* written by a newly arrived immigrant to Philadelphia, Tom Paine, and published in early 1776 may have helped radicals in the Congress, such as Samuel and John Adams, to join with counterparts in the city to overwhelm moderates and conservatives. Pennsylvania's delegates, previously among the most reluctant, voted with others for independence.[35]

Pennsylvania's Assembly, however, never endorsed their decision. Angered that this elite body, dominated by Quakers and their allies from the three oldest counties—Bucks, Chester, and Philadelphia—would not vote for independence, Philadelphia's Committee of Privates declared the government vacant. In late

June 1776, they called a convention to which the hinterland responded. Only Associators who abjured allegiance to the crown and swore an oath of belief in the Holy Trinity (eliminating Quakers) could vote for the new legislature.

Pennsylvania's new constitution was the most radical and controversial of all the states. A unicameral legislature was chosen by all oath-taking taxpayers and their sons over the age of twenty-one. The assembly increased in size from thirty-nine to seventy-four, with representation now weighted toward the more Revolutionary western counties. Legislators could serve only four years out of seven; galleries in the statehouse were opened to the public to ensure account-ability; and laws (except in emergencies) had to be approved by two sessions in a row so voters could inform legislators if they approved of their actions. A council and president had little power. The only institutional check on the assembly came from a Council of Censors, elected by the voters every seven years, which could call the people's attention to abuses of public office or to laws that were in violation of the constitution. By a two-thirds vote, the Censors also could recommend that a new convention rewrite the constitution.[36]

Conservatives were horrified at this constitution, especially the Test Oath. Some local officials construed this so broadly that not only loyalists and Quakers but also anyone who disapproved of the radical constitution was forbidden the vote. From 1776 until the constitution's opponents drafted a new document in 1790, political power in the state seesawed between Radical Constitutionalists and conservative Republicans (also known as Anti-Constitutionalists). The for-mer dominated from 1776 to 1780 and from 1784 to 1786, the latter from 1780 to 1784 and after 1786.[37]

Although the principal activities of both parties' leaders were centered in the capital, and despite the impression that historians may have created, Philadel-phia was not all there was to Pennsylvania. When organizing the colony, Penn created the counties of Bucks, Philadelphia, and Chester around the city and three more to the south (New Castle, Kent, and Sussex). The latter withdrew their delegates from the legislature in 1705 and became the proprietor's colony of Delaware. As colonists moved farther into the interior, the Assembly formed additional counties: Lancaster, 1729; York, 1749; Cumberland, 1750; Berks and Northampton in 1752; and late in the colonial period, Bedford, 1771; Northumberland, 1772; and Westmoreland, 1773. By the eve of the Revolu-tion, the population of the interior counties approximately equaled that of the city of Philadelphia and its surrounding counties.[38]

Readers may be surprised to learn that there is not much evidence that the

Pennsylvania hinterland was involved in the resistance during most of the period between the end of the French and Indian War and the passage of the Intolerable Acts in 1774. Probably the major reason for the apparent disinterest is that they were more concerned about their own immediate problems and blamed them on their provincial government rather than on the British. Frontiersmen in the Juniata Valley felt abandoned by everyone else in their struggle for survival against the Indians. In the Upper Susquehanna Valley, pro-proprietary Pennsylvanians waged three-way battles with Indians, "Yankees" from Connecticut whose Susquehannah Company claimed the area, and anti-proprietary Pennsylvanians who sided with the Yankees.[39] Residents of Berks, York, and Cumberland Counties who experienced Indian attacks during both the French and Indian War and Pontiac's Rebellion, which followed almost immediately thereafter, resented their disproportionately few seats in the colony's Assembly. Had they been adequately represented, they claimed, they could have forced the government to organize a militia that could have protected them. Berks Countians demanded better roads on which to transport their agricultural and industrial products to markets. From Cumberland Countians came protests against provincial judicial officials who attempted to have alleged culprits tried not by their local peers but in distant Philadelphia.[40]

Not until news of the Bostonians' plight reached the interior did its people's hostility to Great Britain became obvious. Of course, the news came from Philadelphia. The city's committees encouraged hinterland settlers to develop their own resistance groups, variously called committees of observation, inspection, and safety. These appeared in Chester, Bucks, and most other interior counties. With the outbreak of hostilities in Massachusetts in April 1775, committees in the interior prepared for action.[41] The Chester County Committee of Safety bought arms and weapons. York Countians already had begun to drill. Militia units elsewhere in the hinterland turned into fighting forces. Some responded to the call of the Second Continental Congress for troops to join General George Washington's Continental Army at Cambridge.

As both rural and urban Pennsylvanians moved, however reluctantly, from "resistance to revolution"[42] between 1775 and 1776, deep fissures emerged within the province. Some pacifist Quakers relinquished their committee posts. The three Quaker members of Bucks County's Committee of Safety withdrew. Chester and Bucks County Quakers disowned those who continued to participate in committee and military activities. The Radnor meeting expelled more than one-quarter of its members. The German sectarians, Mennonites, Amish, and Dunkers—unlike the far more numerous, pro-Revolutionary Lutherans and Reformed, had never been much involved and remained aloof.[43] As a result, Pennsylvania became what Anne M. Ousterhout called "A State Divided."[44] Local committee members observed with suspicious eyes the activities of the pacifists and the loyalists. Berks County officials fined and imprisoned those who refused to swear allegiance to the new government. The county's loyalists, such as its only Anglican clergyman, who remained loyal to the King as the head of the Church of England and who attempted to discourage the rebellion, were harassed, beaten, and imprisoned.

As these divisions indicate, the Revolution in Pennsylvania was a complex event, as it was elsewhere as well. John Adams believed that the Revolution was over before the war began. He claimed that it had occurred in the hearts and minds of the people.[45] Historian Bernard Bailyn developed this point in emphasizing its origins as ideological.[46] To the contrary, Louis Hacker charged that the Revolution was a clash between British and American capitalisms.[47] Carl L. Becker claimed that it was a revolution against both the British and the colonial elite.[48] Daniel Boorstin questioned whether it was a Revolution at all.[49] Moreover, if there was a revolution, it was different in each colony. We should go further and point out that there were different revolutions even within colonies. The following chapters demonstrate amply that this was true of Pennsylvania.

Anyone seeking to generalize about the impact of the American Revolution on Pennsylvania based on the study of a "typical" county or region would be off the mark. Pennsylvania's interior was similar to the interior of the South, as described by Jack P. Greene in his introduction to *An Uncivil War: The Southern Backcountry in the American Revolution:* "There were several southern backcountries, each with its own peculiar Revolutionary experience."[50] This substitution would be appropriate for another reason: historians from Frederick Jackson Turner to Greene himself have referred to the southern backcountry as "greater Pennsylvania,"[51] populated by Scots-Irish, German, and other recent immigrants who made Pennsylvania their first stop. Finding insufficient quantities of land or uncongenial communities in rural Pennsylvania, these immigrants trekked down Virginia's Shenandoah Valley and into central North Carolina in the mid-eighteenth century. Greene warns us, however, that we should not push deconstruction of the South's Revolutionary experience to the point where no coherence can be found among diverse local particularities. For Pennsylvania, three broad regional patterns emerge, each consonant, to a large extent, with a particular time frame and type of revolution.

Philadelphia, Bucks, and Chester, the oldest counties and closest to the metropolis, were weak in their support of the Revolution. The many prosperous Quaker farmers were naturally pacifists; proximity of the Delaware River and the British army during the 1777–78 occupation of the capital made trading with the British easier, as it was more lucrative, than with the rebels. Overrepresented, with eight delegates each in Pennsylvania's colonial assembly, these counties resisted independence and lost heavily when the state's 1776 constitution apportioned seats more equitably.

Loyalist guerrilla warfare plagued both Bucks and Chester, although the terror was sporadic and failed to disrupt economic development.[52] Proximity to both major armies ensured that these rich agricultural counties did not suffer much economically for their lack of patriotic ardor, as did those areas subjected either to prolonged occupation, devastating raids, or the depletion of manpower for the army. In Bucks and Chester, the Revolution's major change was political: to substitute Presbyterian and other dissenters who were mostly Scots-Irish ethnically, although some were English and German, for the predominantly English Quaker colonial elite. Ironically, although more broadly based, the new leaders were less representative of counties that were filled with pacifists, loyalists, and lukewarm patriots whose failure to take required oaths or outright disloyalty excluded them from political life until the Revolution was concluded.

The Revolution near Philadelphia was most like the Revolution in the city itself. It emerged as a by-product of urban resistance to the taxation and customs regulations imposed by the British ministries from 1765 to 1775. Conservative Quaker and Anglican leaders led limited pre-1775 protests, only to be supplanted by more radical figures who supported war, independence, and the constitution of 1776. As in Philadelphia, the Revolution here most sharply divided the population into sizeable contingents of genuine Tories, neutrals, conservative Whigs, and Radical Revolutionaries. It marked the state's greatest internal revolution and division on the local level.

Pennsylvania's middle region—Berks, York, Cumberland, and Lancaster Counties and the Lehigh Valley—saw no internal revolution and not much violence within its communities, despite ethnic and religious diversity. Rather, the central counties joined with newcomers to Philadelphia politics to bring about radical political change at the state level, which shifted power away from the older counties. This variant first appeared in 1775–76, when the interior counties began to take serious interest in the imperial crisis, which culminated in the constitution of 1776 and played itself out by the end of the 1780s as the Federalists took control of the state. The Whiskey Rebellion of 1794 and Fries's Rebellion of 1799 may be seen as vestiges of localist suspicion of outside control, which fueled this aspect of Pennsylvania's Revolution.

Central Pennsylvania provided the core of the state's support for the cause. It sent a large contingent of troops to the Continental Army and contributed heavily to the army by providing food, munitions, and housing for the wounded and prisoners of war. While the British occupied Philadelphia, Yorktown served as the national capital and Lancaster housed Pennsylvania's state government. The population of this region, mainly Scots-Irish and German, had chafed under the elite of the older counties, which had taxed them with very little representation. Active loyalists were few in this part of the state.

That the Continental Army housed large numbers of German prisoners in Berks and Lancaster Counties could have been permitted only if the ethnically German majorities in these areas had been heavily pro-Revolutionary. Many of the soldiers were permitted to wander around at will, and a good number chose to remain in America rather than return to Europe. As historian A. G. Roeber has shown,[53] the majority of German immigrants were Lutherans and Reformed church members who had struggled for ecclesiastical independence from the European churches. They read German-language publications, which had convinced them that liberty included secure possession of their property.

Radicalism came to the Scots-Irish, as to the Germans, through frontier experience, its interpretation in the press, and conflicts with both Pennsylvania and trans-Atlantic hierarchies. At least fifty-eight pamphlets were published following the Paxton Boys' 1764 massacre of the Conestoga Indians in Lancaster, perpetrated in retaliation for the proprietary government's failure to "protect" frontiersmen who were dispossessing Indians. The most notable feature of these pamphlets is a general popular disgust with all the elements of a severely divided elite—both Proprietor Penn and his predominantly Presbyterian supporters, and his chief adversary Benjamin Franklin and his principally Quaker supporters—that had been quarreling among themselves as the frontier burned.[54] The Paxton Boys later moved from Lancaster County to the Wyoming Valley, where they continued their opposition. Cumberland County's Black Boys were other violent frontiersmen who resembled their Scots-Irish compatriots in Northern Ireland, such as the Oakboys and Steelboys. All rejected British domination, which had reduced them to marginal status and deprived them of political rights in both Pennsylvania and Ireland. Two of the most important Revolutionary leaders in Lancaster (General Edward Hand, Adjutant General of the Continental Army) and Cumberland (statesman James Wilson) counties were Scots-Irish immigrants, participants in a tradition of trans-Atlantic radicalism that saw Thomas Paine, scientist Joseph Priestley, French revolutionary Brissot de Warville, and Irish rebel leader Wolfe Tone come to Pennsylvania.[55]

These "Regulators" of Central Pennsylvania, and their country cousins, did not show much political interest in imperial affairs until the Boston Port Bill and the outbreak of war. (This was typical of much of America: Concord, fifteen miles from Boston, also remained aloof from the crisis until the eleventh hour.) Then Pennsylvania's central region joined with Philadelphia "radicals" in engineering the most significant upheaval in the internal structure of any new state government. Dubbed "democratic" by sympathetic historians, it was nothing of the kind, because it excluded Quakers, loyalists, neutrals, and in some cases conservative Whigs who opposed the constitution of 1776. The unpopular test oaths reversed an accommodationist tendency in colonial Pennsylvania that permitted the numerous Quakers and sectarians who objected to taking oaths to instead affirm or declare their allegiance or opinions in court.[56]

But as many of the chapters in this book indicate, while numerically Scots-Irish or Germans may have dominated the Revolution in one or another part of Pennsylvania, the struggle brought the state's ethnically diverse population together. Significant numbers of French Huguenots, Welsh, Germans, and English, including "Fighting Quakers" whom the meeting disowned, also supported the cause. Increasingly, men with non-English surnames served on the committees and were elected representatives from the interior counties. The oaths transformed Pennsylvania into a politically covenanted community until those supporting the constitution of 1776 were ousted from office in the mid-1780s. Not only in the eastern counties were oaths, taxes, and military requisitions unpopular; the overzealous communities that drove the war forward created opposition to themselves among loyal but long-suffering Revolutionaries in the central parts of the state. Only briefly did the "rage militaire" described by historian Charles Royster sustain itself in Pennsylvania, as elsewhere; patriotic fervor needed to be supplanted by coercive institutionalization in order to establish a government and obtain manpower and supplies, whose unpopularity increased in proportion to their effectiveness.[57]

Ironically, while Bucks and Chester flourished economically despite—or even because of—their equivocal stance, many inhabitants of Central Pennsylvania, from one of the most patriotic regions in the new nation, paid dearly for their loyalty. Soldiers lost their lives; farmers went into debt as prices and taxes soared; inflation struck; the British market became inaccessible. To be sure, there were offsetting factors. The war created new demand for iron from Berks furnaces, for guns and gunpowder from the Carlisle Depot, and for Conestoga wagons and Pennsylvania rifles from Lancaster. The city and region surrounding Lancaster, the largest interior town in the thirteen states and the original home of the Pennsylvania rifle and Conestoga wagon, especially flourished as a center for manufacturing munitions. But the infusion of inflated dollars, along with the arrival of the continental and state governments, accelerated the development of a commercial cash economy with an industrial component that was under way before the Revolution. Yet unlike many parts of the country, Central Pennsylvania survived the war in relatively good shape. It was untouched by combat or guerrilla warfare. Its location, fertile soil, industrious inhabitants, and prewar infrastructure ensured that the region, critical for the Continental Army's manpower and materiel, prospered even if the prosperity was unevenly distributed.[58]

For the Juniata and Wyoming Valleys, the Revolution figured primarily as a complicating factor in local wars that began before the conflict with Britain and continued afterward. Accelerating or reviving brutal, sporadic conflicts with Indians and their British protectors (before the war) and supporters (once it began and afterward), the Pennsylvania frontier endured during the Revolution, on a far more protracted scale, a mixture of the guerrilla war found in Bucks and Chester and large-scale military activity such as punitive expeditions and the erection of forts. As in much of the hinterland throughout British North America, settlers found eastern elites alternatively neglectful and intrusive. People in the Juniata Valley had been chased out both by Indians and by a colonial government that was anxious to avoid conflict with them. Neglected by a state that was unable to help so remote a region, even if it could have spared the time from the Revolution, Juniata inhabitants built a chain of private forts and somehow survived. Population declined, and economic development could hardly go beyond subsistence agriculture as warfare with Indians persisted after the Peace of Paris. The Juniata remained a remote, poor region of isolated farms and hamlets, a quality it still retains today. In this it differed sharply from the southwestern region of Pennsylvania in and around Pittsburgh whose development has been well traced by historian R. Eugene Harper.[59] The Revolution cleared the three counties formed in the early 1770s from western Cumberland of Indians and laid the foundation for greatly accelerated agricultural growth.

With the opening of the Ohio Valley after the victory over the Indians at the Battle of Fallen Timbers in 1794, southwestern Pennsylvania, unlike the region that is now the center of the state, became a major staging point for the movement of people into the Old Northwest.

The Wyoming Valley, on the other hand, located along the northern Susquehanna River, was a prize coveted by both Connecticut and Pennsylvania (Pennamite) settlers. A potentially rich commercial region with access to the recently flourishing port of Baltimore, it was fought over by Pennsylvanians moving up the river and by Yankees who claimed that Connecticut's sea-to-sea charter was not nullified by land granted to New York, and therefore Connecticut continued at the same latitude lines at the western edge of New York. This intercolonial war began well before the Revolution. Although Pennsylvanians who participated in the famous Wyoming Valley "massacre" of New Englanders in 1778 were dubbed Tories by their foes, this was basically a dispute over lands in which both sides took what they could get and made alliances that served them best. Historian Anne Ousterhout has written of these Pennsylvanians as "the disaffected" who made alliances with British troops, New York loyalists, and Iroquois to support their claims when the Revolutionary government sided with the fiercely patriotic Yankees.[60] After the Revolution, Congress settled the dispute in the Pennsylvanians' favor, which ironically led to the nullification of land titles held by pro-Revolution Yankees in favor of people who had courted the enemy. The war interrupted the commercial development of a region that Peter Mancall has shown was involved in the greater Atlantic economy beginning with the fur trade, then in the shipment of grain to the South, and ultimately in the production of coal.[61]

The violence of frontier warfare caused Western Pennsylvania soldiers to develop a virulent strain of racism that depicted all Indians—regardless of a nation's[62] history or the personal loyalties of its members—as "red" savages fit to be exterminated. Perceptions of easterners who served on the frontier were more complicated: Indians were sometimes yellow or brown, and discriminations were made among them. As Alden T. Vaughan has shown, the racism that identified Indians as "red" began to solidify only in the late-eighteenth and early-nineteenth century. Western Pennsylvania pioneered a more general post-Revolutionary simplification of what Richard D. White called the "Middle Ground." In this vast region stretching from the Gulf of Mexico to the Great Lakes, from the Appalachians to the Mississippi, different groups of whites and Indians had for several hundred years combined and recombined in changing alliances that precluded the white versus red dichotomy institutionalized once the United States supplanted other white powers in the region.[63]

The chapters in this volume also confirm Edward Countryman's recent observation that Indian relations must be moved from the margin to the center of the Revolution's history.[64] In the Juniata and Wyoming Valleys, the Revolution itself was at the margin. In Cumberland, Berks, Lancaster, York, and the Lehigh Valley, the failure of the provincial government to provide adequate defense beginning in the 1750s was, in some cases quite literally, the burning issue that made underrepresentation in the Assembly a matter of life and death rather than political theory. Conversely, reluctance to organize defense brought down the Quaker elite centered in Bucks, Chester, and Philadelphia Counties.

Reinforcement of racial hostility in a Revolution that effectively ended Indian autonomy in Pennsylvania was but an extreme form of one of the principal unifying themes of Pennsylvania's Revolution: that outside of Philadelphia, ethnic and religious divisions shaped who supported and opposed the Revolution more than class or economic status. Richard A. Ryerson and Steven Rosswurm have effectively built on the older work of Robert Brunhouse to demonstrate class-based political and crowd action in the capital.[65] Yet even there it was more likely that Anglicans would be loyalists, that Quakers would be neutrals or British sympathizers, and that Scots-Irish Presbyterians and German Lutherans and Reformed would be Revolutionaries. And even in the Juniata Valley and Cumberland County, Revolutionaries were well-to-do local landowners, merchants, and lawyers who enjoyed the confidence of their followers. Owen Ireland has persuasively extended such an ethnoreligious interpretation to Pennsylvania's regional voting patterns on the federal Constitution of 1787 as well.[66]

A second theme that emerges from these chapters is the role of the militia and its leaders, working in conjunction with the newly formed Committees—of Correspondence, Safety, and Observation, as they were variously called—in raising troops, obtaining supplies, collecting taxes, checking dissent, and regulating a frequently inflation-ridden and hard-pressed economy. Given the refusal of Pennsylvania's pre-Revolutionary legislature, like all the legislatures from Maryland to New York, to support the Revolution, and given the presence of numerous pacifists, neutrals, and loyalists, Pennsylvania's Revolutionary government understandably instituted a major internal political revolution. It extended representation and expanded the franchise to favor a hinterland that, east of the frontier, engaged in Indian warfare, almost unanimously supported a revolution that the metropolis and its surrounding counties at best partially endorsed. The

"Test Act" became a symbol of the incursions on personal freedom required throughout the state to mobilize people behind a revolution that claimed to be a struggle for both collective and individual liberty.

Politically, Pennsylvania's constitution of 1790 signaled a counterrevolution that modified its 1776 constitution. But while losing a single-house legislature, the Council of Censors, and the weak executive, hinterland Pennsylvanians retained ample representation of their interests. Socially and economically, the Revolution accelerated an evolutionary process that was already under way. The infusion of cash and the demand for supplies and munitions furthered the concentration of wealth and commercial development, as did the defeat of Indians everywhere. Except on the frontier, Pennsylvania did not suffer the economic devastation that a large part of the nation felt. The Juniata Valley, isolated by repeated mountain ranges from the rest of the state, was the exception that proved the rule.

Pennsylvania's Revolution was also a profoundly civil war in the counties along the Delaware, in Philadelphia, and on the frontier, where internal violence accompanied political strife. Only in the central region was there no clash over who was to rule locally. And people there united to oppose the indifferent colonial government they overthrew. To be sure, this civil war took different forms in different part of the state: class conflict in Philadelphia, settlers versus Indians in the Juniata Valley, Pennsylvanians versus Yankees in the Wyoming Valley, the central counties versus the eastern, and Quakers and loyalists versus other dissenters and patriots in Bucks and Chester. Despite unifying elements of ethnic conflict, commercial evolution, and intense popular mobilization, Pennsylvania's American Revolution was as diverse and unique as the colonial experience that preceded it. Like patterns of allegiance in the English Revolution of 1640–49—which recent scholars have persuasively argued must be understood through looking at how larger trends were shaped by circumstances in diverse local communities—we are only beginning to uncover why particular towns, counties, and regions in colonial British America played the role they did in the American Revolution.[67]

1

Chester County

Rosemary S. Warden

On the eve of the Revolution, Chester County was a picture of rural tranquility, with no foreshadowing of the deep turmoil to come. Chester County's fifty-four townships included modern Delaware and Chester Counties, with a population of about 30,000. Stretching forty miles west from Philadelphia to Lancaster County, Chester County was bordered on the north by Philadelphia and Berks Counties and on the south by the Delaware River, Delaware, and Maryland. It was settled in the 1680s. Mixed farming was well established by the mid-1770s, when Chester County farmers were exporting one-third to one-half of their wheat crop through Philadelphia. Family farms of modest size, averaging 130 acres, were typical. Farms were smaller in areas close to Philadelphia that supplied food to the city. Many of the most prosperous farmers were also mill owners.[1]

Except for iron manufacturing in the Schuylkill Valley, Chester County had no large-scale industry. It also lacked any towns of size. Only the county seat, the town of Chester, on the Delaware River south of Philadelphia, had reached a population of 200 by 1800. Tiny hamlets appeared at crossroads and at taverns, mills, and ferries. Blacksmiths, tanners, and shopkeepers also provided natural meeting places. Shopkeepers or affluent farmers sometimes provided local banking services and distilled liquor for their neighbors. Weaving was a cottage industry; itinerant butchers, tailors, and shoemakers traveled the county. Philadelphia, within a day's journey of most of the county, drew its trade, provided professional services, and served as a religious, political, social, and cultural center for the county.[2]

Taverns served as Chester County's most important social centers. Some were mere eating places; others, like Yellow Springs Tavern in West Pikeland Township, owned by Dr. Samuel Kennedy, had greater facilities. This tavern, on the site of the famous mineral springs, once fed 500 people in a single day at the height of the season.[3] Taverns also often served as voting places, meeting places for political caucuses and various Revolutionary committees, recruiting posts for the army, and mustering points for the militia. Some of them, such as the Turk's Head Tavern in Goshen and the Unicorn Tavern in Kennett, became well-known centers of Revolutionary activity. It is not surprising that many tavern owners became important local political leaders who advanced the careers of family and friends. David Coupland, a tavern owner in the town of Chester, was also mayor of the town and a chief organizer of the County Committee in 1774. Robert Smith, a Scots-Irish Presbyterian, Chester County Lieutenant, and later Assembly member, was the most powerful Revolutionary leader in the county after 1776. He gained influence among the Welsh because he married Margaret Vaughn, daughter of the owner of the Red Lion Tavern, an important meeting place for that ethnic group. Charles Dilworth, a Quaker tavern owner from Birmingham Township who served on the County Committee and as Chester County Sheriff, suffered twice for his politics. The Friends Meeting disowned him, and the British army stripped his tavern bare when they marched through the county in September 1777.[4]

Membership in churches or Quaker meetings provided another opportunity for social and political leadership. Almost all state and county officeholders, members of Revolutionary committees, and officers in the Continental Army or

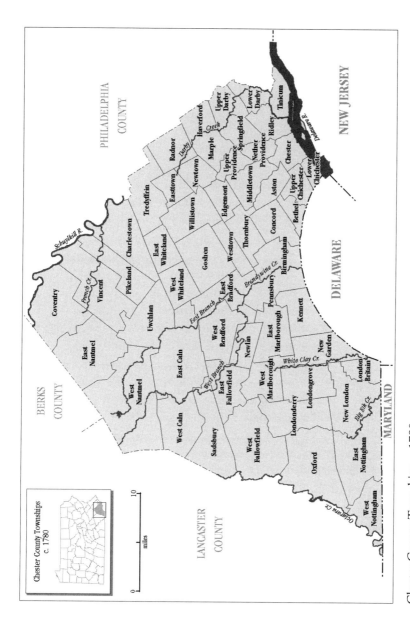

Chester County Townships c. 1780

militia from Chester County were members of churches or meetings, many of them elders or vestrymen. This is impressive, because the county had only about forty churches and meetings for its Revolutionary period population of some 30,000, or one for every 750 inhabitants. Most Chester Countians could not have been active members of any sect or church. Chester Countians showed toleration and enjoyed some mutual assistance in establishing churches. They frequently supported church benefit lotteries for other denominations and occasionally attended the only church in their area, though of a different religion, until a church of their own denomination could be built. For example, Presbyterians collaborated with Anglicans to build the Great Valley Church and accepted a gift of land on which to build Charlestown Church from Job Harvey, a Quaker. Despite generally good relationships among religious groups, a clear religious and ethnic identity marked Chester County's political leaders during this period. Quakers provided most of the county political leadership before the Revolution. Revolutionary leaders were of more diverse religions and ethnic backgrounds, particularly Scots-Irish Presbyterian.[5]

The Quakers were the largest religious group in the county, comprising about 40 percent of the population. As early settlers in the county, they were most thickly settled in the eastern townships near Philadelphia and held the greatest recorded wealth in the county tax lists. Although mostly English, Chester County Quakers included significant numbers of Irish and Welsh. Many other Welsh settlers were Baptists; some were Anglicans or Presbyterians. Religious orientation, not national origin, was the most significant determinant of political behavior for the Welsh. Most Quakers of these ethnic groups conscientiously opposed the ultimate violent split from England. Many non-Quaker Welsh strongly supported the Revolution.[6]

Chester County's inhabitants of English birth or descent were a majority except in the twelve western townships; even there, the English population share was in the range of 25–50 percent. Most non-Quaker English were Anglican. Another important group, the Scots-Irish Presbyterians, about 19 percent of the county's population, were concentrated in the southwestern townships along the border of Lancaster County and Maryland, in areas passed over by earlier settlers, with smaller numbers throughout the county. German settlers were an even smaller minority in the county, about 8 percent of its population, settled mainly in the northern townships abutting more heavily German Philadelphia, Berks, and Lancaster Counties. They remained unassimilated at the time of the Revolution, playing little role in Chester County politics.

The Quaker party thoroughly dominated Chester County politics in the decade before the Revolution. Fifteen of the eighteen Assembly members from Chester County in the decade before independence were Quakers; at least two of the remaining three, though not Quakers in religious affiliation, were Quaker party members. The Quaker party's dominance resulted from more than Quaker wealth and numbers. The party represented effective and tolerant government and opposition to proprietary privilege. It supported talented non-Quakers, such as Chester County's John Morton, in positions of leadership. Another source of Quaker party strength lay in the prestige of the assemblymen themselves. They were drawn from the most substantial families in the wealthier eastern townships, such as Haverford (Charles Humphreys), Upper Darby (John Sellers), Lower Darby (Isaac Pearson), and Ridley (John Crosby and John Morton). Most came from families settled in Chester County before 1700, families that had long records of public service, particularly in the Assembly. They cemented their relationships and power by an intricate network of marriages. Chester County Assembly members served lengthy terms, usually leaving office only because of old age or a disinclination to serve further. No viable opposition to the Quaker party developed in Chester County before the Revolution.[7]

Prosperous and politically content, Chester County was slow to join protests against British policy and reluctant to support the final breach with England. John Morton, Quaker party Assembly member from Ridley, was a delegate to the Stamp Act Congress in New York City in 1765, but no record remains of protests or petitions against the Stamp Act from Chester County. No protest movement developed in the county for almost a decade. Philadelphia merchants directed early protests and nonimportation agreements. Only the town of Chester, on the Delaware River, was directly involved in protest activities. In a notorious incident in November 1771, an unidentified pilot boat stole a colonial ship held at Chester by a British revenue agent. Local officials and townspeople refused to give British officials any information or assistance in the affair. Two years later the town of Chester was the scene of the Philadelphia "Tea Party." When the tea ship *Polly* arrived at Chester on Christmas Day 1773, a town meeting of 8,000 Philadelphians decided to prevent the landing of any tea. In a confrontation at Chester, Captain Ayres of the *Polly* was persuaded to return peaceably to England with his cargo intact.[8]

Chester County formed its first Revolutionary committee after the closing of the port of Boston on June 1, 1774. The Philadelphia Committee, still a force for moderate resistance to British policies, corresponded with prominent Chester Countians concerning ways to influence the Assembly's choice of delegates and instructions for the First Continental Congress, due to meet in the fall. The Philadelphia Committee contacted three Chester Countians: Francis Richardson, a Quaker merchant who moved from Philadelphia to the town of Chester in 1773; Elisha Price, an Anglican lawyer from the town of Chester; and Henry Hayes of Darby, just outside Philadelphia, a Quaker tavern owner and farmer.[9]

Richardson, Price, and Hayes convened a public meeting at the town of Chester on July 13. Following the lead of the Philadelphia Committee, the Chester County meeting approved nonimportation as the best way to counter British aggression. The gathering chose Richardson and Price, along with eleven others, primarily Quakers from the eastern townships, to represent the county at the provincial level.[10]

Ignoring suggestions from the more radical committees, the Pennsylvania Assembly sent to the Continental Congress a seven-man delegation that represented the conservative senior Assembly members from most counties, including John Morton and Charles Humphreys of Chester County. Chester County's voters approved the Assembly's determination to channel and restrain radical protest, returning their county's Assembly delegation almost unchanged in October. The single new member was Anthony Wayne, replacing an elderly Assemblyman who retired. Though an Anglican, the wealthy twenty-four-year-old Wayne was the son of a former Quaker party Assemblyman and not widely known as a radical at the time.[11]

The new Assembly sought no open rupture with the protest committees; it only insisted on leadership of a moderate, nonviolent constitutional protest. The Assembly adopted the nonimportation program of the First Continental Congress early in December and called for the formation of County Committees to put the Continental Association into effect. On December 20 a public meeting at the courthouse in the town of Chester chose a new, larger County Committee of seventy-four members to enforce nonimportation. However, while most of this large committee were from eastern townships and more than half (forty-three members) were Quakers, the western townships were well represented, as were other religious groups, especially Scots-Irish Presbyterians (fifteen members). This marks the first appearance of the Scots-Irish as a driving force in the county's protest movement.[12]

A month later the Quaker Meeting for Sufferings that assembled at Philadel-

phia formally stated Quaker opposition to the resistance movement. This was
the result of years of gradually eroding support among Quaker leaders in Philadelphia for extralegal means of protest. Now they condemned "every measure
tending to excite disaffection to the King" and "all combinations, insurrections,
conspiracies and illegal assemblies." They further hoped that they would be able
to "maintain our testimony against any requisitions which may be made of us,
inconsistent with our religious principles. . . ." This strong and vocal position
resulted in a storm of opposition from non-Quakers. It also led to dissent within
the society. Philadelphia-area Quaker meetings eventually disowned almost
1,000 Quakers in the Philadelphia area.[13]

Chester County meetings reacted immediately to this formal declaration of
principle by the Meeting for Sufferings. In March 1775, Darby and Chester
Meetings recorded the disownment of the County Committee delegates to the
Provincial Committee. These Quaker delegates all remained active in the resistance in spite of this, but many other Quaker Committee members dropped out
rather than face being disowned.[14]

Meanwhile, the Chester County Committee made no move to carry out the
resolves of the January Provincial Committee meeting for military preparations
at the county level. The committee's main effort was the enforcement of nonimportation, which mostly involved the town of Chester.[15]

In the Pennsylvania Assembly, a conservative reaction against the power of
the Continental Congress was growing. Until the beginning of March, members
from Chester County hesitated, waiting for a sign to indicate whether they
should continue to support the Congress. The Revolutionary situation fragmented the eight-member Quaker party Assembly delegation from Chester
County. Joseph Pennock always assumed conservative positions, and the radicals
could count on Anthony Wayne and Benjamin Bartholomew. The other five
members, James Gibbons, Charles Humphreys, John Jacobs, John Morton, and
Isaac Pearson, were swing votes, giving the Chester Countians the potential
balance of power in the Assembly for the next months.[16]

The tensions within the Chester County delegation were soon more than
matched by a new outside pressure. By late April, news from Lexington and
Concord electrified Pennsylvania. In the radical reaction that followed, the
Chester County Committee recommended a military association to the people
of the county. On June 30, the Assembly appointed a provincial Committee of
Safety to direct military preparations. The Chester County members of that
committee, Anthony Wayne, Benjamin Bartholomew, and particularly Richard

Riley and Francis Johnston, both from the town of Chester, feared a possible naval invasion of Pennsylvania up the Delaware River. They pushed for construction of forts along the Delaware and the sinking of chevaux-de-frise in the river as a defense against the British fleet.[17]

By the fall of 1775, the Chester County Committee was purchasing powder and ammunition, arranging to have flintlocks made in compliance with the quota established by the Committee of Safety, and organizing local militia units. Through the recruiting and equipping of the militia, the County Committee gained a quasi-legal status as an agent of the Assembly (through the Committee of Safety). At the same time, local officials worked closely with the County Committee to create a militia. Chester County Commissioners and Assessors, most of whom were Quakers, laid a tax to finance the militia and purchased military goods, occasionally reimbursed by the Committee of Safety through the County Committee.[18]

To counter fears of increasing radicalism and growing support for independence, the Chester County Committee published a strong statement of opposition to independence, signed by Anthony Wayne as chairman, in the *Pennsylvania Gazette* on September 25, a week before the annual Assembly election. Regarding independence, they declared "their abhorrence of an idea even so pernicious in its nature," and expressed their desire for "nothing more than a happy and speedy reconciliation, on constitutional principles," with England. In the October election, Chester County voters rejected suspected radicalism by making a single change in their Assembly delegation. They replaced Anthony Wayne with Joseph Pyle, a particularly conservative Quaker. On November 9 the Assembly agreed; it "strictly enjoined" its Congressional delegates to "dissent from, and utterly reject, any Propositions, should such be made, that may cause, or lead to, a separation from our Mother Country, or a Change of the Form of this Government." No list of a roll-call vote on these instructions exists, but it is clear that the Chester County delegation stood strongly, and possibly unanimously, against independence at this juncture.[19]

The main issue debated in the Assembly in the fall of 1775 was not independence but militia service. Under intense pressure from the "Associators" (those who accepted the "Association," or boycott, of British goods by the First Continental Congress) and committees, the Assembly passed an act requiring universal military service and even laid a light tax on non-Associators. In the fall of 1775, universal military service forced every adult male Quaker to make an immediate choice between support for the resistance movement and adherence to Quaker principles. By October 1775, the County Committee had only twelve Quakers, none of them in good standing, among its thirty-five members.[20]

Western-township Presbyterians moved into the gap in leadership created by the withdrawing Quakers, in part because they were politically cohesive and well led. Some lists of wardens and trustees of Presbyterian churches contain almost exclusively names of men prominently involved in the Revolutionary movement. The Presbyterian ministers in the county also vehemently supported the County Committee and the militia. In the spring of 1776 the Reverend John Carmichael preached on the need to defend New York, and most of his congregation enlisted, leaving the women to reap the harvest. A year later, informed of the need for bandages at Valley Forge, Carmichael preached that Sunday "They must have this linen, and you women can spare this much," indicating with his hand the proper width, "from your shifts." The next day little rolls of linen came to the parsonage, and Carmichael delivered them to Washington's army. Carmichael's church at Brandywine Manor was used as a rebel arsenal during the war, which made it a target of enemy raids, particularly during the British occupation of Philadelphia. Another pastor, the Reverend William Forster of Upper Octoraro church, also preached recruiting sermons for the army. Joseph McClellan, later a prominent citizen of the county—County Lieutenant, Sheriff, and State Senator—testified years later that he had joined the Continental Army as a result of hearing one of Mr. Forster's fiery recruiting sermons. Forster was so involved in the Revolutionary movement that a Tory plot to kidnap him was thwarted only when his congregation spirited him out of harm's way.[21]

The militia was a major factor in the increasing radicalization of county and provincial politics early in 1776. Chester County's militia mustered at Chester starting in January. Inevitably, power gravitated to the militia—especially to the militia officers, who had broad responsibility and considerable leeway in providing for their troops. The militia's importance as an independent political force also came in part from control of its own officers, who were elected annually by their units. For many militia officers, militia leadership was a bridge between membership on the County Committee and later political office. Most militia officers were substantial farmers. The rising power of the militia in Chester County brought an ethnic and geographic change to county leadership, but no immediate economic or social democratization of county leadership.[22]

As the militia grew in size and influence, the Chester County Committee could no longer deny the push for independence in the Congress and by the Philadelphia Committee. In March 1776, Francis Johnston, secretary of the

County Committee, wrote to Anthony Wayne, the chairman and his old friend, that he had been warned of "a most dangerous scheme in agitation" by two of the delegates to the Congress and other gentlemen as well.

> I am convinced that such a scheme (I mean a proposed State of Independency, and the appointment of a Convention, with a view of annihilating the power of our Representatives in Assembly) will without doubt promote Disunion among ourselves, and totally put an end to the friendship of those Worthies in Britain who have heretofore generously stood forth in our Cause.

Johnston, representing some of the Committee members, went on to ask Wayne to call a meeting of the County Committee very shortly to deal with the situation. Francis Johnston was a committed County Committee member, had served as a member of the provincial Committee of Safety, and later became a colonel in the Continental Army. Yet three months before the Declaration of Independence, Johnston and his connections were shocked by the drive for independence and the destruction of the Charter government, and especially felt that the Committee lacked information concerning these "schemes" to which they might be opposed.[23]

Meanwhile, in the course of the spring, the struggle between the Radicals and the Assembly had reached its peak. To gain support for independence, the Radicals forced a special Assembly election on May 1, adding representatives from the more radical western counties. They still failed to create a proindependence majority in the Assembly. Chester County's Assembly delegation split evenly on the question of independence. Joseph Pyle, Joseph Pennock, Isaac Pearson, and Charles Humphreys, four of the Quaker assemblymen, did not support independence or serve in the Revolutionary government. Benjamin Bartholomew and John Morton, as well as Quakers John Jacobs and James Gibbons, supported independence and participated in the new government. The split among Chester County's leaders on the issue of independence reflects the persistent attachment of many Chester Countians to the pre-Revolutionary political system, and a reluctance to jeopardize the county's security and prosperity. The Chester County leaders who supported independence did so because of a fear of recent British political and military aggression and in reaction to the movement toward acceptance of independence in the colony as a whole.

The ultimate Radical response to the Assembly's intransigence was to pull down the Charter government, calling for a Provincial Committee meeting to organize an election for delegates to a constitutional convention to establish a new state government committed to independence. The Provincial Committee meeting, bowing to pressure from the militia, required all prospective voters to take a "test oath" abjuring allegiance to George III and promising to support a government based "on the authority of the people only." In Chester County, not only Quakers but also many others opposed to independence or attached to Charter government refused to take such an oath. Because the "test oath" resolution gave discretionary power to judges and inspectors of elections as to whether or not to administer the oath to an individual, it gave them considerable control over the electoral process. This left the choice of delegates in the hands of the Radicals.[24]

Another important factor in the choice of Chester County's delegates to the constitutional committee was the loss of Anthony Wayne, Francis Johnston, and other influential County Committee leaders to the military. Troops from Wayne's Continental command, the Fourth Pennsylvania Battalion (later the Fifth Pennsylvania Regiment), largely raised in Chester County, joined the Canadian campaign in the summer of 1776, fought at Trois Rivières in Canada, and then remained at Ticonderoga in New York until joining Washington in New Jersey in the summer of 1777. Wayne's Continentals did not return to Chester County until the British invasion in the fall of 1777. Some Chester County militia units marched to Washington's aid on Long Island in the summer of 1776. Many Chester Countians were captured or killed at Flatbush in August and in the fall of Fort Washington in November. The loss of experienced leaders to the military, in several cases for long periods, left local politics to less experienced and less well known leaders. By the late summer of 1776, Chester County found itself led by political newcomers.[25]

The summer and fall of 1776 marks an important step in the democratization of Chester County politics, as new political leaders from the previously under-represented western townships emerged. The new Presbyterian leadership permanently ended Quaker party domination of the county's political life. Five of Chester County's eight delegates to the constitutional convention were Presbyterian, as were three of the new assemblymen elected in the fall. The new Radical party, without the Quaker tradition of leadership, also lacked a strongly organized base of the size the Quakers had been able to rely on. The Radicals necessarily had to expect competition and lack of support from the more conservative groups they displaced.[26]

The implementation of the new state constitution in the fall of 1776 inspired fierce opposition within Chester County's Revolutionary movement. Thomas Bull wrote to Anthony Wayne decrying the "Danger and folly of the constitution. . . . It has substituted a mob government to one of the happiest governments in the world. Nothing more was necessary to have made us a free and happy people than to abolish the royal and proprietary power of the State." Furthermore, Bull pointed out that "a majority of the Presbyterians are in favor of the constitution, and in no part of the state do they discover more zeal than in Chester County." Bull claimed that this faction was hampering the military effort "by urging the execution of their rascally government in preference to supporting measures for repelling the common enemy." He urged Wayne to counter the Constitutionalist faction, "to add your weight to the zeal of opposition, especially in your native county."[27]

The opposition to the constitution, which formed around devoted Revolutionaries like Thomas Bull and Anthony Wayne, expressed discontent with the Scots-Irish "novices at the helm" of the state and specific grievances like the arbitrary "test oath" and militia fines, as well as the loss of the Charter government forms. While support for the new constitution centered around western township Scots-Irish Presbyterians, Anti-Constitutionalists were found among many different ethnic and religious groups. Anglicans, such as Anthony Wayne, John Morton, Francis Johnston, and Thomas Bull, were strongly Anti-Constitutionalist. The small number of Quaker supporters of independence also probably objected to the destruction of Charter government and to the "test oath." Even a few Presbyterians strongly opposed the new constitution. This bitter split among Revolutionaries left them less able to cope with the strong opposition to independence developing in the county.[28]

Chester County's large Quaker population provided a core of passive resistance to the Revolutionary government. Quaker meetings required that their members refuse to vote, hold office, pay taxes, serve in the militia, pay militia fines, or otherwise acknowledge the new government to avoid disownment. In the early years of the Revolution, some townships raised no militia, paid no fines, and underpaid taxes. Because most Quakers also refused to accept Congressional paper money, Colonel Francis Johnston wrote at the end of 1776, "Most of the Tavern Keepers who are friends on the Lancaster Road have pulled down their signs, refuse the Soldiery Provisions or drink . . . ," adding to the increasing economic disruption. By 1777, Chester County's government had effectively ceased to function; the British invasion in September 1777 added to the political chaos. As late as May 1779, the Supreme Executive Council received a report that no justices of the peace were serving for three Chester County districts comprising thirteen townships—the whole more conservative Quaker eastern portion of the county. A few other Chester County pacifists, such as German sectarians in the northern townships, and some individual passive loyalists added to the Quaker passive resistance. For example, William Currie, the Church of England minister of St. David's, Radnor Township, refused to hold services until after the Revolution, rather than to pray for the Congress and betray his ordination oath.[29]

A significant number of active loyalists also plagued the Revolutionary effort. The eastern and southeastern townships, with their relative wealth, largely Quaker populations, and long-standing disproportionate officeholding under the previous regime, were the areas of strongest loyalist sentiment. However, loyalist activity occurred throughout the county. Active loyalism did not center on any one ethnic or religious group. The small minority of Chester County Quakers disowned for military activity were more likely to serve with the Americans than with the loyalist troops raised in Chester County during the British occupation of Philadelphia. Even families were politically split. Two of the sons of the most prominent county loyalist, the Quaker former Sheriff Nathaniel Vernon, served as Continental officers. A third son served in the loyalist light dragoons raised in Chester County. The Thomas family of West Whiteland offers another example of the cleavages wrought by the Revolution. Richard Thomas IV, the most prominent member of this old Quaker farming family, was a noted patriot and militia colonel. His brother George, who remained a Quaker in good standing, held Quaker meetings in his home when meetinghouses were being used as military hospitals and cooperated with Revolutionary authorities by serving on committees for the relief of the poor in the county. The black sheep of the family was George's father-in-law, John Roberts, also a Quaker, later hanged by the rebels for guiding the invading British through Chester County.[30]

As Chester County's government disintegrated in late 1776, county Radicals became dependent on the state Constitutionalist leadership to support the Revolutionary movement within the county. In the spring of 1777, the Supreme Executive Council created a new militia organization headed at the county level by a lieutenant to recruit, train, muster, and supply the militia. The Chester County Lieutenant, Robert Smith, stepped into the breach left by ineffective local government and the official disbanding of the County Committee after independence. Smith became the most powerful Revolutionary political leader in the county.[31]

While some Chester County Revolutionaries struggled to organize their political institutions, others were making the county's most substantial military contribution of the war. As a result of the losses of Chester County militia in Washington's New York campaign in the summer and fall of 1776, Chester County suffered to a disproportionate extent from the rapidly shrinking size and enthusiasm of the Pennsylvania militia after summer 1776. In spite of the near debacle of Washington's army in December 1776, and numerous alarms of impending invasion of the state in the spring of 1777, the county militia did not again assemble in force until August 1777, when the British invaded Pennsylvania via the Chesapeake Bay, Maryland, and Delaware.[32]

On July 23, Lord Howe sailed from New York with fifteen to eighteen thousand soldiers. Washington, expecting Howe to attack Philadelphia by way of the Delaware River, proceeded southward from North Jersey. Possibly deterred by exaggerated reports of fortifications and chevaux-de-frise on the Delaware, Howe sailed south to Chesapeake Bay. He landed on August 25 at Head of Elk, Maryland, about fifty miles southwest of Philadelphia.

The preceding day, Washington had marched his army through Philadelphia, then continued marching farther south to place himself between Howe's army and Philadelphia. On September 9, Washington positioned the bulk of his army at Chad's Ford on the north side of the Brandywine, a shallow stream about 150 feet wide at that point. Anthony Wayne's brigade of Continentals, largely raised in Chester County, deployed at the center of the American line near Chad's house. Light earthworks and a redoubt protected Wayne's troops and the rest of the American center. Last-minute support by the Chester County militia raised the total number of militiamen under Washington's command at the Battle of Brandywine to 3,000. Washington posted the militia downriver to protect his flank; they took no active part in the battle.[33]

On September 11 the British forces took up positions on the south side of the Brandywine across from the Americans at Chad's Ford. Howe left a Hessian force under Knyphausen to distract the Americans. Flanking Washington's position, Howe planned to ford the Brandywine and attack the surprised Americans from the northwest.

As the British army passed, the countryside turned out to see them. Joseph Townsend, a Quaker youth of twenty who visited British headquarters before and after the battle, recalled seeing the British emerge from a stand of woods:

". . . In a few minutes the fields were literally covered with them. . . . Their arms and bayonets being raised shone as bright as silver, there being a clear sky and the day exceedingly warm." Washington heard mixed intelligence reports and refused at first to credit reports of the British flanking maneuver. Thomas Cheney, a substantial local farmer and militia leader, galloped into Washington's camp to warn him of the impending attack. Some of Washington's staff sneered at the warning of the excited middle-aged farmer, who had fled his home half dressed to warn the Americans. Even Washington, aware of the hostility of many Chester Countians to the Revolution, courteously doubted Cheney's word. Furious, Cheney demanded to call Anthony Wayne and Persifor Frazer, Continental officers and neighbors, as witnesses to his good character and patriotism.[34]

Washington had no time to investigate further. The British had reached his rear. Washington moved troops to face the new threat, leaving Wayne among those remaining to face Knyphausen across the Brandywine. At 4:30 in the afternoon, Knyphausen's artillery opened fire, and the battle was joined on both fronts. After an hour and forty minutes, the Americans meeting the flanking attack gave way and began a panicked retreat to the town of Chester.[35]

Notwithstanding his defeat at Brandywine, Washington's army was still between the British and Philadelphia. Washington marched north from the town of Chester to the Falls of the Schuylkill on the edge of Germantown on September 12. He feared that Howe would seek to cut off the American army's access to military supplies in Reading or that Howe might trap the Continental Army between the Delaware and the Schuylkill. Washington also sought another chance to fight the British army before letting it into Philadelphia. Howe had two goals following his victory at Brandywine: to occupy Philadelphia and, more important, to maneuver into another more decisive victory over Washington's army.

The 17,000 British troops who devoted the autumn of 1777 to campaigning in Chester County "Committed Many Robberies and Plundering of the Inhabitants of the several Townships . . . they Passed through," as Colonel Thomas Cheney later wrote to the Supreme Executive Council. The British, he reported, carried off "Horses, Cattle, Sheep & Swine, and all kind of Poultry, Wearing Apparel, Bedding, Household Goods, Grain and Provisions of all kinds," and "in many Places what they could not carry off they wantingly [wantonly] destroyed, which has greatly distressed [the] inhabitants." The British often stripped a farmhouse of everything of value; for example, they robbed Nathan Norton of Kennett of silver teaspoons, several dozen buttons, and two copies of the "Arabian Nights." The invaders looted even Quaker areas, although there "the English soldiers were friendly and sociable, asking many questions and allowing a good deal of liberty to the people."[36]

Washington crossed the Schuylkill and marched southwest as Howe moved north. On September 16 they met in the hills near the White Horse Tavern. The two armies formed in such fog and driving rain that the encounter became known as "The Battle Above the Clouds." Neither army could fire their muskets because of the dampness. The British were not able to try a bayonet attack; the ground was too wet to permit a charge. Frustrated, the armies disengaged.

Washington marched northwest to Reading Furnace to replace his soaked powder. Howe took advantage of Washington's withdrawal to seize Continental stores at Valley Forge and to send raiding parties south to Newtown Square and north to Phoenixville. Still unsure of Howe's immediate objective, Washington moved east again to Perkiomen Creek, east of the Schuylkill. He sent a warning to the Continental Congress in Philadelphia that Howe might move on the city at any time. Congress quickly left the city, later settling in the town of York, to the west. Many other refugees, including the state government, fled the city.

On September 25, the British army reached Germantown, five miles north of Philadelphia. The following day, Lord Cornwallis led 3,000 British troops down the Germantown Road into the city, leaving the bulk of the British army in Germantown. General Sir William Howe further dissipated British strength by sending forces to reduce the Delaware River forts and to escort supplies from Maryland. Washington attacked the British army at Germantown on October 4, seeking to take advantage of their reduced members. His complex strategy failed to win the Battle of Germantown, and the British settled into Philadelphia for the winter.

After weeks of fruitless maneuvers by both armies, the hungry and bedraggled Continental Army limped to winter quarters at Valley Forge, twenty miles northwest of Philadelphia on the northern border of Chester County, arriving in late December. The Valley Forge encampment was protected on the north by the Schuylkill River, which runs east to west at this point, and on the west by Valley Creek. Washington's men fortified the heavily wooded hills with a series of earthworks. From Valley Forge, Washington hoped to prevent large-scale British movements into the Pennsylvania countryside.[37]

The Chester County militia played a vital military and political role within the county during the winter of 1777–78. As General John Armstrong, in command of the Pennsylvania militia, reported to the Council of Safety, Washington was concerned with "the much exposed Situation of the Eastern parts of the State . . . [particularly] the extensive Country this Side the Schuylkill." According to the general, Washington hoped the militia would be "taking a variable Station on every leading Road betwixt Schuylkill and Delaware . . . to compete with Smaller parties of the Enemy, prevent Such from proceeding into the Country and intercept the business of Marketing or any other intercourse of the disaffected with the enemy." Armstrong believed that this could best be accomplished by pickets on every road, as well as patrols aided by "a few light Horse to proceed as near the Enemy as may be reasonable."[38]

The militia did not succeed in isolating Philadelphia from Chester County. British gold, more appealing than inflated continental currency, attracted ample provisions to the occupied city. Refugees streamed out of the city both before and during the occupation. Militia leaders were warned of spy activity and tried unsuccessfully to control access to Philadelphia by issuing passes.[39]

The militia was only partly effective as a deterrent to small-scale British raids into the county. Prodded by loyalists, the British sporadically attempted to harass prominent rebels by confiscating and destroying their property. They burned County Sheriff Charles Dilworth's tavern, but they spared Waynesboro, Anthony Wayne's fine stone mansion in Easttown, though British troops were in the vicinity more than once. Kidnapping was a favorite weapon against rebel leaders. The British kidnapped the elderly mayor of Chester, David Coupland, and confined him on a prison ship in the Delaware River until they abandoned Philadelphia. Captain John Crosby, home on leave from the Continental Army, was captured and sent to New York, where he was confined on the prison ship *Jersey*. Some prominent rebels, such as Robert Smith, took to sleeping in the barn or in different houses to foil would-be kidnappers.[40]

At least once, in December 1777, Cornwallis led a large force on a three-day raid into the county as far as Radnor and Newtown Townships. Apart from harassing rebels, skirmishing with groups of local militiamen, and gathering provisions obtainable with less risk in Philadelphia, the British achieved no military advantage by their expeditions into Chester County.[41]

At least the British were usually willing to pay for provisions they confiscated, except in the case of the property of known rebels. Washington's rapidly dwindling army at Valley Forge also depended on supplies from Chester County, which it paid for in inflated paper currency. Anticipating the British invasion, in July 1777, the Pennsylvania Supreme Executive Council ordered an inventory taken of all grain, livestock, wagons, and other stores in Chester County within twenty miles of the Delaware River. That winter the state government requisitioned the inventoried provisions and wagons, as well as arms, blankets, and clothing. In November the Council of Safety appointed a committee of twenty-two Chester County militia officers to collect supplies from those who "[had] not taken the Oath of Allegiance and Abjuration, or who have aided or assisted the enemy." Quakers, who could not conscientiously take the Oath of Allegiance, were an obvious target of such collections. Since they could not accept the compensation offered in such cases, collecting supplies from Quakers usually amounted to confiscation.[42]

Furthermore, the American army foraged almost as energetically as the British in marching through the countryside. Henry Melchior Muhlenberg wrote that, as the American army passed, "farms were being drained of wood, hay, and crops, and they are being ruined." Muhlenberg reported that the Lutheran Church in Pikestown, Chester County, "which had cost so much to build," suffered the fate of many substantial buildings in the Valley Forge area. It had been "occupied by American Troops, its interior was ripped out, the wood was made into beds, and the building was used as a hospital for the wounded and sick.[43]

Anthony Wayne, who returned to Chester County with Washington, advised him not to alienate the local minority who warmly supported the Revolution by allowing Continental troops to confiscate their produce essentially without compensation, or to waste his recruiting efforts in unsympathetic Chester County. Wayne eventually led a successful "grand forage" to New Jersey and brought back substantial provisions to Washington. Wayne's knowledgeable advice on local conditions could have been a great asset to Washington had his usefulness not been temporarily destroyed by the "Paoli massacre." In September 1777, after Washington's defeat at Brandywine, Wayne was ordered to post his division of 1,500 men near his home in Easttown Township. The following night, probably aided by a local loyalist, the British launched a bayonet attack on Wayne's camp, creating panicked flight among the American troops and, according to the British, killing 300 and taking 70–80 prisoners. Though a court-martial exonerated Wayne, Washington temporarily posted him to Lancaster County on a recruiting mission, to reduce tensions in the American camp.[44]

Chester Countians had more to fear than the losses to both armies and the frequent small-scale fights between British soldiers and loyalists, and between Continental soldiers and militia. The British invasion brought politically disunited Chester County a further breakdown of order and increased violence. Personal revenge and pure banditry flourished, often disguised as political acts. Tax collectors and militia recruiters were often targets of beatings and physical harassment; one of the several murders in the county during this period was that of a tax collector, William Boyd.[45]

Loyalist gangs operated in the county, contributing to the breakdown of law and order. The Doan gang was one such large gang that operated more in Bucks County than in Chester County. James Fitzpatrick was the most important Tory bandit in Chester County. A deserter from the American army, the handsome and athletic Fitzpatrick helped guide Howe's army through Chester County. Then Fitzpatrick began a series of raids in Chester County. He targeted militia recruiters, tax collectors, and those who made any attempts to capture him. He enjoyed not only robbing them, but also physically punishing them and making them look ridiculous. Fitzpatrick robbed one tax collector, Captain McGowan, tied him to a tree and flogged him, and then carefully cut off his queue, of which the captain was known to be inordinately vain. Characteristically, however, he returned the watch he had stolen from McGowan when the officer mentioned it was a family heirloom. Protected by local Tories, and inspiring fear of retaliation among potential informers, the dashing "Fitz" terrorized rebels until he was caught and hanged in 1778.[46]

The Pennsylvania Supreme Executive Council remained troubled by these problems and by possible Tory plots in Chester County after the British occupation ended. Most of the handful of Chester Countians who became active loyalists left Pennsylvania with the British army in May 1778. Yet humble loyalists persisted in hopes of a second invasion. Patriots frequently reported their poorly laid plots to the Council.[47]

The Supreme Executive Council relied on Robert Smith, the County Lieutenant, his sub-lieutenants, and the militia to counter violence and loyalist activity, to support Washington during the British invasion and his encampment at Valley Forge, and to uphold the new Pennsylvania constitution politically. In late 1777 the Council commissioned the militia to raise companies of light dragoons to counter the most serious loyalist threats, such as the recalcitrance of the southeastern townships and the attacks of mounted armed loyalists on rebel leaders.[48]

The Constitutionalist state government supported Chester County's western township Scots-Irish Presbyterians in county politics. When two sets of election returns were made from Chester County in 1778, the Supreme Executive Council accepted the Constitutionalist returns. In the first three years of independence, the county's Assembly delegation strongly supported Constitutionalist positions in state politics. These delegates, who in 1777 and 1778 were all new to the Assembly, were overwhelmingly western township Scots-Irish.[49]

As the British invasion passed into memory, opposition to the constitution became a stronger political position. In Chester County the "test oath" and the attempts of the militia to deny non-Associators voting rights were grievances shared by more than half the population: Quakers, pacifist Germans, active and passive loyalists, and Anti-Constitutionalists. Chester County returned Radical assemblymen in the early years of the war partly because voter turnout was extremely light both because of the "test oath" and opposition to the new government. By the last years of the war, Chester County voter turnout was double that of the early years of the Revolutionary government. In 1784 the top vote-getter received 1,790 votes, and all six assemblymen elected polled more than 1,000 votes each, compared with 284 votes for the most successful candidate in 1777. In fact, judges of elections must have been permitting considerable numbers of unqualified voters who had not taken the "test oath" to vote, to account for the turnout in 1781. In the last years of the war, Chester County returned more moderate Assembly delegations, which were committed to the repeal of the "test oath" and the overthrow of the Pennsylvania constitution of 1776.[50]

Several years passed before these goals were reached. The "test oath" was not repealed until 1787; the constitution was not replaced until 1790. However, by 1783 the Anti-Constitutionalists, also known as Republicans, were firmly entrenched in the Assembly delegation from Chester County. Some who had withdrawn from politics in 1776 took Assembly seats, among them former Quaker Assemblyman Charles Humphreys and the former non-Quaker Justice of the Peace, Richard Riley. Anthony Wayne briefly served as an Assemblyman and signaled the return to local political influence of Continental officers. Another Republican Assemblyman was Richard Willing, who had served as a militia colonel but whom Constitutionalists resented because of his family's well-known hospitality to the British during the occupation of Philadelphia.[51]

The Constitutionalists became a minority party in Chester County. The Republicans pressed their advantage within the county and in the Assembly. As the Chester County Constitutionalists had used Assembly support to underpin their position in the first years of independence, the Chester County Republicans used their stronger position in the Assembly to humiliate their adversaries in the 1780s. In 1784, Chester County Radicals complained to the Assembly that many who had not taken the "test oath" were being permitted to vote in the county. The Assembly appointed a Republican-dominated committee to investigate the charges; the committee claimed it could not judge the situation unless the complainants submitted more specific charges. The well-known Constitutionalists Samuel Cunningham, John Culbertson, and John Boyd duly submitted the required information. In a lengthy closed session, the pro-Republican committee attacked and humiliated the petitioners. When Cunningham, Culbertson, and Boyd complained to the Assembly of the committee's unfair and rude treatment, the Assembly, by a strictly party vote, found the accusations unjust and ill-founded.[52]

The Republicans again used their strong position at the state level to punish former Constitutionalist adversaries in 1786. The Supreme Executive Council ordered Chester County Lieutenant Robert Smith to appear to answer charges from his political enemies concerning the improper levying of militia fines. The Council removed the aged and ill Smith from office, then reinstated him, then finally revoked his reinstatement. His forced retirement marked the ignominious end of the Constitutionalists' great role in the Revolutionary struggle in Chester County.[53]

As politically disruptive as the Revolutionary years, particularly the early years of the war, were to Chester County, their economic impact was minimal in the long run. Unevenly felt hardship such as the loss of personnel to the Continental Army and to the militia, and the destruction and confiscation of property in the county by both sides in the struggle, had a largely short-term economic impact on Chester County as a whole. The interruption of county government in the early years of the Revolution, particularly 1777–78, also had a primarily short-term economic effect. Peace eased the longer-term economic problems such as inflation and the interruption of the export trade through Philadelphia, which by 1789 had again reached prewar levels. A comparison of prewar and postwar tax assessments shows that many Chester County farmers flourished during the Revolution. Inventories of estates suggests a continued increase of wealth during the period. Substantially settled for decades, Chester County felt no serious economic loss from the interruption of immigration into the county. The substantial emigration from the county to western Pennsylvania and down the Appalachian chain slowed only slightly during the early years of the Revolution, and it increased in the early 1780s. Emigration for the decade 1775–85 reached levels that were substantially unchanged from high prewar levels.[54]

The chief long-term effects of the Revolution on Chester County were not economic but political. As a result of the Revolution, Chester County permanently lost political power at the provincial level. Its Assembly representation was proportionately reduced at the outset of the Revolution. The creation of new counties to the west in 1781 and afterward further decreased Chester County's relative weight in state politics. The Quaker party, which dominated the Pennsylvania Assembly before the Revolution and which magnified Chester County's influence there, was gone.

Political changes within the county were even greater. The increased political influence of the western townships led to a transfer of the county seat from the town of Chester on the Delaware River to what is now West Chester, in the middle of the county, in 1786. This move increased the east-west political tension and precipitated the splitting of Chester County into two counties in 1789: Delaware County in the east with the town of Chester as its capital, and Chester County in the west, with its capital at West Chester.

Several Revolutionary changes increased democracy in the county. The abolition of property qualifications for voting expanded suffrage, despite the limitations on suffrage imposed by the requirement in the first years after 1776 that voters swear allegiance to the new constitution, eliminating, among others, Quakers, who could not take the oath. The Revolution also gave access to leadership positions to Chester Countians from western townships and to ethnic groups, such as the Scots-Irish, previously unrepresented. In their constitution of 1776, the Radicals also sought to end the long unchallenged terms of pre-Revolutionary assemblymen, such as those from Chester County, limiting Assembly terms to no more than four out of any consecutive seven years. This provision did not directly limit the terms of Chester County assemblymen in the 1780s, as no Chester Countian served more than three years in seven during the period. Still, it created the perception of holding a seat in the Assembly as a temporary service, not a long-term career. Finally, the two-party politics that emerged after the destruction of the Quaker party advanced democracy in the county. At first, the parties that emerged were little more than two factions loosely organized around a handful of issues, such as the repeal of the constitution of 1776 and of the "test act." Nevertheless, the new system opened Chester County politics to broader public debate and more representative leadership.

Politics were no longer the preserve of eastern township Quakers or of their Revolutionary successors, western township Presbyterians, but were inclusive of these groups and others as well. Chester County's political tranquility was lost during the Revolutionary period, but a livelier democracy was the result.

2

Bucks County

Owen S. Ireland

The War of the American Revolution divided the people of Bucks County, Pennsylvania. It turned neighbor against neighbor and precipitated a decade or more of physical and political violence. On one level, we know that war is a "scourge," a "blood-swollen god," often a tragic experience for those closest to it. Yet all too often we have allowed the contest between Great Britain and its thirteen North American colonies to become a bloodless abstraction, a clash of ideologies or classes. The history of Bucks County between 1774 and 1780 reminds us that the Revolution brought pain, suffering, death, and widespread social disruption to many.[1]

The people of Bucks County united in rejecting British claims to unlimited power, but they also divided sharply and deeply over how best to resist. The full magnitude of this division remains to be defined and explained. Preliminary analysis, however, suggests that the key to it lay in the ways different religious groups within the county responded to the war. In broad terms, between 1774 and 1778 well-to-do men, principally Presbyterian, Baptist, and Reformed (Dutch and German), displaced an equally well-to-do group of men, largely Quakers. The first supported the use of arms against the British; the second did not. Both groups were politically experienced. Most of the men in the new group had received appointed offices in the County from the proprietary government of Pennsylvania. Most of those in the old group had held popularly-elected office. The new group seemed to speak for a minority of the residents of the County; the old group, for the majority.

Bucks County on the eve of the Revolution was one of the most English, most Quaker, most rural, and most politically stable counties in Pennsylvania. Located north and east of the city of Philadelphia, its broad, gently rolling farm-land had attracted a heavy influx of diverse peoples. The English Quakers predominated, however, with eight Meetings located strategically in every section of the county. Alexander Graydon, born and raised in Bristol in southern Bucks County, later recalled that in the village of his youth "the principal inhabitants were Quakers."[2] General John Lacey, a Revolutionary military and political leader, claimed that where he grew up in Bucks "none but Quaker families resided." In 1772, a Philadelphia Anglican clergyman, William Smith, lamented that Bucks County had "not a single" Anglican minister and described the Quakers as "the most numerous body" in the county.[3]

Bucks County also was home to a variety of Dutch and German settlers. The Dutch, mostly from New York, adhered principally to the Reformed tradition. The Germans, many of whom spilled over from the heavy German settlement areas to the west, in Philadelphia County, came from a more diverse religious background. Mennonites (sometimes described as German or Swiss Quakers) and German Dunkers (Baptists) came first, then a variety of pietistic sects followed by an increasing flow of Reformed and a smattering of Lutherans.[4]

In the central areas of the county, especially in the vicinity of Neshaminy, a small number of Presbyterians, many of Scots-Irish background, settled. Here, at the now famous "Log College," the Tennent family had sparked and fueled the Great Awakening among the Presbyterians in the mid-eighteenth century. English Baptists also had staked out a place for themselves in the central portions

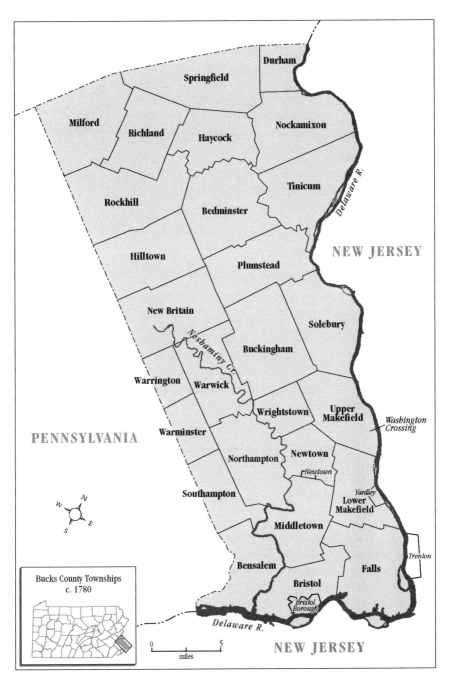

Bucks County Townships c. 1780

of the county. Most, apparently, had moved into the Baptist fold from one or another of the more numerous denominations, especially the Quakers.[5]

Bucks County was predominantly rural and agricultural. Its two sleepy villages together contained no more than a thousand souls. Bristol, the county's first administrative center, was situated about twenty miles northeast of Philadelphia on the direct land route to New York. Its location and its function had promised to make it into a major urban center, but the promise remained unfulfilled in the eighteenth century. One native of the village looking back from the early nineteenth century wrote: "There are few towns, perhaps, in Pennsylvania, which . . . [from 1756 to 1811] . . . have been so little improved, or undergone less alteration."[6] The second county seat, Newtown, was slightly more isolated and, if possible, more somnolent.[7]

Bucks farmers produced wheat, eighteenth-century Pennsylvania's principal cash crop, as well as meat and truck for Philadelphia. The county's proximity to the Delaware River and to the city facilitated its participation in the growing consumer culture and in the international market.[8] Bucks County had other, though relatively less important, economic assets. For example, the Durham iron mines and iron works in the northeastern corner of the county produced pig iron and shot for the patriot cause, but the county's iron production was greatly overshadowed by that of the Schuylkill and Susquehanna Valleys.[9]

This largely rural, commercial, agricultural population exhibited a marked degree of economic equality.[10] Well over 40 percent of the county's taxables held between 100 and 299 areas of land. Probably 70 to 80 percent held enough land to constitute a viable farmstead capable of supporting a family.[11] The vast majority could thus maintain the independent and autonomous ideal toward which large numbers of eighteenth-century Americans aspired.[12] About 25 percent of Bucks households held no land, but not all of these were necessarily poor. Families struggling on the edge of subsistence undoubtedly constituted part of this landless population. Most likely, the propertyless households also included young men who in time could expect to acquire land, and an indeterminate but significant number of tenants of varying degrees of affluence, including those Lucy Simler and Paul Clemens have labeled "cottagers."[13] Thus we might say of Bucks County what Jackson T. Main said of Connecticut. It was "a land of plenty for some and of sufficiency for most people," and "the great majority . . . did not simply escape poverty but enjoyed real plenty."[14]

Bucks County's heterogeneous population appears to have lived together easily and peacefully. Historian Sally Schwartz argues that there was a widespread commitment to the ideal of liberty of conscience and toleration in eighteenth-century Pennsylvania. She concluded that most Pennsylvanians "came to take pride in the way all colonists lived harmoniously with their neighbors."[15] Alan Tully attributes much of this harmony to the deliberate efforts of the Quakers to build and maintain an inclusive and balanced political coalition that cut across ethnic and religious lines and tempered public disagreements.[16]

If that were the case, then, nowhere did this policy of accommodation produce a more successful outcome for Quakers than in Bucks County. Before the Revolution, voters in the county sent Quaker or Quaker-backed Anglicans, Germans, and Dutch to the provincial legislature, where they regularly supported the Assembly or the Quaker party.[17] Furthermore, among Quakers, political and religious leadership overlapped. Many men elected to the provincial Assembly from Bucks County were also conspicuous in the Quaker Meetings.[18] The attachment of county voters to Quaker party was unassailable, as one of their challengers discovered. Samuel Purviance, a Presbyterian merchant from Philadelphia and a zealous organizer for the "New [anti-Quaker] Ticket," traveled the county court circuit in 1765 recruiting anti-Quaker support. "I went lately up to Bucks Court," he reported optimistically before the election, "in order to concert measures for their Election in pursuance of which we have appointed a considerable meeting of Germans, Baptists, and Presbyterians to be held next Monday at Neshaminy."[19] Purviance's efforts, however, came to nothing. Bucks voted the Quaker ticket in 1765 and in every year thereafter until October 1776.

Between 1764 and 1774 a succession of crises disrupted the British Empire and pitted the North American colonies against their mother country. In the early stages of this conflict, Bucks County appears to have shared the general American concern about the intrusion of Parliamentary authority into the internal domestic affairs of the colonies. There is, however, no evidence of concerted anti-British action in the county before 1774.[20]

In December 1773, Boston's reaction to the Tea Act provoked a new crisis. Parliament had earlier, in the Declaratory Act, defined the colonies as subordinate political bodies for whom it could and would legislate as it saw fit. In 1774, Parliament acted on this principle. Its new enactments, labeled "Coercive" by the English and "Intolerable" by the colonists, closed the port of Boston and altered the structure of government and the administration of justice in Massachusetts. The harshness of these acts and the threat they posed to the other colonies united most Americans in opposition. The people of Bucks County were no exception. They too saw the "Intolerable Acts" as a threat to their collective freedom and to the local autonomy they had long enjoyed. They too reacted vigorously and negatively. On July 9, 1774, many of the traditional political leaders of the county assembled in an ad hoc meeting at Newtown. Gilbert Hicks, a well-to-do landholder, a county commissioner, a justice of the peace, and the presiding judge at the Court of Quarter Sessions, chaired the meeting. Under his leadership, these men condemned the British claims and declared it the "Duty of every American" in "this time of public distress" to resist the "Claims of the British Parliament to make laws, binding on the inhabitants of these Colonies . . . without their consent." They also demanded that a "general Congress" define and secure the "Liberties of the Colonies" and restore "that Harmony so necessary for the interests and happiness of both." And finally, they chose delegates to attend a "meeting of the several Committees of the respective Counties of Pennsylvania" scheduled to convene in Philadelphia on July 15.[21]

In Fall 1774, the First Continental Congress met in Philadelphia and committed itself to the Continental Association, an agreement to use economic coercion against the British. Bucks County followed suit. On November 27, 1774, its leaders, again assembled at Newtown, explained the Continental Association to their constituents and then called for the popular election of a Bucks County Committee, to "observe the Conduct of all persons touching" on the boycott.[22] On December 15 the voters of the county chose twenty-nine men to perform that task. This group, referred to variously as the "Committee of Observation," the "Committee of Inspection," or the "Committee of Safety," guided the patriot effort in the county for the next year and a half.

A bad snowstorm on December 29 prevented the first scheduled meeting of the new Committee, but it convened on January 16, 1775, and demonstrated its resolve to support the American cause. It declared that it "highly approve[d] of the pacific measures recommended by the Continental Congress"; it pledged the people of Bucks County, "bound, in justice to ourselves, our posterity, our King, and our Country, . . . to keep the Association"; and it committed them "both as Christians and as Countrymen, to contribute toward the relief and support of the poor inhabitants of the town of Boston, now suffering in the general cause of all the Colonies."[23] During the next few months, Bucks demonstrated its commitment in a concrete way. In conjunction with Berks, it contributed in excess of £200 for "the sufferers under the Boston Port Act."[24]

Three aspects of the Committee's composition and stance shed light on the popular response to the "Intolerable Acts" in Bucks County. First, the Committee, elected by the same voters who traditionally chose the county's provincial and local officers, was the first popularly elected, extralegal, Revolutionary body in the county.

Second, the membership of the Committee included many, if not most, of the county's powerful political figures and reflected much of its ethnic and religious diversity. Of the thirty men who served on the first Committee and/or represented the county in the provincial conference in the summer of 1774, at least seventeen had collectively held at least twenty-two major public offices in the county, ranging from assemblyman through coroner to justice and county commissioner. In addition, at least nine were Quaker, two were Presbyterian, and one each came from Baptist, Anglican, and Dutch Reformed backgrounds. More telling, perhaps, is that the five-man Committee of Correspondence, the effective leadership cadre of the larger Committee, contained three Quakers, one Baptist, and one Dutch Reformed. At least four of these five men had held prominent county offices.[25]

Third and equally important, Bucks County's first popular elected Committee defined its position rather precisely. On the one hand, it took a radical stance in challenging the claims of the British Parliament. Given the prickly nature of that legislative body and the naked power it could assemble in its own defense, the Committee's direct defiance was courageous. These Bucks County farmers threw down the gauntlet to one of the most proud and powerful governing bodies in the eighteenth-century world.

On the other hand, they were determined to contain that challenge within relatively narrow limits. They recognized the need for collective action. They repeatedly defined themselves and their fellow American sufferers as "countrymen." They committed themselves to "the pacific measures recommended by the Continental Congress for the redress of American Grievances," but they would not support violence.[26]

The Committee's response to Philadelphia's call for action reflected that attitude. The Philadelphia Committee had announced a provincial convention for January 23 to consider additional measures, and some Pennsylvanians talked of making military preparations. The Bucks Committee refused to participate. It informed the Philadelphia Committee rather abruptly: "[We] cannot conceive . . . the necessity of such Provincial Convention or that any good effects can be produced thereby."[27]

Thus, in January 1775 a popularly elected and widely representative body of traditional political leaders defined Bucks County's position. They saw themselves as part of an identifiable group called Americans. They unequivocally rejected the Parliamentary claims of unlimited authority over them. They joined their fellow Americans in peaceful economic coercion to obtain redress of their grievances, and they contributed liberally to the relief of those in Boston suffering in the common cause. They would not, however, go beyond this. In short, they would neither submit nor rebel. Unfortunately for the future peace and harmony of the county, mounting pressures from the evolving military activities, from the Continental Congress, and from Philadelphia made this position increasingly untenable. Bucks County soon divided into hostile factions.

News of the battles at Lexington and Concord arrived in Philadelphia on April 24, 1775. The British troops had marched into the Massachusetts countryside; blood had been shed. Protests and petitions had given way to violence. This outbreak of hostilities destroyed the unanimity with which the heterogeneous population of Bucks County had earlier responded to Parliamentary claims of omnipotence.

On the provincial level, a mass meeting at the State House in Philadelphia on April 25 agreed to "associate, for the Purpose of defending with ARMS their Property, Liberty, and Lives."[28] This decision radically changed the Association and its adherents, the Associators. Back in the fall of 1774 many in Pennsylvania had associated together to boycott British goods. Organizing on a county-by-county level, they had called their agreement the Association and themselves the Associators. Now, many of these same people had agreed to take up arms. This act transformed the Association into a military commitment and Associators into citizen soldiers.

In early May 1775, the Pennsylvania legislature moved in the same direction, and by mid-summer it had committed itself to military defense. It authorized an issue of paper money to cover the Associators' expenses; it urged Associators, now transformed from peaceful boycotters into an armed force, to "bear a tender and brotherly Regard" toward those "conscientiously scrupulous of bearing arms," and it encouraged pacifists to provide financial assistance to the Associators "cheerfully" and "in Proportion to their abilities."[29]

Pennsylvania's Quakers, however, moved in the opposite direction. They refused to support armed rebellion against the King. Over time, they took an increasingly intransigent, if not belligerent, stance in opposition to the patriot cause. Back in September 1774 the Quaker Yearly Meeting had assumed a moderate stance, but clearly one that foreshadowed its future opposition. It had urged trust in God and respect for the King, from whom Pennsylvania had received its charter and under whom, the Meeting said, Pennsylvania had been well governed.[30]

Then, in December 1774 the Pennsylvania "Meeting for Sufferings" (an official voice of the Quaker religious body) pressured Quaker legislators to oppose the Association. In January 1775, the "Meeting for Sufferings" took a position that historian Richard Bauman has called "tendentious, defiant, and provocative." It condemned both the Continental Congress and Congress's support of an economic boycott (i.e., the Association) as "repugnant to the peaceable Principles of our Christian Profession," and it made disaffection to the King a matter for discipline.

One year later, in January 1776, as Thomas Paine's *Common Sense* urged repudiation of the King and the British connection, the Quaker "Meeting for Sufferings" took a defiant stand. It blamed the current calamities on sin, praised the past government under the King, and prohibited writing or acting in a way designed to break the connection with Great Britain. In the fall of 1776, the Yearly Meeting took the final step toward an outright break with the patriots. It forbade Quakers in good standing with the Meeting from having "any Share in the Authority and Powers of Government," from participating in the militia, or from paying fines in lieu of that service.[31]

In Bucks County, the Quaker leadership took this injunction seriously and moved forcefully to ensure compliance. On November 28, 1776, for example, the Quarterly Meeting at Middletown, responding to the "Weighty Matters" of the "last Yearly Meeting," appointed a committee to "visit the Several Monthly Meetings belonging to the Quarter" to counter the "instability and Deviation of some . . . in this time of Commotion" and to "afford them Such help and Assistance for the removing Disorders and the Maintaining and supporting the testimony of truth and our Christian Discipline."[32]

Between the fall of 1774 and the fall of 1776, the patriots and Quakers in Bucks County took increasingly incompatible positions. At the beginning, in the winter of 1774–75, Quakers elected and were elected to the County Committee, which in turn had organized the local Association. By May 1775, many Quakers in Bucks had begun to distance themselves from the Association. In the next few months the Quakers and the patriots went their separate ways.

The core of the County Committee, the five-man Committee of Correspondence, divided. Its three Quaker members withdrew, while the other two members, an English Baptist and a Dutch Reformed, continued. These two, believing that "something should be done towards warding off the oppressive measures . . . against us . . . ," called for a meeting of the full Committee on May 8. Those who assembled committed themselves to military preparation and called on the people of Bucks County to "form themselves into Associations . . . to improve themselves in the military art."[33]

Despite its brave words, the County Committee was disintegrating. The minutes of its May 8 meeting indicate that those present acted "unanimously," but the records do not tell us how many participated. Attendance at the next three meetings suggests that only a fraction of the original membership supported the shift from peaceful to violent protest. At the June 12 meeting, only ten of the twenty-nine members attended. The minutes of the August session claimed that "a large majority" was present but offered no names. By September, only about half the original group remained active; eight had formally resigned and an additional five or six had simply stopped attending. The bulk of the absent men were Quakers. The Committee itself behaved in an increasingly militant and determined fashion. It assumed general direction of the now militarized Association. It also struggled with petty jurisdictional disputes and with personal squabbles among competing aspirants to military titles. Most important, it worked to silence dissent and to disarm opponents.

Initially, suppressing verbal opposition took precedence. Some of the individuals hauled before this tribunal for uttering "expressions derogatory and injurious to the general American cause" quickly repented. John Hoff, for example, "voluntarily" appeared, "acknowledged the charge," and "made such concessions as were considered as a sufficient atonement for his former errors."[34] In the same vein, Thomas Meredith, when confronted by an array of hostile accusers, groveled before the Committee, demeaning himself in a public act of contrition whose religious overtones speak volumes: "Whereas, I have spoken injuriously of the distressed people of the town of Boston, and disrespectfully of the Measures prosecuting for the redress of American Grievances; I do hereby declare, that I am heartily sorry for what I have done, voluntarily renouncing my former principles, and promise for the future to render my Conduct unexceptionable to my Countrymen."[35]

The Committee dealt severely with those who resisted. Thomas Smith of Upper Makefield, for example, stood accused of uttering "expressions derogatory to the continental Congress and inimical to the Liberties of America." He denied those charges but asserted that "the Measures of Congress had already enslaved America" and "that the whole was nothing but a scheme of a parcel of hot-headed Presbyterians." The Committee investigated further and then denounced Smith for casting "the grossest indignities upon the Honourable the Continental Congress" and for raising "invidious Distinctions between different denominations." Smith should be considered, the Committee declared, "An Enemy of the Rights of British America," and it urged all persons to "break off every kind of dealing with him." Within a month, Smith capitulated.[36]

Silencing dissent continued to absorb a fair portion of the Committee's time but, prodded by Philadelphia, it also began to disarm probable opponents. It first encouraged each of its members to purchase the weapons from those who would be "willing to part with [them] on reasonable terms." In time, however, it created a formal structure for seizing arms by force. In April 1776, it empowered the "Collectors of the Arms" to call on the militia to deal with those who refused to surrender their weapons. The need to disarm dissenters by force suggests that, by 1776, opposition to the patriot cause extended beyond pacifist Quakers and German sectarians. The later behavior of the Doan gang (see below) points toward the same conclusion, as does the organization in 1777–78 of a loyalist troop of mounted Bucks County men under the leadership of William (possibly Evan) Thomas, a Welshman from Hilltown, and Owen Roberts, from New Britain.[37]

By late summer 1776, two determined bodies of men contended for dominion in Bucks County. On the one hand, the Committee of Safety and its adherents sought to organize a military defense, convert its burgeoning extralegal organization into a working government, and intimidate its opposition. A complex group of Quakers, pacifists, loyalists, and feisty individuals resisted. At least some of these had undoubtedly been alienated by the coercive tactics of the Committee of Safety.

There is insufficient data to define precisely the composition of the competing groups, but a number of indicators suggest that between 1775 and 1778, Quakers and other principled pacifists constituted the core of the opposition. Patriots represented a more heterogeneous collection of Presbyterians, Baptists, and Reformed and included at least some Anglicans and Lutherans and a handful of disowned Quakers.

A comparison of the delegations that represented Bucks County on the state level before and after 1776 suggests the ethnic-religious dimension of this shift in power. The men chosen in the last five elections under the old provincial charter (1772–76) came from middling economic backgrounds. One was rich, one held very little land, and the rest had substantial but moderate landholdings, mostly between 200 and 300 acres. Few held slaves. The men chosen to represent Bucks County in the Revolutionary government in 1776 and 1777 came from similar economic backgrounds. One was wealthy; nine held between 200 and 500 acres. Six had more modest assets, but four of the six had other sources of income: mills, tanneries, or professions. Moreover, the majority owned slaves.[38]

Thus, both before and after the Declaration of Independence, Bucks County voters sent men of substantial property to represent them on the state level. If anything, the patriot representatives were somewhat better off than their provincial predecessors. They also had a greater investment in slaves, which is another reflection of the declining political power of the Quakers who led Pennsylvania in freeing the state of the sin of slaveholding. Although the two elected groups of men came from roughly the same economic strata, they differed dramatically in their ethnic and religious backgrounds. In simple terms, Quakers and their Anglican, German, and Dutch allies dominated the early legislative delegation. Presbyterians, Lutherans, Baptists, Reformed, and disowned Quakers predominated in the later group.

The actual picture was more complex. The pre-1776 delegation had three distinguishing characteristics: a high degree of continuity, an unequivocal Quaker complexion, and two apparently "token" minority seats. Fourteen men filled the forty legislative seats (eight a year for five years) between 1772 and 1776, and four of these men won election in all five years. One Anglican, the future loyalist Joseph Galloway, led the Quaker party in the Assembly and won election from Bucks County until he withdrew from politics in 1775. A Quaker replaced him. For all intents and purposes, "Quakers" regularly controlled at least five of the eight Assembly seats in each of the five years. Furthermore, some of these Quakers also held prominent positions within the Quaker religious organization.[39]

Quakers, however, did not monopolize these positions of power. Possibly by chance, more likely by design, the Germans and the Dutch each had at least one seat. Peter Shepherd had held the "German" seat since the 1760s. In 1774 he passed it to John Heany, who kept it until 1776, when, in opposition to the Revolution, he withdrew from elective office. Henry Krewsen, of Reformed Dutch background, passed the "Dutch" seat in 1774 to Gerardus Wynkoop.

Unlike the German Heany, the Dutchman Wynkoop accepted independence and later sat in the Revolutionary legislature.[40]

In sharp contrast, the men elected to statewide office in the Revolutionary era (1776–77) were much more diverse. Six were Reformed or Presbyterian, two were Baptists, two were disowned Quakers, one was a German Lutheran, and one was an Anglican. These men also reflected a much more unstable situation. Over two years, nineteen men filled twenty-five seats in four bodies: the Provincial Convention of June 1776; the state constitutional convention of July 1776; and the State Assembly in November 1777 and 1778. Most of these men served only once; only one won election to three of the four bodies. Despite its heterogeneity and its apparent instability, the composition of this Revolutionary delegation suggests the core of a new coalition made up of three hitherto excluded groups:

1. Powerful and well-to-do men such as Joseph Hart and Joseph Kirkbride, whose conflicts with the Quaker meeting before the Revolutionary era had deprived them of the popular elective office to which their wealth and status otherwise would have entitled them.
2. Prominent leaders of the Dutch Reformed community, including Henry and Gerardus Wynkoop, who had cooperated with the Quakers before 1776 but broke with them in 1775–1776, and then continued to enjoy popular support among the Reformed, Presbyterian, Baptist, and Lutheran groups that now made up the bulk of the participating electorate.
3. Men from groups not represented in the immediate pre-war years, such as Lutheran John Keller, Baptist William Van Horn, and Presbyterian John Crawford.

In the broadest terms, the shift in power in Bucks County in 1776 reflects the emergence of men of social and economic stature previously excluded from elected office because of their alienation from the dominant Quakers. The Bucks County Revolution apparently brought to power a non-Quaker economic elite.

The degree of public support enjoyed by the two contending groups eludes precise measurement, but voter turnout in two elections in the fall of 1776 suggests the relative electoral strength of each. The first election occurred on October 1, 1776. Historically, Pennsylvanians had gone to the polls early in October each year to elect representatives to the Assembly. By early Fall 1776, however, radical changes had transformed the political landscape. Congress had declared America's independence; British and American forces faced each other on the field of battle; and Pennsylvania's state constitutional convention, elected in July, had assumed responsibility for governing the province while it drafted a new fundamental law for the state. In September this convention published its proposed constitution and scheduled the election of representatives to a new state legislature for early in November.

A sizeable portion of Bucks County's eligible voters chose to act as if none of this had happened. Operating expressly under the authority of the old provincial charter, the county's prewar election officials held the annual fall legislative election at the customary time and place. Led by the old county sheriff, Samuel Biles, and by Gilbert Hicks, the judge who had organized the first patriot protest meeting two years earlier, about 600 men risked calumny, public harassment, violence, and possible imprisonment to come to the polls. There they voted, with near unanimity, to reelect almost the entire slate of Quaker party representatives who had served in the last (1775) colonial legislature.[41]

A month later, the patriots in Pennsylvania held their first legislative election. The new state constitution had extended the franchise to all adult male taxpayers. Thus, for this November 1776 election Bucks County's potential electorate had been expanded to about 3,500. However, only about 100 men chose to demonstrate their commitment to the cause by casting a vote.

Many factors combined to produce this extraordinarily low rate of participation. It would be unwise to view this turnout as a direct measure of patriot support and to conclude that antipatriots exceeded patriots in Bucks County by a 6 to 1 ratio. On the other hand, in October 1776 more than 600 men risked much in a public demonstration of dissent, while in November 1776 only 100 took a parallel risk to demonstrate their revolutionary zeal. Equally significant is that at no time before Yorktown in 1781 did the voter turnout in Bucks county match that of the antipatriots of October 1776.[42]

Additional evidence reinforces the conclusion that in the early years of independence (1776–78) the bulk of Bucks County's people remained opposed or indifferent to the patriot cause. In the winter of 1776, for example, Washington complained incessantly about the lack of support he received from Bucks. He and the remnants of his army had beaten a hasty retreat from New York across New Jersey toward Philadelphia. The British followed at a more leisurely pace. By December 1776, Washington had crossed the Delaware into Bucks County, from which he would, at the end of the month, recross the river to engage the

British at Trenton and Princeton. While in Bucks, as he wrote to his brother John, he discovered himself "in a bad situation." He was "in a very disaffected part of the Province" in a "Neighbourhood of very disaffected People." "The public Spirit and Virtue of the People . . . has manifested," he said, "but too small a Regard to their Rights and Liberties." He demanded that the Pennsylvania Council of Safety give its serious attention to the problem and warned his General Officers to take care "that . . . these Persons do not . . . betray us." On December 21 he described his situation as "critical, and truly alarming." He later wrote to General Philip Schuyler that the degree of disaffection was "beyond anything you might have conceived."[43]

Most discouraging and most threatening, the patriot militia also failed Washington. He had originally entertained "little doubt of receiving considerable support from the Militia" in Bucks, he said, but he was disappointed: "But few . . . have yet come out." He appealed again and again to the state Council of Safety and to the Bucks County Lieutenant, Joseph Kirkbride, to little avail. The local militia not only refused to obey, but, Washington heard, "exulted at the approach of the Enemy." The American commander-in-chief, worrying "whether such people are to be trusted with Arms in their Hands" and fearing that they might use their weapons "against us, if the opportunity offers," urged the state to consider disarming the Bucks militia.[44]

Bucks County grain farmers and millers posed another problem for Washington: they refused to sell wheat or grind it into flour for the army. Washington suggested that only fear could remedy the problem. In December 1776, he authorized his deputy commissary general to confiscate grain, to seize mills, and to "Imploy [them] for the use of the Public." In spite of all Washington might do, however, a month later he was still complaining of a lack of flour. In January 1777, he declared that "A Scarcity of Flour in Pennsylvania must be fictitious and not owing to any real Want" and concluded that the farmers and millers acted "either from disaffection or an unwillingness to take Continental Money in pay, which . . . is the same thing." He condemned "those Millers who have Wheat and refuse to grind it." They should, he declared, be "treated as the worse Enemies of their Country."[45]

Bucks County's overall manpower contribution to the Continental Army in these years reflects the same lack of enthusiasm for the Revolution. In the early stages of the war, Bucks lagged far behind every other county in Pennsylvania save Bedford, which was isolated in the far western mountains. During the entire course of the war, Bucks, with about 7 percent of the state's taxpayers, manned approximately 3 percent (5 of approximately 155) of the infantry companies of Continentals recruited in Pennsylvania.[46]

On the local scene, Bucks County produced an equally unimpressive military showing. Between 1775 and 1778 the County Association, the military arm of the patriot cause, probably never commanded the loyalty of the majority of the county's residents. Certainly, in these years it did not enjoy the participation of the majority of the eligible men in the county. In the late summer of 1775, in the first flush of the war fever, a "rage militaire" may have inflamed the war spirits in most places, but not in Bucks. An official tabulation found that non-Associators outnumbered Associators among the county's adult male residents.[47]

In the fall of 1777, the patriot lamp flickered low in the county. The British occupied the city of Philadelphia while Washington took the Continental Army into winter quarters at Valley Forge. The course of the war and the close proximity of the British troops further reduced the martial spirit in Bucks, and in December 1776, Washington had called in vain for militia support from Bucks. A year later, in December 1777, General John Armstrong could muster only about 1,000 men to patrol the entire area between the Schuylkill and Delaware Rivers. Early in 1778, when General John Lacey commanded these local forces, their numbers ranged between 60 and 600 men.[48]

By early Spring 1778, what Lacey had described earlier as a "sullen, vindictive and malignant spirit" infecting "a large portion of the People" of Bucks had spread and intensified. The patriot forces had little or no control of the county within a 20-to-25-mile radius of Philadelphia. Loyalists took their revenge, using such guerrilla tactics as arson and kidnapping. Organized bands of irregulars roamed the countryside, "burning of houses of those who act vigorously in the militia, receive stores, etc. . . ." or who held civil office under the Revolutionary authority. In addition, "a few deluded inhabitants" as the Congress resolution calling for the death penalty labeled them, "have associated together for the purpose of seizing and secretly conveying to . . . the British . . . loyal citizens, officers and soldiers . . . as may fall into their power."[49]

These roving bands terrorized the civilian and the military population. One group took Captain Francis Murray prisoner in February 1778 within sight of his home in Newtown. Mrs. Joseph Reed, living in neighboring Philadelphia County, constantly feared for her husband, the future president of Pennsylvania and a current member of Congress. "Indeed," she wrote at the end of February 1778, "I am easiest when he is from home. . . . There are so many disaffected to the cause . . . that they lay in wait for those that are active in it."[50]

Probes by British troops heightened the uncertainty and the brutality. Howe's regulars supported loyalist raids into Bucks, seizing "prominent Whigs, lawyers, committeemen, and militia recruiting officers." On May 1, 1778, the Queen's Rangers, under the command of Robert Simcoe, carried out a vicious assault on General Lacey's militia in camp in the central part of the county. In this so-called "Battle of Crooket Billet," the British reputedly killed many, bayoneting the wounded and burning the dying on heaps of straw. Lacey reported in the spring of 1778 that he "was mortifyed to find the Whigs . . . were seeking hiding places, and some of them even Courting the Tories for Safety."[51]

Equally reflective of widespread popular disaffection was the continued economic intercourse between the Bucks countryside and the British occupying the city. During the Valley Forge winter, farmers in southeastern Pennsylvania starved the patriots while they fed the British in Philadelphia. Gouverneur Morris concluded that "the free, open and undisguised communication with Philadelphia debauches the minds of those in its vicinage. . . . The state is sick even unto death."[52]

Joseph Reed reported that farmers in the area refused to sell to the Americans forces, because "the hope of getting to market . . . induces them to keep it [food] back and deny they have it." In December 1777, Washington had warned farmers that they must thresh their grain or risk "having all that shall remain in sheave . . . seized . . . and paid for as straw." The next month, in desperation, Washington wrote to Colonel Walter Stewart: "If any particular mode of cutting off this pernicious intercourse [with Philadelphia] strikes you, be pleased to communicate it to General Lacey." Washington suggested the seizure of the property, as well as the horses and carriages that carried it, and also severe punishments for some who were "proper objects to make examples of." Nothing worked. Grain continued to flood into the city while armed countrymen drove herds of cattle through the British lines. As the patriots suffered hunger, the glut on the market depressed food prices in Philadelphia.[53]

General John Lacey, charged with stopping this trade, finally resorted to desperate measures. In his fury, he commanded his troops to patrol the roads leading to Philadelphia night and day, and if you meet "any persons whatever going to the city, [who] . . . endeavor to make their escape, you will . . . fire upon the villains. You will leave such on the road, their bodies and their marketing lying together. This I wish you to execute on the first offenders you meet, that they maybe a warning to others."[54]

Patriots roundly blamed "the cursed Quakers and other inhabitants" who seemed to have no "more idea of Liberty than a savage does of Civilization." However, probably few farmers in southeastern Pennsylvania, regardless of political sentiment or religious orientation, could resist the lure of British gold. Even those who sympathized with the rebels faced the problem of the rapidly depreciating continental currency. The Congress' money had lost about 25 percent of its value by November 1776. By Fall 1777 it had declined even more. Joseph Reed reported that beef in the Schuylkill Valley was selling for paper money at 100 percent markup over specie. As long as the British army occupied Philadelphia, the outcome of the contest remained uncertain, and the value of Continental currency declined, few farm families in Bucks could afford to ignore the Philadelphia market.[55]

Little quantitative evidence documents the extent to which farmers in Bucks County traded with the British, but logic suggests that it was extensive. By December 1777, the state militia had conceded the better part of lower Bucks County to the British. During the following winter, Lacey himself admitted that "an almost open and uninterrupted intercourse existed between the disaffected in the lower parts of Bucks and Philadelphia Counties . . . and the Enemy in City of Philadelphia."[56]

Bucks County's trade with the British in Philadelphia during the winter and spring of 1778 was consistent with its military and political behavior. Initially, the people of the county had united in peaceful opposition to the British encroachments on colonial liberty. Soon, however, as the resistance movement shifted from peaceful economic boycotts to physical coercion and then war, significant numbers of people, principally Quaker and German pacifists, drew back. Then, the repressive tactics of those who assumed power undoubtedly alienated others and further exacerbated the internal divisions. In sum, between Fall 1776, and Spring 1778, the county's halfhearted and ineffectual military record, its tacit support for British raiding parties and collaboration with antipatriot vigilantes, and its wholesale commerce with the enemy in Philadelphia all suggest that Bucks County was considerably alienated from the patriot cause during the first three years of the war.

In June 1778, the British evacuated Philadelphia. By fall, the patriot forces were once again in control in Bucks County. The Court of Quarter Sessions resumed its periodic meetings in June 1778, regularly impaneling a grand jury and facing a docket crowded with such traditional and mundane responsibilities as licensing taverns and overseeing roads. Prosperity, social peace, and political reconciliation came more slowly.[57]

The economy apparently recovered most quickly. On the national level, the war had devastated the standard of living. Historians John McCusker and Russell Menard concluded: "If the results of current research stand future scrutiny, something 'truly disastrous' happened to the American economy between 1775 and 1790." Overall per capita gross national product, they estimate, may well have fallen as much as 40 to 50 percent, a drop comparable to that occurring during 1929–33, the first four years of the Great Depression. McCusker and Menard caution, however, that the data are limited, that we lack a body of systematic local studies, and that there was pronounced regional variation. Moreover, they indicate a slightly more optimistic picture for the mid-Atlantic region.[58]

No systematic analysis of Bucks County's relative or absolute prosperity is possible here, but some bits of evidence suggest a mixed picture. Bucks farmers produced grain, flour, and meat for the market. Demand for these staples remained high, and as the war itself moved south and then ended, the military impediments to local production and to trade declined. Between 1783 and 1787 the wholesale price of wheat on the Philadelphia market generally remained strong despite wide monthly fluctuations. Bucks farmers, with easy and cheap access to Philadelphia, certainly should have benefited from these prices.[59] On the other hand, the county's principal iron furnace was producing nothing. The Durham furnace had closed by 1791, possibly because of the legal complications flowing from the confiscation and resale of the property belonging to loyalist Joseph Galloway.[60]

The number of slaves in the county provides us with another hint. Despite powerful counterforces, the slave population in Bucks apparently increased between 1775 and 1790. The war itself had threatened this complex institution. In addition, by the 1770s, Quakers in good standing with the Meeting could not own slaves. Most dramatically, in 1780 the Revolutionary government of Pennsylvania had legislated the gradual abolition of slavery. Nonetheless, the number of slaves listed for Bucks County in the U.S. Census of 1790 (approximately 260) exceeded the probable number of slaves in the county at the beginning of the war (approximately 245–50).[61]

The persistence of slavery suggests the continued prosperity of that relatively small proportion of Bucks residents who held slaves. Although the slave population in Bucks was widely dispersed, slaveowning tended to concentrate in a relatively small number of areas. Slaves held in Bristol Borough, Bristol and Newtown Townships, and by men associated with the Durham furnace made up more than 40 percent (about 55 of 130) of the total recorded in the incomplete records of 1775. Adding the 20 slaves held by six wealthy families living in affluent Falls Township, adjacent to Bristol, increases the proportion concentrated in these five political subdivisions to just short of 60 percent of the total recorded in the fifteen political subdivisions for which we have records. In short, these fragmentary records of slaveholding do not confirm the "truly disastrous" economic decline suggested by McCusker and Menard for the period 1775–90.[62]

Tax arrearages for the county also suggest a mixed picture. During the 1780s, residents of Bucks County did fairly well in paying their taxes. In the winter of 1787–88, John Nicholson, the comptroller general of Pennsylvania, reported that across the state approximately £354,651 in back taxes remained unpaid. This figure represented about £3.2 for every adult white male in the state sixteen years old or older. Bucks County residents owed an average of about £1.4. While considerably below the mean, this amount was higher than the averages in a number of other counties. In the same vein, in late winter 1788 a number of people from Bucks County petitioned the legislature for relief from debt.[63]

If the Bucks County economy showed signs of healing in the early 1780s, the wounds in the body politic continued to fester. Some of the more belligerent patriots had migrated. John Lacey, who issued the shoot-on-sight orders against farmers trading with Philadelphia, married and moved to the vicinity of Mount Holly, New Jersey. Even there, however, violence followed him. Well after the war, he apparently shot and killed Joel Cooke behind the Quaker meetinghouse after what some thought was a business dispute.[64]

Other violent men remained and continued to disrupt the county. Among these, the Doans stand out, robbing, burning, and spreading terror over a wide geographic range. They reputedly robbed a horse from Mr. Shaw in Plumstead, and when he complained they returned in the dead of the night, beat him bloody, and took the rest of his horses. They also were given credit for robbing tavernkeeper Robert Robinson, and for stripping the corpulent businessman naked and whipping him. Public opinion as well as petitions to the government credited the Doans with pillaging houses and stealing horses and cattle in the lower parts of the county.[65]

Separating fact from fiction here is not easy, but the Doans' most notorious deed is fairly well documented. At about 1:00 on the morning of October 27, 1781, Aaron, Levi, and possibly Moses Doan, along with Robert Steele and a number of "brown figures, in linsey-woolsey coats, knee-britches . . . and small felt hats with round crowns," robbed the county treasury at Newtown. Armed with cocked pistols, clubs, swords, and flintlock muskets, they forced their way into the home of the treasurer, ransacked his dwelling, and compelled him to open the county's coffers. At the end of three hours, the gang of fifteen to twenty men made off with more than £650.[66]

In the next few years a number of the known members of the gang died violently. At least one was shot resisting arrest, and two were hanged in 1788. Others fled, some to Canada where, it was later rumored, they joined the British in fighting against the Americans in the War of 1812.[67]

Who the Doans were, how much of the county's endemic violence they caused, and why they took to arms remain matters of conjecture. Most of the families with that name lived in the northern parts of the county, in and around Plumstead and Bedminster Townships. Of English descent, the first inhabitant of that name arrived in Bucks in the seventeenth century from Puritan New England, where his conversion to Quakerism had made him unwelcome. In Bucks the family had a checkered religious career. Some were disowned from the Quaker Meeting for their experiments with astrology, others for marrying out of the Meeting. By 1778 at least one branch of the family were widely known loyalists. Whether led to that position by their Quaker religious principles, or by disputes with patriot forces over the confiscation of property or by compulsory military duty remains unclear.[68]

Whatever the cause, from 1778 well into the 1780s the Doan gang earned credit for terrifying and abusing substantial numbers of people in all sections of the county. These exploits, whether real or fictional, illustrate the violent and unsettled status of the county long after the British and the patriot armies had moved on.

Other kinds of hostilities persisted. The departure of the British loosed a torrent of patriot abuse on loyalists, neutrals, and trimmers. The legislature authorized the confiscation of loyalist property. Ironically, one of the victims was Gilbert Hicks, who had chaired the meeting in the summer of 1774 that had inaugurated the Revolutionary movement in Bucks County. Between 1777 and 1779, the state legislature, dominated by Scots-Irish Presbyterians, enacted a series of Test Acts that disfranchised all who would not abjure the King and pledge allegiance to Pennsylvania. At first persuasive rather than punitive, the final Test Act permanently disfranchised all who did not take the oath by the fall of 1779.[69]

Quakers categorically refused the oath, as did most Mennonites and other German sectarians. Many Lutherans remained ambivalent, cautious, and on the sidelines as long as possible. Bucks Country, because of its high concentration of these groups, may have had the highest proportion of nonjurors in the state.[70]

In Bucks County, as across Pennsylvania, the Constitutionalist party championed the state loyalty oaths. They pursued and punished Tories and nonjurors during the war, and then, after the end of hostilities, resisted the reincorporation of these men into the political life of the community. As a "Plain Common Freeman" cautioned: "In this day of our triumph, when the rewards of victory are to be dispersed to the victors, we must not be surprised to see crowds pressing forward to share the fruits of our perseverance and sufferings whose past services have been a steady opposition to our efforts."[71]

The patriots were determined that those who did not share in the struggle would not enjoy the results. Of the hated Tories and traitors, Quakers were singled out for particular attention. Meeting on May 29, 1783, the Philadelphia militia protested the return of "such persons as have joined the enemy or have been expelled [from] this or any other of the United States." Two weeks later, a mass meeting at the State House in Philadelphia resolved to keep the disaffected from returning, to ensure the prompt payment of the public debt, and to create a revivified Committee of Correspondence to carry out these resolutions. This committee then warned the disaffected that "unless they depart this state within ten days, . . . such as may be found within this district, after that time will be dealt with in a proper manner."[72]

Similar meetings took place in Bucks County. On July 29, representatives from throughout the county assembled at Bennet's Tavern in Northampton Township on the road to Yardley. Acting under the guidance of Joseph Hart, they condemned traitors and Tories, then charged their legislators, recently reduced to five by reapportionment, to protect the state constitution of 1776 and "to oppose with your strongest efforts, any attempt . . . to repeal the test laws now in force."[73]

In 1784, the county's dominant Constitutionalists again publicly supported the Test Acts. The state legislature was about to reopen the test rolls when nineteen legislators withdrew from the house, broke the required two-thirds quorum, and prematurely ended the legislative year. At a meeting at Newtown on November 1, 1784, some twenty-one leaders from sixteen of Bucks townships commended their assemblymen for keeping the Test Acts in force, and declared their approval of the continued exclusion of those who had not supported the war.[74]

A year after the conclusion of the peace, a decade after the Revolution had divided the people of Bucks County, a considerable number—most Quakers, a fair portion of pacifist German sectarians, and possibly others—remained outside the new political community created by the American Revolution. The patriots who had struggled for liberty continued to infringe on the basic liberties of large numbers, possibly the numerical majority, of the residents of Bucks County. A remark by James Allen of the prewar Proprietary party highlighted the irony. He had championed the colonial cause through 1774 and 1775, but he could not accept independence in 1776. Isolated and threatened at his estate in Northampton County, he wrote in his diary in January 1777: "to oppress one's countrymen is a love of Liberty."[75]

On the basis of this preliminary study, it would appear that the people of Bucks County had initially united in opposition to the claims of the British to legislate for them in all cases. Living in a relatively prosperous commercial farming region, they joined their fellow British colonists in 1774–75 in peaceful resistance to Parliament's challenge to their local autonomy and traditional rights. As the contest progressed from protest and boycotts through coercion to war, the people of Bucks County divided sharply. The Quakers, and probably most of the pacifist Germans, held back, then refused to participate. The patriots, operating through the Committee of Safety, silenced and disarmed their dissenting neighbors. The tactics of the patriots alienated additional groups in the county.

The men who had achieved dominance by 1776 differed from their opponents (and from their former Whig colleagues in the original County Committee) in neither sectional residence, nor occupation, nor social-economic status, but rather in their ethnic and religious backgrounds. By 1776 a new political coalition of Presbyterians, Reformed, Baptists, and possibly Lutherans had replaced the old Quaker hegemony in Bucks County. Furthermore, even though it included of a variety of groups, this new political coalition probably spoke for a minority of the county's residents.

Thus, the evidence now available from Bucks County seems to suggests a great irony. In this county's internal revolution of 1776, one ethnic-religious-based elite displaced another ethnic-religious-based elite. The violent vanquished the peaceful, "the few" triumphed over "the many," and untold numbers suffered in a war fought ostensibly to protect liberty from tyranny.

3

The Lehigh Valley

Eugene R. Slaski

Saving church bells from being melted down into cannonballs, dressing combat wounds and caring for the sick and captured, weeding out traitors, fining and harassing the uncommitted, and providing and storing weapons of war—such was the history of the Revolution in the Lehigh Valley. As throughout the colonies, the valley's residents—pacifists, loyalists, patriots, and others who reluctantly and often under duress supported the Revolutionary cause—felt the impact of the American Revolution. Unlike in the French and Indian War, the valley south of Blue Mountain did not suffer from any military engagements. That earlier experience, however, had helped to develop some communication between the various and widely scattered settlers who had moved into the area after the Walking Purchase of 1737. Thus, when the War of Independence did break out, the area was able to respond readily to the new threats.

The Lehigh Valley, or at least that portion south of Blue Mountain (the Kittatinny Ridge) and north of South Mountain (Lehigh Mountain), was the southern end of Northampton County, created in 1752. Within that area, by 1763, were the principal Moravian settlements of Bethlehem, Nazareth, and Emmaus, the county seat at Easton at the forks of the Delaware and Lehigh Rivers, and Northampton Town (Allentown), the residence of James Allen, a son of William Allen and friend of the Penn family. Both Thomas Penn and William Allen had substantial landholdings in the area.[1] During the Revolution, the valley (some fifty miles north of Philadelphia), essentially served as a safe area to which the sick and wounded could be taken and from which supplies for the war could be requisitioned.

By the 1770s, perhaps 10,000 people had settled in the area; the three main settlements in 1776 were Bethlehem with 575 people, Easton with 450, and Allentown with 350.[2] Agricultural production had increased significantly before the Revolution and had coincided with the dramatic increase in the numbers of Germans of the Lutheran and Reformed faiths who settled in the rich, limestone-based region. At the same time, earlier groups of settlers, especially the Moravians, had declined in number as births lagged behind death rates and Europe sent no replacements. From 1761 to 1771, the population of Bethlehem, the central Moravian community, decreased from 669 to 560.[3]

Tax lists of 1772 indicate that nearly 75 percent of the taxables who listed an occupation were farmers; another 20 percent were identified as laborers (generally farmhands). Frame and stone buildings on land farmed by the Germans, Moravians, and Scots-Irish could be seen throughout the area; wheat, buckwheat, rye and other grains, hemp, flax, potatoes, cabbage, and various fruits, especially apples, pears, and peaches, were the chief products of these developing farms. Every township had the services of several millers, blacksmiths, weavers, and shoemakers, although few shops or shopkeepers existed outside the three main towns.[4]

Records of the period just before the Revolution indicate that the Lehigh Valley, though near major trade and industrial centers, was essentially autonomous. The close ties that had developed between its leaders and those of Philadelphia and outlying townships as a result of the French and Indian War loosened once that danger had passed. Indeed, basic transportation within the

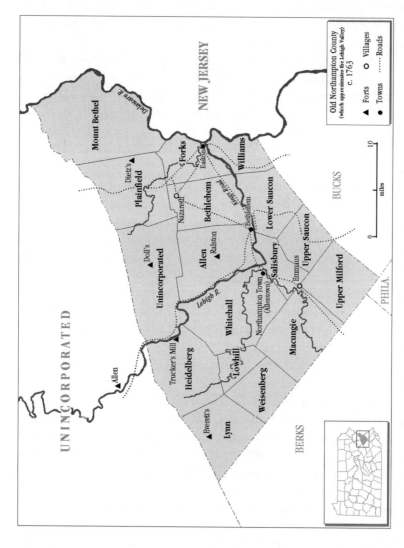

Old Northampton County (approximating the Lehigh Valley region), c. 1763.

valley and to major trade regions like Philadelphia remained primitive. No bridges crossed the Delaware or Lehigh River; only ferries connected major arteries. Crossing most other streams meant fording on foot, horseback, or wagon. A good day's travel was needed to transport supplies or produce within the valley from one of its towns to another, even though the entire trip from Easton through Bethlehem to Allentown was a mere twenty miles.[5]

When the war began, valley leaders responded in various ways; patriots quickly emerged, although some still hoped for reconciliation; loyalists urged continued attachment to the Crown; pacifists sought to avoid confrontation with either side. Many in the valley, as elsewhere, tried to conduct business with as little interruption in their daily routine as possible, but most residents felt the war's impact. Families, as in any revolution, divided. Stories of broken families abound, but trends could be seen developing among people with similar national backgrounds. Generally, the area's Scots-Irish Presbyterians were among the more active revolutionaries, as were members of the German Lutheran and Reformed churches, particularly in the Saucon Valley area just south of Bethlehem.[6]

There is little recorded evidence of the response of Northampton County residents to British taxes and regulations between 1763 and 1774. Philadelphia newspapers, including a German-language paper, Heinrich Miller's weekly *Staatshote,* certainly kept the townspeople informed. The county's representative to the Pennsylvania Assembly, ironmaster George Taylor, annually reelected from 1764 through 1769, remained responsive to the political debates unfolding in Philadelphia and presumably kept the best interests of his constituents in mind. He joined in the colony's opposition to the Stamp Act and the movement to have it repealed.

While Taylor represented the county, most inhabitants occupied themselves in their work building their farms and engaging in business ventures. News of the "Intolerable Acts" in 1774, however, caught the attention of many residents. After Governor John Penn refused to convene the Assembly to consider sending delegates to a Continental Congress, the Philadelphia Committee of Correspondence called for a July meeting of delegates from the counties. Prominent Northampton citizens met on June 21 to discuss the June 1 closing of the port of Boston and to respond to the "oppressive Acts of Parliament, . . . tending to destroy the liberties of North America." With Taylor as chair of the meeting, several resolutions were adopted.[7] Closing the port was labeled "an act of the highest oppression and a violation of the liberties of America." Since Bostonians were "suffering in the common cause of American freedom," the convening of a general congress of representatives to respond to harsh British policy received strong support. In the interim, the men agreed to create a county committee of correspondence. Those selected, William Edmonds, George Taylor, Lewis Gordon, John Okely, Peter Kichline, and Jacob Arndt, were to communicate with similar committees and cooperate with them "for the common good." As for the immediate crisis in Boston, the committee readied itself to accept contributions for the relief of citizens of the New England port. Edmonds, then the county's representative to the Pennsylvania Assembly, was instructed to attend any Assembly meetings to keep the county informed. On July 15, four of the six-man committee met in Philadelphia with others to urge the Assembly to appoint delegates to the First Continental Congress.[8]

In late December 1774, Northampton County organized its own Committee of Observation, as did other counties. The county was responding to the call from the Pennsylvania Assembly in its support of recommendations of the Continental Congress to collectively resist increasingly restrictive British policies. These county groups, generally known as Committees of Safety, were coordinated by an overall Pennsylvania Committee of Safety. Their responsibilities included raising troops, securing military supplies, and identifying those who did not support the cause. Armed with such extraordinary power, they came to govern their areas on behalf of the Revolution.[9]

Northampton's committee, initially consisting of thirty members, including nearly one for each of the twenty-six townships, also selected a Standing Committee of Correspondence. Most key members of these two committees were from Easton. Of those appointed to the Committee of Correspondence, former Assemblyman Taylor served as chairman. Lewis Gordon was the first chair of the main committee and its treasurer. Robert Traill, as clerk, kept the minutes for the Committee of Observation. Kichline, Okely, Arndt, and Henry Kooken rounded out the Standing Committee. Membership on both committees changed, often reflecting the pressures of the war; more radical members replaced the more conservative as the push for independence clearly overcame any lingering hope of compromise. Meeting as needed from December 1774 through 1777, the Standing Committee, even more than the larger Committee of Observation, gradually assumed greater responsibilities. As colonial government broke down, the committee kept order and acquired a quasi-judicial function.[10]

In May 1775, following the skirmishes at Lexington and Concord, the County Committee of Correspondence responded to orders from the Pennsylvania Committee of Safety and created a local military system directing the townships to establish armed companies called Associators. Anyone who failed to join these companies was labeled a non-Associator and his actions were watched closely. Associators chose their own officers: a captain, a lieutenant, and an ensign. Each member of the company received "one good fire lock, one pound of powder, four pounds of lead, and sufficient quantity of flint, and a cartridge box." These Associators were standby units to be used in an emergency situation in or near their homes. Though none ever had to be used in Northampton County, more than 2,250 Associators signed up; a year later, those numbers were increased by a "flying camp" of regulars from Bucks and Northampton Counties under the command of Lieutenant Colonel Peter Kichline, a member of the Northampton Committee of Observation.[11] In overall charge of the Associators was Captain Abraham Miller.[12]

A year later in May 1776, the County Committee of Observation selected seven members of the Committee of Correspondence to attend a provincial convention in Philadelphia to help in "forming and establishing a new government."[13] The six who actually participated on June 18 were Robert Levers, John Wetzel, Neigal Gray, David Deshler, and Nicholas and Benjamin Depui; Wetzel and Deshler, original members of the County Committee of Observation, represented the western region of the county, including the Allentown area. Out of that conference emerged new election districts, with Northampton County having four. One included Allentown and the townships that eventually would become Lehigh County. This development proved popular because residents of Allentown and nearby townships no longer had to travel all the way to Easton to vote—a major complaint in previous years. Several weeks later, on July 8, Levers stood on the courthouse steps in Easton and read the Declaration of Independence to those who had gathered. On the same day, the county voters elected their delegates to the Pennsylvania constitutional convention, including two from the new Allentown-Whitehall area: Peter Rhoads and Peter Burkhalter.[14]

Following independence, the Revolutionary committees tightened control. The Committee of Correspondence sought out the enemy. Informers, agents of the Committee, filed reports on non-Associators, and the Committee began to act as a judiciary, though without a jury. All firearms were ordered confiscated from non-Associators, and those who refused to hand them over or who spoke out against revolutionary activities had to recant, on pain of being jailed or paying heavy fines. The names of recanters appeared in the English and German area newspapers.[15]

The local Committee of Correspondence assumed other powers as well. In July 1776 it levied taxes to support the militia; in August it declared that it would "keep the peace and call offenders to justice . . . until it shall otherwise be ordered by the Convention or any other Superior Authority of this State." As a result, any English-colonial government in the county officially came to an end.[16] Among those who offended the committee, three men bear some closer scrutiny, for their plight suggests the difficulties that arise within a community in the midst of war and revolution. Nathaniel Vernon, tavern owner and ferry-boat operator in Easton, joined the militia and drilled with it, despite being a Quaker. After the Quakers disassociated with him for bearing arms, he faced another dilemma. Though angered by British policies, he could not support such a drastic measure as complete separation. He openly denounced the independence movement and its leadership at local gatherings and was declared a traitor. His local property was seized—he owned land, operated a sawmill locally, and raised livestock in Chester County as well. Before he could be tried, he escaped to Philadelphia, where he received British protection and became a valuable informer to the British in planning their troop movements. After the war, he was compensated with land in Nova Scotia. His sons remained loyal to the Revolutionary cause and obtained the rights to his local property.[17]

Lewis Gordon, like Vernon, had backed the various tax protests and generally despised British policies. Gordon, a native of Aberdeen, Scotland, had supported the boycotts and even served as a principal member of the county's Committee of Observation. With others he had hoped to be able to persuade British officials to change their policies, but he saw no reason to seek independence. As a lawyer he struggled with the whole notion of rebellion, yet he retained his membership on the Committee of Observation until late in 1776, when successive defeats suffered by the Continental Army apparently convinced him of the futility of the patriot cause. He resigned his committee position in December as George Washington's troops were fleeing New Jersey. Gordon tried to remain neutral; initially he refused to take the state's Test Oath of 1777 and did not support the British cause. But as the prothonotary of the county (and thus an officer of the King), he was arrested in the summer of 1777 by order of Pennsylvania's Supreme Executive Council. He was put on parole, with restricted travel privileges. Before his death in 1778, he took the oath of loyalty to the United States.[18]

Both Vernon and Gordon were residents of Easton and early supporters of grievances against British authority. James Allen fit a different mold. His father, Pennsylvania Supreme Court Judge William Allen, one of the beneficiaries of the Walking Purchase of 1737, had founded Northampton Town (Allentown) in 1762. William was both a friend and a staunch supporter of the Penns. His son, James, born in Philadelphia, was educated in London. Once he moved to Northampton Town in 1770, he did much entertaining at his stately home, Trout Hall, above the Jordan Creek, which teemed with many varieties of fish. Both Governor James Hamilton and John Adams were among the many prominent guests at his home.

While still residing in Philadelphia in 1765, James Allen had called for the resignation of Stamp Distributor John Hughes. A month later, in October, meeting with others opposing the Stamp Act, Allen had helped convince Hughes not to deliver the stamps until other colonies had put the act into effect.[19] In the election on May 15, 1776, to fill the Assembly seat for Northampton County, Allen received an overwhelming endorsement in a vote of 853 to 14, but that legislative body's future was cut short by the successful political maneuvers of the provincial convention. In his brief tenure, he declared himself "very obnoxious to the independents and . . . determined to oppose them vehemently."[20] After admitting to himself that a vote for independence was inevitable, he left for New Jersey in June 1776 to discuss the crisis with George Washington. Conscientious and open-minded, Allen remained unconvinced that independence was either necessary or wise. He returned to Trout Hall on parole and continued to live the life of a country squire.[21] In poor health, he never did choose sides in the conflict,[22] though the very road his home adjoined served as a constant reminder. Called by John Adams "the most traveled road in America," most of the Congress passed him on the Easton-Reading Pike (Hanover Avenue, Union, Jackson, Walnut and Hamilton Streets in Allentown). War supplies moved past Allen's house in a steady stream.[23]

During the war, Easton became an important center for dealing with British prisoners of war. With Robert Lettis Hooper Jr. in charge locally, the jails and other buildings used to hold them were severely overcrowded in 1777–78. Many of those captured were sick or wounded, but food and fuel were scarce. Many died in confinement. Some attempted escape. In December 1777, due to a shortage of labor, Hooper allowed a group of prisoners to cut wood, and several escaped from the guard. On the other hand, Hooper found Hessian prisoners useful: "They are hired with our farmers and behave well." Indeed, after the war many Hessians stayed with German farm families and became citizens.[24]

Among the prisoners, enlisted men were treated differently from officers. Most of the officers were men of property and social status and were quartered in the homes of local leaders like Lewis Gordon. They were essentially on parole and seldom placed in a jail. Most of the enlisted men were simply imprisoned. Though the prison areas were overcrowded and undersupplied, treatment appeared to be civil. According to records kept, rations varied from three-quarters to one pound of bread and meat per day per man. Generally prisoners were allowed to walk through the town whenever they wished and to buy their own supplies if they had money. As with the Hessians, some were allowed to work on neighboring farms and earn a dollar a day.[25]

At times during this period, Bethlehem also served as an overflow area for prisoners, though its chief role was to provide hospital care. In September 1777 some 218 British prisoners, mostly Highlanders, were held in the Family House; the town's waterworks served as a barracks for the guards. Later, eight loyalists chained together by two's arrived from New Jersey via Easton and were added to those already confined.[26]

Fortunately for the entire Lehigh Valley region, no military skirmishes occurred there. Men of the valley did fight at the battles of Trenton and Princeton, and in the first engagement on Long Island under the command of Colonel Daniel Brodhead and Captains Peter Kichline and Melchior Hays. The Reverend John Rosbrugh of Allen Township's Presbyterian Church commanded a company of militia and supported Washington's troops at Trenton. Rosbrugh was killed there in January 1777.

The Lehigh Valley also served as a temporary encampment for detachments of the Continental Army moving to and from the war front. After crossing the Delaware in retreat after the Battle of Long Island, part of the American army under General John Sullivan camped overnight just a week before Christmas, across the Lehigh River from Bethlehem in nearby fields, and then joined Washington's troops in the attack on Trenton. Moravian Bishop John Ettwein estimated that by December 17 approximately 5,000 or 6,000 soldiers were being housed in Bethlehem, with several thousand more camped on the outskirts of the community.[27] Bethlehem also hosted Maryland and Virginia troops one night on their way to Boston.[28] Between December 1775 and the summer of 1779, a Moravian community at Nazareth, some nine miles north of Bethlehem, became a convenient area within which to confine British and Hessian prisoners and to serve a steady influx of Continental forces.[29]

Because the enemy was so close in the campaigns of 1776 and 1777, the Delaware River had to be securely defended. As commander of the troops at Easton, Colonel Abram Labor had that assignment. His men were scattered all along the river from Easton to about thirty miles northward at the Delaware Water Gap near present-day Stroudsburg.[30]

Later, in September and October 1777, Continental forces suffered devastating defeats at Brandywine Creek in Chester County and at Germantown. Northampton troops under Brodhead, Captain John Van Etten, and Colonel John Siegfried (sheriff and tavernkeeper and later a military supplier to the encampment at Valley Forge) experienced heavy casualties. As a direct result of those two setbacks, the three towns in the county became increasingly important as safe havens caring for the sick and for gathering and storing military supplies.[31]

At Easton, Robert Levers, who once had taught school near Philadelphia and had attended the Pennsylvania provincial convention for the county, was now a county lieutenant and a colonel in the militia. He was given the responsibility for raising troops and the monies to maintain them. He also requisitioned wagons to transport the troops and supplies. During the winter of 1777–78, he found it very difficult to locate flour, meat, and salt for the troops at Valley Forge and for the sick and wounded housed in Bethlehem and Easton. At times, horses and wagons were rented or impressed if the owners failed to lease them. Raising troops following unsuccessful encounters with the enemy was not an easy task for Levers either. Many potential recruits thought it was more important to tend to their farms and families than to fight for something that did not benefit them directly. During harvesting and planting, or following an American military defeat, desertions were common. To add to Levers's troubles, money was scarce. Farmers put little faith in the paper currency of the Revolutionary government, whereas the British exchanged gold for farm products. Levers and other procurers often resorted to threats or actual confiscation in order to obtain foodstuffs from farmers and supplies from local merchants.[32]

But Levers was fortunate in one sense at least; the county had many skilled blacksmiths, gunsmiths, and cabinetmakers who combined their talents in producing rifles and muskets. Among the German and Swiss gunsmiths of the county were John Golcher, Abraham Berlin, Stephen Horn, John and Henry Young, Matthias Miller, and William Henry. A Nazareth resident, William Henry continued to make accurate rifles after the war, and his plant remained vital as late as the Civil War.[33]

Because Easton was a warehousing area for food, munitions, and clothing, Levers also was responsible for their proper storage and protection. He even had to safeguard the ferry runs across the Delaware at Easton. He meted out punishment to wayward militiamen, tended to the prisoners who came to Easton, and helped identify suspected traitors. At least one observer judged him to be the "local dictator of the new government." In fact, when the Continental Congress had to abandon Philadelphia to the British in 1777, the official papers, records, and public funds of the Congress were delivered to him in Easton for safe-keeping.[34]

Two other men who contributed greatly to the Revolutionary cause were Robert Traill and George Taylor. Traill, who served as the clerk of the Committee of Observation, was a Scotsman, born in the Orkney Islands. He had come to Easton in 1763 and for some time worked for a merchant and taught school. Eventually he studied law under Lewis Gordon and gained a solid reputation as a lawyer. In 1781 he became sheriff and later rose to associate county judge. At various times he served as a major in the militia, an assistant deputy quartermaster, a member of the General Assembly, and a member of the Supreme Executive Council of Pennsylvania.[35]

Taylor, who served as a member of the County Committee of Correspondence, arrived in America from northern Ireland as a redemptioner, as had many other emigrants who could not afford to pay their own way across the Atlantic. Initially he worked for the ironmaster in Durham, Bucks County, just south of Easton. By 1755, he had become one of the principal operators of the Durham Iron Works, which during the Revolutionary War produced round shot, cannonballs, and small cannon for the Continental Army. In 1763 he moved to Easton and rented the Parsons House (home of the founder of Easton, William Parsons). By 1768 he had built a summer home on 331 acres in Allen Township (now Catasauqua). In 1780 he owned two slaves at his Easton residence.[36]

During the Revolutionary period, Taylor accepted numerous responsibilities. As a member of the General Assembly in 1765, he sat on the committee appointed to draft the instructions for the delegates attending the Stamp Act Congress. He also helped draft the "thank you" note to the King for the repeal of the act.[37] A decade later he became a colonel, though his legislative duties curtailed his active involvement in the military. In 1775 he served on the very important State Committee of Public Safety. In early November 1775 he helped prepare the report that provided the instructions for the colony's delegates to the Continental Congress. At that time, the instructions did not favor independence. Yet near the end of July 1776 he took his seat as a delegate to the Continental Congress and became the only resident of the Lehigh Valley to sign the Declaration of Independence. Later he was elected to the Supreme Executive Council of the state and served on a number of committees in 1777.[38] Four years later he died poor, but with a continuing passion for his comrades in the Revolutionary cause. Among his few remaining possessions were a pair of pistols, which he willed to Robert Traill; a silver mounted small sword, passed on to Robert L. Hooper; and a silver mounted double-barrel gun, given to Robert Levers.[39]

As already noted, caring for the sick and wounded during the war was a major activity for many in the Lehigh Valley. Beginning in late 1776, churches in and around the three towns, the courthouse in Easton, and the Easton jail became emergency hospitals. In Bethlehem, under orders from General Washington, an army general hospital was set up as part of the Middle Medical Department of the Continental Army.[40] Originally only the Single Brethren's House of the Moravian community was to be used, but, as casualties increased, other Moravian buildings were forced into service. Two doctors, Surgeon-General John Warren and William Shippen, director of the Hospitals of the Continental Army, supervised the activities that first winter. Expectations were that some 250 men would be cared for in Bethlehem, but by December 8 between 500 and 600 were in various facilities in the town, including hospital tents, while a thousand others were taken across the Lehigh River to the Crown Inn and nearby buildings, or to Easton or Allentown, or into the homes of neighboring farmers. Because of the heavy casualties and the need to use so many additional and widely scattered facilities, General Horatio Gates arrived to monitor and control the situation. Some 110 men died in Bethlehem between December 1776 and March 1777. The battles of Long Island and later Trenton had strained the valley's ability to serve the cause. A smallpox outbreak in February hastened the decision in March to close the hospital.[41]

Later that year, due to heavy Continental Army casualties at the battles of Brandywine and Germantown, William Shippen, director-general of the Continental Hospital, on September 19 informed the officials in Bethlehem, Easton, and Allentown that the Continental Congress wanted each of these communities to set aside its largest buildings to house some 2,000 "sick and wounded" soldiers and to expect their arrival in a few days.[42] In Easton, as earlier during the battle of Trenton, the Reformed Church was put into service; the Zion Reformed Church served as the chief care facility in Allentown.[43] Emmaus, a Moravian community only some five miles to the southwest of Bethlehem and with less than 100 residents (of whom 36 were adult males), was used to care for 132 war casualties between October 10, 1777, and the third week in January 1778. On January 20, the remaining wounded were moved to Allentown.[44]

Bethlehem received the largest number of wounded from the battlefields at Brandywine and Germantown. Within a week of Dr. Shippen's orders, more than 400 wounded had arrived in Bethlehem. Six weeks later, more than 700 were housed in the Brethren's House alone, while others were bedded in some fifty tents nearby. Officers filled the Sun Inn and the Gemein Haus in town or were ferried across the Lehigh River to the Crown Inn and nearby buildings. Every vacant space in the area surrounding Bethlehem and the other towns in the valley was filled.[45]

Among those in Bethlehem, though not by choice, was the Marquis de Lafayette, who had been wounded at Brandywine. He stayed at the home of George Frederick Boeckel, superintendent of the Bethlehem farm. Boeckel's wife and daughter nursed Lafayette back to health,[46] although local lore claims that he overstayed his visit for "personal reasons."[47]

Lafayette was not alone in his appreciation of the good works provided by the residents of Bethlehem. After a number of members of the Continental Congress visited the town for varying lengths of time, an order was issued on September 22, 1777, by sixteen Congressional delegates attesting to the basic humanity of the Moravian people:

> . . . Having here observed a diligent attention to the sick and wounded, and a benevolent desire to make the necessary provision for the relief of the distressed, as far as the powers of the Brethren enable them, we desire that all Continental Officers may refrain from disturbing the persons or property of the Moravians of Bethlehem, and particularly, that they do not disturb or molest the Houses where the women are assembled.[48]

Despite the best efforts of the Moravians, without benefit of appropriate medicines or adequate numbers of physicians, and with the overcrowded conditions, death occurred most frequently over the months from September through the harsh winter of 1777–78. Of one group of 500 soldiers, more than one-third died. Out of 40 men from the Ninth Virginia Continental Regiment, only one survived to return to duty.[49]

Cramped and unsanitary conditions increased the death rate. In fact, Bishop John Ettwein's son, John, died of typhus at age nineteen, and other local residents succumbed while caring for the sick and wounded at the Brethren's House. The situation was so bad that locals trading in the area were cautioned against coming too near to the hospital facilities. Observing the overcrowding, several members of the Continental Congress arranged for the transfer of a number of British prisoners who also had been confined in the area. An epidemic of spotted fever killed so many that coffins could not be built fast enough; several hundred bodies were buried in a common grave just west of the town across the Monocacy Creek on a low hilltop (near First Avenue).[50]

While Washington's men were dealing with the hardships at Valley Forge, Bishop John Ettwein recorded his observations about conditions in Bethlehem:

> Long before the winter passed, the chests and drawers of the houses in Bethlehem were emptied of all material that could be spared for lint and bandages, in the preparation of which the women contributed their share to the public service. Three or four times we begged blankets from our people for the soldiers and distributed them to the needy; likewise shoes and stockings, and old trousers for the convalescents whose clothing had been stolen in the hospital or had come into the hospital with nothing but a pair of ragged trousers, full of vermin.[51]

To add to these problems as the British occupied Philadelphia, refugees from the city streamed into the valley along with hundreds of supply wagons, most of them carrying military stores, much to the displeasure of the Moravians. Earlier in July an order was sent to get all available boats and wagons to Easton. In August, 200 wagons were requested for conveying women and children from Philadelphia. Among the cargo in the wagons in late September was a bell taken from the State House (now Independence Hall) along with other bells, generally from church steeples. Fearful that British occupational forces would melt down all those bells in Philadelphia and turn them into musket balls and cannon balls, the city's bells were removed to Bethlehem, except for the "Liberty Bell" and the bells of Christ Church, which were moved farther west about five miles to Allentown and stored beneath the floor of Zion Reformed Church. Key Revolutionary leaders in Northampton County were members of that congregation: Peter Rhoads, Nicholas Fox, and John Griesemer.[52]

Accompanying the wagons were remnants of troops and camp followers, all adding to the press of people in the immediate area of Bethlehem and Emmaus.[53] Military stragglers began to cause trouble for the many visitors and residents and eventually increased guards had to be maintained. Marauders west of the town were brought under control. Troops broke into the hospital supplies. And on March 17, 1778, a riot erupted.[54]

By then, though, the worst was over for the valley, and particularly for the Moravians of Bethlehem and Emmaus. Members of these two communities had learned much more than their leaders would have preferred from the encounters both settlements experienced with those passing through.[55] At least by early April 1778 the remaining patients had been moved to Lititz. All baggage and military supplies actually had been removed earlier, as well as the more rowdy troops.[56]

Visible horrors of war present in the hospital beds, and the disruptions that resulted from the numerous nearby military encampments, were especially difficult on the Moravians of Bethlehem, a pacifistic religious mission community. Local patriot committees viewed it with suspicion because most of the Moravian men refused to enlist in the militia. But the town's strategic location, its abundant housing, and its thriving economy made it an excellent choice for the army's needs.

Although pacifism had been a guiding principal for the Moravians since their founding in the middle of the fifteenth century in eastern Europe, their experiences in America while conducting their mission work among the native American Indians during the French and Indian War had helped to modify this position regarding pacifism. Early Moravians had considered bearing arms unchristian, but the bloody confrontations during the 1750s and 1760s caused them to take a defensive stance; in fact, they built "an efficient armed defense system in case of attack against their town."[57] They agreed that the use of weapons could not be avoided under certain circumstances, but when troubles began to escalate into actual military confrontation between the British and the colonists, most Moravians, and particularly their leaders, determined that the conflict did not constitute a defensive war. Thus they declared their neutrality.[58]

Indeed, the Moravians refused to take an oath of allegiance, which they considered blasphemy, to either side. They had no quarrel with their revolutionary neighbors or with the British who had permitted the Moravians to settle in America, to worship freely, and to remain exempt from military service. Moravians in Bethlehem retained close ties with a number of Christians in England. Some feared that supporting the patriot cause could jeopardize their mission work in other areas of the empire and might provoke the British to interfere with further emigration of Moravians to America.[59]

Although the Moravians' decision to remain neutral was a reasoned one, local

Revolutionary committees responded with suspicion and open hostility. As the fighting intensified, so did actions against the Moravians and others who refused to support the war effort. Early in 1775, Moravian leaders had formally agreed not to take up arms. As a result, their property was searched, and any weapons found were confiscated for military use.[60]

When Moravians refused to take the oath of allegiance to Pennsylvania and the new nation under the 1777 Test Act, Revolutionary agents quickly enforced its provisions. Punishment could mean loss of citizenship. Anyone who left his community without a certificate of oath could be jailed until he took the oath. Although 4,821 valley residents took the oath, among the fifty-nine who refused a majority were Mennonites or Moravians.[61] In June 1778, county authorities confiscated and sold the properties of several Mennonite families in Upper Saucon Township, and two wives appealed to the Assembly for aid because the seizure of the property had left them destitute.[62] Upset by such a dramatic impact of the Test Act, the Assembly modified it in December to remove the power to confiscate the property of those who refused to take the oath. The new law did continue to deny the right to vote, to serve on juries, or to hold office to recusants. Some of those who had refused to take the oath were imprisoned and released only after paying heavy fines. Others became the objects of rough treatment, harassment, intimidation, and even extortion by Revolutionary government officials and overzealous and unruly neighbors.[63]

Reaction to such repressive actions caused the Moravian leadership to attempt to tighten community discipline. Church leaders decreed that any brethren who took the oath would not be permitted to receive Communion. But because each Moravian congregation had the power to make its own decisions for its own members, some congregations simply chose not to have a Communion service during the war. Moravian leaders also appealed to the General Assembly, asking that the Moravian brethren be excused from the oath-taking, but the request was denied. Eventually, however, the Pennsylvania Committee of Safety did instruct Robert Levers, justices of the peace, and constables not to be "unusually severe" with Moravians in fining or imprisoning them and to avoid "all tumultuous and riotous treatment."[64]

Nonetheless, laws that levied fines on those who refused military duty continued to be strictly enforced. Non-Associators initially were fined 50 shillings and eventually 70 shillings.[65] Indeed, the combination of fines "strained the finances of the congregation."[66] Overall, the Moravians were treated with contempt by local revolutionaries.

Within the congregation, controversy existed also. By 1776, generational differences had surfaced. Older Moravian ministers and church elders urged a strict adherence to pacifist principles, while some of the younger brethren talked of their patriotic duty to bear arms.[67] Bishop John Ettwein not only opposed the bearing of arms, but also rejected the practice of paying for a substitute, an action he considered comparable to hiring a murderer.[68]

The plight of the Moravians may have been complicated by the lack of communications between the home church in Germany and the mission settlements in America, which had been shut down from 1776 until the spring of 1779.[69] In this crucial period, the once splendidly isolated and structured Moravian community at Bethlehem became a hub of activity. Neutral at the beginning of the war, most Moravians supported the Revolutionary cause by the end. In fact, by the end of the war several Moravians held offices in the county government.[70]

When Bishop John Frederick Reichel and his party arrived from the home church in Saxony to visit Bethlehem later in the war, he clearly demonstrated his support for the decisions made by the local church leadership in his written *Brotherly Agreement:*

> We will cordially subject ourselves to the government that is in power over us, and will conform to all human ordinances of the land in which we live; and we will by no means evade the payment of the taxes required of us for the support of our State or County. Being called to maintain peace, we will follow after peace with all men, and in no way will permit ourselves to become entangled in political agitation or controversies, but, if such take place . . . [we] will strive to approve ourselves as orderly and quiet citizens.[71]

Such practical reasoning essentially vindicated the position of the local Moravian leaders, who had struggled to maintain their faith during the early years of the fighting.

In several ways the Moravians made solid contributions to the Revolutionary cause despite continual harassment. Mechanics and artisans provided key service to local patriot committees as they tried to meet requests from the state committees and the army. Moravian flatboats shipped grains down to Easton. The grist and linseed-oil mills and tannery in Bethlehem were heavily used during the war. The spinning, weaving, and knitting skills of the Moravian women proved critical in caring for the war victims and some of the poorly outfitted troops that moved through their community. Unfortunately, most of the monies that might have been realized from the wartime prosperity were consumed by the heavy fines the community had to pay to local officials.[72]

Moravians, and other valley residents, cautiously looked forward to the return of normality once the sick and wounded and other military personnel had left the area. Most of the area's people resumed their normal subsistence farming relatively quickly. Not so for the Moravians, whose motto had been "We pray together, we labor together, we suffer together, we rejoice together." Dramatic and divisive changes occurred within their community.[73]

After sending a bill to the Continental Congress for services rendered,[74] the Moravians of Bethlehem repaired the Brethren's House once its status as a hospital was rescinded on June 1, 1778. But some repairs could not be made, at least physically. After the army left, local revolutionaries again began persecuting and harassing the Moravian community. There were threats of land confiscation, and several brethren were imprisoned illegally. Others were assessed fines beyond those prescribed by law. Because Bethlehem, Emmaus, and Nazareth did not have a justice of the peace from the time that proprietary government fell in 1776—when the commissions lapsed—until 1787 (incredibly), Allentown's justices ordered Bethlehem's and Emmaus's single brethren to go to Allentown to take the oath or be fined; [75] the county sheriff continued to compel the Nazareth Brethren to pay fines. At times Brethren sat in jail in Easton for weeks or months at a time.[76]

Many changes disrupted the values that had sustained the Moravian community, including a "crisis of discipline." Reports of excessive drinking, profanity, and less regular church attendance abounded. Many young men left Bethlehem following the war, in part influenced by the soldiers and other outsiders who had intruded on their lives. In 1783, about 100 young Moravian men remained in Bethlehem, but by 1806 that number had dwindled to 38. The community would never recover from such a loss.[77] In Nazareth, quite a few Brethren had taken the oath of allegiance to the state of Pennsylvania, and a number from the area congregations actually enlisted and served in the army. Unlike the settlements in Bethlehem and Emmaus, the Moravian communities in Nazareth grew between 1774 and 1786, hitting a high of 312 in 1785.[78]

What were the overall consequences of the war on the Lehigh Valley? Prices skyrocketed; an 18¢ bushel of salt in 1774 cost $6 in 1781. Sugar sold for $12 a pound, coffee cost $20 a pound, and tea $75 a pound. A spelling book sold for $20, a scythe for $130, a skein of thread for $4, and a silk handkerchief for $120 dollars.[79] Local Allentown merchant Peter Rhoads, much aware of the fiscal crisis, began in 1779 to record customer sales in British pounds, whereas during the prewar period individual purchases totaled only shillings and pence.[80] Indeed, because of the quickly decreasing value both of state and national currency, bartering prevailed. A number of people lost everything by selling their property for continental currency at the time of its greatest depreciation.[81]

As early as May 1776, James Allen lamented: "Every article of life is extravagantly dear." In January 1777, he complained: "Every article of consumption is raised six fold." As Washington's troops fought at Brandywine, Allen analyzed the runaway inflation: "The quantity of paper currency has, together with the total stoppage of trade, risen all articles to a monstrous pitch." He begrudged the way his estate was being destroyed by high prices and taxes.[82]

Even collecting taxes proved difficult. County tax commissioners for Northampton County advised the Supreme Executive Council in August 1783 that taxes were not collected because the "effects of war . . . do not yet cease to operate. Lack of currency remained the major problem, for . . . money has not yet begun to circulate at this distance from the Capitol, and it is yet too early for the inhabitants to have received any profit from their late harvest."[83]

Some Lehigh Valley industries collapsed, while others flourished due to the decline in imported goods from Europe and especially England. Small shops for manufacturing saddles, clothing, bayonets, scabbards, cartridges, and even rifles were established in Easton, Bethlehem, and Allentown, among other places. Some businessmen made fortunes supplying the army with food and clothing. Given the small number of loyalists, the loss of those who fled or were forced out did not cause long-term damage to the local economy or leave the valley short of skilled government personnel. Supreme Executive Council proclamations between 1778 and 1781 identified some thirty-five traitors from the county. Few properties were confiscated under the state law of 1778, which forfeited the property of traitors.[84]

Most civilians continued to live a harsh existence in the later years of the war, but no one starved because most residents lived and worked on farms that recovered their productivity quickly. Indeed, a perusal of Peter Rhoads's account books reveals that in Allentown, and certainly in Easton, consumers had access to a wide variety of foodstuffs, dry goods, hardware, and stationery supplies. In variety and quality, townspeople in the valley enjoyed a comfortable standard of living.[85]

Overall, the people of the Lehigh Valley survived the war well, though the mix of peoples was somewhat less diverse at the war's end. Many of the Scots-

Irish moved on to the west or southwest into western Maryland, seeking new lands to clear. Smaller groups, such as the Moravians and Mennonites, declined in numbers and at least in the valley lost their exclusivity. Indeed, the valley became more Pennsylvania-German, and its distinct dialect exaggerated the isolation of the area from the rest of the new nation. Adding to this insularity was the inclination of the Pennsylvania-German subculture to marry within its own community, to remain wedded to the soil, and perhaps to be somewhat more religious, superstitious, and suspicious of the outside world than others.

By 1783, Allentown had emerged as a politically vital area to rival the county seat at Easton. Before 1775, few Germans had held office in Pennsylvania. The Revolution changed that, and Allentown reaped the benefits of the emerging leadership by local German residents. As in Easton, those elected to various offices were middle-aged, affluent, and influential farmers and businessmen. Throughout the war, political control in the valley's towns remained in the hands of individuals who had been active locally in the Revolutionary War. As the fight for independence wound down, the desire for economic stability and security increased. Thus, in Northampton County the supporters of the war also favored the new federal and state constitutions. Indeed, Lehigh Valley delegates to the constitutional convention had to pledge support for the new federal government. County delegates all approved the 1790 state constitution. Thus, by 1790 the Federalists in Northampton County had helped defeat anti-Federalists in the national debate and had helped unseat the radical Pennsylvania Constitutionalists of 1776.[86] No leading anti-Federalist or 1776 Pennsylvania Constitutionalist achieved political power in the county.[87]

The Lehigh Valley could embrace Federalism because its people had already gained new political privileges through the revolution. Voting had been extended; greater representation existed.[88] After the war, they sought the stability and order that proceeded from strong state and national central authority in keeping the peace, sharing the tax burden, and offering financial security and more stable investment opportunities.

The high degree to which the local Revolutionary committees intruded in people's lives certainly had its impact, for most residents eagerly awaited the end of that scrutiny and interference. They had experienced more than enough of a society in which wagons and buildings were requisitioned by the government, in which people spied on their neighbors, and in which trade was restricted by forces beyond those of the marketplace. But such intrusions also demonstrated the power of petition, skilled organization, and experienced and active leaders to ameliorate these hardships. Local leadership remained the choice over external interference. Had that not been what the war was all about anyway? Many Lehigh Valley residents were happy to anticipate being their own bosses again, under the protection of a strong central government that would be ready to contest external and internal foes alike.

4

Berks County

Karen Guenther

> The said County has very much increased in large well
> cultivated Farms, and in the Number of its Inhabitants, by
> whom very great Taxes, and other Duties to the Government,
> are regularly paid and performed, and near the Centre of the
> said County there is a large flourishing and increasing Town,
> settled by an industrious, thriving People, who carry on a great
> Trade with the adjacent Country, and with the City of
> *Philadelphia.* . . .
> —*Votes and Proceedings,* . . . *Province of Pennsylvania,*
> March 29, 1763, 255

The above description of Berks County by petitioners for an additional representative in March 1763 serves as a vivid statement of the attributes of Pennsylvania's seventh county. The early settlers were not great agitators; all they wanted was the representation they believed had been guaranteed in King Charles II's charter to William Penn. Their initial grievances against the government of the province, however, ultimately led them to become the "First Defenders" of American liberty. After British soldiers fired on Massachusetts militiamen in April 1775, Berks soldiers were among the first to report to Commander-in-Chief George Washington.[1]

The European immigrants who settled in the region that became Berks County represented nearly every part of northern and western Europe and the

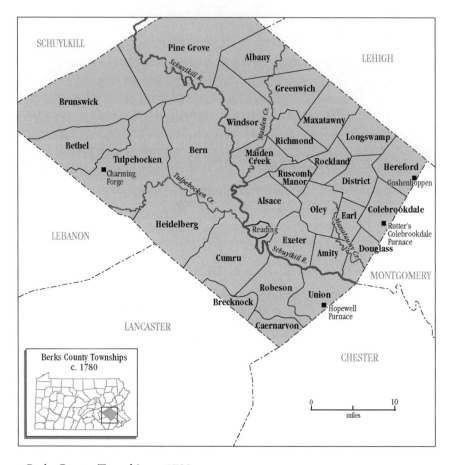

Berks County Townships c. 1780

British Isles and practiced almost every religion known to Europeans at the time. Immigrants from central Europe were the earliest settlers in the area and included several Swedes, who established a community near the mouth of the Manatawny Creek, and French Huguenots, who had fled from their homeland to the Palatinate following the revocation of the Edict of Nantes in 1685 and settled in the Oley Valley. These settlers had arrived in the province through the port of Philadelphia and from there proceeded up the Schuylkill River. By 1720, enough immigrants had settled in the Oley Valley in what became eastern Berks

County for the settlers to petition the legislators in Philadelphia for the establishment of a township in the region.[2]

Germans, however, were the most significant ethnic group to settle in the region. These Palatines came from both Europe and the Schoharie Valley in western New York. The earliest German migrants from New York established homesteads in western Berks County along the Tulpehocken Creek; the later waves settled throughout the county. By 1776, Germans comprised a majority in almost every township and accounted for at least 80 percent of the population.[3]

The final group of Europeans to settle in the region that became Berks County were immigrants from the British Isles. English Quaker families, among them the ancestors of the famous pioneer Daniel Boone, settled between the Manatawny Creek and the Schuylkill River. Welsh Quakers and Baptists, many of whom migrated from Chester County, settled in the eastern and southern sections of the county. A few Irish also moved to the area during the eighteenth century; Irish Quakers tended to locate near Maiden Creek in central Berks, while Irish Catholics mostly resided near the Roman Catholic mission at Goshenhoppen. Unlike the German settlers, the British generally concentrated their settlements along the southern border and in central and eastern Berks County. Some English did own land in the northern and western sections of the county, but few lived in those areas.[4]

Berks County had a diversified economy during the colonial period. The land along the Schuylkill River proved to be part of the most productive agricultural region in colonial America. Berks County farmers labored earnestly on their land, producing foodstuffs for their own consumption. Superior irrigation from the numerous creeks that flowed into the Schuylkill River, combined with limestone-rich soil, provided an ideal environment for the growth of cash crops like wheat and rye. Farmers also raised cattle for milk and meat and planted orchards for home use.[5]

Berks County, however, was more than just a bountiful agricultural region. Each community had a blacksmith shop and a wheelwright shop, and many farmers had gristmills on their property to process the wheat into flour. Local entrepreneurs also operated sawmills, paper mills, fulling mills, and oil mills throughout the county. In addition, county tax lists during the 1760s and 1770s reflected a diversity of occupations, with more than two dozen vocations identified.[6]

More important, however, were the iron-making furnaces and forges that produced pig iron and bar iron. During the colonial period, the large number of iron furnaces and forges resulted in Berks County becoming one of the largest industrial areas in North America. Ironworks were essentially self-sufficient enterprises like Southern plantations, for they included land suitable for farming (once cleared) in addition to timber and ore reserves. The first charcoal blast furnace in Pennsylvania, Thomas Rutter's Colebrookdale Furnace along Iron Stone Creek in eastern Berks County, supplied pig iron for his forges in northwestern Philadelphia County. Among the other products of the iron industry during the colonial period were horseshoes, plowshares, wagonwheel rims, and stove plates. The growing population of the Philadelphia region, along with Great Britain, provided markets for these items.[7]

While thousands of Europeans migrated to the interior of the province during the colonial period in search of religious freedom and economic opportunity, they did not find a democratic society. The availability of land enabled the recent immigrants to fulfill the property requirements for voting (ownership of 50 acres of land with 12 acres cleared, or personal property worth £50). Many of the farmers, however, were not British citizens and also had to meet naturalization requirements, which included owning 100 acres of land, a personal income of £10 per year, and approval of the Provincial Council. Even though inhabitants in the interior of the province outnumbered the residents of the Delaware Valley by mid-century, political control continued to rest in Philadelphia. The only new counties established by the legislature were Lancaster in 1729 and York in 1749, both along Pennsylvania's southern border. Part of this reluctance stemmed from fears that the frontiersmen would try to overturn Quaker political control and upset the colony's economic stability.[8]

Berks County was one of several counties established after mid-century, in 1752. Since the late 1730s, residents had been active in efforts to form a new county in the region, mainly because of the difficulty in traveling more than forty miles on the crude roads to Philadelphia to handle legal matters. In the settlers' requests for a new county, they claimed that distance prevented them from profitably marketing the crops grown on their farms. The nearest market was Lancaster, almost thirty miles away. The petitioners also emphasized that the Schuylkill River, which cut through the proposed county, would provide an effective natural means of shipping goods to Philadelphia—a means of transport that became crucial during the War of Independence.[9]

The establishment of the town of Reading in 1748 was the key in the making of Berks County. Proprietors Thomas and Richard Penn, sons of the province's founder, saw the region's potential. They laid out a seat for the proposed county, naming it after their family's ancestral home. Government officials viewed the town, situated near several trading paths, as ideal for conducting negotiations with the Indians. These advantages combined to persuade the legislators to establish Berks County, with its borders ultimately extending from approximately forty miles northwest of Philadelphia to the southern border of New York, a distance of about 200 miles. For the next twenty years, Berks County served as Pennsylvania's northwestern frontier, and its settlers learned to cope with the problems of frontier life—particularly visits by unfriendly natives.[10]

In some ways, Berks County resembled other regions of Pennsylvania during its early years. While German settlers outnumbered the others from the earliest settlements, the only political positions they held were appointive. Most elective offices were held by English settlers; Anglican James Read alone served as a county judge, recorder, register, clerk of the orphan's court, clerk of quarter sessions, and prothonotary during the first quarter-century of the county's history, holding most of these posts concurrently. By the early 1760s, the concern for defense had become so important that voters had begun to elect members of the more militant religious groups to public office instead of members of the Society of Friends. The English settlers remained dominant, as Anglicans assumed control of most county and provincial positions during the decade before the Revolution. German Lutheran and Reformed settlers, having become more self-conscious ecclesiastically and politically, also began to run for office. The election of the German Heinrich Keppel from Philadelphia to the Provincial Assembly in 1764 was followed by that of Adam Witman, a Berks County German, in 1765. When Berks County finally received two assemblymen in 1770, an Englishman filled one seat; the other seat went to a German. Although the Anglicans were a small minority, the continuation of the deferential society enabled them to hold prominent political posts in the county until the Revolution.[11]

Berks County did not see much agitation against the British during the 1760s and early 1770s, but there was some dissatisfaction with the provincial government. The lack of proportionate representation excited much interest, resulting in at least nine petitions for additional legislators between 1763 and 1776. In February 1764, residents of Berks County joined with fellow hinterland settlers from Lancaster, York, Cumberland, and Northampton Counties to petition the assembly for representation equal to that of their brethren in Philadelphia,

Bucks, and Chester Counties. Each time the westerners made these pleas during the 1760s, the Assembly tabled the discussion until an unspecified later date.[12]

By 1773 the focus had shifted from acquiring additional representatives to the creation of a new county. Settlers along the border between Berks and Lancaster Counties requested this because their safety had been "rendered very insecure from disorderly and wicked Persons" who fled there to escape the local magistrates. The inhabitants repeated their requests again in 1774 and 1775, with no success.[13]

Even though Berks Countians perceived that they were being treated unfairly because of inadequate representation, they had few other grievances against the actions of the Assembly after 1765, when the need for frontier defense declined. Typically, most of their petitions during peacetime reflected commercial interests. For example, in January 1768, inhabitants requested permission to build a road from Reading to Fort Augusta, near present-day Sunbury, "to advance the Trade and Commerce with the Indians who are Settled at the heads of the Susquehanna River, and to preserve the Friendship and Peace with them." The Provincial Council denied the petition because the land in question had not yet been purchased from the Indians, but its members did permit construction of a road to the purchase line. A year later, the road commissioners reported that they had completed construction of this "King's Highway, or Public Road."[14]

The decade after 1774 proved to be a testing time, not just in Berks but in the entire colony. The passage of the Boston Port Bill, one of the "Intolerable Acts" approved by Parliament, initiated Berks County's protest against British oppression. Even though residents of the county had not experienced any turmoil personally, community leaders met in July 1774 to decide how they should respond to the crisis. After acknowledging that they still owed their loyalty to George III, the Berks patriots resolved that "the Boston Port Bill is unjust and tyrannical in the extreme, and that the measures pursued against Boston are intended to operate equally against the rights and liberties of the other colonies." The settlers supported an intercolonial meeting to "settle with precision the rights and liberties of America." Furthermore, they agreed to contribute money and supplies to relieve the people of Boston.[15]

Proceeding from protesting against the "utter destruction of the liberties of America," Berks Countians moved to action. Seven prominent citizens, including future Speaker of the Assembly Edward Biddle, formed a committee to correspond with leaders of other counties. This group, however, did not represent a cross-section of the ethnic and religious diversity of the county. A majority were English Anglicans; only two Germans were selected. It is not surprising, therefore, that only Christopher Schultz, a Schwenkfelder, provided a pacifist opinion at these gatherings.[16]

A leading actor during the early stages of the agitation, Edward Biddle, was a Philadelphia native who had moved to Reading in the early 1760s to practice law. From 1767 through 1775, he represented Berks County in the Provincial Assembly, joined by Henry Christ in 1771. On October 15, 1774, the assemblymen gathering in Philadelphia selected Biddle to be speaker, and it was during his tenure in early 1775 that the Assembly became the first legislative body to ratify the acts of the First Continental Congress. In addition, Biddle was a Pennsylvania delegate to the Continental Congress from 1774 through 1776, although he was not present when that body adopted the Declaration of Independence because of injuries he had suffered in a boating accident during the previous year.[17]

English citizens like Biddle directed Berks' Revolutionary movement. Five of its six representatives to a provincial meeting in 1774 were of English ancestry. Delegates to the Provincial Convention that met in January 1775 included two Germans, one French Huguenot, and four English settlers. Two of the seven members of the County Committee of Correspondence formed that year were Germans, but both were from Reading and probably had little in common with the typical Berks County farmer. Only the County Committee of Correspondence elected by the citizens of the county in December 1774 had a German majority. There was, however, a great deal of opportunity for the young patriots to participate in the process of plotting the rebellion, for only Edward Biddle and Dr. Jonathan Potts belonged to all the above committees.[18]

The pace of preparations for a conflict with England increased. On January 16, 1775, the Standing Committee of Berks County issued a request to its farmers "not to sell any Sheep whatsoever to any Butcher from Philadelphia, or elsewhere, till the first day of May." The primary purpose of this conservation measure was to have the wool ready and available locally in case of urgent need—undoubtedly for uniforms. If farmers wanted to dispose of excess wool, Mark Bird, a member of the Standing Committee, would compensate them 14 pence per pound of wool. A week later, the Provincial Convention expanded the regulated items and ordered the preparation and preservation of supplies of saltpeter and gunpowder.[19]

For residents of Berks County, the outbreak of hostilities was momentous. Within a week of the Battle of Lexington in April 1775, two companies of soldiers commanded by two members of Reading's German Reformed congregation had been formed to aid the patriot cause.[20] Even before the Continental Congress could issue a general call to arms, the Reading committee informed that body of the status of preparations in the county: "We have raised in this Town two Companies of Foot, under proper Officers; and such is the spirit of the people of this free County, that in three weeks time there is not a Township in it that will not have a Company raised and disciplined, ready to assert at the risk of their lives the freedom of America."[21] Captain George Nagle's company left for Boston when it learned of the call to arms on June 14. The men arrived at Cambridge on July 25, among the first troops to report to the newly appointed commander-in-chief, George Washington.[22]

By July, Berks Countians had organized at least forty companies to resist British authority. Over the course of the war, local militia and Continental regulars from the county participated in campaigns in Massachusetts, Canada, New York, New Jersey, Pennsylvania, and along the frontier. More than 3,000 men from Reading and Berks County had volunteered to serve in the Pennsylvania militia or the Continental Army by 1781.[23]

For many of the German "church people," the War of Independence represented an opportunity to demonstrate support for their new homeland. A vast majority of the men, including some pastors, enlisted in the armed forces. Officers of the county's regiments included members of the Lutheran and Reformed churches. Reformed pastor Philip Jacob Michael, who ministered to at least twenty-four congregations in the county between 1750 and 1786, served as a chaplain for the local militia. Two prominent Continental Army surgeons, Dr. Bodo Otto and Dr. Jonathan Potts, hailed from Berks County. The non-Quaker British settlers of Berks County, however, generally held civil rather than military posts. Prominent Anglicans of Reading during the war included Edward Biddle, Edward Burd (a Reading attorney who became prothonotary of the Supreme Court in 1778) and James Read, who served as an executive councilor and register of the Court of Admiralty.[24]

Not all residents of the county supported the developing rebellion. After hostilities began in 1775, a group of "divers Inhabitants of the County of Berks, being conscientiously scrupulous of bearing Arms," met in Reading. The chairman of the gathering, William Reeser, a member of the German Reformed congregation of Reading and of the County Committee of Observation, wrote to the Pennsylvania Committee of Safety on September 11, 1775, and stated that, although this group opposed taking up arms, they realized the "justice of

the cause" and promised to contribute to its support. In the county, Mennonites, Moravians, Amish, Schwenkfelders, and Quakers all had theological reservations concerning the war. The German sects stated that they would neither
fight nor pay militia fines, but they would provide supplies for the war effort.
Demonstrating the good intent of these pacifists, Reeser forwarded the sum of
£152 collected at this meeting to the Committee of Safety. With most of the
Germans and Anglicans supporting independence, little contrary sentiment existed in the county.[25]

After the Second Continental Congress voted to declare independence from
Great Britain, Pennsylvanians moved quickly to overthrow the control of the
Penn family and to create a government that would provide for a more equitable
distribution of power throughout the Commonwealth. The resulting state constitution of 1776, unquestionably the most democratic of the state constitutions
adopted after the separation from England, met considerable opposition in
Berks County, but political maneuvering gained the support of the populace.
The new state constitution did enable Berks County to gain four additional
seats in the Assembly for a total of six, but some county political leaders were
reluctant to endorse all the document's provisions.[26]

Although Berks County's delegation did not include any of the prewar activ-
ists, it did consist of men who had a stake in the Revolution. Valentine Eckert
and John Lesher were ironmasters whose businesses had been affected by the
changes in British policy and whose industries now supplied ammunition for
the Continental Army. Jacob Morgan had become colonel of the Berks County
militia and would later serve on Pennsylvania's Supreme Executive Council and
on the Council of Safety. Furthermore, Gabriel Hiester and Thomas Jones Jr.
became majors in the county militia.[27]

These delegates, however, were reluctant supporters of the 1776 constitution
they helped devise. One, in fact, refused to sign his name to the finished product. For the county, Mark Bird, a conservative, guided revolutionary sentiment
and supported the actions of the Philadelphia city conservatives in their opposition to the document. When it came time for Berks Countians to indicate their
preference, however, the Radicals (also known as Constitutionalists) outsmarted
the conservatives and gained victory. All the new assemblymen elected from
Berks were Radicals, resulting in an unsuccessful protest against the election by
the defeated conservatives.[28]

Opposition to the document continued to grow during the late 1770s. Daniel
Hiester, brother of Gabriel, declined to accept a political appointment in 1777

because it would imply support for the Revolutionary government. Two of the Berks County assemblymen elected in 1777 openly declared their dissatisfaction with the new Pennsylvania constitution and took the oath of loyalty to the new government, with reservations. By October 1780, conservatism had become so entrenched in the county that three of the six assemblymen elected that fall were wealthy ironmasters who, although firm revolutionaries, had opposed the new state constitution.[29]

During the Revolution, the strategic geographical location of Reading along the Schuylkill River induced the Continental Congress to select the town as a general depot for storing supplies. Berks County artisans and businesses produced and manufactured many military supplies during the early years of the war. Among these provisions were saltpeter, cartridge boxes, muskets, canteens, and knapsacks. Berks County gunsmiths proved to be especially helpful to the cause by fashioning high-quality muskets for the army. Ironmaster Mark Bird also shipped more than a thousand barrels of flour from Reading down the Schuylkill River during the winter of 1777–78 to aid the troops at Valley Forge.[30]

Berks ironmasters proved to be some of its staunchest patriots. The Iron Act of 1750, and the addition of iron to the list of enumerated products in 1764, adversely affected the success of their plantations. Ironmasters Daniel Udree, Christian Lower, John Patton, and John Lesher served in the Continental Army as colonels. In addition, Valentine Eckert, John Lesher, and Christian Lower were responsible for purchasing supplies for the army. During the first two years of the war, George Ege of Charming Forge and Mark Bird of Hopewell Furnace provided the American cause with cannon, shot, and shell. By September 1776, Bird had manufactured more than forty usable cannon of varying sizes, in addition to another three dozen pieces that could not be shipped because of defects.[31]

The contributions of Mark Bird and others caused the Continental Congress and the Continental Army to recognize the defense of Reading as crucial to the success of the war. Because of the vital importance of the food and industrial production of Berks County, beginning in late 1776, some troops had to remain in the Reading area in order to protect the supplies and to defend the interior of the state. In November 1776, the Council of Safety ordered the Berks County militia to be ready to march to Philadelphia at a moment's notice, an order repeated two months later. When the war reached the province in summer, 1777, almost 2,000 men of Berks County fought in the battles in the vicinity of

Philadelphia, half the number eligible for duty. In the meantime, James Biddle (Edward's brother) received £15 from the Pennsylvania Assembly "to defray the Expence of conveying the public Papers to Reading" in order to put them out of reach of the occupying British forces.[32]

The importance of Reading also affected the location of a winter camp in 1777. After General Washington withdrew his army from Philadelphia in 1777, he kept his forces between British General William Howe and the town to protect the storage depot. In January 1778, Congress noted that 8,000 barrels of flour would be deposited at Reading to feed the troops. Washington remarked in a letter to Pennsylvania President Thomas Wharton that he had also received word of "a considerable quantity of cloathing collected at Reading," which he hoped would be made available to the troops wintering at Valley Forge. It is not so surprising that, in March 1778, Congress ordered 200 Pennsylvania militiamen to be stationed at Reading to defend "magazines of military, & other stores & provisions . . . & to keep the communication secure from any sudden incursions of the enemy."[33]

The British invasion and occupation of Philadelphia in 1777–78 had other effects on life in Reading. Many supporters of the Revolutionary cause fled there for safety. William Hall, whose presses in Philadelphia had printed Continental money for the government, brought his equipment with him when he moved in early 1777. The German Reformed ministers and elders met in Reading that fall, in part because the location was safe from the advancing British army. Exeter Monthly Meeting's representatives to Philadelphia Quarterly Meeting could not attend the session that November because the American army prevented their travel.[34] Alexander Graydon, a Philadelphia lawyer, recorded in his memoirs: "The [Philadelphia] society was sufficiently large and select; and a sense of common suffering in being driven from their homes, had the effect of more closely uniting its members. . . . Besides the families established in this place, it was seldom without a number of visitors, gentlemen of the army and others. Hence the dissipation of cards, sleighing parties, balls, &c., was freely indulged."[35] The British occupation of Philadelphia also forced the Reverend James Sproat to follow his Presbyterian congregation to Reading when they fled the city, so he could continue to offer worship services in an area that had no Presbyterian church.[36]

The war affected Reading's religious institutions in other ways. Private houses served as hospitals, as did the town's "public places of worship." After the Battle of Brandywine in September 1777, the Lutheran and Reformed church build-ings and the Quaker meetinghouse housed the sick and wounded soldiers, with the consent of the congregations.[37]

During the war, Reading was also a prominent center for keeping prisoners. Among these men and women were Hessian troops and their followers captured at the Battle of Trenton and Quakers from Philadelphia interned for their con-scientious scruples. Neighboring ironmasters hired some of the Hessians during their imprisonment to produce munitions for the patriot cause. The records of Trinity Lutheran Church in Reading indicate that some of the mercenary sol-diers who had been imprisoned remained in the town after the Revolution.[38]

Reading became a site for internment in December 1775 when the Continen-tal Congress ordered British prisoners captured by General Richard Montgom-ery at St. John's in Canada to be sent to Reading, Lancaster, and York. The first batch arrived in early February 1776, some accompanied by their wives and children. Reading's Committee of Correspondence, however, had not yet re-ceived word of the town's designation as a prison camp, so they placed the prisoners in the homes of local residents. The committee also quickly appointed Henry Haller to be in charge of the prison camp, a position he held for most of the war. It became Haller's duty to provide the prisoners with food, shelter, and firewood.[39]

The prisoners attracted little notice until September 1776, when several in-habitants of the county petitioned the Committee of Correspondence to disarm them and place them under a curfew. The commander of the Hessian troops agreed to turn over their weapons, but not until they had been destroyed to prevent their use by the patriots. Meanwhile, the Council of Safety, which had authorized the use of Hessian prisoners as laborers in the county's iron industry a few months earlier, replied that members of the local militia would remain in Reading as long as the prisoners were stationed in the town.[40]

Part of the concern about the conditions of imprisonment by Berks County's political leaders stemmed from Reading's status as a depot for supplies. Citizens feared that the Hessians might sabotage the powder and ammunition, which not only would hinder the prosecution of the war but might also lead to the destruction of the town. Another problem stemmed from inadequate provisions for the prisoners; Haller often wrote to the Board of War requesting funds to purchase food for the prisoners, perhaps to prevent an uprising.[41]

Nevertheless, the prisoners seemed content with their stay in Reading. In May 1779, Captain P. Pitcairn wrote to John Jay, president of Congress, that he and the other prisoners preferred to remain at Reading rather than relocate. Pitcairn recognized that some animosity had previously existed with the towns-people, but now "the People here wish to be upon a better footing with us." Later that month, however, Pennsylvania President Joseph Reed informed the Board of War that the situation had become tense once again, and he recommended that the British prisoners be removed to New Jersey. Richard Peters, secretary of the Board of War, had received Pitcairn's letter in the interim and denied Reed's request. Peters recognized the sincerity of Pitcairn's promise for better behavior and thought that the transfer was an avoidable expense.[42]

By 1781—nearly five years after the first arrival of the captives—a prison camp had finally been established near Reading, with prisoners "hutted at some small Distance from the Town where Wood & Water are convenient." The site selected was "a Peice of Ground which belong'd to the late Proprietaries" on the east side of Mount Penn. Unlike their predecessors, this last batch of prisoners (almost 1,000 of them Hessians) received favorable mention by the local magistrates because they had "behaved themselves very orderly and Peaceably." In spite of their good behavior, however, they still required guards. The inhabitants of Reading were just as reluctant to quarter the militia as they were to house the Hessians; that forced the local commander to request assistance from the state in locating housing for his men.[43]

Residents of Berks County faced other problems as a result of the war. The county's most prominent lawyers—Edward Biddle, James Read, and Edward Burd—had taken positions in Philadelphia serving in the new state or national government. Consequently, the legal system in the county was in disarray by 1778. James Read remarked in a letter to Timothy Matlack in February 1778 that no attorneys were practicing law in Reading anymore. The court dockets were backing up because of the scarcity of barristers, and the disposition of cases had slowed to a trickle. Not even the arrival of lawyers fleeing Philadelphia during that winter alleviated the situation.[44]

Financial irregularities emerged also, in a plan "to depreciate the Continental Currency." Two Berks Countians were brought before the County Committee of Observation and imprisoned for their offense. After spending some time in the county jail, the two men publicly recanted their actions. One of the accused sought to "beg pardon of my justly incensed countrymen" for the "heinousness and horrid tendency" of his conduct. The other, a Quaker, expressed remorse not only for the crime but also because his actions were "inconsistent with the religious principles of the Society with which I profess." Neither of the two faced further criminal charges, but their imprisonment showed the extent that Berks County patriots would go to encourage Revolutionary sentiment among the populace.[45]

Money was certainly of interest to Berks County's volunteers in the state militia. In December 1776, Henry Haller reported to the Pennsylvania Council of Safety that most of his battalion, including some officers, had deserted. Haller contended that his troops had been promised the same pay as regulars in the Continental Army, but the paymasters instead had merely responded to his requests with "all the delay in their power." Haller's battalion was not the only one to depart because of unfulfilled promises. Connecticut General Israel Putnam noted less than a month later that two companies of Berks County militia "have runaway to a man, except a Lieut. & Sergt., & a Drum[mer]." Putnam expressed concern "that this spirit of Desertion should be crushed in its Infancy, & the Militia taught that there is a Power that can & will detain them." He did not, however, mention why the troops had deserted—they had been ordered to march to New Jersey without any provisions or supplies.[46]

The most obvious open opponents of the Revolution in Berks were two Anglicans—John Biddle, a political officeholder who had become wealthy through numerous government appointments, and the Reverend Alexander Murray, recently sent by the Society for the Propagation of the Gospel in Foreign Parts as an Anglican missionary to Berks County. The outbreak of the American Revolution ruptured relations between Murray and his patriotic parishioners. His ordination vows made him pledge loyalty to the King as well as to the Church of England and obligated him to include prayers for the monarch in the services. Consequently, Murray believed that he "thought it was his duty as a Preacher of peace to discourage" the revolutionary activity in the town and province, "but his voice was drowned in the Genl Cry of Liberty, Property and no Taxation. . . ." Within months of the onset of the rebellion, Murray's congregation ceased to attend his services until he omitted the public prayers for the King. The next step for the patriots was to begin harassing the parson. In April 1776, "an Armed Mob . . . with a Murderous intent attacked his house." Rumors of plots by British prisoners to torch the town and murder the inhabitants with Murray's assistance abounded. An excited mob planted weapons at Murray's country estate to implicate him in one of these supposed attacks. Fortunately, the Town Committee arrived on the scene and prevented any physical harm at this time, but their presence was not enough to protect Murray and his wife from "repeated alarms" over the next two years. Murray finally fled to

England in June 1778, after being imprisoned and beaten for his loyalty to the Crown and seeing his home used as a powder magazine, a guard house, and hospital for the local militia.[47]

While not favoring the Crown, Berks pacifists were hostile to the war. By not supporting the Revolution, however, sectarians, such as the Quakers, Amish, Mennonites, and Schwenkfelders, were branded as "tories" and persecuted for their beliefs. Such perceived "toryism" encouraged the Revolutionary leaders of Pennsylvania to pass an Act of Allegiance (known as the Test Act) in June 1777. All white male inhabitants of the state were required to take the oath of allegiance to the Commonwealth of Pennsylvania if they wanted to preserve their civil rights. By the beginning of July, almost 5,000 Berks County males over eighteen years of age had sworn allegiance to the new government.[48]

Most members of the Society of Friends refused to take the oath; the minority of Friends who complied with the provisions of the Test Act faced possible excommunication. Those who kept to the teachings of their faith and refused to swear allegiance, however, faced secular rather than religious problems. Between August 1777 and December 1778, Berks County officials took from an unidentified Quaker "a cow for the £3.10.0 fine," which they then sold for £10.10; 36 bushels of wheat to pay a tax of £20; "a great coat" worth £10; a horse valued at £200 for a £30 tax; and "four cows for forty pounds fine said cows would at that time have Sold for £20: each." In July 1778, the Berks County sheriff imprisoned three Quakers and fined them 16 shillings each for refusing to take the Oath of Allegiance. Undersheriff Conrad Foos arrested George Rush for failing to pay a militia fine; Rush stated that he refused to comply with the law because he did not believe it was "Right for me to pay or contribute to the Sheding of human Blood." At least a dozen members of Exeter Monthly Meeting faced imprisonment and/or property loss for refusing to comply with the law.[49]

By 1779 the pacifists in the county had taken their objections one step further. Thirty-two residents refused to pay the assessed taxes, thus earning the distinction of being labeled Tories on the official tax rolls. In fact, this number is quite minuscule in relation to the county's population. A census of men eligible for service in 1777 revealed that approximately 4,000 Berks Countians were available for military duty. All the townships that had so-called Tories did have some Amish, Brethren, Mennonite, Moravian, or Quaker settlers.[50]

A year later, high taxes became another burden for both conscientious objectors and patriots. By 1780, tax resistance had become widespread in western

Berks County. German farmers who had fought in the war and had seen their farms destroyed by foraging troops could not afford to pay the high levies assessed that year. The state government, however, did not show any mercy to the oppressed patriots. That November, the Supreme Court convicted almost 150 German settlers in Bern, Bethel, and Tulpehocken Townships of "associating together to oppose the collection of the publick taxes." The inhabitants of these townships were mostly Lutheran and Reformed, so the morality of paying taxes to support the war did not appear to be the issue. The resisters comprised about one-fifth of the total number of taxpayers for these townships, and they did not include any pacifists. Furthermore, two dozen township tax collectors refused to collect taxes that year, and seven others would not collect militia class fines. The revolt, then, was not only led by taxpayers but also extended to those responsible for enforcing the laws and receiving payments.[51]

The arguments employed by government officials to punish the farmers recognized the severity of the situation. They considered the actions of the Berks Countians treasonous and seditious. Supreme Court Judge George Bryan, however, noted that all involved had "been active in the marching of the militia" and recommended that a plea bargain be arranged. Nevertheless, the courts responded with heavy penalties on the conspirators, fining them £300 each for their part in the revolt.[52]

The taxpayers, in contrast, consistently maintained that they remained "strongly attached to the liberties of America" and were upset because they could not afford the tax, much less the penalty. In a petition to the Supreme Executive Council in January 1781, the settlers feared that the punishment meted out by the courts would further "reduce your Petitioners and their innocent Families to distress and Want." Subsequent requests to the Council led to a reexamination of the case, and by the end of January the Council had agreed to reduce the fines by 50 percent. The revolting taxpayers were still guilty, but the penalty became more affordable.[53]

Even though the Society of Friends lost control of the Assembly with the internal revolution in 1776, and faced persecution for not following the provisions of the Test Act, their influence continued to affect public policy. In 1780, the Assembly passed an Act for the Gradual Abolition of Slavery. The culmination of the Quakers' efforts for over four decades, that law codified what the Philadelphia Yearly Meeting had mandated for its members. Friends in Berks County, however, had not joined their co-religionists in freeing their slaves.[54]

The slow rate of manumission by the Friends in Berks County reflected the overall opposition to the abolition of slavery in the county. Approximately 100 Berks Countians owned slaves when the Assembly passed the law in 1780. Only two of Berks County's five representatives who attended the 1779–80 Assembly session supported the Act. The three who voted against the measure were Germans, while the two supporters were French and Welsh. All the opponents of the law were slaveholders, as was one of its supporters.[55]

This lack of support for abolition by Berks County's legislators paralleled the two other German-dominated counties in Pennsylvania. Representatives from Northampton and Lancaster Counties, part of the "German arc" of southeastern Pennsylvania, opposed the Gradual Abolition Act. Here, slaves were used both on farms and in industry, where they provided some of the labor force at the growing number of iron plantations in the region. The iron industry in Berks County employed both indentured servants and slaves in its labor force. In fact, ironmasters held the largest numbers; Mark Bird of Hopewell Furnace, John Lesher of Oley Forge, John Patton of Berkshire Furnace, and George Ege of Charming Forge all possessed at least ten slaves in 1780.[56]

Germans opposed the Gradual Abolition Act for a variety of reasons. Many of the recent immigrants were laborers, and while they themselves might not have owned slaves, they did recognize the status associated with the institution. Opponents of abolition, meanwhile, argued that the law would invite discontent within the nation and that it presumed incorrectly that the freedmen could integrate peacefully into Pennsylvania society with little difficulty. In spite of the opposition of many German settlers, the law still passed. It did not, however, provide for immediate emancipation; Berks Countians continued to own slaves legally into the early 1800s.[57]

In 1781, the focus in Berks County shifted once again from political to military affairs. All was not quiet on the local front, even though the brunt of military operations had shifted to the southern colonies. In May, residents of Brunswick and Pine Grove Townships north of the Blue Mountains petitioned the Supreme Executive Council for assistance against Indian attacks from the upper Susquehanna Valley. The state government ordered the local militia to defend the county's frontiers from the natives. A year later, the Council ordered an additional 150 men and officers from Berks to rendezvous with other troops at Muncy in Northumberland County, to defend the northern frontier of the state from attacks by Indians in the Wyoming Valley.[58]

By 1783, everyday life in Berks County had once again become quiet. Most prisoners had been evacuated from Reading, while a few Hessians remained to start their lives anew in Pennsylvania. Soldiers had returned home to work on their farms and in their shops. Many farms returned to their prewar productivity, although the nationwide economic depression affected the prices of crops. Ironmaster Mark Bird typified the financial straits that some faced; he went bankrupt in 1783 because he could not collect debts owed by the American and French governments. His brother-in-law James Wilson bought some of his lands, including Hopewell Furnace, and the rest the county sheriff sold at a public auction.[59]

Politically, Pennsylvania's internal revolution following the overthrow of the proprietary government in 1776 changed Berks County forever. No longer would the English settlers dominate elective offices; the Germans had begun to assert political independence at the same time that the colonists had declared theirs from Great Britain. More than 80 percent of the justices of the peace elected between 1777 and 1780, and all the county sheriffs and treasurers, were German settlers. Henry Christ replaced James Read as the register of wills by 1776. After Berks County gained a total of six seats in the Assembly in 1776, Germans comprised almost two-thirds of the men who served as state representatives.[60] The agitation for equal representation that had begun in 1763 ultimately enabled the German majority of Berks County's settlers to participate in the legislative process—and as a result have a greater voice in their own destiny.

The War of Independence had other effects on the people of Berks County. More than three-fourths of all eligible men served in the war, either in civil or military posts. Pacifism, rather than loyalism, characterized the opposition to the war, and even then it was not widespread. The men of Berks County, men who had volunteered after receiving the news of Lexington and Concord, had successfully defended American liberty and had proven that William Penn had not erred in inviting the oppressed peoples of the European continent to live in his colony.

5

York County

Paul E. Doutrich

The American struggle for independence came to York County during the spring of 1774. Although the Stamp Act controversy initiated some local protest, news about the Intolerable Acts and Parliament's attempt to punish Boston transformed York Countians into active patriots. In the months and years that followed, the county became actively involved in the struggle with Great Britain. For a time, the county played a crucial role in the American struggle for independence. And as a result of its participation in the war, York County experienced an internal revolution of its own. The American War of Independence rapidly accelerated socioeconomic and political development. In some ways the changes were a product of wartime military participation. More important, the unique experience of Yorktown (now York) as the temporary seat of the provisional American government generated profound change throughout the county. As a result, by the mid-1780s the county was well on the way to making the transition from a region of remote cultural settlements to an economically progressive "modern" American community.

York County in 1774 was a sparsely populated region at the edge of British American civilization. In an effort to appease the Indians, Pennsylvania authorities prohibited European settlement in the area until the mid-1720s. Even after provincial restrictions were lifted, expansion into the western part of the lower Susquehanna was slow. Throughout most of the 1730s, the colony's border conflict with Maryland discouraged potential settlers. Not until 1739 was the region's population large enough to justify assigning a Pennsylvania justice of the peace to the area. Two years later the Assembly approved laying out York-town. Supportive local residents and Philadelphia speculators proposed that the town might someday become a commercial crossroads and possibly serve as the seat of a future county government should the need arise. That need became a reality in 1749 when York County, which until 1800 also included Adams County, was created.[1]

Despite the organization of a new county, the threat of Indian attack and troubles with the French slowed migration into the new region during the 1750s. With the successful resolution of the problems, the county's population grew steadily though not rapidly to almost 5,000 residents by 1770.

The ethnic heritage of the county's initial settlers played an important role in determining the character of York County. Between 1730 and 1755, European immigrants established several loosely organized and remote communities. By the time of independence, the county had become a collection of relatively isolated cultural enclaves.

German was the county's dominant nationality, accounting for perhaps 50 percent of the total York County population.[2] Many of region's earliest residents were first-generation immigrants who had come from the Palatine district of Germany. Before relocating west of the Susquehanna, many had spent time in eastern Pennsylvania refilling empty pockets and adjusting to life in a British colony. When relocating to the county, they maintained their indigenous cultural habits, thus establishing York as the western extreme of Pennsylvania's German region. German settlers generally entered the county at Wright's Ferry (now Wrightsville) and created a band of farmsteads and villages stretching from the Susquehanna to Yorktown and then south and southwest to the Maryland border.[3]

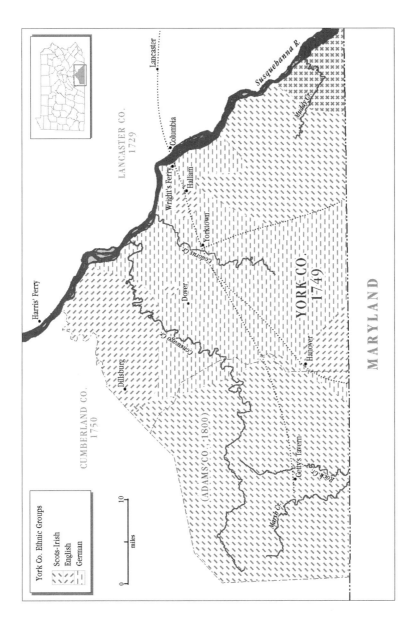

York County Ethnic Groups c. 1749

Scots-Irish settlers constituted about one-third of the county's early population. Unlike the Germans, many Scots-Irish migrated north from western Maryland and northwestern Virginia into the western part of York County (the part
of the county that would later become Adams County). At the same time,
other Scots-Irish entered the county from eastern Pennsylvania by crossing the
Susquehanna at Harris's Ferry (now Harrisburg). These migrants usually stayed
north of the Germans who occupied the central part of the county. Generally
the Scots-Irish established small farmsteads in the western portions of the new
county as well as along the county's northern periphery.

The Germans, though less numerous than either the German or Scots-Irish migrants, pockets of English settlers, scattered throughout the county, comprised a third important York population. Principal concentrations included settlements along
the Susquehanna north of Wright's Ferry and in the north-central part of the
county. The English were predominately small farmers, although a few sustained
themselves through commerce.

Whether German, Scots-Irish, or English, Europeans came to York County
for similar reasons. Early settlers were, for the most part, yeomen farmers of
modest means who had come to America in search of economic security and
opportunity. The land west of the Susquehanna was affordable and available,
and while the soil was not quite as rich as Lancaster County soil, it was potentially productive. In York County, settlers maintained traditional farming activities that could sustain families for generations to come.

The relative isolation of York County also attracted migrants. The county was
a three-day journey from provincial authorities in Philadelphia. The Susquehanna River, which separated York County from eastern Pennsylvania, was a
barrier that at times became almost impassable. This isolation enabled immigrants, Germans in particular, to maintain cultural traditions with little fear of
interference.

Though less important than economic opportunity, Pennsylvania's tolerant
religious policies also drew settlers to York County. For many, the church was
an integral part of daily life. Church affiliation was a critical factor that, along
with ethnic heritage, determined where an immigrant family would ultimately
settle. Likewise, church organization was one of the first tasks communities
within the county tackled.

Among Germans, the Lutheran and Reformed churches were dominant.
Scots-Irish settlers usually formed Presbyterian congregations, while Englishmen
were either Quakers or, to a lesser extent, Anglicans. Denominations often cre-

ated cultural barriers that occasionally alienated one community from another and generated minor local squabbles. While in the long run, church differences did not seriously divide the county, sectarians and Moravians were not really welcome in the county. On the few occasions that clergy with ties to the Moravian church did attempt to lead local congregations, the community acted quickly. In Yorktown, both the Reformed church, led by brothers Caspar and Baltzer Spengler, and the Lutheran church, led by, among others, Bartholomew Maul with assistance from Henry Muhlenberg, expelled ministers who had previously preached to Moravian congregations.[4]

During the quarter-century between the creation of York County and passage of the Intolerable Acts, life within the county stabilized through the evolution of several villages. Most important was Yorktown, the county's government headquarters as well as its commercial focus. In the southwest, Getty's Tavern became the core of the Marsh Creek community that evolved into Gettysburg. Roughly midway between Yorktown and Getty's Tavern was Hanover, a speculative land venture that grew to village status by 1770. Five miles north of Yorktown, a crossroads tavern served as the axis of Dover. East of Yorktown were two other settlements: Hallam and Wright's Ferry on the Susquehanna. These villages all became sites of local commerce and society by 1774.

A slowly but steadily growing economy characterized the county between 1760 and 1774. During that time, Yorktown became a hub from which commercial spokes stretched to virtually all corners of the county. In addition, unlike Pennsylvanians east of the Susquehanna, York residents had the option of trading south with Baltimore. Although trade eastward would remain primary, southward trade provided opportunities that York Countians occasionally explored. To facilitate commerce, a number of wagon paths that linked farmsteads with grist mills, mills with villages, villages with Yorktown, and Yorktown with Lancaster and Philadelphia, were created.

Economic expansion also included diversity. Virtually all county residents did some farming. The typical holding was between 100 and 300 acres, but only a small portion of a farmstead's acreage was cultivated. York County farmsteads were subsistence enterprises that grew primarily wheat, barley, and corn while maintaining minimal livestock. Once established, a farmer usually planted a small portion of his land, perhaps 10 percent, with a cash crop such as hemp or tobacco.

By 1774, York also included a small nonfarming population consisting of craftsmen, tavernkeepers, and merchants. They resided in the county's villages, particularly Yorktown. Until the late 1770s, village residents were no more prosperous than their farming counterparts; and, like their agrarian neighbors, the nonfarming population confined its economic activity primarily to local trade.

Politically before 1774, York Countians focused almost exclusively on local issues. In other political matters, they usually deferred to provincial leaders. Local government was administered by a leadership that had evolved during the county's first quarter-century. Once a resident became a community leader, he generally held a variety of local offices for a decade or longer. Qualifications for leadership included economic sufficiency, though not necessarily wealth. Most township and county officials held several hundred acres of land and were often among the more prominent local entrepreneurs. While ethnic background was a somewhat important factor in determining community leadership, church affiliation was critical. Most local leaders were either German church people (Lutherans or Reformed) or Scots-Irish Presbyterians, depending on the community.

At the top of the county political hierarchy were elected representatives to the Provincial Assembly. By 1774, provincial offices had become positions that required local prominence as well as the ability to function within both the English culture of Philadelphia and the German/Scots-Irish cultures of York County. Few county inhabitants possessed such abilities, but two who did were James Smith and Thomas Hartley. While Smith had arrived in the county before Hartley, both were of English descent but had been reared in Pennsylvania's German hinterland. Both were economically secure lawyers who often represented the legal interests of local citizenry, and both carried the American struggle for independence into the county.[5]

James Smith was perhaps the first York Countian actively to protest British legislation. A backwoods lawyer, the operator of an iron furnace, and a land speculator, he was affected in several ways by British actions during the 1760s. Responding to the Stamp Act, he organized an informal committee to keep the county informed about the unfolding colonial dispute with the King and Parliament. Through the early 1770s, he enlisted a half-dozen locally prominent residents into his committee. Nevertheless, his early protest organization was of little significance to most York Countians.

Aside from Smith's group, York Countians during the early years of the imperial crisis remained far more interested in local matters than in imperial debates. The Revenue Acts (Townshend Acts) of 1767 brought virtually no reaction within the County. Likewise, the Boston Massacre and the Tea Act elicited only a ripple of dissent. No doubt some were at least mildly troubled by the British actions—York Countians certainly discussed the growing problems among themselves informally. However, there are no records, official or otherwise, of such discussions, debates, or concerns.

The Intolerable Acts began to transform the county into a hive of patriot activity. Shortly after news about the closing of Boston Harbor reached Yorktown, James Smith and his fellow patriots formally organized a Committee of Correspondence. Announcing its creation, Smith proclaimed: "We want our words to express the high sense we have for [the Bostonians'] conduct and virtue: few men in the world would have opposed despotism and stood the torrent of ministerial vengeance with so much steadiness, intrepidity and resolution as the inhabitants of your town and country have done. You have true notions of liberty."[6] Elsewhere in the county, food, blankets, and various other supplies were collected and sent to Boston to help fortify "our brothers and sisters." Even British sterling, always a limited commodity throughout the county, was collected to provide New Englanders with additional aid.[7]

As new reports of ever worsening conditions in New England were posted at the courthouse and circulated throughout the county, local residents informally began to prepare themselves militarily. Even before the First Continental Congress advised that a colonial militia be created, York County prepared its own defense. During the summer and fall of 1774, voluntary drilling became a regular activity in several communities.[8] In December, Yorktowners organized the Committee of Freemen and Inhabitants "to protect the lives and property of those who are either away with the army, or are too young, or for some other reason are unable to protect themselves, also to keep law and order and collect funds and materials for the [volunteers]."[9]

Formal mobilization of the county began during the following summer. In June 1775, responding to the call of the Second Continental Congress for a battalion of eight Pennsylvania rifle companies, the York County Committee of Correspondence issued a call for volunteers. James Smith, the committee's president, informed prospective riflemen that, once created, the unit would march to Massachusetts and join the newly formed Continental Army under the command of George Washington.[10]

At the same time that the committee issued a call for volunteers, it chose Michael Doudel, a Yorktown tanner, as captain of the future company. Henry Miller of Yorktown, John Dill from the Monaghan settlement, and James Matson were also enlisted to serve as Doudel's lieutenants. With officers selected, recruiting began in three locations, all three in the western portions of the county. Two sites were Getty's Tavern in the Marsh Creek settlement and the Monaghan settlement (near present-day Dillsburg). Another site, not specifically identified, was in the southern part of the county.[11]

Despite requiring volunteers to agree to serve for a year, the Committee of Freemen had no problem enlisting the 77 men (68 privates, 4 sergeants, 4 corporals, and a musician) needed to fill out Doudel's company. Smith claimed that "the spirit of the people on this occasion gave the committee much encouragement. The principle [*sic*] people here have caught the spirit of the honorable Congress and in their small circle have done everything in their power to animate their neighbors to stand forth . . . and resist the arbitrary and unjust measures of Parliament."[12] So many York Countians volunteered that the committee considered accepting only the best marksmen. However, it was decided that virtually all who volunteered should be welcomed and that additional companies could be formed for future service as needed.[13]

On July 1, 1775, just two weeks after the call for volunteers, Doudel's rifle company met in Yorktown and attended services at the German Reformed Church. After a farewell meal, the volunteers, carrying a banner that proclaimed "Liberty or Death," marched off to become part of the Continental Army. Three weeks and three days later, the York rifle company arrived in Cambridge and became one of the first Pennsylvania rifle companies to join the Continental Army. Initially part of Thompson's Rifle Battalion, the York company was later redesignated as part of the First Continental Regiment.[14] During the next eighteen months, the York Countians were involved in battles against the British near Boston as well as in the struggle in and around New York City. They also retreated with the Continental Army through New Jersey and participated in the battles at Trenton and Princeton in early 1777.

Doudel's rifle company reflected a general cross-section of the county's ethnic population. While it appears that more Scots-Irish than Germans volunteered, both groups were well represented. In terms of socioeconomic status, the unit can best be described as part of colonial York County's aspiring middle class. A majority were eighteen-to-twenty-five-year-old farmers whose families held farmsteads of less than 100 acres. Many were unmarried, though at least a few had families of their own.[15]

As Doudel and his men marched into New England, the York County Committee of Safety took further steps to organize defensively. In late July 1775, the committee divided the county into five military districts. Battalions of volunteers, known as Associators, with their own officers were established in each of the five districts. The first battalion included men from townships surrounding Yorktown; the second and third were from the western part of the county; the fourth was from the southeast; and the fifth battalion was from the northern part of the county. These community-based units were designed to provide a local defense as well as a pool of volunteers who might later join Washington's army.

At the same time, the Committee of Safety responded to a request from the Pennsylvania Council of Safety and created one more battalion that would defend the county at a moment's notice. Composed of select members from each of the five community battalions, this "minuteman" unit created some administrative confusion but it also provided York Countians with a another layer of defense. By the end of 1775, some 3,349 men from the county, or about 75 percent of the male population between the ages of fifteen and fifty-five, were enlisted in some way for the defense of the county.[16] During the next three years, many of the local Associators would become, if only temporarily, part of the Continental Army.

For many in the county, support of the American cause meant more than simply military service. Baltzer Spengler Jr., a prominent Yorktown innkeeper and farmer, spent part of the fall of 1775 in Philadelphia manufacturing gunpowder for the Pennsylvania Council of Safety.[17] Other residents provided goods ranging from iron cannonballs to saltpeter and wheat. Most clergy urged their congregations to support the patriot cause. Speaking on behalf of his flock, one Yorktown minister assured the local Committee of Safety: "You will find us eager and willing to fight for 'our rights as Englishmen' just as other colonists are doing."[18] As independence neared, sermons implored listeners to do their duty to their community, to Pennsylvania, and to the colonies. Men were encouraged to volunteer for service if they were physically able. Women were instructed to tend the homes and businesses of absent volunteers.[19]

Mobilization in York County also meant identifying those who opposed the colonial cause. When suspected loyalists were discovered, the County Committee of Safety took swift action. In mid-1775, one disgruntled resident who "gave vent to his feelings by insulting Congress and its measures for the institution of defensive warfare" was tarred and feathered. The committee required that another resistor publicly "express his sorrow" for doubting the Continental Congress. William Rankin, perhaps the county's most outspoken opponent of independence, was declared "Inimical to the Liberties of America" and strongly encouraged to leave the county (which he wisely did). Anglican clergyman Daniel Batwell also experienced the wrath of York County patriots. Upon his arrival in the county in late 1774, he was labeled a Tory, and over the next two years was officially denounced, physically threatened, jailed, and dunked in the Cadorus Creek by "the friends of Liberty in Yorktown." Like Rankin, Batwell soon fled the county.[20]

While successfully limiting loyalist activities, the Committee of Safety remained somewhat sympathetic to religious objections to armed conflict from York congregations. Of particular concern were pacificistic local Moravians and Quakers. To avoid "infringing upon the rights of Conscience," the Committee of Safety contemplated issuing a tax that could be paid by "those People who conscientiously scruple bearing Arms." Those who refused either to serve in the militia or to pay the tax would be tagged as opponents of America. Eventually community service rather than a tax was used to determine who supported the patriot cause and who did not. As a result, many "who did not draw a sword did the Civil State quite a valuable and indispensable service" within the county. This alternative to military service enabled virtually all county residents eventually to support American independence. By May 1776, James Smith boasted that not a single dissident could be found within the county.[21]

The initial year of the war was a time of change and adjustment for York Countians. While many local volunteers remained at home through July 1776, the slow but steady socioeconomic growth that had characterized the county since the early 1760s ended. On many farmsteads, production declined to subsistence levels because the primary labor force—fathers and sons—had journeyed off to war. Likewise, merchants, artisans, and craftsmen temporarily ceased operations. By mid-1776, one Yorktown resident observed that throughout the county "all businesses and every occupation are prostrate, all shops are closed."[22]

Despite the growing hardships, York Countians remained staunch supporters of the American cause through the first year of war. As tensions between the Continental Congress and the Pennsylvania Assembly grew during the spring of 1776, York Countians came down squarely on the side of those who sought sweeping reforms within the provincial government. Spurred by local patriot leaders—particularly James Smith, who was a member of the Continental Congress—the county joined the growing revolt against Pennsylvania's proprietary administration. York Countians sought to expand democracy within the colony and in turn to support further the colonial independence movement.

News of American independence came to the county on July 4, 1776, and touched off a day-long celebration. The focus of the festivities was the courthouse square in Yorktown, where James Smith and fellow patriot Archibald McClean led a group of men to a makeshift bell tower that had been built. The bell had been sent to St. John's Church, the Church of England in Yorktown, two years earlier but was too big for the church's belfry. On the first day of American independence, Smith and his companions hoisted the bell into the improvised tower and alerted everyone within hearing distance that important news awaited at the courthouse. Learning about the recent events in Philadelphia, gathering county residents erupted into spontaneous celebration. The rest of the day was used to salute, in various forms, General Washington, the Continental Army, patriots everywhere, and American independence.[23]

In contrast to that joyous July 4th, the weeks and months that followed were increasingly difficult for county residents. Inspired by independence and General Washington's plea for more men, a second wave of local volunteers marched off to war by the end of July. In all, about 4,000 York Countians served in the Continental Army. The exodus pushed many families to the brink of ruin. All county government functions were suspended, and Yorktown, the busiest village in the county, was "quite deserted on account of the departure of all men under fifty years of age. . . . Only the old and women are left."[24] Some families had to move in with parents and grandparents. Others simply moved in with neighbors. Wives assumed the family duties previously performed by their husbands, which included operating shops or inns and, in most cases, tending fields. By early 1777, agricultural production barely met county needs. Some families were compelled to sell their possessions, including lots and homes, in order to sustain themselves.[25]

Regular reports of dead, wounded, and captured York Countians added to the melancholy. During the first two years of the war, York Countians participated in every important battle from the siege of Boston to the Battle at Germantown. In November 1776, almost 400 York Countians were captured at Fort Washington, and many died during their captivity. Other York County volunteers were part of the unsuccessful American invasion of Canada. Eventually the county contingent, under the command of Colonel Thomas Hartley, limped back to Carlisle, where in March 1777 most survivors reenlisted for three more years. By the end of the war, every cemetery in York County (and Adams County) carried the abbreviated story of local volunteers.[26]

Amid the growing travails, York Countians were called to play a unique role in the American struggle for independence. Late in August 1777, the British began a march from the Chesapeake Bay toward Philadelphia, where the Continental Congress was meeting. With the threat of a British attack imminent, American leaders decided to abandon Philadelphia in favor of a safer location. Easton, Reading, and Lancaster were among the cities Congress considered, but it chose the more remote Yorktown for its refuge.

Yorktown became the temporary headquarters of the Continental Congress for several reasons. Perhaps most important, the town was a four-day march from Philadelphia, thus providing plenty of time to flee should the British army move inland. In addition, Yorktown was located on a primary north-south road with good access to other colonies as well as an emergency escape route. The Susquehanna River served as an excellent natural barrier that would deter an approaching army. Unlike most eastern counties, York, despite the disappointing course of the war, still supported the American cause almost universally. There were no rumors of loyalist conspiracies like those that swirled through Lancaster County during the summer of 1777. In lieu of the suspended county government, the York County Committee of Safety administered local defenses and saw to it that the county was free of loyalist opposition.[27]

Most county residents hoped that the Congress' decision would breathe new life into the stagnant local economy. For innkeepers and Yorktown homeowners, the temporary residents meant customers and boarders. With a good number of townsmen still away on active duty, many dwellings could accommodate the Philadelphians, for a price. Likewise, town lots were spacious by eastern standards. The profitable subdivision of a lot and the anticipated boom in the local building industry would help recoup recent losses. County farmers, some of whom had recently returned from two years of service, were anxious to balance family accounts. The visitors were expected to provide a profitable market for county agricultural production as well as for local artisans and craftsmen.[28]

Despite a relatively warm reception, the visitors soon became disillusioned with life in the Pennsylvania hinterland. Many of the complaints were the combined product of long hours of work and culture shock. Like several of his cohorts, John Adams lamented: "The house where I am is so cramped that I cannot enjoy such accommodations as I wish. I cannot have a room as I used, and therefore, cannot find opportunities to write." He later moaned that York "is the dirtiest place in the world" and that "the People are chiefly Germans, who have [church] schools in their own Language, as well as Prayers, Psalms, and Sermons, so that Multitudes are born, grow up and die here, without learning the English. In Politics they are a breed of Mongrels or neuters and be-numbed by a general Tupor."[29] Benjamin Rush called the town "The Damnedest Hole in the World." North Carolina representative Cornelius Har-nett charged that Yorktown "is the most inhospitable scandalous place I was ever in." Another visitor called it simply "a vile quarter." Local water was blamed for having "torn many countrymen's bowels out and had forced some delegates home to their native springs." Henry Laurens grumbled that he was regularly compelled "to dine on bread and cheese and a bit of grog!"[30]

While conditions of life in Yorktown were often the sources of complaints, the cost of goods in the county was even more vociferously condemned. Many of the sixty-four members of the Continental Congress who eventually came to Yorktown reported that their daily stipends of $5 to $8 would barely begin to cover the cost of living in the village. "A Man must pay ten dollars for glancing at a Tavern, and ten or twelve shillings a night for his horses gnawing rock" wrote Massachusetts representative James Lovell. Another visitor complained caustically: "The people here are not obliging. . . . The horrid scene of extortion is shocking."[31]

A portion of the Philadelphians' animosity was no doubt generated by the impression that York Countians were profiting from the plight of their guests. Congressmen were living on allowances that had been appropriated before the rampant inflation of late 1776 and 1777. Furthermore, the ability of representa-tives to supplement their stipends was severely limited by life so far removed from a commercial and communication center such as Philadelphia. Meanwhile, the infusion of new money had an invigorating effect on a local population whose economy had been in a steady decline for two years. While not outland-ishly pursuing their potential windfall, York Countians were not prepared to foot the bill for the guests. Instead, local residents intended to regain fiscal balance by meeting the needs of their new customers by charging what the market would bear.

Like their visitors, York Countians had some complaints of their own. The most common gripe involved what many local residents considered frivolous entertainment required by the Philadelphians. In February 1778, as Washington and his men, including some York Countians, were suffering through the worst days at Valley Forge, it was reported: "Balls have now begun to be held in this town. . . . They are frequented by officers of the army and even members of Congress, beside many improper people."[32] Despite remonstrances from the local clergy and officials, the galas continued. Local residents also labeled the

Shakespeare plays that were performed on the second floor of the county court-house "unnecessary diversions." In addition, York Countians increasingly complained about the haughty attitude of the visitors. Finally, locals feared that, with the Continental Congress in Yorktown, the entire county would become a target for Tory conspiracies.

The primary activity of the Continental Congress while in Yorktown was the day-to-day administration and management of the war. Filling troop quotas, maintaining supply levels, and grappling with money problems dominated the representatives' work days. A couple of exceptional matters also came up. In November 1777, after lengthy discussion, the controversial tentative draft of the Articles of Confederation was sent to each state government for ratification. While not intended to create a new nation, the proposed document was a step on the path toward uniting the thirteen states. Also, news of the crucial American victory at Saratoga arrived while Congress was meeting in Yorktown.[33] The victory set in action a chain of events known as the "Conway Cabal" that gave the town a bit of lasting notoriety. This alleged plot was a maneuver by friends of General Horatio Gates to have Congress replace Washington with Gates. The scheme fell apart at a dinner party given by Gates when the Marquis de Lafayette, in Yorktown to discuss his own possible command of continental forces, pointedly rebuked the conspirators and defended Washington. In the days that followed, Gates's popularity faded.[34]

Clearly the time during which the Congress was meeting in Yorktown were trying days for all involved. The long-term results for the local population were profound. Most important, the Yorktown area, and to a lesser extent the entire county, took a major step toward becoming a market economy rather than a barter economy. This transition was generated by a vastly expanded amount of hard money available within the local economy. Before independence, York Countians rarely used the small amount of available specie in their everyday commercial activities. Instead they had devised an informal though somewhat complex system of credit notes and bartering. Market prices were recognized for most goods, but cash infrequently changed hands when purchases were made. In lieu of specie, goods and services were traded, and if there was a balance due to one of the traders, a promissory note was issued. These notes became an unofficial tender in various York County communities. By the mid-1770s, notes dating back a decade or more were being used within the county.[35]

Before 1777, the local economy operated on at least two levels. On one level were county residents who bartered almost exclusively and restricted their commercial activities to their neighbors. On a second level were York Countians who also did business on a limited basis within the market economies of Lancaster and Philadelphia. Because they functioned in a market economy and had at least minimal access to specie, they were able to determine cash values for most local commodities. At the same time, because they were dependent on local barter partners, county entrepreneurs were limited in their ability to manipulate prices for their own benefit. The result was a tightly knit commercial network within the county.[36]

The Continental Congress brought a significant amount of specie to York County and to Yorktown in particular. Because they had few goods with which to barter, the Philadelphians purchased with specie virtually all the goods and services they required. Further, York Countians were generally unwilling to accept the credit of their prestigious temporary residents. For permanent residents, access to new specie meant that the ties that bound them to the local barter system began to weaken.[37]

The business and capital that Congress brought bred socioeconomic divisions within the county. With a few exceptions, there was little distance from the top and to the bottom of York County society before 1775. In addition, while the estates of county residents grew slowly between 1750 and 1775, the growth was consistent throughout the county. Estate records indicate that, aside from the land they held, most York Countians owned little more than a few basic pieces of furniture, necessary work implements, and a change of clothing. By 1780, however, the estates of residents in the immediate Yorktown area had grown significantly. An assortment of tableware, kitchen utensils, clothing, and decorative household furnishings became part of many Yorktown homes. Likewise, such luxury items as jewelry, watches, looking glasses, and books written in English, items that could only be purchased for cash from Lancaster or Philadelphia merchants, were found throughout the immediate Yorktown area. Meanwhile the estates of most county residents beyond the immediate influence of Yorktown showed little growth through the 1780s.[38]

The debts owed to Yorktown entrepreneurs further reflected the evolving economic dominance within the county of the town's population. Before 1775, townsmen held as many of their county neighbors' credit notes as they owed. Typically a townsman owed between five and ten creditors a debt of a few pounds each. By the late 1770s, Yorktowners owed to their neighbors far less than their neighbors owed to them. Several townsmen, notably George Irwin and Thomas Hartley, had amassed long lists of local debtors. In essence, by 1780 a balance of trade that favored the Yorktown population had developed.

The increasing value of land was yet another indication of the evolving economic conditions. The migration of the Continental Congress to Yorktown set off an unprecedented period of land speculation during which individual town holdings shrank significantly while the assessed value of town lots soared. Before 1777, most townsmen held either full lots or half lots. Residents considered a half lot the minimal acreage capable of providing the basic needs, including space for a garden and a cow, required to sustain a family. Therefore, townsmen were reluctant to divide their holdings beyond the half-lot size.[39]

When Congress came to town, all that changed. The Philadelphia population generated great pressure on existing housing and services. To accommodate the temporary residents, some chose to subdivide their holdings down to quarter-lot, eighth-lot, and sixteenth-lot sizes. They then either sold the scaled-down holdings or built houses and rented to incoming population. When townsmen chose to sell a portion of a lot, as they often did, they were paid in specie much more than the entire lot had been valued before the migration to Yorktown. The initial windfall profits created a land rush within the town, especially to its center. In at least one instance, a lot at the intersection of the town's two primary thoroughfares (George and High Streets) was bought, subdivided twice, and the parcels were resold at a considerable profit, all on the same day.[40]

While residents beyond the town's limits did not experience a real-estate boom, York Countians within approximately ten miles of the town did benefit from the new wealth. Numerous craftsmen were employed to construct houses and other facilities within the town. Often these tradesmen were contracted by Yorktowners on behalf of a Philadelphia lot-holder. Likewise, farmers in the townships surrounding Yorktown usually had no trouble selling whatever produce they grew or whatever livestock they had available.

The changes generated within the Yorktown area during the nine-month visit by the Continental Congress accelerated previous trends begun before the congressional migration. The experiences of 1777–78 simply compressed into only a few years the growth that may have taken a generation or more. However, this growth was not consistent throughout the county. With several exceptions, the farther away a community was from Yorktown, the less likely it was to have experienced these changes. The result was that the Congress' sojourn severely divided York County. In the immediate Yorktown area, the county had begun to embody the qualities of an early commercial American community: a greater population density, increased social stratification, vocational specialization, and a market economy. Meanwhile, most York County communities more than half a day's ride from Yorktown continued to reflect the traditional lifestyles of a region that remained a collection of relatively isolated enclaves.[41]

Yorktown bade farewell to the Continental Congress in late June 1778. During the war years that followed, York Countians continued to serve in Washington's army, though not in the same numbers as at first. After two- and three-year tours of duty, many volunteers chose to spend the rest of the conflict passively defending their homes. Likewise, county residents continued to support the concept of American independence, but they had also begun to question patriot leadership within Congress and radical leadership within the state.

When the first state constitution was drafted in 1776, York Countians generally applauded the reforms the document embodied. The Declaration of Rights, which promised religious freedom, expanded enfranchisement, and instituted proportional representation was enthusiastically endorsed by county residents. However, at least one element of the constitution of 1776 troubled York Countians.[42]

In September 1776, the state constitutional convention announced that, before they could vote in the fall elections, all voters would be required to take an oath pledging to uphold the new frame of government. In addition, elected officials would be required to take a second oath affirming their belief in God. Some York Countians, like others throughout the state, feared that such voter declarations would limit individual rights and commit oath-takers to supporting the radical government unconditionally. Public opinion was further molded against the oaths by an appeal circulated throughout York and Cumberland Counties. Fortunately, enforcement of the oath was lax during the 1776 election, but the controversy remained important.[43]

By the time of the 1777 fall elections, a loosely organized protest against the oaths had evolved within York County. Providing momentum was the Militia Act of 1777, which the State Assembly passed in June. The act included yet another oath that renounced fidelity to George III and required oath-takers to inform authorities about any potential conspiracies against American independence. Again all voters were required to take the new oath before they could vote. Reaction was almost immediate within the county. In early August, one York Countian reported: "Numerous of Inhabitants of this place are prepossessed against the said Oath [because] it is replete with gross falsehoods, and misrepresentations and facts."[44] In Hanover, 200 Germans united to oppose the oath and to encourage fellow county residents to do the same. By late August, Yorktown residents were calling the pledge "impolitic, severe, cruel, unjust breathing tyranny and injudicious."[45]

York Countians opposed the oaths primarily for two reasons. Some contended that the pledges were merely devices that enabled those in power to remain in power. One Yorktowner lamented that the Militia Act was "not founded in public good, but is made to continue the present members of the Assembly in power."[46] For many German immigrants within the county, the oaths compromised the naturalization oath requiring loyalty to the British Crown they had taken when they arrived in Pennsylvania. Even Germans who had come to York County as children, and who therefore had not been required to pledge their allegiance, complained that by taking the new oath they were denigrating their parents.

As the elections of 1777 approached, the rancor created by the oath controversy had begun to dilute York County support of the state's radical leadership. One Yorktown patriot observed: "The Test Oath, instead of strengthening us, hath weakened us very much."[47] In Yorktown, only one-quarter of the eligible voters took the oath. Throughout the rest of the county, less than 20 percent confirmed the pledge. With so few qualified voters, and even fewer potential candidates, the election became a sham.[48] Local Radicals retained control of county offices, but then realized that they would be unable to enforce not only the oath but also any other locally unpopular legislation.

While the test oath controversy flared on, another crisis erupted. By early 1779, economic instability plagued the county. Rampant inflation, coupled with a rapidly depreciating currency, generated much concern. Likewise, the unavailability of various essential commodities, including wheat and salt, brought a growing number of complaints from county residents. At the heart of the problems seemed to be an emerging network of entrepreneurs, including some Yorktowners, who were manipulating commodity prices for their own profit.

After struggling with the unstable local economy for more than a year, the Radicals who were running York County pursued a course at home that had been charted by Radicals in Philadelphia. Blaming the problems on "monopolizers, forestallers and engrossers," Philadelphia organized a committee to oversee commercial activity. Ultimately, the committee was instructed to establish fair prices and ensure that merchants adhered to them. Those who did not were to be punished. During the summer of 1779, York Countians, like residents in several other counties, organized their own committee to manage the local economy.[49]

The attempt to solve the county's economic problems began with a pamphlet that announced the creation of a new committee. Borrowing rhetoric used to justify the Philadelphia committee, James Smith, on behalf of the local Committee of Safety, insisted that there was operating within the county "a set of extortionists, forestallers, engrossers and depreciators of our currency who, like a swarm of locusts from a bottomless pit threaten to obscure our political horizon and eat up every plant of liberty." Smith blamed the "extortionists" for creating "an artificial famine . . . [for] the virtuous and brave who have been sacrificing life and fortune to procure the blessings of liberty for their countrymen and posterity."[50] Thirteen York Countians were assigned to the committee to oversee all commercial matters within the county.[51]

The Committee of Thirteen, like price-control committees in other counties, was a failure. Throughout late 1779, inflation continued almost unabated. Depreciation of the currency became so severe that by the spring of 1780 many York Countians refused to accept Continental dollars. Meanwhile, although agricultural production generally remained healthy, inflation pushed commodity prices far above the ability of the average York Countian to purchase them. In addition, fair implementation of price controls proved almost impossible.[52] The Committee of Thirteen was unable to stay abreast of commercial activities and often had little idea about the actual prices paid for goods. Some local merchants used the regulatory committee to check competition, others complained that the committee punished only its critics. Even though local Radical leaders continued to insist that price regulation would lead to recovery, a growing number of York Countians disagreed. Instead, regulation was producing higher prices and seriously devalued currency.

By 1780, the problems of administering the economy and the war had begun to produce a deep-rooted discontent throughout the county. While continuing staunchly to support the philosophical foundations of American independence, county residents became ever more disillusioned by American leadership. The economic problems and the test oath controversy demonstrated that the state government was incapable of maintaining order. The use of legislative procedures that deterred any revision of Pennsylvania's new constitution further confirmed flaws in the government. Dissatisfaction with the state government adversely affected the attitudes of York Countians toward the Continental Congress, which seemed to support Pennsylvania's Radical Assembly rather timidly. According to a growing number of York Countians, self-serving members of the Congress were responsible for many of the problems encountered by the Continental army and by communities throughout America. Like Radical leaders in the Pennsylvania Assembly, the Continental Congress appeared to be oblivious to the plight of most Americans.

One obvious reflection of the changing mood within the county involved military participation. After 1778, recruiting became an arduous task.[53] Pennsylvania's Supreme Executive Council repeatedly pleaded with county recruiters: "As you regard the honor of your government, the character of your State in general, and your Country in particular, the good of the great cause in which we are now engaged, and your name, [we] pray that you make every argument to induce the Militia of your County who have been ordered out to join" the Pennsylvania forces. A few months later, York Countians were told: "We make no doubt but you will exert yourself . . . and save the [county] from the Mortification and Disgrace of acknowledging your Inability to do what others have done at short Notice and with Dispatch."[54] These requests and taunts brought few results from the county. York Countians continued to serve in the army, but in ever lower numbers.

At times the Continental Army's quest for recruits entailed confrontation with York Countians. On one occasion during the spring of 1779, four Continental regulars led by Lieutenant William Reynolds came to a tavern near Hanover searching for recruits and deserters. When one of the tavern's patrons, Daniel May, refused to enlist in the unit, May was declared a deserter and bound by the regulars. Immediately the tavern owner sent for a nearby justice, Daniel Messerly. Finding the tavern guarded by two of Reynolds's men, Messerly entered the building cautiously and announced his intentions to escort May back to Yorktown for a hearing. Despite the pronouncement, the justice was seized, dragged outside, and "beat and Abused in a cruel manner" by the guards. With May and Messerly tightly fettered, the Continentals and their prisoners began a march toward Reynolds's unit, which was encamped near Yorktown. Along the way, four other York Countians were beaten with clubs and swords as they watched the procession. Eventually local officials were able to arrest and jail Reynolds and his band, but the incident enraged county residents.[55]

Despite the recruiting problems, York Countians continued to assist Continental forces in various ways through the end of the war. Because of its location along a primary north-south route, the county periodically became a rendezvous site for the army. York Countians on a regular basis were called on to supply food, wagons, horses, and other goods to the various units that passed through the county. Three local iron forges provided bar iron to the Continental Army. British prisoners were also held in the county during much of the war. By early 1781, the need for prisoner facilities had grown to such proportions that the Pennsylvania Assembly ordered construction of a prison camp, Camp Security, just east of Yorktown. Many residents were unhappy about having several hundred British and Hessian prisoners concentrated within the county, but the local population reluctantly built and administered Camp Security.[56]

Certainly York County's most disheartening encounter with the Continental Army came in early 1781. Before marching south to reinforce Nathanael Greene's army, Anthony Wayne was instructed to resupply his men and to recruit in the Yorktown area. Relations between Wayne and local residents became strained almost immediately. The general complained that "the conduct of the inhabitants tends to inflame [the troop's] minds by refusing to part with anything which the soldiers need." The source of Wayne's complaints centered around the unwillingness of York County residents to accept Continental dollars as payment for goods needed by the army. Likewise, merchants denied credit to the Continentals. Furthermore, local residents encouraged Wayne's men to ignore their commander's orders until the regulars received back wages, which in some cases meant more than six months' pay.

The admonitions affected at least a few Continentals. Two weeks after arriving in York County, Wayne was alerted to an alleged uprising brewing within his ranks. He took swift action to remedy the potential rebellion. Within hours his officers had "knocked down and confined" the suspected insurrectionists. They tried them by a court martial and sentenced six of the accused, four of whom were publicly executed. The incident horrified the local population. Many of Wayne's men, and York Countians as well, watched "through tears that rolled down their cheeks in showers" as a firing squad carried out the sentence. After the executions, there were no further troubles among Wayne's men, and local resistance was muted. However, the episode left a permanent scar on many York Countians. They had witnessed the abuse they believed was perverting the struggle for independence. For county residents, the patriot cause was deteriorating into a regime sustained by its military.[57]

British General Lord Charles Cornwallis surrendered at Yorktown, Virginia, five months after Wayne and his men left Yorktown, Pennsylvania. When the war officially ended in 1783, York Countians, like Americans in all thirteen states, rejoiced. However, neither the end of fighting nor the Peace in Paris concluded the Revolution within the county. The war had jolted York Countians out of their hinterland refuge and pushed them much closer to the mainstream of American civilization. Adjusting to the new realities, while at the same time maintaining the principles on which independence had been founded, became a task that York Countians found almost as difficult as the war with Great Britain. The Radical government that had appeared so attractive in 1776 was, by 1783, unacceptable to many within the county. Local political leaders, many of whom had fought in the war, moved toward the moderate policies proposed by James Wilson and Gouverneur Morris, among others. American independence and individual liberties were still dear to York Countians, but the methods through which those ideals were being achieved were not. Likewise, the war created within the county a much more complex socioeconomic structure. Adapting to a market economy and to the increasingly powerful local merchant class generated internal community conflicts. Most important, the struggle for independence forced the county population to recognize that they could no longer isolate themselves, that they had joined a much larger community. During the struggle for independence, York Countians had become part of the American republic.

6

Cumberland County

Robert G. Crist

In 1750, Pennsylvania west of the main stem of the Susquehanna River, except York County and its future offspring, Adams, became the new county of Cumberland. However, during the Revolutionary era Cumberland lost two-thirds of its territory. First, in 1771 the province sliced off fourteen townships from the western end and erected Bedford County. Then it created Westmoreland County from Bedford in 1773. By 1776, Cumberland County was reduced to twenty-three townships. Westmoreland five years later lost its western end when Washington County came into being on its southern flank in 1781 and when Fayette was created in 1783. Accordingly, by 1783 four county seats covered the Cumberland County of twenty years earlier.

The entire province was said to have had a population of 220,000 in 1755,[1] but it is impossible to state with accuracy how many lived in the single county in 1763 and in Cumberland and its four divisions two decades later. Population was sparse indeed. Not until 1758 did much of the land west and north of the Blue Mountain edge of the Cumberland Valley become free from Indian claims and legal white settlement begin. Only a few traders and squatters inhabited land west of modern Bedford. Five years later, in 1763, about ten named settlements existed west of the Susquehanna, most of them near provincial forts. Also, a substantial number of people lived in mountain valleys and other areas. When the settlers fled for their lives in 1763 to avoid Indian incursions, excited observers stated that there were "upwards of 1,500 plantations evacuated"[2] and that everyone to the west had abandoned his farm. A reasonable guess is that the total 1763 population was 6,000.

Of these, virtually all were Scots-Irish, most of whom scratched a marginal living off soils they did not understand, or engaged in commerce in or around the several settlements. Individuals of German descent first appeared in the records around 1764 following the end of Pontiac's War.[3] The first Germans appeared to be servants indentured by their English-speaking predecessors, but by 1770 they began to take up certain unpatented or unwarranted lands and to purchase from the original Scots-Irish settlers the worn-out farms they were abandoning for fresh starts to the south or west.

The immigration of German Reformed and Lutheran people grew to major proportions after a pause occasioned by the War of American Independence. When the first federal census was completed in 1790, the territory that once was Cumberland included 25 percent of the state's population, 110,068 individuals in eight counties. Keeping in mind that a rush to settle began in 1783 at the end of the Revolution, it is therefore likely that the population of the four-county area in 1783 was in the range of 50,000 to 60,000.

Until 1771, this half of the province was governed out of its only frontier town larger than a hamlet, Carlisle. Actually, it was not governed, given the vast distances separating farms and the absence of either militia or civil police officials. That there was any sense of community at all had to do with the periodic appearance of threats to economy or freedom.

Military Presence and Prosperity

The twenty years spanning 1763–83 were alternately times of feast or famine for Cumberland County and its seat, Carlisle, depending on the presence or absence of war. Military spending, when it occurred, became a major element

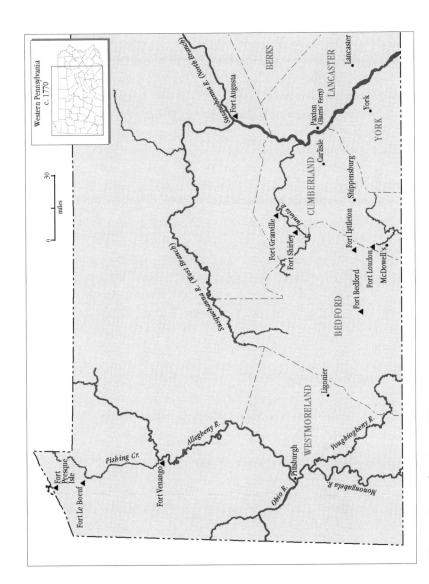

Western Pennsylvania c. 1770

in stimulating the economy of the land west of the Susquehanna River. The first great wave of defense expenditures accompanied the French and Indian War. As early as 1755, Mayor Edward Shippen (Chipping) of Lancaster was urging Governor Robert Hunter Morris to use "a Strong Stone House, 30 feet Square" (the future Fort Morris) at Shippensburg to store supplies for the Braddock Expedition. He asked that cattle be sent to Tobias Hendricks's "Fortt Pleasent" on the Manor of Lowther (present-day Camp Hill).[4] Furthermore, a stockade for twenty to thirty soldiers went up at McDowell's Mill, which was later designated Fort Loudoun in present Franklin County.[5] George Croghan, Sir William Johnston's deputy for Indian affairs in Pennsylvania, threw up a fort at Shirleysburg and a second one on Burd's Road in present Fulton County, which was renamed Fort Lyttelton. The Reverend John Steel created a defensive position east of Mercersburg, and Benjamin Chambers created another at the settlement he named for himself. Shippen's son-in-law James Burd suggested that "a Fort would be immediately erected" at Raystown (Bedford) to bar the French from the road west he had been constructing.[6] In Carlisle itself, in the aftermath of the Braddock fiasco, the governor ordered the construction of a wooden fort on the public square.[7] Into these public and private forts and magazines flowed a succession of men and their followers: militia units, ranger companies, Colonel John Stanwix's Royal Americans, part of Colonel William Clapham's Regiment of Provincials, and Colonel John Armstrong's Provincial Regiment.[8]

When peace came in 1762, the several thousand people at the forts who were spending the King's coin or accepting the provincial paper dwindled to a few hundred. Colonel Henry Bouquet, and his battalions, regimental trains, and quartermasters, were tending to business elsewhere in western areas that the French had left to the British and Indians. Farms were abandoned and mills were closed, their owners' markets having disappeared. Ironmongers, forgemen, smiths, wheelwrights, harness makers, and artificers of all types had fewer calls on their talents.

In 1763, however, Cumberland County experienced another boom. This time it was a product of the continental-wide Indian uprising. A population that had by now twice experienced Indian depredations retreaded its war veterans and generated faster responses from provincial and imperial authorities than had been the case eight years earlier. Armorers went to work again in the "Grand Magazine" at the edge of Carlisle.[9] Supplies had to be gathered, and various implements of war manufactured. The town became the supply base for the posts at Bedford, Ligonier, Bushy Run, Presqu'Isle, and the forks of the Ohio. It was also a rendezvous for expeditions going westward and a reception center. Companies of provincial troops arrived to begin construction and to perform garrison and guard duties throughout western Pennsylvania. All recruits went to Carlisle to be equipped and trained. A Forty-second Highlander battalion arrived in July at the Carlisle camp to join the Royal Americans, who were already there.

Adding to the melee was a civilian population in a state of panic. In mid-summer 1763, Colonel Henry Bouquet wrote Governor James Hamilton to report of 40 known dead and 19 wounded within sixteen miles of Carlisle: "The desolation of so many families reduced to the last Extremities of Want and Misery; the Despair of those who have lost their Parents . . . with the Cries of distracted Women and Children who fill the streets, form a Scene of Horror painful to Humanity impossible to describe. . . . The whole of the Country to the West of this Place is chiefly abandonned, with the Harvest, Cattle and Horses and this Town entirely become the Frontier on that Side."[10] As bad as the facts were, rumors were worse as a source of panic. George Croghan had written from Shippensburg on June 11:

> Yesterday and this Day a report prevailed in this Cou[ntry] that all the People in the Path Valley were Murde[red by] the Indians and their Houses Burn'd, & that Fort Ligonier was likewise taken and Burn'd, the People in General was flying from their Habitations but just now I recived [*sic*] a Letter from Bedford by which I find that the Indians have not prevail'd against Ligonier, tho' they had fired some shot at the Fort, & two Men is come from the Path Valley who say that no Indians has appear'd there as Yet, but say the People are much allarmed.[11]

A contemporary description of future Perry County told of Indians that

> had set fire to houses, barns, corn, wheat, rye, and hay; in short to everything combustible; so that the whole country seemed to be in one general blaze; that the miseries and distresses of the poor people were really shocking to humanity, and beyond the power of language to de-scribe; that Carlisle had become a barrier, not a single inhabitant being beyond it; that every stable and hovel in the town was crowded with miserable refugees, who were reduced to a state of beggary and despair; their houses, cattle, and harvest destroyed . . . and become real objects of charity and commiseration. the woods were filled with poor families and their cattle, who made fires, lived like savages, exposed to the in-clemancies of the weather.[12]

The forts at future Franklin, Waterford, and Erie fell. Croghan estimated that about 2,000 settlers were killed, nine forts were burned, and traders lost £100,000 worth of goods. Bouquet and Armstrong immediately reduced the threats by defeating the Indians at Bushy Run and raiding the North Branch of the Susquehanna River.[13]

The letters and newspaper reports exaggerated. Not all settlers fled. James Smith of the Conococheague Valley, for example, in 1763 raised a company of fifty rangers whom he taught to fight in Indian fashion. Nicknamed the Black Boys, they patroled the gaps and valleys that raiders might use.[14]

Smith was not entirely successful. In the spring of 1764, Indian attacks resumed, striking at McDowell's Mill and Brown's near Greencastle. These new raids caused production to drop and commerce to decline. Bouquet marched westward again beyond Fort Pitt with enough show of power to persuade the Delawares and the Shawnee to negotiate a peace and return more than 200 prisoners.[15]

Rights Become an Issue

By 1765, Western Pennsylvanians began to concentrate on new concerns. The Indians were relatively peaceful, and the French were gone, but the east continued to ignore the west. Looking for allies, it supported the Proprietary party in opposition to Benjamin Franklin and his Quaker faction.[16] To increase its political influence, Cumberland County elected William Allen of Philadelphia, leader of the Proprietary faction, as its representative in the legislature and kept him as its assemblyman until a 1770 law made such a choice illegal.[17]

A cause célèbre was George Croghan's decision to resume trading with the Indians by dispatching westward from Carlisle a pack train carrying not only the provincial public gift of presents but also, for his private account, $3,000 worth of ammunition, liquor, and knives. Without any official authorization, James Smith and the Black Boys attacked the train, killed the animals, and burned the goods, which they did not want the recently pacified Indians to have.[18] Not bothering to call on the civil authorities for warrants, a detachment of the Forty-second Black Watch who were still stationed at Fort Loudoun responded by seeking out the Black Boys, catching and incarcerating seven of them. Smith responded in March 1765 by investing the fort with 300 armed men. He captured fourteen soldiers who ventured beyond the palisade, and demanded an exchange of prisoners. Lieutenant Charles Grant, his fort not supplied for a siege, complied.

The implications for civil government of a military usurpation of its functions caused Governor John Penn personally to ride out to Carlisle to investigate. A grand jury refused to indict anyone, and the frustrated governor returned to Philadelphia. Colonel Bouquet had to swallow the indignity of mere civilians besting his professional soldiers.

The following month, Smith's band stopped a second supply train near Fort Loudoun and seized and burned contraband. Grant ordered out a detachment to deal with the Black Boys. After capturing one of them, the soldiers returned to Fort Loudoun. Smith and 200 men accompanied by three civilian magistrates surrounded the fort once again. The three justices informed Grant that they had come to inventory goods at the fort and that, if they found among them the items authorized for sale to the Indians, they would certify them accordingly and the Black Boys would disperse.

Here was another civil-military confrontation. Grant was not ready to submit to civilian authority. On the other hand, one of the magistrates, William Smith, shown a pass signed by Bouquet, stated that he was not subject to military orders. Furthermore, James Smith announced his unwillingness to honor a pass from a military commander unless validated by a civilian magistrate. The reasons for refusal were made clear: Burd's Road was not the "King's Road" but merely a road built across the proprietor's territory; Fort Loudoun was "not the King's fort" but a provincial installation; authority claimed by Lieutenant Grant was merely "English law" that had reference only to prohibition against killing "the King's deer"; and such laws did not apply in the colonies.[19]

Later in the month, James Smith captured Grant. Charged with being a rebel, Smith rejoined that he was as ready for a rebellion as the British were ready to oppose it, but he released the British officer. Subsequently, he and his boys again invested Fort Loudoun and forced the British officer to surrender seven firearms that they had confiscated from the local people. On June 4, 1765, Governor Penn ordered Magistrate William Smith to Philadelphia, quizzed him, and concluded that he, not Grant, was in the right. James Smith then ceased his harassment of the pack trains, noting in his journal: "This [series of confrontations] convinced me, more than ever, of the absolute necessity of the civil law in order to govern mankind."[20]

The Stump-Eisenhauer affair of January 1768 once again found the people of the hinterland invoking English rights to justify their murder of Indians. The controversy began when Pennsylvania's Chief Justice William Allen ordered the senior magistrate of Cumberland County, John Armstrong, to send Frederick Stump and his indentured servant John Ironcutter (Eisenhauer) to Philadelphia to answer allegations that they had murdered ten Indians. A member of the county bar and future signer of the Declaration of Independence, George Ross, counseled that to try the prisoners in Philadelphia would be an invasion of their civil liberties.

Faced with major dissent on the part of his neighbors, Colonel Armstrong hesitated to comply with the Chief Justice's order: "An Alarm is raised in the minds of many, touching their Privileges in this and in any future case, which they allege would be infringed by this Measure . . . that these Men would not be remanded for Tryal to the County where the Fact was committed, but the Whole Process carried through at Philadelphia."[21] Governor Penn replied angrily: "I am astonished at the impertinent insolence of those who have taken upon them to Suggest or even to suppose that the Government or Judges intended to do so illegal an Act as to Try the Prisoners in any County or place than where the Fact was committed."[22]

After a mob of eighty men intervened and released the two prisoners, Armstrong was chagrined, the governor was enraged, and the provincial government mobilized in a futile effort to recapture Stump and Eisenhauer. The reaction never quite extended to the dispatch of military forces to find the two, although fear spread throughout the frontier that they would be so used. The governor certainly considered the idea. A proprietary man, Edward Shippen, thought this would be a good idea: "Nothing less than the Appearance of regular Troops will check the Insolence of these people."[23]

A third clash between soldiers and frontiersmen occurred. In 1769 a new group of men organized in Cumberland County revived the name Black Boys and intercepted a caravan of the trader Robert Callender that carried whiskey, arms, and ammunition for the Indian trade. In retaliation, British soldiers at Fort Bedford seized several men whom they suspected to be part of the Black Boys. The action rejuvenated that almost-rebel James Smith, who this time had not been involved in the interception: "Yet I concluded that they should not lie in irons in the guardhouse, or remain in confinement, by arbitrary or military power. I resolved, therefore, if possible to release them, if they should be tried by civil law afterwards."[24] Release them he did, but quickly thereafter a civilian force captured James Smith. Magistrate William Smith commented: "They were put under confinement, but for what crime they knew not, and treated in a manner inconsistent with the laws of their country and the liberties of Englishmen."[25]

Men of Cumberland had begun to speak of rights, to differentiate among them, and to note their opinion of where the King's writ ran and where it did not. How much was pure disinterested commentary on political theory and how much was mere justification for lawless behavior is not clear. Cumberland was a rough-and-tumble frontier, and people there were angry that the British were friendly with Indians that they had just fought or who had recently killed their friends and devastated their farms. In the period 1750–76, Cumberland County courts of oyer and terminer tried eleven people for murder between 1776 and 1799. The rate for "brutal and audacious felonies" doubled after 1776 and during the entire half-century was substantially higher than in Berks and York Counties. York County counted 1,690 crimes, of which 474 were violent, whereas Cumberland, with about half the population, had 2,148, some 648 of which were violent.[26] Cumberland women were not much more law-abiding than men. Some 11 percent of all crimes were committed by women. Seven women were tried for infanticide and five for other species of murder; four were convicted. How many more perpetrators never came to justice cannot be estimated, but certainly there were many in a territory that had no police force and a high tolerance for violence.

Inevitably the people of the Pennsylvania frontier are compared with their contemporaries in the western reaches of North Carolina: the Regulators. An account of their activity speaks of their being "marked by strife and turmoil, . . . isolated from the outside world, . . . Scotch-Irish and Germans . . . particularly oppressed by the laws drawn up by an assembly largely composed of eastern landowners . . . referred to as 'the mob'. . . . ripe for revolt."[27] But such comparisons are inappropriate in other respects. Unlike in Pennsylvania, matters in North Carolina clearly got out of hand. There 1,461 militiamen faced down 3,700 armed Regulators, mobs burned government and private property, and dissidents whipped public officials and terrorized towns. Unlike the North Carolina Regulators, Pennsylvania's backcountry elements would for the most part staunchly support the Revolution.

Interbellum Years

The decade ending in 1774 saw the appearance of a new element in the Cumberland County population. The almost exclusive domain of feisty Scots-Irishmen became an area with a heavy mix of the more taciturn Germans. A tally of churches gives a rough approximation. In 1762 there were no German Lutheran or Reformed churches in the sixty-mile stretch of the Cumberland Valley, but there were nine Presbyterian meetinghouses.[28] By 1775, three Lutheran and three Reformed congregations had appeared, while the number of Presbyterian churches grew only to ten.[29] In the intervening years, the number of taxables had increased from 1,501 to 3,521.

Most of the arrivals were German, the second and third sons of families whose land to the east had been taken up by older brothers. Most of those who left were Scots-Irishmen who had little luck with an unfamiliar type of limestone soil. Having worn out the farms or seen them wash away, they conveyed the land to Germans, who knew about draining and manuring. Felling trees, digging out the stumps, and putting more land under cultivation, they soon were heavy customers for the millers and drovers. In short, the growth in the German population caused the economy to flourish.

Politically, the Germans tended to support Pennsylvania's establishment, those individuals in Proprietary favor who held most of the public offices. Although they cast their votes with the Penns, they did not seek office themselves, at least in Cumberland County during the eighteenth century. They supported the Scots-Irish politicians.

They had reason so to do, for it was those Scots-Irishmen who defended them in the wars from 1755 to 1781. They had retained their ancestors' martial skills from Scottish border days and the Ulster years. A number of the leaders in the American Revolution had learned military and leadership roles in the earlier contests. Major General John Armstrong had risen to the rank of colonel by 1757, had led the expedition that suppressed the Indians at Kittanning, had headed a battalion during the Bouquet Expedition, and had commanded the military posts in Carlisle.[30] Cumberland's field grade and general officers of the Revolution learned their military skills during the earlier war. For example, Major General John Potter and Brigadier General William Thompson served under Armstrong. Major General Arthur St. Clair, former prothonotary of Bedford County, began service with the Royal Americans in 1757. Brigadier General Frederick Watts, of future Perry County, and Commissary General Ephraim Blaine first gained experience in the French and Indian adventures, as did Colonels Joseph Armstrong, James Smith (who had moved to Westmoreland County by 1777), Robert Magaw, and John Montgomery. The last two, except for the accident of being captured by British forces, would also have won generals' stars. The whole breed from Armstrong to Watts did nothing to diminish the stereotype of Scots-Irishman as doughty fighters.[31]

The Cumberland Scots-Irish resented the Philadelphia establishment because of its failure to defend the backcountry. Several factors widened the east-west division. The easterners did little to make the transportation of western farm products to Philadelphia easy. In response, the west forged commercial links with a closer city, the port of Baltimore, which had been founded in 1729. Maryland authorities constructed roads north to Pennsylvania locations, including Middletown in Lancaster County and York.[32] The Susquehanna became a conduit: it was easier to float rafts south to Baltimore's ice-free harbor than to pay tolls to the Susquehanna ferry operators and drag farm goods over rutted roads to the ice-clogged Delaware. Also, the Scots-Irish were comfortable with the western Marylanders, who were of the same ethnic and religious stock and whose legislature was more responsive to hinterland demand than that of the Englishmen of Philadelphia. Soon the principal trade with the east was to send taxes there.

Furthermore, the west took umbrage at unbalanced representation in the Assembly. In 1760, the three counties on the Delaware River had 51 percent of the taxables but held twenty-six seats in the legislature. The west, with 48 percent, elected only ten.[33] Representation was not changed until March 8, 1776, when Cumberland got two more representatives and Bedford and Westmoreland acquired one each.[34] However, even at this date only four months before Independence, the eastern element narrowly retained control with its thirty votes; the Scots-Irish and German hinterland areas were represented with twenty-eight votes. Nothing substantial was done about east-west roads until 1794, when a corporation was chartered to improve the road from Lancaster to Philadelphia. To reverse the priority of Carl Becker's famous dictum about the Revolution, the west was concerned about "who shall rule at home" long before it turned its attention to home rule. The west stayed calm during the east's storm over the Stamp Act, the tea monopoly, and the taxes of the Townshend duties, rising up only when it felt its civil rights were threatened, as in the case of the Black Boys, Paxton Boys, and Stump-Ironcutter incidents.

Revolution Looms

The march of Pennsylvania, including its trans-Susquehanna region, to rebellion and independence intensified on June 18, 1774. An extralegal assembly in Philadelphia, having learned from Paul Revere of the Bostonians' request for aid in responding to the British Parliament's "Intolerable Acts," voted to help the New Englanders and started a provincewide association, the Committee of Correspondence. Twelve days later, the Assembly asked the counties to see to their inchoate militia organizations. The legislature hoped that they would support the organization, arming, and equipping of as many inhabitants who joined the Revolutionary forces as tax levies would permit.

Perhaps stimulated by one of the three men whom the Philadelphians had sent to the frontier "to discern sentiments," Cumberland County responded. The Carlisle establishment called a meeting in the First Presbyterian Church for July 12. It was not by accident that the participants avoided the German Reformed, Lutheran, or Anglican church buildings. In the back of many Presbyterian minds lay the fear that a newly active British government would impose a bishop on America and institute tax support for a single religion. Fears of an episcopacy increased in 1768, when many Quakers were seen to "declare themselves highly desirous of seeing the [Anglican] Church flourish, for a fear of being run over by Presbyterians." Both the *Pennsylvania Gazette* and the *Pennsylvania Journal* ran a series of articles on the matter.[35]

Called to preside at the town meeting was John Montgomery, incumbent assemblyman, sheriff, and longtime elder of the church. His sketchy spelling suggests the typical rough-and-tumble Scots-Irishman who loved both Johns (Calvin and Barleycorn) and kept the Ten Commandments and everything else he could lay his hands on.

Several resolutions emerged from the Carlisle meeting:

1. That the British statute that closed the port of Boston was "subversive of the rights and liberties" of Massachusetts and that the principle on which it rested was equally obnoxious to the other colonies
2. That the colonies should speedily adopt vigorous and prudent measures to obtain redress of that statute and others that that principle might generate
3. That "a congress of deputies from all colonies will be one proper method for obtaining these purposes"
4. That the colonies should not import, export, or consume British goods
5. That they would send relief to Boston
6. That a committee be established to correspond with Philadelphia or other provinces [*sic*]

The implication was that if the key committee in Philadelphia were to be captured by the ultraconservatives, Cumberland County would turn elsewhere for direction.[36]

As a seventh resolution, the group chose as its Committee of Correspondence James Wilson (whose home was in Carlisle after 1770), John Armstrong, John Montgomery, William Irvine, Robert Callender, William Thompson, John Calhoon, Jonathan Hoge, Robert Magaw, Ephraim Blaine, John Allison, John Harris, and Robert Miller, "or any five of them." By August, certain members left the committee and others were added, including John Agnew, John Byers, and James Pollock.

The group was no band of frontier ruffians. Six had been officers in French and Indian War military units. Wilson had learned his law from John Dickinson in Philadelphia. Magaw and Harris also were attorneys, and Irvine was a University of Dublin graduate and a former naval surgeon. Agnew, Allison, Armstrong, Byers, Hoge, Miller, and Thompson were incumbent justices of the peace; Callender had just retired from that appointive post. Blaine had recently completed three terms as Cumberland County sheriff. Montgomery was serving his eleventh term in the Assembly. Callender was a mill owner and a commissary during the earlier wars. Ten owned slaves, seven had been county judges, and six were trustees of the local Latin School, from which Dickinson College was to emerge. Five of the fourteen Presbyterians were elders; two others of the group were Anglicans. In short, the committee, all of whom lived in or near Carlisle, was the Proprietary party leadership of the county.[37]

The Carlisle meeting appointed Irvine, Magaw, and Wilson to meet with the deputies from the other counties at Philadelphia in order to take in concert measures preparatory to the general congress. At this convention, Wilson was selected to a committee of eleven, which prepared a report titled "Instructions on the present situation of public affairs to the representatives who were to meet in the Colonial Assembly next week." The conservative-controlled Assembly accepted some of the written suggestions of the convention but failed to select anyone from the trans-Susquehanna region to serve in the general congress, which convened in September 1774. The frontier, based on long experience, did not trust the constitutional representative body of the province, the Assembly, to adequately reflect the public need in its actions. Accordingly, it continued to create and support a series of extralegal organizations.

In Carlisle the informal Committee of Correspondence in the fall of 1774 asked voters to gather at the county seat and select a Committee of Observation that would oversee public affairs. John Byers chaired the Cumberland Committee. Its main task was to establish smaller organizations in each district to enforce the economic boycott of British goods. An indication of the fervor in Cumberland County was the appointment of nearly 100 people to serve as enforcers.

On January 23, 1775, a second extralegal provincial convention gathered. Blaine, Irvine, Magaw, and Wilson from Cumberland attended, although neither Bedford nor Westmoreland County sent representatives.[38] The principal action taken was to authorize a standing body in Philadelphia to call still another provincial convention if that seemed necessary. Of greatest importance for the frontier was the decision to speed the manufacture of war supplies, including woolen goods, hemp, saltpeter, and the iron and steel that Cumberland County once produced for army use and could manufacture again if a market were to materialize. Westmoreland County was among the earliest areas to call for action. On May 19, 1775, a meeting convened at Hannastown at which the people subscribed to a series of resolutions advocating liberty and independence. They formed an association out of which later arose a regiment commanded by Thomas Proctor.

The frontier obtained representation of a sort in May 1775 when the Assembly added James Wilson to the Pennsylvania delegation in the Second Continental Congress. Back in Philadelphia, Wilson quickly allied himself with Robert Morris and his old mentor John Dickinson, although he frequently exhibited even more moderate views than those two stolid conservatives did. The first actions even remotely attributable to him concerned his participation in two committee recommendations on June 9, 1775. In the first, he urged the extralegal Provincial Congress of Massachusetts to take up and exercise the full and plenary powers of civil government unless the King agreed to revoke Parliamentary laws of the past decade that had violated the province's charter. In the second action, he asked Congress to take over the army around Boston.

Competing Governments

Through the remainder of 1775 and until September 1776, two bodies competed for leadership of Pennsylvania: the legally constituted General Assembly and the extralegal continuum of the Provincial Conference and the state constitutional convention. Separating the competitors was the issue of independence.

When in March 1776 it became apparent to the recalcitrant Assembly that independence as an issue was linked with the matter of underrepresentation for the western counties, the Assembly voted thirteen more seats for the frontier and called for a May 1 election to fill them. A fortnight later the new faces in the Assembly included individuals of radical persuasion, such as Jonathan Hoge and Robert Whitehill, of Cumberland County. Not part of the establishment in the beginning, they remained in opposition to the traditional leaders of the county. Whitehill, an alumnus of the Allison Academy, quickly rose to lead the Radicals in the Assembly, receiving support from such allies as George Bryan, James Cannon, and Daniel Roberdeau. Christopher Marshall noted in his diary seeing Whitehill huddling in city taverns with Samuel and John Adams and other independence-minded individuals in the Continental Congress. He rotated in and out of the Assembly, the Executive Council, the State Senate, and the Congress until his death in 1813.[39]

Probably as a result of their contact with the independence-minded Congress, the Radicals, who found themselves still a minority in the Pennsylvania Assembly, walked out. Led by Whitehill, they destroyed its quorum and permanently paralyzed it. This accomplished, the Radicals supported a substitute legislative body, the Provincial Conference. Meeting at Carpenters Hall on June 18, 1776, that extralegal conference consisted of 108 delegates, including 10 from Cumberland, 9 from York, 3 from Bedford, and 2 from Westmoreland counties. It took a number of steps the Assembly had avoided. Perhaps most important was the advice issued to the Congressional delegation to vote for independence. The conference also named a committee that included James McLean of Cumberland to "devise a ways and means for raising . . . 4,500 men."

To provide legitimacy and permanency for what they were doing, and to replace the legal Assembly, the Provincial Conference called for the election of delegates to a convention to draft a new constitution for Pennsylvania. To ensure that the conservatives would not seize control by reviving the Assembly or otherwise, the conference formed a Committee of Safety to "exercise the whole executive powers of government, so far as it relates to the military defense and safety of the province."[40]

Meanwhile, the Assembly was in session concurrently with the Conference. Cumberland County sent it a resolution:

The arbitrary and unconstitutional claim, of the British Parliament to bind by its acts, the British colonies in all cases whatsoever, and the cruel exertions of the British Administration to carry, by force, that claim into execution, drove America into the present unhappy, but on her part, just and necessary war. . . . If those who rule in Britain will not permit the colonists to be free and happy, in connexion with that kingdom, it becomes their duty to secure and promote their freedom and happiness, in the best manner they can, without that connexion. . . . It will soon . . . be necessary to advise and to form such establishments as will be sufficient to protect the virtuous . . . [in the land] these establishments may be construed to lead to a separation from Great Britain. . . . [There-fore,] we petition this honorable house, that the last instructions which it gave to the delegates of this province in Congress wherein they are enjoined not to consent to any step which may cause or lead to a separa-tion from Great Britain may be withdrawn.[41]

The sense of the petition became a resolution of the Assembly. Thus, the Congressional delegation was free to vote for a separation seventeen days short of July 4, 1776. If any were unsure about the matter, they received a reminder. General John Armstrong, Wilson's sponsor in Carlisle, rode into Philadelphia in mid-June with a troop of noisy, armed pro-independence Cumberland Coun-tians. Wilson and others were given the message of the backcountry: although their chief concerns once were with a high-handed proprietor and a low-budget legislature, now they opposed an arbitrary and unconstitutional Parliament from which they would be pleased to be separated.

If Cumberland County's voice carried far, it had to do with its size and reputation. As early as 1764, Governor John Penn epitomized the matter: "Every man in Cumberland County is a rioter at heart . . . that ten thousands troops could not bring one to trial."[42]

Militia Organized

With the removal of Indian threats after 1763, all militia units, irregular bands, and ranger units soon disappeared from western Pennsylvania. An organized militia force began to reemerge on May 4, 1775, two weeks after the news of Lexington and Concord arrived. Representatives of nineteen Cumberland County townships met that day, in response to a call from the First Congress to form companies of "Associators." Cumberland reported that about 3,000 men enlisted, a figure to be compared with the quota for the entire province, which was only 4,300. One hitch, however, was that only half the men had firearms.[43]

Of the 3,000 Associators in Cumberland County, the county authorities immediately formed 500 men and officers into a force to march at the first emergency call. They would be paid from a tax on all estates, which the county calculated would amount to £27,000 a year. To administer the proposed army, the Assembly named a twenty-five-man Committee of Safety to sit permanently in Philadelphia. Assemblyman John Montgomery represented Cumberland County from July 23, 1775, to July 22, 1776, when a new state government emerged. The committee determined when the units should go on active duty, paid and supplied them, and appointed the field-grade officers.[44]

Companies of about sixty-eight men elected their own officers, who nominated the men of higher rank that led the battalions or regiments. (The words were used interchangeably.) Where privates called to active duty did not have arms of their own, the counties attempted to supply the shortage by buying weapons from people staying at home, or in one instance by seizing a supply of French and Indian War firearms found in storage in Paxton, Lancaster County.[45] To pay for these weapons, Cumberland County collected £300 from people who preferred not to be mobilized. Other funds became available after November 1775, when the Assembly imposed a fine of £2, 10s. on "non-Associators." Enlistment was also encouraged by a law of May 1776 that decreed that non-Associators were required to surrender all their weapons.

An "emergency" for the organized militia arose in June 1776 when Congress called on Pennsylvania for 6,000 men, of whom 4,500 would be "Associators" to serve until November 30 to augment the regular army forces in northern New Jersey. To select that force, on July 4, 1776, a delegation of two enlisted men and one officer from each of the fifty-three associated battalions assembled in Lancaster. Representing Cumberland County were Colonel John Armstrong, Lieutenant Colonels William Blair, William Clark, and Frederick Watts, and sixteen others.[46] Later in the war, John Armstrong of Carlisle as a militia major general commanded all Pennsylvania state forces.

Two Cumberland County regiments were designated as first emergency troops, or "The Flying Camp." Commanded by Montgomery and Watts, they hurried across the Jerseys to General George Washington on Long Island.[47] The Bedford companies, however, were not dispatched east, presumably because they might be needed at home to fend off the Indian attacks that were anticipated. After the Americans withdrew across the East River, the Cumberlanders were promptly captured by the British when they took Fort Washington on Manhattan Island.

The record of the Cumberland militia during the rest of the war is not clear. After Congress authorized a separate Continental force, a substantial number of militiamen enlisted. Washington tended to use these units of regulars for main battle duty, which became the raw material for history, while assigning state forces to guard duty and other supporting roles. An example of such use involved a unit of Westmoreland County militia that in 1778 moved against certain Indians in the "Squaw Campaign," which did not rate plaques and plaudits; their bag was one old man, three women, and one boy. In the same year, Cumberland County militia chased other Indians who with loyalist units had raided the Wyoming Valley. In still another militia campaign, Colonel Archibald Lochry raised two Westmoreland County companies to accompany George Rogers Clark in his campaign against Fort Detroit. Lochry's units were ambushed and wiped out in Ohio.

Continentals

In May 1775, Congress, having organized the Continental Army, asked the Middle Colonies to begin the process by providing ten companies. Thirteen men who were destined to become captains immediately recruited their own seventy-man companies. Two were raised in Virginia, two in Maryland, and nine in Pennsylvania, of which two came from Cumberland County and one from Bedford. The company mobilized in eastern Cumberland County by William Hendricks marched first to Cambridge and later in 1775 was among the expeditions sent up the Kennebec River and across Maine to attack Quebec.[48]

The other trans-Susquehanna units remained under Washington's eye outside Boston. In July 1775, the units recruited by James Chambers, by Robert Cluggage from the Bedford County area, and by Hendricks plus five other companies became a battalion. It was placed under the command of William Thompson, who had been commissioned a colonel by Congress on June 25. During the winter, it was reorganized as the First Pennsylvania Regiment of the Pennsylvania Line, a unit mustered on February 13, 1776. Thompson took the regiment as part of his brigade on the 1776 campaign against Canada; he and part of the First Pennsylvania were captured at Trois Rivières. Some members of the units reenlisted and served in various campaigns through the surrender at Yorktown and subsequent mop-up operations through May 11, 1783.[49]

Many trans-Susquehanna Cumberland County men served throughout the war in the prestigious professional Continental regiments. Seven of the thirteen regiments raised in Pennsylvania during the war were led by colonels from Cumberland County. In addition to Thompson's riflemen, who were designated the First Continental Regiment, Congress raised the Second Pennsylvania Battalion, which it assigned to Colonel Arthur St. Clair of Bedford.[50]

Robert Magaw organized the Fifth Pennsylvania Battalion of the Continental Army, which departed Carlisle on March 17, 1776.[51] Washington posted it to cover the retreat of his army following the battle of Long Island. After being assigned to defend Fort Washington on Manhattan Island, Magaw and the Fifth were obliged to surrender to the British. He, Watts, Montgomery, and 2,815 others went into thirty-five months of captivity on November 16, 1776.[52] In 1781 the Fifth Continentals went under the command of a colonel who lived in both York and Carlisle, Richard Butler.[53]

In December 1775, the Cumberland County Committee of Correspondence organized what Congress on January 9, 1776, designated the Sixth Pennsylvania Battalion with William Irvine of Carlisle as commander.[54] It went to Canada, where it too was captured at Three Rivers. The remnants and new recruits were organized into the Seventh Pennsylvania Regiment, placed under Irvine (who had been exchanged) and kept in existence until early 1781.[55] Irvine, who had become a brigadier general in May 1779, left to serve under Anthony Wayne.

As for the Ninth Pennsylvania, its colonel during four of its five years of existence was Butler, formerly of the Fifth Regiment.[56] The Tenth Pennsylvania Continental Regiment was for a time commanded by James Chambers, who had started his career under Thompson in the First Regiment.[57]

Still another unit of regulars was recruited by Thomas Proctor of Westmoreland County and initially designated the Pennsylvania State Artillery Company.[58] By 1778, it was offered to Congress and came to be designated the Fourth Battalion of Continental Artillery. By this time, Proctor was a colonel commanding a regiment consisting of nine companies of Pennsylvanians, two of Jerseymen, and one of Marylanders.

Between militiamen and Continentals, Pennsylvanians served in very large numbers, although most of them for short hitches. Some served in both forces— for example, Armstrong served as a major general of Pennsylvania troops and as a brigadier general of Continentals. Some of the veterans awarded state pensions survived long enough to permit early county chroniclers to get their stories. (A typical sum, received by Sergeant Robert Prendergast of Cumberland County, was $48 a year.) One of the last of these, William Heim, was buried on March 2, 1856.[59]

Any assessment of the American War of Independence should take into account the story of the seven Continental battalions that marched under the eyes of Scots-Irish Cumberland County commanders, particularly Thompson's, as one of the first regiments of the regular army, which fought from Quebec to Charleston and served until Yorktown and beyond.

The Other Side

By no means was there unanimity west of the Susquehanna. Within the band of patriots there was strong opposition to the state constitution that the Radicals, with Robert Whitehill as floor leader at the convention, had forced on the people. The exact division of opinion cannot be ascertained, but from the fact that the Radical ticket won the various elections in 1776, we can infer that the moderates were solid losers. And they were not silent about their loss.

Acting as a group, the moderate Anti-Constitution faction dashed off a "Declaration of the Inhabitants of Cumberland County," which said: "We are of Opinion that the Constitution formed by the late Convention is Inconsistent with the principles of free government."[60] Individually, various members of the moderate group gave their opinions. William Thompson, for example, wrote James Wilson: "The Sensible and vertious [*sic*] part of this County, have since you left us, been endeavoring to set this Villanous Constitution aside, and we had great reason to believe we should have been successful, had not Blaine brought up and reported that two thirds of the People below liked and would support the Constitution, Land said it would be inforced by fixed Bayonets."[61]

John Armstrong wrote Thomas Wharton: "The greatest opposition by much that I have heard to the present Governmt happens to be in this County, where temper hath had too great a lead of reason. . . ."[62]

Robert Galbraith of Bedford County, a Radical, displaced the Anti-Constitutionalist Thomas Smith from his various offices because of his opposition, and Radicals remonstrated for the selection of a new assemblyman who would support the 1776 state constitution.[63] In a subsequent tiff, the prevailing party had to jail Smith to get him to relinquish his records. Party divisions grew even wider after the Radicals forced everyone to take an oath before they were permitted to vote. George Stevenson, a moderate, wrote Wilson that Carlisle would vote for Andrew McKee, "who will swallow the oath, if there were as many Fish Hooks in it as there are letters" and that the reason the oaths were legislated was that the Radicals sitting in the convention wanted to ensure themselves seats in the next Assembly.[64]

Court activity was disrupted by the Test Oath. James Pollock had to leave his position in Westmoreland County because he refused to take it.[65] John Agnew in Cumberland County refused to deliver the prothonotary's papers to his Radical successor. John Montgomery, who had been defeated by Whitehill for an Assembly seat, asked Wilson: "will you advise [us] to Submit our neck to the Yoak like [an] ass. I trust not. . . . We shall have a blessd set of Justices in this County. . . . The Town will be full and Stink[in]g with yellow w[h]iges. . . . I am afraid if they are once alowd to Open the Courts, it will be over with us. . . ."[66]

Wilson, back in Carlisle in March 1777, circulated a petition condemning the "Arbitrary and Unreasonable Oath" and calling for a vote by the people on the new constitution.[67] Blaine refused to head the militia because of his initial opposition to the 1776 constitution; two Bedford County sub-lieutenants refused reappointment on similar grounds.[68]

Besides being divided as Radicals and Moderates, Constitutionalists and Anti-Constitutionalists, the hinterland was split on the very issue of separation and war against the British. Embedded in the records are descriptions of incidents ranging from simple reluctance to accept the new radicalized state government, to outright opposition and treason. During six years of fighting, a substantial number of potential militiamen chose to pay money in lieu of service. In reference to Cumberland County, General Irvine wrote: "the Monied & luke warm are beginning to procure Men. . . . This goes down hard with people who are fond of militia."[69] George Stevenson, who in 1776 took on the leadership of the Cumberland County Committee of Correspondence, complained of public apathy, corruption, laggards, and instances of farmers selling grain to distillers rather than to army commissaries.[70]

Pinning down active loyalist opposition to the Revolutionary government in

Cumberland County is more difficult. Occasional court records mention the seizure of the real estate of some individuals attainted by treasonable activities. They also tell about people accused of "going to the enemy" and "speaking inimical to the United States."

A threat arose in 1776 to the military installations at Carlisle. John Holmes, a storekeeper there, stated in a deposition that a Scot and deserter from the British army, Alexander McDonald, was raising a force of 100 loyalists to raid the Carlisle works and burn the stores.[71] Getting word of this, Stevenson stated: "There are divers treasonable and dangerous designs of levying men and destroying the public stores at Carlisle."[72] He had also heard that there were political prisoners in the Carlisle jail who allegedly had incited other inmates to do mischief and tried to stir up discontent among wagoneers working for the army, who had organized to demand prepayment for their services. Perhaps he had heard of a brisk trade that had developed in the Chambersburg area by which horses and cattle were stolen, driven south, and sold to British agents in Virginia. Patriots heard that victims who complained to the legal authorities found their crops and outbuildings burned.

Learning of the threat in Cumberland County, Washington suggested: "Two cos., each to consist of 60 men at least, under proper officers, should be raised immediately to guard the laboratory and stores at Carlisle."[73] Congress complied by authorizing the raising of two regular army companies. These measures were successful, as no sabotage occurred.

In late 1778, printer Christopher Sauer III wrote Sir Henry Clinton that the backcountry loyalists expected help from a member of Pennsylvania's Supreme Executive Council who said they had already been sounded out. It is impossible to identify beyond a doubt the individual to whom Sauer referred, but one distinct possibility is Colonel Matthew Smith, onetime leader of the Paxton Boys. By 1780, Sauer was claiming that there were 6,000 potential loyalist men "spread all over the country,"[74] although he did not delineate what counties he meant.

There is little of record that tells us what the patriots knew about these amorphous, irregular bands of men and their grand plans. When they found a suspected loyalist, they acted quickly. Thus, the Anglican missionary Daniel Battwell, who was working Cumberland and York Counties for the Society for the Propagation of the Gospel, was tossed into an icy river when the locals suspected him of opposing them.[75] The fate of his acquaintance Dr. Henry Norris of York, whom he termed "madly loyal," is not apparent, but Battwell claimed that he also raised a band of 500 loyalists and used five horses to conduct loyalist business, in the course of which he was captured three times. At the Carlisle depot a court martial was in almost continuous session for the trial of spies and deserters and other military offenders. It was not an empty gesture for the citizenry to name the place "Washingtonburg" as early as 1779, reputedly the first use of the name anywhere in America.[76]

Motivation and Mobilization

Regarding the general population and their reasons for participation in the patriot causes, records are also scarce, and it is necessary to surmise. An economic motive for supporting the Patriot party is evident; safe behind the Susquehanna, they were free to produce and sell to the rebel army great reserves of food and supplies that were amassed at the Carlisle quartermaster depot and in cellars, barns, and private houses leased as emergency storage spaces. They did not have access to the British or they might well have sold to both sides, as Americans had done during the wars of the 1750s. Of further interest to the farmers was the fact that the army was in the market for dray horses for purchase, and for teams and wagons for lease. On one occasion an observer saw 1,200 horses at the Carlisle corrals.[77]

The army was able, without dragooning, as had been the case during the Braddock expedition, to hire wagons and employ artisans to make harnesses, knapsacks, canteens, potash, and other items.[78] There was no reported difficulty in recruiting for the commissary magazine at Carlisle 40 carpenters, 40 blacksmiths, 20 wheelwrights, 12 harnessmakers, and an unspecified number of turners and tinsmen.

On the other hand, the yeomanry, seeking maximum profit, grew wheat and rye to make whiskey, rather than the hay and grain for the flour that the army needed so urgently.[79] The farmers made so much alcohol that the Assembly ordered the confiscation of hay and ordered that a portion of acreage be devoted to raising cereal grains that would not be converted into liquor. Halfway between the capital and Fort Pitt, where the patriots anticipated Indian raids, Carlisle became the site for a number of military activities. For example, it was a place to lodge spies, such as those found between Carlisle and Harris's Ferry in Callendar's Tavern, as well as Dr. John Kearsley, John André, and others.

"Retained loosely" would be a better choice of words, for André with his own servants journeyed as far as Lancaster while on parole, and eight prisoners of war captured in Canada had freedom to hunt and exercise on their own recognizance within six miles of the town square.[80]

Also lodged in Carlisle were about 40 Hessians taken prisoner during the raid on Princeton, New Jersey, who were kept busy cutting wood, tending stables, and, according to tradition, constructing a powder magazine. Regular army regiments spent time at Carlisle being resupplied, trained, and brought up to strength. In addition, an artillery school was started in Carlisle in February 1777, and a hospital and recruiting station the year following.

After the British captured Philadelphia in September 1777, Congress ordered the construction of a gunpowder factory at Carlisle and designated the old French and Indian War public works as a Quartermaster Depot and Commissary Magazine. It soon was providing food for 5,000 men and forage for 1,000 animals based at the various installations. When space became a problem, a substation was opened at York and another at Shippensburg. Carlisle supplied the French forces at Newport, Rhode Island, and the Sullivan expedition into New York, shipping cargo on flatboats up the Susquehanna.

Colonel Ephraim Blaine, a Cumberland County miller turned infantry officer, demonstrated a knack at feeding his regiment. This rare ability caught the eye of Washington, who transferred him to the Commissary Department and assigned him to Carlisle to handle the feeding of the entire army in the north. Blaine's innovation was to eliminate the practice of sending live cattle along with the marching units. They tended to walk off the tissue that made for good eating. He substituted instead the system of slaughtering the animals in Carlisle and shipping them in wagons as salted beef. Each brigade got ten vehicles drawn by four horses each.

In late 1776, Washington directed the opening of an artillery school at Carlisle, probably the first in the American army.[81] Stored there were ordnance as big as 9-inch mortars and 24-pound cannon. At least four furnaces were part of the operation. Producing iron pigs was the Mary Ann Furnace, run by the three brothers-in-law, George Ross, George Stevenson, and William Thompson, at Manheim Township, Lancaster County. The Boiling Springs furnace made cannon castings, Mount Holly bored cannon, and Pine Grove produced cannonballs and shot. A boring mill at the works using Letort Spring power manufactured cannon of up to 3,000 pounds. It is not hyperbole to suggest that

Carlisle ranked near the top of the list of important ordnance and quartermaster bases in America.

Summary

Cumberland County and its people played important parts in the events of 1763–83. Leaving aside some extremist roughnecks, such as the Black Boys, the hinterland initially followed the lead of a politically moderate squirearchy that endorsed efforts to seek redress of grievances against Great Britain. However, when most of the traditional leaders left the county to take major military and civilian posts, new and more Radical leaders stepped in to the vacuum. They took the county to the side of the Radical city faction that superseded the legal Assembly and reorganized Pennsylvania under a new state constitution that virtually eliminated the executive branch, lavished much power on the legislative, but reserved much more for the people in an innovative Declaration of Rights.

There is little direct evidence regarding why Cumberland County sought independence and greater latitude in running its own affairs. One can infer, however, that the people were angry with an eastern establishment that provided little defense against the Indians (who were a greater threat than the redcoats), that outvoted them in the Assembly, that built them no roads to market their crops, and that in 1776 waffled on the issue of independence. To the nation, the trans-Susquehanna area was generous. It furnished James Wilson as a congressman and signer of the Declaration of Independence. It provided two rifle companies and the commander of one of the first regiments of the first professional army, William Thompson, as well as a large number of others who won generals' stars or headed regiments as colonels. These included two major generals: Arthur St. Clair, a future senior officer (the commanding general) of the regular army, and John Armstrong, who held both regular and militia posts.

The public works in Cumberland County, which had originated in the wars of the 1750s, were refurbished to become storage places for ordnance, supplies, forage, and food, as well as factories for the manufacture of weapons from muskets to the largest cannon, barrels, and casks, knapsacks, haversacks, and valises. A Shippensburg subdepot rounded up horses, wagons, saddles, harnesses, and forage. In large numbers, Cumberland County men and at least two "Mollie

Pitchers" (Margaret Corbin of Chambersburg and Mary Ludwig Hays Mc-Cauley of Carlisle) marched off to battle.[82] The enemy from within waged mostly a war of recalcitrance and threats; the enemy from without never actually trod the acres of old Mother Cumberland. Had it done so, there is little doubt that a population tempered by frontier struggle would have given a good account of itself.

During the Revolutionary period, the county, by allying itself with the Radicals, won increased representation in the Assembly and for the first time gave a leader to the Assembly and the Council: Robert Whitehill. Propertyless individuals won the suffrage; after the repeal of the Test Oath, virtually every adult male could vote if he wanted to. In Presbyterian hearts, any lurking fear of an episcopate died; in Lutheran and Reformed minds, a hope for an establishment, if it ever existed, died unfulfilled. The militia lapsed into its usual desuetude, its members living with hopes of land grants and pensions.

By 1783 the traditional conservative and moderate squirearchs, bearing honorable records for wartime military service, regained their positions of influence in local and state governments as well as in voluntary organizations. Their day in the sun ended, the Radicals who had created and sustained eight years of civil revolution quietly yielded place and subsided.

7

The Wyoming Valley

Frederick J. Stefon

> The romantic theory of revolution, in which all the lowly
> unite to rise against the oppressors, is embarrassed by the
> American Revolution's multiplicity of variously oppressed and
> exploited peoples who preyed upon each other; what most
> aggrieved the poor frontiersman was his sovereign's ban on
> robbing the even poorer Indian, and the first target of the
> Indian's hatchet was the frontiersman's skull . . .
> —Francis Jennings, *Empire of Fortune*

In the early eighteenth-century prehistoric Indian mounds, the ruins of former
Indian settlements, and vibrant new settlements of displaced natives, dotted the
North Branch Valley of the Susquehanna River from Shamokin to Tioga. Until
1763 the bustling Indian town of Wyoming was haven to refugees placed there

*I am grateful to the Scholarly Activities Committee of the Wilkes-Barre Campus Faculty Senate
for awarding me two small grants from the annual fund to pursue research on Sullivan's March
and the Seneca culture at the Genesee Valley Room and the Letchworth Collection at SUNY,
Geneseo, New York. My thanks also to Mary Ellen Calemmo, Director of the Lackawanna Historical Society, the staff of the Wyoming Historical and Geological Society, and Head Librarian Joan
Diana, retired, and her staff at the Penn State Wilkes-Barre Campus Library for their assistance in
this project.

by the Six Nations Iroquois Confederacy with the approval of Pennsylvania colonial authorities. From 1763 to 1784, the Wyoming Valley brought fortune to many diverse cultural groups of people, and disaster to others. To white settlers from Connecticut and Pennsylvania, the Wyoming Valley was a new frontier, a rich river plain to be possessed, tamed, and profited from. The only regrettable feature of this potential homeland was that it was isolated from established colonial communities. Both Easton and Bethlehem were sixty-five miles away. To the Indians, and in particular the Iroquois League, it was not only a valuable hunting ground, but also a warrior's path of communication, a middle ground from the southern door of the Seneca nation at Tioga (Athens) to the colonial powers in Philadelphia and their interests in Virginia. The Wyoming Valley was a buffer to the unfettered white incursion that threatened Iroquois geopolitical order.[1]

As early as June 1754 at the Albany Congress, the Iroquois League and colonial authorities, especially from Connecticut and Pennsylvania, were already mapping out the fate of the Wyoming Valley. On April 19, 1763, the last Indian settlement of displaced Delawares, Mohicans, and Shawnee, headed by the astute Delaware chief, Teedyuscung, was burned to the ground by an advance party of Connecticut settlers acting under the auspices of the Susquehannah Land Company. These Connecticut settlers assassinated Teedyuscung and turned his people into refugees. Teedyuscung's settlement, Wyoming, had been financed by the Quakers and placed there at the behest of both the Iroquois and Pennsylvania governments, who feared and resented the coming onslaught of Susquehannah Company settlers. The Connecticut settlers who destroyed Teedyuscung's village laid claim to the same territory by virtue of a deed surreptitiously obtained by John Lydius, an agent of the Susquehannah Company, during secret negotiations at the Albany Conference nine years earlier.[2]

The Onondaga Council, speaking for the Iroquois Confederacy, later declared Lydius's negotiations fraudulent.[3] On October 7, 1763, the Crown issued a royal proclamation that limited colonial settlement to a line agreed on earlier at the Treaty of Easton in 1758. The proclamation sealed the fate of the North Branch Valley to the refugee Indian communities who lived there by the grace of both Iroquois and Pennsylvania colonial authority. On October 15, 1763, many of the Susquehannah Company settlers responsible for the destruction of Wyoming were massacred; the remainder were either captured or driven from their encampment by an Indian raiding party led by Teedyuscung's vengeful son, the noted Delaware war chief, Captain Bull. Before Captain Bull's com-

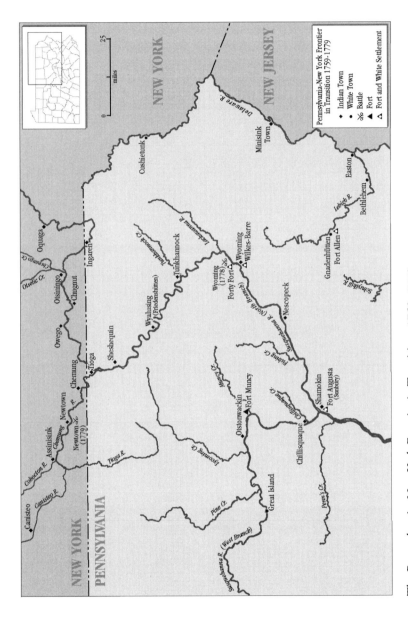

The Pennsylvania–New York Frontier in Transition, 1759–1779

bined force of more than 100 Shawnee and Delaware warriors destroyed the nascent Connecticut settlement at Wyoming and turned it into a no-man's-land, it had wreaked havoc and devastation throughout the Pennsylvania frontier. Captain Bull's raids were part of the Ottawa chief Pontiac's pan-Indian war of liberation to drive the whites and their alien ways from the Indians' dwindling havens of refuge.[4]

In 1768, at the Treaty of Fort Stanwix, the Iroquois Confederacy ceded the Wyoming Valley to Pennsylvania. After 1768, the valley became embroiled in a bitter land war between competitive speculators from Connecticut (Yankees) and Pennsylvania (Pennamites). This struggle over land, sometimes called the Yankee-Pennamite Wars, lasted from 1769 to 1784 and was the major preoccupation of the settlers of the Wyoming Valley before and throughout the Revolutionary period. From 1776 onward, the Connecticut Susquehannah Company settlers, victorious in this internecine strife by that time, sought to use their communal participation in the war effort as a way to further justify and perpetuate their land claims in the region. From 1776 onward, the political leadership of the Susquehannah Company at Wyoming propagandistically labeled all Pennsylvania claimants since driven from their homesteads in the valley, or now settled sixty miles upstream on former Indian land near Wyalusing, as "Tories." Throughout 1776, the vigilance committee or committee of inspection at Wyoming constantly threatened, harassed, and arrested the Pennsylvania claimants upriver under the existing Connecticut laws against treason.[5] Even after the valley was devastated by a joint force of British Rangers and Iroquois on July 3, 1778, the hatreds and disputes over land lingered on past the signing of the Treaty of Paris in 1783.[6] At the same time, the Iroquois claimed hegemony over the valley and opposed the coming incursion of white settlement and colonial powers that sought to and eventually did extinguish their claims.

On November 5, 1768, at Fort Stanwix (Rome, New York) a treaty was negotiated with the Iroquois Confederacy by Sir William Johnson, the Crown's agent for Indian Affairs. The Iroquois, in an effort to contain white settlements at their southern door, ceded the entire Wyoming Valley and millions of acres of land at cut-rate prices to Pennsylvania in an effort to limit the threatening machinations of the Susquehannah Company.[7] This company of white land speculators and settlers had plagued the Iroquois ever since their initial arrival in the Wyoming Valley in 1754. In 1768 the Iroquois Confederation believed its strategy was sound as it acquiesced in the skillful political manipulation of Sir William Johnson in the matter. The Iroquois hoped that Pennsylvania claimants under the political control of the provincial government would be settled systematically in the Wyoming Valley and ward off the more aggressive and despised New Englanders.[8]

Neither the illusory Royal Proclamation of 1763 nor the Treaty of Fort Stanwix held back the white invasion of prime Indian lands by zealous settlers, greedy speculators, traders, and missionaries in search of Indian souls. Within two years of the Fort Stanwix Treaty, the Iroquois confederated leadership recognized that it had made an unwise decision. By 1770, white settlers were spilling into areas beyond the guaranteed boundaries. The Six Nations also realized the real cash value of the land they ceded for white settlement. Their resentment over their new predicament increased with time, and they continued to look on the Wyoming Valley at their southern door anxiously. Moravian missionary John Heckewelder noted that in 1770 the Six Nations sent emissaries to the resettled Munsee-Delaware converts at Friedenshütten (Wyalusing). The messengers brought them two Spanish dollars as their symbolic portion of the monies for land ceded to the English under the Fort Stanwix Treaty and asked them to move their settlement to Assinisink, to draw them farther away from white influence and bring these Christian converts under their watchful eye. Heckewelder rejected such a plan and feared that renewed pagan influences over his new converts might lead them astray.[9]

Even before the ink dried on the Fort Stanwix Treaty and the Six Nations Confederation was laden with £10,000 worth of treasure, Pennsylvania's proprietary government ordered its surveyors in December 1768 to map out its new domain in the Wyoming Valley over the ashes of Teedyuscung, his brethren, and the bones of those New England martyrs. The proprietary surveyors divided the Wyoming Valley into the manors of Sunbury on the west side of the North Branch of the Susquehanna and Stoke on its east side. Meanwhile, agents of a rejuvenated Susquehannah Company, believing the Indian menace had been politically neutralized by the Stanwix boundary line, also made plans to resettle the Wyoming Valley.[10]

Signals from its agents at the Fort Stanwix Treaty Conference encouraged the Susquehannah Company shareholders to make plans to settle the Wyoming Valley quickly. On December 28, 1768, the shareholders voted to send an advance party of forty men to settle the Wyoming lands by February 1769. Two hundred more settlers were scheduled to follow in early May. The shareholders, at that same meeting, approved the layout of five townships, each five miles square, within the bounds of the Wyoming purchase. In each of these the company set aside land shares for "a Gospel ministry and schools."[11] Governor John Penn received word from his agents of the Susquehannah Company's immediate designs for Wyoming, and he set out to thwart them. In early January 1769, Penn offered a seven-year lease on Wyoming lands to Amos Ogden, Charles Stewart, and Sheriff John Jennings of Northampton County. The three men received 100-acre tracts of the rich bottomlands mapped out in the manor of Stoke. Naturally, these leases occupied land originally settled by the Susquehannah Company in 1762, one mile from Teedyuscung's former town of Wyoming.[12] Ogden, Stewart, and Jennings built a small blockhouse at Mill Creek and awaited the inevitable arrival of the Connecticut claimants. By the end of January, Penn granted leases to at least forty men from Northumberland County and New Jersey. When the weary New Englanders arrived at the Mill Creek site on February 8, 1769, they found, much to their chagrin, Ogden's blockhouse occupied by proprietary tenants. After a brief altercation, Sheriff Jennings arrested three of their leaders and carted them off some sixty-five miles to the Easton jail.[13]

Around March 1, 1769, the remaining Connecticut claimants journeyed to the mouth of the Lackawanna River (Pittston) and built a number of crude log huts in preparation for the expected arrival of 200 more settlers in the spring. On February 13, Governor Penn sent a letter of protest to the enfeebled Governor of Connecticut, William Pitkin, asking him to avert the Susquehannah Company's "deluded" and "unwarranted designs" on Wyoming.[14] The Yankees persisted, and John Penn ordered Sheriff Jennings and Justice of the Peace Lewis Gordon of Northampton County to gather a sufficient posse to arrest the New Englanders at the mouth of the Lackawanna River. This posse of more than 100 armed men reached the crude settlement on March 14, 1769, and easily captured thirty one of the forty settlers. Although some of these escaped on the journey to Easton, the majority of those arrested found themselves in jail awaiting bail. The Susquehannah Company met on April 12 and decided to move quickly to overcome the recent obstruction to their plans by the Pennsylvania authorities. The shareholders voted to send an additional 300 settlers to Wyoming.[15] In April, 110 men left for Wyoming under the command of Major John Durkee, a bankrupt merchant from Norwich, Connecticut.[16] By May 12, 1769, they decided to encamp over the remnants of Teedyuscung's town of Wyoming. There they were joined by another 146 men with heavily laden packhorses and cattle. The settlers decided to build their houses at this location. Years before, these rich flatlands, now derelict, had been cleared and cultivated by the Delaware and other natives.[17]

Throughout the summer of 1769, the valley was divided into two armed camps: the Connecticut claimants under John Durkee at Wyoming, and Amos Ogden's Pennsylvanians one mile away at Mill Creek. Both groups made improvements on the land, and hostilities between them erupted in September. A small party of Ogden's group skirmished with some Connecticut men on September 22. On November 14, Ogden's men at the Mill Creek blockhouse were reinforced by Sheriff John Jennings's posse of 200 men. The settlement of Fort Durkee surrendered to this superior force.[18] Thus, the first year closed on this dispute for precious Wyoming lands. Jennings and his men returned to their homes. Ogden left a skeleton force of ten men at Fort Durkee and journeyed triumphantly to Philadelphia to celebrate his victory.

In January 1770, Lazarus Stewart and a group of men from the town of Paxton—the "Paxton Boys," who in December 1763 had massacred in cold blood the last men, women, and children of the Conestoga tribe—made a deal with the desperate shareholders of the Susquehannah Company, led by Zebulon Butler and Ebenezer Backus, to dispossess the Pennsylvania claimants in return for promises of land along the North Branch of the Susquehanna.[19] This unholy alliance between Stewart, his notorious band, and the Susquehannah Company's leadership stirred John Penn to remind his Uncle Thomas Penn that many of these same "banditti" were those "lawless villains" who had massacred the Indians at Lancaster.[20] With Stewart's help, the Connecticut men regained control of Fort Durkee on February 11, but this did not mean that the Connecticut forces had possession of the area. The Wyoming Valley changed hands many times throughout 1770 and 1771. There were deaths, some maimings, and much looting associated with this bitter struggle for land rights.[21]

In the end, Lazarus Stewart's men and the Connecticut men under Zebulon Butler proved victorious. On August 15, 1771, Ogden's Pennsylvania claimants surrendered. As they left Wyoming, the victorious Yankees confiscated their livestock, grain, and other possessions. Fear of possible reprisals by posses instigated by Pennsylvania's provincial government gave the Wyoming community the demeanor of a virtual armed camp.[22]

Not only were Governor John Penn, the Provincial Council, Pennsylvania claimants, and greedy speculators disgruntled by the loss of the Pennsylvania forces at Wyoming in August 1771, but so was the Iroquois Confederacy, whose southern door no longer seemed secure. The Six Nations felt hostility toward the New Englanders for upsetting their fragile balance of diplomacy and the chain of friendship they had so carefully forged with Pennsylvania over the years. The Confederacy also bitterly remembered the Yankees' fraudulent purchase of Wyoming lands and their murder of Teedyuscung, the Confederation's Delaware cousin and prop in the Wyoming Valley, and the mayhem his death unleashed up and down the Susquehanna with the revenge of his son, Captain Bull. An Indian delegation journeyed to Philadelphia and on September 24, 1771, held a conference with the Provincial Council. Cheahogah, a Cayuga chief, spoke for all the natives present, including the Six Nations. The New Englanders, Cheahogah said, claimed that the Indians gave them the Wyoming lands, but, he stated, "we who are here of several Nations namely, the Six Nations, Shawanese, Delawares, Mohickons, Nanticoke, and Conoys, we all declare that the Indians never did give this land to the New England people, but we gave it to the proprietor Onas [Penn], and to no other person, and we not only gave Wyoming to him, but a great space of land round about it, except the places where Indians live."[23]

In June 1772, the Moravian Munsee-Delaware converts living at Friedenshütten (Wyalusing) and Sheshequin (Ulster), both in the area of the Susquehannah claim, determined to leave for the Ohio country. Their neutrality in the early years of the struggle for the Wyoming Valley had been for naught. White people were invading their lands, and the Six Nations wanted them well beyond the Stanwix Treaty line so no conflict would break out.[24]

The provincial threat abated during the years 1772–75, which found the Susquehannah Company vigorously advertising the lush plains of Wyoming. Many Connecticut newcomers made their way into the Wyoming Valley, having been assured that they would find paradise. On June 2, 1773, a meeting of the Susquehannah Company at Hartford drew up a law code for Wyoming called the "Articles of Agreement," which established a system of local government for each town and provided for a three-man directorate to maintain order, levy taxes, and raise a militia. Now any settler who felt that his legal rights, especially his property rights, were being violated by a town's directorate could appeal his case to a quarterly meeting of directors from all the towns.[25]

In 1773, the Susquehannah Company sent 140 settlers to plant a town on the West Branch of the Susquehanna, but they met with stiff resistance from a Pennamite posse comitatus and were expelled. William Plunket, a Northumberland magistrate and the leader of the posse, reported to the governor that he and his comrades could not "hope for peace" while Susquehannah Company claimants kept possession of Wyoming.[26]

Proprietor John Penn, for his part, issued proclamation after proclamation against the Susquehannah Company's incursion into Wyoming lands. Finally, in December 1773, Pennsylvania claimants from Northumberland County appealed to Penn and the assembly to take a strong hand and drive out the "lawless intruders," but the assembly failed to appropriate funds to send troops against the settlement.[27] Penn answered the protests and pleas from the frustrated Northumberland petitioners with yet another proclamation, which he issued after the Connecticut General Assembly had met in January 1774 and created the town of Westmoreland and attached it to Connecticut's Litchfield County after years of intense lobbying by Susquehannah Company agents.[28]

The protracted debate over Wyoming lands also raged on in the British courts until the Revolution. Penn used harsh words in his February 28, 1774, proclamation against the colony of Connecticut and its "emigrants," who had in a "hostile" manner taken possession of Wyoming under a pretended "right to lands" within the boundaries of Pennsylvania's Royal Grant and without a claim confirmed by the King's Privy Council. Penn did not recognize the town of Westmoreland, and he called Connecticut's appointment of Zebulon Butler, the Susquehannah Company's principal agent at Wyoming, as justice of the peace an illegal act and "pretense." He concluded that any settler without a "grant or license" issued by the province would be brought to justice.[29] The dispute festered, and Penn's continuing war of words seemed hollow to Pennsylvania claimants who were expelled from Westmoreland by Zebulon Butler and his settlers' committee in November 1774. When the year 1775 found the British Empire threatened by its rebellious American colonies, the Second Continental Congress became the court of last resort for this continuing quarrel over Wyoming lands. The Continental Congress sought an expedient political solution to the troublesome matter through compromise but could satisfy neither party.[30]

On July 27, 1775, Zebulon Butler and a large delegation of Susquehannah Company settlers conferred with a group of thirty natives and several headmen from the Six Nations. The Indians journeyed to Wyoming from Oquaga (Windsor, New York), a bustling polyglot village principally of Oneida and Tuscarora. The leader of the Six Nations delegation, a Tuscarora chief, gave the principal speech. He said the delegation attending the treaty Conference of Oswego, conducted by Colonel Guy Johnson (William Johnson's nephew and successor), had then decided to trek to Wyoming. "We come," he continued, "also to let you know the Six Nations have been somewhat afraid, but now are glad to see all things look like peace, and they think there will be no quarrel among yourselves, with one another. And you must not believe bad reports or remember times pass'd that have been unfriendly."[31] On a more practical note, the chief requested that safe passage for the Iroquois be ensured along the main path from the headwaters of the Susquehanna through Wyoming and down to Philadelphia, for the purpose of hunting, trade, and travel.

Butler and his delegation also seemed satisfied with the demeanor and promises of neutrality made by the natives in the present strife between the colonies and Great Britain. In his official response to the Tuscarora chief's message, Butler said: "Your young men are welcome to hunt in our neighborhood, and we are glad to trade with them for their skins, but you must caution them not to make our women and children afraid, either by word or action."[32] The Indians stayed at Wyoming until August 3 and were given provisions for their journey home. It is significant that wampum, the accepted device for recording and establishing cross-cultural contact and agreement, was not exchanged at this conference. These were perilous and swiftly changing times. Had Butler but known what would transpire at Albany a mere twenty-eight days after the close of the Wyoming Conference, he would not have been so elated about prospects for peace with the Iroquois on the Wyoming frontier.

Following this conference at Wyoming, the Continental Congress commissioners for Indian affairs, Oliver Wolcott, Philip Schuyler, Turbott Francis, and Volkert Douw, next treated with the sachems of the Six Nations Confederation. They met in Albany on August 25 to secure their neutrality in the ongoing dispute with Great Britain. On August 31 the Onondaga sachem Tiahogwando (Teyohaqueande), a close ally of the late Sir William Johnson and a man of great influence in the Six Nations Confederacy, made an important speech that totally repudiated the Connecticut claims and was designed to influence the events in the Wyoming Valley anew in favor of Pennsylvania. If both Pennsylvania and the Iroquois considered the New Englanders' pretensions to Wyoming lands fraudulent, perhaps the new government of the united colonies would drive the interlopers out. The Iroquois then could renew their chain of friendship with Pennsylvania and secure the southern door to their homeland. But the renewal and peace Tiahogwando hoped for never came to pass.[33] In July 1776, after Congress announced American independence, the British-American conflict broke the Iroquois Confederacy asunder. After 1777, the Great Council fire was covered at Onondaga. Most of the Six Nations supported the British, although a majority of the Oneidas and Tuscaroras allied with the Americans.[34]

By September 1775 the Susquehannah Company moved to establish a settlement along the West Branch of the Susquehanna River that did nothing to soothe the apprehensions of the Pennsylvania settlers already there. On September 22, 1775, an angry Northumberland County official, William Maclay, sent a message to Joseph Shippen, secretary to Pennsylvania's governor. He warned Shippen that the Wyoming settlement soon planned to send 300 settlers to the West Branch and that Connecticut controlled "every motion of the people at Wyoming."[35] On September 25, an armed force of 150 Connecticut settlers from Wyoming made its way to the Pennamite settlement at Freeland Mills, some thirteen miles from Sunbury. Around 200 armed inhabitants rushed to disperse the invaders. A fight ensued. One Wyoming settler was killed, two were wounded, and seventy-two were captured. The Pennamites also confiscated 130 firearms and thirty horses.[36]

The threat from Wyoming agitated the already rankled Pennsylvania freeholders of Northampton and Northumberland Counties. They petitioned Pennsylvania's Committee of Safety to protect them and their property from further "hostile invasion" by "lawless intruders" from Wyoming.[37] On November 20, the sheriff, William Scull, and a few magistrates of Northumberland visited Zebulon Butler and other leaders of the Wyoming settlement and asked them to submit to the laws of the province. The leaders said they would never do so, as long as the "common people" of Wyoming threatened and cursed the magistrates.[38]

The Pennsylvania Assembly did not accept this insult. On November 25 it asked the governor to coerce the leadership of Wyoming to comply with its laws. The Wyoming expedition, composed of more than 500 well-armed men, left Fort Augusta (Sunbury) around December 15 under the command of Magistrate William Plunket and Sheriff William Scull.[39] They planned to journey up the Susquehanna via Wapwallopen and Nanticoke Falls to Wyoming, where a forewarned Zebulon Butler, Lazarus Stewart, and a force of 400 men awaited their arrival. There, on Christmas Eve and again on Christmas Day, the Yankees repulsed the Pennamites with some lost lives and many wounded on both sides. The Yankees referred to the Pennamite expedition as a Tory invasion.[40]

By December 25, 1775, the Pennsylvania government's feeble attempt to destroy the Connecticut claimants' foothold in the Wyoming Valley had ended in shambles. The quarrel between the two colonies continued to fester throughout the Revolutionary War, threatening the political stability and unity of the Second Continental Congress. The Congress, for its part, hoped to draw up some compromise resolution that would put off a decision over jurisdictional soil rights until the indefinite future after the "present troubles in the colonies" had passed. Ironically, on December 20, 1775, as Plunket's force moved up the Susquehanna toward Wyoming, Congress ordered that "the contending parties immediately cease all hostilities and avoid every appearance of force, until the dispute can be legally decided."[41] Again, on December 23, it recommended to Connecticut "not to introduce any settlers on the said lands till the further order of this congress."[42] Although the colony of Connecticut had already agreed to the latter recommendation, the Wyoming settlers were unaware of this decision.

By 1776 a number of Pennsylvania claimants had already settled upriver from Wyoming on lands in and around Wyalusing, the former productive settlement of Munsee-Delaware Moravian converts. The Moravians had left the forsaken settlement to the oversight of Job Chillaway, a well-known Indian guide and trapper who held a Pennsylvania claim in the area. Thomas Willing, a rich Pennsylvania claimant, and Alexander Patterson, a staunch Pennamite leader, owned large Pennsylvania land grants in the area. John Depue and some other disgruntled Connecticut claimants moved up to Wyalusing from Wyoming shortly after the Munsees left in 1772. In 1775, Chillaway sold some land to the son of Henry Pauling, a member of the Pennsylvania Assembly. John and James Secord, Frederick Vanderlip, and a number of other wealthy farmers were working grants in the area. According to Alexander Patterson, these predominantly Pennsylvania freeholders could not live in peace with settlers at Wyoming.[43] In March 1776, the Wyoming settlers' Committee of Inspection, acting under the existing Connecticut laws against treason, arrested a number of upriver Pennsylvania claimants who were suspected of Toryism. First, John Secord was brought in on charges of spying and of harboring and provisioning escaped British prisoners. The outraged Secord petitioned the Pennsylvania Assembly on March 6 and the Continental Congress on April 15, 1776, and was freed. The committee also arrested Philip and Abraham Van Gorder and shipped them off to Litchfield, Connecticut, for trial. Eight other people also were rounded up and sent to Hartford, Connecticut, where their cases were ultimately dismissed.[44]

By Fall 1776 the Connecticut settlers in Wyoming realized that to the north, and no more than a few days' journey by river, were the bustling Indian communities of Tioga, Chemung, Newtown, Otsiningo, and Owego. The Wyoming leadership recognized that they sat on the brink of a hostile frontier at the edge of civilization, and they began to fear the gathering storm. In order to control their destiny and keep a watchful eye on the Pennsylvania claimants near the northern Indian borderlands, they decided to erect a fort at Wyalusing. The Six Nations Confederacy heard about this and immediately protested that they were "unwilling" to have fortifications built upriver. "A fort at Wyalusing will block up our new made, wide and smooth road," they insisted, "and again make us strangers to one another."[45] Two days later, Zebulon Butler responded to the sachems' message. "The fort We think of building at Wyalusing," he said, "is for your defense as well as ours; for if [the loyalist forces of John] Butler and [Sir John] Johnson do come down the River we think they will likely fall upon you—in which case you can flee to Wyalusing and be safe with our people, your brothers."[46] Butler's stilted words (Zebulon Butler was not related to John Butler) did nothing to assuage the Six Nations' angry complaint.

Throughout the remainder of 1776, the Wyoming authorities constantly sent militiamen to check on the Pennsylvania claimants and continued openly to harass them. Finally, when Pennsylvania settlers refused to journey the sixty miles to Wyoming to train for the militia under Yankee officers, they were branded as Tories and forcibly taken to Wyoming with all their movable property. Indian neighbors from the Wyalusing area interceded on their behalf and warned that they would complain to the Continental Congress if their good neighbors were not released. The upriver Pennsylvania settlers were released without their property and ambushed on their journey home. The Pennsylvania claimants, wrote Patterson, were so tormented by the Yankees "that they were driven to seek an asylum with the Indians and at length retreated to Niagara for protection."[47] Many of these tormented upriver settlers found their revenge against the New Englanders at Wyoming by fighting on the side of the British. During the winter of 1776–77, a disgruntled John Depue committed himself to the British cause and made his way through the harsh cold to Fort Niagara to meet with Captain John Butler. He carried with him letters from seventy upriver Pennsylvania settlers who desired to serve the Crown. Depue eventually became Butler's leading recruiter of upriver settlers for the British cause.[48] Soon many other upriver settlers, entire families like the Augers, the Windrons, and the Vanderlips, encouraged by Depue and with assurance from John Butler, abandoned their farms and trekked to Niagara.[49] Beginning in early 1777, upriver Pennsylvania claimants from Tunkhannock to Wyalusing kept in constant communication with the Indians at Tioga and Newtown and with many of their brethren now at Niagara. In August, many upriver Indians and yet another group of settlers, this time under James Secord, marched off to join the British at the Battles of Fort Stanwix and Oriskany.[50] By the end of that year, the remaining upriver Pennsylvania claimants and their families, once branded as Tories by the New Englanders in Wyoming, in fact pledged their honor to the Crown, deserted their homesteads en masse, and made the bitter pilgrimage to the refuge of Fort Niagara.[51]

On September 2, 1776, the Congress had called on Wyoming to raise two military companies. This was done, and by January 1777 the Wyoming (Westmoreland) independent companies and other settlers who joined the main army totaled almost 300 men. These soldiers saw battle that year and the next away from Wyoming. By August 1777, the majority of the Iroquois Confederacy had sided with the British, and the 300 able-bodied men fighting in the Continental Army away from the valley left the settlement of less than 3,000 people in a vulnerable position.[52] Throughout the summer of 1777, detachments of settlers busily engaged themselves in building new or strengthening old forts, and sending scouting parties upriver on reconnaissance missions. At the same time, the Seneca and Cayuga grew worried over unconfirmed reports that the Wyoming settlers, known for their unscrupulous treatment of Pennsylvania people, planned to attack their villages along the upper reaches of the Susquehanna.[53] The Seneca, as did most of the Six Nations, still harbored resentment of the fraud perpetrated by the Susquehannah Company in 1763 when it burned out Teedyuscung and his people. In April 1777, the Seneca received a message to parley with the leaders of the Wyoming settlement. Before the meeting took place, a party of Seneca men and women were set upon five miles from the settlement by one of its scouting parties; one woman and two men were murdered and scalped.[54]

To combat the Yankee settlement of Wyoming, John Butler called a great conference at Niagara in December 1777 to bind the Six Nations tightly to the British cause. By March and April 1778, small groups of Indians and "enemy whites" began to attack scattered homesteads on the periphery of the main settlement. On March 12 the terror-stricken settlers petitioned the Continental Congress, stating that the Indians had recently made "repeated depredations" on the inhabitants and that recent intelligence showed that they planned to increase their hostilities. The petitioners requested that the two Wyoming Companies be re-stationed in the valley for its "defense and protection." Soon thereafter, Butler held another council with the Confederacy at Canadasaga (Geneva, New York) on May 12, 1778. All was set for a scourge to descend on the Wyoming Valley.[55]

Butler and his combined force of more than 500 Indians and Rangers floated down the Susquehanna on rafts and in boats, and on June 30 they reached the highlands surrounding the Wyoming settlement. Warriors from the Seneca and Cayuga tribes dominated this force; their southern door was at stake. Still stinging from their heavy losses at the Battle of Oriskany, the Seneca, led by the renowned war chief Sayenqueraghta, looked forward to the upcoming battle.[56]

On July 1, the Indians and Rangers surrounded Wintermoot and Jenkins Forts at the upper end of the valley and obtained their immediate surrender. Forty Fort, commanded by Colonel Zebulon Butler and Nathan Denison, rejected similar surrender demands. On July 3, more than 400 Connecticut militiamen marched out to meet the enemy. "This pleased the Indians highly," wrote John Butler later, "who observed they should be upon an equal footing with them in the woods."[57] Between four and five o'clock the Wyoming men came within a mile of the invaders. At this point, Butler ordered the captured forts set afire as a ruse of retreat. It worked; the Wyoming rebels rushed toward an open wood and opened fire at 200 yards on the Indians and Rangers who awaited them there. Waiting until the advancing force came within 100 yards, the Indians and Rangers began a two pronged attack. Their well-directed fire soon caused many casualties and resulted in a confused rout of the Wyoming militiamen. The battle lasted only thirty minutes: John Butler reported that 227 scalps and 5 prisoners were taken on the field of battle, while fewer than a dozen of his Indians and Rangers were killed or wounded. Zebulon Butler fled downstream; Nathan Denison retreated to Forty Fort, where the next day he signed the surrender agreement. John Butler promised the valley's inhabitants their physical safety, while Denison pledged Wyoming's neutrality throughout the rest of the war—a promise he did not keep.[58]

Soon John Butler's forces set about their task of devastating the Wyoming settlements. He ordered the eight existing forts destroyed and had 1,000 dwellings and the existing mills burned to the ground. More than 1,000 head of cattle were either butchered for food or driven away.[59] In their panicked exit from Wyoming, the survivors left the bodies of the dead unattended on the field of battle until October 21, when a returning Zebulon Butler ordered a contingent of his militia to inter "the remains of the men killed in the late battle."[60]

With Wyoming in ruins, the lamenting men, women, and children made their long and bitter exodus from the valley with fictitious stories of a hideous massacre. Rumors of the "savages'" wanton torture, rape, and mutilation of women and children made their way into the sensational newspaper accounts of the day. "Wyoming" became a well-worn battle cry for rebel revenge throughout the remainder of the Revolutionary War. Even today the folklore of the Battle of Wyoming continues to fascinate Wyoming Valley residents, despite the reality that not one noncombatant was harmed after the surrender. John Butler wrote to Colonel Mason Bolton that it gave him "the sincerest satisfaction" that "not a single person has been hurt of the inhabitants but such as were in arms."[61] After word of the Wyoming debacle and some small enemy raiding parties reached settlers living on the West Branch of the Susquehanna, they also deserted in droves. The "Great Runaway" was on.[62]

In September 1778, Colonel Thomas Hartley took the 200 men of the Sixth Pennsylvania Battalion and raced up the Susquehanna in a raid of retribution. Twelve vengeful Wyoming settlers joined Hartley's invasion into Indian country. His men burned the deserted town of Tioga and some surrounding villages to the ground. Hearing there was a superior force of Rangers in the area of Chemung, he then retreated downstream. While in retreat, Hartley's troops also killed and scalped a number of persistent Indian resisters in and around Wyalusing.[63]

In 1779, General George Washington, determined to pacify the chaotic New York and Pennsylvania frontier, chose Major General John Sullivan to lead a huge and meticulously planned expeditionary force against the Iroquois. On May 31, 1779, Washington recommended to Sullivan that he establish a post in the middle of Indian country "whence parties should be detached to lay waste all settlements around, with instructions to do it in the most effectual manner; that the country may not be merely overrun but destroyed."[64] John Sullivan met General James Clinton, his second in command, over the ashes of Tioga on August 22, 1779. Clinton's forces had already destroyed a number of Indian communities en route. Now Sullivan and Clinton began their "scorched-earth" campaign against the verdant communities of the Iroquois. Colonel Daniel Brodhead was also poised in Pittsburgh to destroy every Seneca and Munsee-Delaware town on the Allegheny River in Pennsylvania and New York. As Sullivan's forces made their way through Iroquois country, the women, children, and elderly fled in terror before them. Except for one notable battle at Newtown (near Elmira, New York) and a few skirmishes, Sullivan's force encountered little resistance.[65]

The journals kept by Sullivan's men describe the lush landscapes surrounding the Seneca and Cayuga communities: the fertile soil, the well-built houses, the extensive acres of vegetables, tall Indian corn, and abundant orchards.[66] Sullivan's men scrupulously turned this abundance into ashes. On September 30, 1779, Sullivan reported the success of his campaign to John Jay, president of the Congress. He wrote that his army had destroyed forty Indian towns, vast fields of vegetables and fruit trees, and 160,000 bushels of corn.[67] Mary Jemison, a white woman and Seneca adoptee who fled from Sullivan's wrath, recalled that when she returned to her Seneca lands "there was not a mouthful of any kind of sustenance left, not even enough to keep a child one day from perishing with hunger."[68] Ironically, some native communities escaped Sullivan's torch, and some buried caches of food aided the communal renewal of the Seneca and Cayuga in the summer of 1780 following Sullivan's invasion. That summer, incensed warriors embarked on raids of revenge that stretched along the borderlands of New York and down the Susquehanna to Wyoming. The Sullivan/Clinton campaign to quell the Indian danger in the hinterlands of New York and Pennsylvania proved a failure. For the next two years, Indian and loyalist attacks intensified and nearly depopulated the Susquehanna and Mohawk valleys.[69]

Before Sullivan's troops left the Wyoming Valley at the close of his campaign, one of his men, Lieutenant Erkuries Beatty, wrote in his journal: "Chief of the inhabitants have left this settlement [and] what few there is here erected small hutts [*sic*] where they live very uncomfortable."[70] They were protected by a Continental garrison at Fort Wyoming (Wilkes-Barre) that consisted of 125 officers and men. Colonel Zebulon Butler, perhaps the largest landowner in Wyoming, commanded the fort. Later that year, the Yankee-Pennamite controversy over land claims erupted again.[71] Connecticut's continued obstinacy and legal maneuvering frustrated a Continental Congress that was unable to reach a compromise. By November 20, 1780, President Joseph Reed of Pennsylvania's Supreme Executive Council wrote the Board of War a justification for his refusal to send supplies to Colonel Butler's garrison at Wyoming: Connecticut had refused to submit the land controversy "to amicable settlement by Congress agreeable to the terms of the Confederation." Noting that the entire command of the garrison "is a claimant of Lands under Connecticut Title,"[72] he insisted that Pennsylvania take over the running of Fort Wyoming. This ongoing discontent worried Congress, which directed George Washington to remove the existing Pennsylvania garrison and replace it with soldiers from neither side.

Washington then replaced Butler's men with a detachment from the Jersey Line.[73]

When Congress publicly proclaimed the ratification of the Articles of Confederation on March 1, 1781, Pennsylvania saw its chance to petition Congress to oversee a final solution to the Wyoming lands question. Under Article IX of the Confederation, whenever two or more states claimed jurisdiction over the same rights to the soil, controversies could be decided by specially appointed commissions or courts. The state's petition was forwarded to Congress on November 21, 1781. Congress consented to Pennsylvania's plea to arbitrate and, in January 1782, Connecticut grudgingly accepted Congressional auspices to settle the dispute.[74] The hearing held at Trenton, New Jersey, to settle the controversy lasted from November 12 to December 30, 1782. After weeks of lengthy arguments, the five commissioners rendered their decision: "We are unanimously of opinion that the State of Connecticut has no right to the lands in controversy."[75]

Although the Continental court awarded jurisdiction over the disputed territory to Pennsylvania, another bloody phase of the Yankee-Pennamite contest followed quickly. After the Trenton decree, Connecticut state politicians lost interest in the settlers' cause. Also, early in 1783 the Jersey Line detachment was withdrawn and replaced in March by Pennsylvania troops.[76] The Connecticut settlers realized that they faced an ominous future, as Pennsylvania claimants prepared a number of legal suits to eject the Connecticut settlers from Wyoming lands. In February the Pennsylvania General Assembly ordered a commission to journey to Wyoming to investigate land titles and soil rights, temporarily holding lawsuits over settlement of the valley in abeyance. The commissioners arrived in Wyoming on April 15, 1783.[77] Ironically, on April 19, 1783, twenty years to the day on which Teedyuscung was assassinated and most of his town of Wyoming was reduced to ashes by Connecticut settlers, the Pennsylvania commissioners told the Connecticut claimants that Pennsylvania would not "deprive her [own] citizens [or Connecticut claimants] of any part of their property legally obtained."[78] This signaled the eventual expulsion from Wyoming of the Connecticut claimants, who refused to compromise over rights to the soil. In August 1783, the Wyoming commissioners made their formal report to the Pennsylvania General Assembly, which in turn accepted the harsh recommendations of the commission, stating: "Our hopes of a friendly compromise seem now vanished."[79] On September 9, the Assembly repealed its Act of March 13 "to prevent and stay suits" against the Connecticut claimants at Wyoming.[80]

In early August 1783, a German traveler named Johann David Schoepf spent a week in Wyoming and recorded the following description of the inhabitants:

> Since the garrison was placed here . . . the Commanding officer has at the same time acted as a Justice, without any recourse to military law. The inhabitants hear his opinion and adjust their dealings thereby, if that seems good to them. But the people of Wyoming, with all their freedom, and living on the most productive lands, are pauper-poor. The war was something of a [setback], but their sloth is still more so. They live in miserable block-houses, are badly clothed, farm carelessly, and love easeful days.[81]

The Wyoming settlers' "easeful days" were destined to end with a number of tragic events that would befall them. In September, Alexander Patterson, a Pennamite claimant, returned to the Wyoming Valley as justice of the peace, reorganized the community, and used the two companies of state militia stationed at Fort Wyoming to coerce rent payments from the inhabitants; to harass and jail Zebulon Butler and his cronies; and to turn people out of their dwellings and replace them with Pennamites.[82] On March 15, 1784, days of rain, a rough winter, and an early thaw caused a flood to inundate the settlements situated on the plains close to the Susquehanna River. Patterson took advantage of the people's distress, and on May 13 and 14, according to John Franklin, a major resistance leader during Patterson's reign of terror, the settlers were forced from Wyoming at the "point of the bayonet" by the militia at Wyoming and the Pennamites. Patterson's men confiscated the property of more than 500 men, women, and children, who "were compelled to march on foot eighty miles through a wilderness unsettled country" to settlements along the Delaware River.[83]

By June 1784, Patterson's forces had cleared Wyoming of Connecticut settlers. John Dickinson, president of the Supreme Executive Council of Pennsylvania, feared the escalating civil unrest at Wyoming.[84] In late May, Dickinson, troubled by the renewed violence executed by Patterson's Pennamite followers, sought an equitable end to the Wyoming controversy. In a spirit of compromise and conciliation, Dickinson ordered the Pennsylvania Supreme Court to investigate the ongoing violence against the Connecticut settlers at Wyoming by Pennsylvania claimants. The Court was unsympathetic to the rampant vigilantism instigated by Patterson and brought indictments of riot against Patterson and forty-five other Pennamites.[85] By the end of November, with the Pennsylvania militia ordered back to Philadelphia, the Connecticut Yankees returned to the valley and settled down to an uneasy truce with the Pennsylvania authorities.[86] In August 1786, Timothy Pickering, noted Revolutionary war veteran and wealthy Massachusetts entrepreneur, traveled to Wyoming to survey some land he had purchased with a group of speculators. He found the culture of the Connecticut people impoverished, "ordinary," and of "the most slovenly kind." The settlers' dwellings were "wretched beyond description"; children and entire families went about ragged and dirty. "Indeed," he wrote, "I did not imagine such general apparent wretchedness could be found in the United States."[87]

The Wyoming controversy between Connecticut and Pennsylvania claimants over soil rights lingered on into the nineteenth century. The Confirming Act of 1787 sanctioned the soil rights of Connecticut claimants settled at Wyoming before the Trenton decree; the Compromise Act of 1799 offered Pennsylvania claimants compensation in lands in Luzerne County; finally, the Act of 1807 permitted Connecticut claimants to receive soil rights regardless of the Trenton decree.[88] The half-century dispute over ownership of the rich bottomlands of the Wyoming Valley frontier finally came to an end.

What was the fate of the Iroquois at the close of the Revolutionary War? During the eighteenth century, the colonies of Pennsylvania, New York, and Connecticut recognized the Iroquois League as the legitimate landlord of the Wyoming Valley through their official policies and treaty protocols. The Six Nations Confederation, of course, sold the Wyoming lands to Pennsylvania at Fort Stanwix in 1768 in order to keep the ever-encroaching Anglo-Americans away from its southern door. At the end of the Revolutionary War, the broken Confederation found itself stripped of its former geopolitical power. The Treaty of Paris in 1783 ended the war but made no provisions for the Indians. The Treaty of Fort Stanwix on October 22, 1784, proved disastrous for the Seneca, the Cayuga, the Onondaga, and the Mohawk. Under the harsh terms of the treaty, these people ceded their lands as rights of conquest to the United States. The nations were forced to abandon all claims to Ohio lands, and the Seneca lost their fertile lands in western New York and Pennsylvania. The Confederation later rejected the treaty. In future treaties the Iroquois were defrauded of their best lands and dispersed to a few small reservations in the United States and Canada. Indian society collapsed amid the growth of this alien reservation culture.[89]

8

The Upper Juniata Valley

Tim H. Blessing

For the first quarter-century of settlement, those who inhabited the Juniata Valley lived beyond the reach of sovereign authority, but ever since they have lived beyond the limits of historical scholarship. It is a rare history of Pennsylvania that does more than glance at the seven counties—Bedford, Blair, Fulton, Huntingdon, Juniata, Mifflin, and Perry—that the Juniata River drains. In some ways this lack of attention seems peculiar, for the history of the region has been anything but unremarkable. The valley, which makes up 10 percent of the land area of Pennsylvania, provides a natural corridor between the Susquehanna and the Delaware Valley and the Ohio Basin (see Map 1). In the early years, Indians used the Juniata Valley as a military highway to strike at more settled parts of Pennsylvania, and squatters used it as a pathway to pass beyond the boundaries of the law. The Germans and the Scots-Irish found it a convenient route for passing beyond the gaze of British and American authorities. Sectarians hid in its nooks and crannies. During the nineteenth century, the valley became, first, a key segment of most highways crossing the state, then the centerpiece of the Pennsylvania Mainline Canal system, and later the route through which the Pennsylvania Railroad ran its trunkline, and the location at which the railroad placed its headquarters, shops, and yards.

Yet the Juniata Valley is a lacuna in the history of Pennsylvania. Unlike the northern and lower Susquehanna Valley, the Delaware Valley, and the Ohio Basin, there are few instances in which this Appalachian hinterland has been studied in and of itself. It would be fair to say that at present we know more about the Frankish Kingdom of Clovis than we know about any historical period of the Juniata Valley. Some of the valley's history does appear incidentally in descriptions of other topics—such as the transportation history mentioned above—but few who live outside the valley have even heard of the different fort systems that once controlled access to the watershed, the tangled web of railroads that dominated the region, or the complex of socioeconomic groups that live in

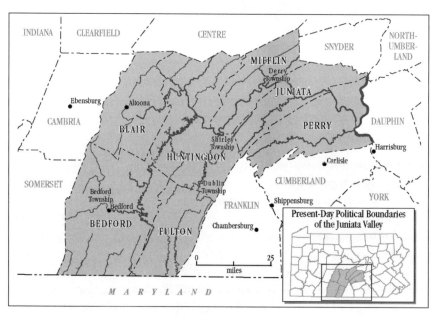

Present-Day Political Boundaries of the Juniata Valley

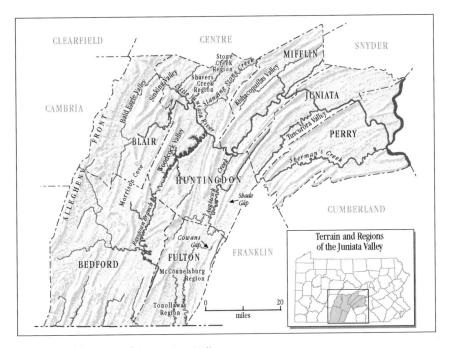

Terrain and Regions of the Juniata Valley

the valley. In part, this ignorance has occurred because the inhabitants of the Juniata Valley have effectively removed themselves from the sociopolitical development believed to be characteristic of Pennsylvania. As a result, the valley has merged into the mass of Pennsylvania history—the mass exemplified by those whose voices have been heard and recorded mainly within their regions, their locales, and their families.[1]

This chapter penetrates part of the why and wherefore of the Juniata Valley's retreat into itself—in this instance, the Revolutionary period of the upper valley (the modern counties of Bedford, Blair, Fulton, and Huntingdon). During this period, a movement toward an entrenched and defensive localism was solidified, confirming traditions of autonomy, resistance to outside authority, self-defense, and resilience that dated back to the 1740s and the earliest Juniata settlements. Indeed, the first Juniata settlements rested on defiance of outside authority, existing as exemplars of "squatter" settlements and "squatter sovereignty."

These settlers established their own communities, and maintained their own authority, for at least a decade before the Penns officially purchased the region from the Iroquois.[2] These settlers did not move into a region in which the Iroquois had only nominal interest, but rather into a region over which the Six Nations sought to maintain control and where active European settlement could be accomplished only by defying them. Moreover, the first white settlers antagonized not only the Iroquois but also their own government, as the colony of Pennsylvania openly sided with the Iroquois' claim to the region. Once the settlers moved in, they refused to leave, and the Iroquois could not get them out without open warfare. This squatter intransigence caused the Six Nations to appeal to the Pennsylvania government. The colony's leaders then determined to follow a course that lacked subtlety, understanding, or foresight, and this deepened and embittered the division between the Juniata Valley and the rest of Pennsylvania.

In the summer of 1750, the provincial secretary, Richard Peters, led a body of militia and sheriffs from more eastern counties to remove the valley's European settlers by force. His army evicted them, burned their cabins, and laid waste to their fields, leaving behind mostly only memories for later generations. One group passed through Cowan's Gap, near the present-day town of Burnt Cabins (a name that memorializes the actions of Peters's men) and then divided into two and perhaps three small bands. One group moved south, past what is now the Fulton County seat of McConnellsburg (incidentally burning out McConnell himself), and then probably down the Tonoloway Creek toward the Maryland border. Another band moved north, most likely passing through southern Huntingdon County before turning eastward and proceeding up the Tuscarora Valley toward the main branch of the Juniata River. A third band may have gone farther west, reaching the Raystown River, east of the present-day town of Bedford. By the time they returned home, Peters's men had destroyed settlements in three of the four counties that presently comprise the Upper Juniata Valley.[3]

Shortly after the Peters invasion, the Penns acquired title to the Juniata Valley from the Iroquois, and the Europeans resettled the area, this time with the approval of the colonial government. Unfortunately, the Iroquois had signed away lands belonging to the Delaware (over whom they had only nominal control), the Shawnee, and the Wyandot (over whom they had virtually no control), and the Seneca (who belonged to the Iroquois, but whom the other nations had not seen fit to consult before the purchase).[4] The result was catastrophic for settlers, who had returned to a region that the Pennsylvania government had declared secured. The size of the Indian columns that struck in the fall of 1754 cannot be determined, but the attacks emptied the valley as though the region had been a potato sack from which the bottom had been suddenly ripped.[5]

In 1758, Pennsylvania managed to negotiate a peace that by authorizing their control over the regions directly to its north and west left the Iroquois looming over the Juniata Valley. This settlement, negotiated in a full and impressive conference at Easton, restored a paper peace to the region but left the borders of the valley open to attack should something go wrong.

In 1763, Pontiac's rebellion broke over the Juniata Valley. The exact dimensions of the disaster to the white settlers cannot be measured. The regions south of the valley, particularly around Shippensburg and Carlisle, were turned into refugee camps. For a third time, the valley was emptied of white settlers. The evidence does suggest that Pontiac's Rebellion struck with even greater ferocity than the earlier attacks of the mid-1750s, and that the attacks continued long after the rebellion had been broken near Detroit and Pittsburgh.[6] After 1764, a nominal peace was achieved and the Juniata region once again began to fill with settlers.[7]

These early settlements have traditionally been assigned primarily to the Scots-Irish, followed by Germans and second- or third-generation Anglo-Americans, followed by several waves, after the Revolution, of Anabaptist Germans.[8] This view is not seriously wrong, but an examination of the 5,832 families, single males, and "inmates" enrolled on the tax lists of 1776, 1779, and 1783 suggests a more diverse mixture.[9] The ethnic backgrounds of 53 percent of the settlers on the tax lists could be readily identified.[10] The largest bloc of settlers was English, and by wide margins in most places. The next most numerous group, making up more than 25 percent of the populace, was the Scots-Irish. Contrary to popular belief, however, it appears that they remained behind the cutting edge of the settlement and the fighting edge of the frontier. The more exposed regions of the valley held a disproportionate number of German families, with 30 or more percent of the ascertainable families or individuals on the western borders of the upper valley and more than 40 percent on the northern borders of the valley being of identifiable German origin. In less-exposed regions, the Germans were irregularly distributed; in the older, more settled regions, in particular, the Germans often made up less than 10 percent of the populace. In some of the older townships, clusters of settlers originating in the

Northumbria, York, and Strathclyde regions of England and Scotland are relatively easy to identify on the tax records, but it is difficult to determine whether they constituted a separate ethnic/cultural group.

Given these settlement patterns, it is unlikely that the tenacity of the valley's defense can be attributed to "Scots-Irish" bellicosity. Nor did German pacifism hinder the valley's defenses, because only a few of the upper valley's Germans seem to have been pacific. Indeed, German and English families led the defense of the embattled northwest corner of the valley. Ethnicity, settlement patterns, and their impact on the life of the Juniata Valley need to be explored at much greater depth than is possible in this chapter. It may well be that, by relying too much on impressionistic literary sources, historians have overestimated the importance of the Scots-Irish on the frontier, turned too many Germans into pacifists, and failed to appreciate the diversity and importance of the English who lived on the frontier.

It is also not clear whether those in the Juniata Valley, at first, saw the Revolution as being different from earlier wars. The valley's population had recovered only slowly from the first three wars, and it had had little involvement with most events of the pre-Revolutionary period. When the British issued the Proclamation of 1763, the Juniata Valley was still shuddering under the Indian breakthroughs of 1763. The upper valley had only begun to be resettled at the time of the Stamp and Townshend Act crises of the mid-1760s.[11] It seems likely that, in the latter stages of the crisis, most settlers would have simply been trying to establish themselves. They had no time for concerns many mountains, and many more unbridged streams, away; and there is little evidence that the general population had became exercised over British revisions of colonial policy.

Once the Revolution was under way, the majority of the population supported the rebel side if doing so helped local interests. This may appear to be a faint bond with the Revolution, but it is not. The people of the Upper Juniata did not have to support the rebel side at all; some worked out accommodations with Britain and its Indian allies. A number of residents actively joined Indian-attacking columns against local rebels. Their names have not generally been preserved, but there is evidence that "loyalist" populations did exist, with their centers in the more recently settled regions.[12] Nevertheless, the imperial crisis did find the upper valley and its leaders siding with home rule over accommodation. A few inhabitants of the Upper Juniata participated in the various extralegal committees that formed in Philadelphia in 1773 and after.[13] As will be discussed below, most Juniata Valley inhabitants did support, and vote repeatedly for, leaders who had records of favoring the Revolution. The residents persecuted those who did not support the rebellion, and at one point they raised their own army and launched their own attack on a loyalist/Indian center in the Allegheny Valley.[14] Such support, while certainly not smacking of a great commitment to the rebel side, does indicate that, all things being equal, the majority preferred those fighting for independence to the British.

Nevertheless, the relationship may well have been somewhat less a matter of commitment than of convenience. What evidence exists indicates little enthusiasm for *authorities* outside the local region, but reveals a perception of the Revolution as a fight for local autonomy. For instance, after less than a year of revolution, the upper valley's representatives withdrew from Pennsylvania government in 1777, publishing an appeal against what they clearly felt had been dictatorial actions on the part of the eastern revolutionaries, who dominated the Assembly, and holding that the popular sovereignty demanded by their own constituents was not being upheld. "As the Representatives of this county [Bedford] have declined sitting in the House of Assembly, you have a right to know the reasons that induced them to take that step. They think themselves responsible to you, *and to you only* [emphasis added], for this part of their conduct."[15]

The Bedford delegation, which represented the Upper Juniata Valley, stated in their appeal that the provisions that kept the 1776 Pennsylvania constitution from being amended for seven years (found in Section 47) were directly opposed to the idea of rule by the people and that hence they could not support the constitution as written. They also refused to take part in a government that had excluded from the polls most of the people of Pennsylvania by a test oath that required a promise to uphold a constitution that could not be amended; "those members who now sit, and assume to themselves the powers of the Assembly, are not the representatives of the people," having been chosen by a small number while the great majority of voters had been excluded by "an arbitrary oath."[16] They noted, moreover, that, while in Section 40 of the constitution all members of the Assembly were required to swear not to "directly or indirectly do any act or thing prejudicial to the constitution," some members of the Assembly had taken the oath and some had not. Clearly some assemblymen would obey and some would not; thus, no one had any idea which actions would be considered legitimate and which would not. The departing representatives then concluded their note, attributing devotion to popular sovereignty as the motive for leaving: "As we from the manner of our election, were to consider ourselves as under express instructions, to alter and amend when necessary, we could not justify ourselves to you, if we had sat upon a different principle . . . [except in] the last necessity."[17]

After that withdrawal and a reapportionment in 1779 (which cut the region's representation by two-thirds), the area's representatives made only occasional wartime appearances in the Assembly. They seem to have regarded the Pennsylvania government as a distant and rather undependable ally in a developing crisis. Once again, the settlers in the valley and the Indians had locked together in furious combat.

The Military Background and Juniata Valley Localism

The attackers in this fourth round of settler-Indian conflict (counting the Peters expedition, the French and Indian War, and Pontiac's Rebellion) apparently came from the west. The peak period of the fighting (1779–82) occurred after the Sullivan expedition's attack on the Iroquois to the North. During this time, when the residents tried to mount a counterattack, their forces marched over the mountains westward, toward the Indian town of Kittanning.[18] Moreover, when loyalists fled the valley, they fled to the west,[19] so it seems likely that the nations maintaining the attack on the upper valley were the Shawnee and Delaware.[20] Although Kittanning did act as a meeting point for the British and Indians, no references yet uncovered indicate the presence of British soldiers or leaders of any rank in the valley.

Regardless of the source of the attacks, and without intending to do so, the inhabitants of the Juniata Valley found themselves forming the wall that Indians had to cross in order to reach the more settled regions of Pennsylvania. The people of the Juniata thus yielded invaluable, if inadvertent, service to the more settled, if inattentive, regions of Pennsylvania. The upper valley's self-reliant system of defenses and its settlers' many years of frontier experience allowed the Juniata Valley to resist effectively. It never crumpled completely, and native offensives that could have imperiled more settled regions, such as the Lower Susquehanna heartland, never penetrated beyond the upper valley. The state of Pennsylvania and the U.S. Congress rewarded the valleyites by removing troops stationed there for regions that were not defending themselves as well—an understandable military decision, but one that residents remembered with bitterness decades later.[21]

Left to themselves, Juniata residents turned their hands to self-defense and proved that the harsh schooling of the previous wars had not been forgotten. In particular, they built a series of fortifications that fragmented Indian forces before they could sweep south and east. The region's defenses were based on a shield of forts and blockades that began at the western end of the valley and curved away into the northern extremes.[22] These standing defenses started with a small private blockade—Fort Martin—ten miles east of Bedford. Fort Martin blocked the approach to the Raystown Branch of the Juniata Valley, closing off the easiest approach to the central valley while sitting astride the best path into what is now Fulton County. John Piper, one of the most important of the upper valley's Revolutionary leaders, built another fort somewhat to the north of Fort Martin and astride Yellow Britches Creek—another access point to the Raystown Branch of the Juniata Valley.

Between Yellow Britches Creek and the northwest corner of the Upper Juniata Valley lay a broad valley now known as Morrison's Cove.[23] The cove offered a series of access points to much of the Juniata Valley, and controlling it was essential to holding the upper valley. The permanent loss of Morrison's Cove, on the other hand, would have caused the abandonment of the Bedford region and what is now Blair County, Fulton County, and the northern section of modern-day Huntingdon County. The northern entrance to this valley was guarded by a private stockade, Fort Lowery, while the western entrance and the approach to another entrance to the central Juniata Valley, the Frankstown Branch of the Juniata, was guarded by Fort Fetter, a fort apparently established by the Hollidays, one of the larger families of the region. This fort had the dubious distinction of being located between a major Indian trail, the accesses to Morrison's Cove, and the headwaters of the Frankstown Branch. Slightly above Fort Fetter, near where the Frankstown Valley and the northernmost approach to the Juniata Valley (Bald Eagle Valley) met Morrison's Cove, lay Holliday's Fort. This fort formed the northwest apex of the valley's stockade shield and, indicative of the pressures that built up on the northwest corner, Holliday's Fort had to be abandoned in 1779 under Indian attack.

To the east of Holliday's Fort, and south of the Bald Eagle Valley, Fort Roberdeau blocked the northern approaches to the Juniata Valley. Fort Roberdeau was the sole fort in the valley built with government funds; the Continental Congress ordered its construction at a site behind the first row of mountains south of the Bald Eagle Valley. The concern of the Congress, however, was to secure a quantity of minable lead near the Bald Eagle Valley, not to protect the settlers of the Juniata. By good fortune, though, Daniel Roberdeau, the officer-in-charge, had placed his stockade near the top of a valley, Sinking Valley, which guarded the confluence of the Frankstown Branch and the Little Juniata. Their juncture creates the main branch of the Juniata and marks the point where the northern plains of the central valley of the Juniata begin.[24] Roberdeau's Fort, for a while, blocked access to this Juniata Valley heartland. Near Fort Roberdeau, settlers erected another private stockade, Fort Roller, to guard other entrances to Sinking Valley and to provide one more rallying point for settlers in the northwest corner. Fort Roller seems to have been still in use when Congress abandoned Fort Roberdeau a year after its opening.[25]

Fort Roller's and Fort Roberdeau's positions were very close to the edge of the Euro-American/Indian boundary. The workers at Fort Roberdeau's mines were driven off by Indian attacks. Fort Roller was heavily used by the locals, and the abandoned buildings of Roberdeau were taken over by the settlers of Sinking Valley and the Bald Eagle Valley and turned into one more base for private operations.[26] Neither site could be held long, however. In short, the heavy use of Fort Roller, the evacuation of Forts Holliday and Roberdeau, and the thinning of population in that region indicates that the pressure on the northern border of the Juniata Valley had approached the limits of toleration by 1779. With the abandonment of this northern line, the fighting moved south onto the plains of the Upper Juniata.

As these forts were abandoned, the settlers were forced to build six more private strongholds to block access across these plains. This line of defense approached Fort Fetter near the top of Morrison's Cove, thereby linking this interior northern line of forts to the western line. Fort Hartslog was closest geographically to Morrison's Cove and protected the western approach to the central valley. McCormick's Fort, Anderson's Fort, Fort Lytle, and Crum's Fort boxed in the confluence of the Frankstown Branch and the Little Juniata below that confluence. McAlevy's Fort anchored the eastern approach to the central region. Potter's Fort, in what is now Centre County, although technically not in the Juniata Valley, protected both the middle section of the Juniata Valley[27] and the northeastern accesses to the upper valley.

Spread across what is now four counties, these lines of stockades could not offer perfect protection. Nor does it seem likely that their construction was coordinated. Most seem to have been built in ad hoc fashion in response to the exigencies of the moment. Nevertheless, the mere erection of so many strongpoints through private resources suggests a desperate situation. Certainly life near Fort Hartslog or Potter's Fort could not have been secure with Indian raids occasionally penetrating between the forts.[28]

Nevertheless, the lines of forts apparently furnished sufficient security to allow settlers to hang on, if just barely and under severe conditions. Most of present-day Blair County seems to have been severely contested, and its northwest corner was lost. Western Bedford County was raided repeatedly. White possession of what is now northern Huntingdon County had slipped away by 1780 with the abandonment of Roller's Fort and Fort Roberdeau.[29] Moreover, the de facto boundaries between Indian and Euro-American control apparently remained in a state of flux. In the Bedford County commissioners' minutes of 1780 is a brief indication that tax returns could not be obtained in many areas: "in some townships no assessment has been made since the Revolution began, . . . the frontier townships being some of them altogether depopulated & others mostly so & that on account of the present distressed situation of the County by the Indians, it is impossible to procure any return from them."[30]

In another instance, George Ashman, a militia lieutenant reporting on a defeat near Holliday's Fort, wrote: "This country . . . is in a Deplorable sittuation. A number of Familys are flying away daily ever since the late damage was dun, I can assure Youre Excellency that if Immediate assistance is not sent to this County that the whole of the frontiere inhabitants will move of in a few days. . . . I shall move my family to Maryland in a few days, as I am convinc'd that not any one settlement is able to make any stand against such Numbers of the Enemy."[31]

In addition, letters from the leaders in the valley are replete with anguished appeals to the authorities to send help, any help. Little was offered.[32] Ashman's letter noted that the militia of Cumberland County (the lower Juniata Valley) had no orders to move to the assistance of the Juniata frontier. In another instance, eastern commanders sent a detachment of troops to Huntingdon (called Standing Stone) near the center of the valley. They seemed to have hoped to send them on through the western part of the Juniata region, and then either westward or north over the Allegheny front. This move would have relieved considerable pressure on the beleaguered northwest flank of the valley. The powers-that-were, however, suddenly ordered the troops eastward to protect other Pennsylvanians from other Indians, a move that certainly suggests that the valley was not uppermost in the minds of those in charge.[33] Nevertheless, despite fluid boundaries and the fact that the settlers were often pushed to despair and desperation, the Juniata Valley's people held off war parties at the very edge of the region's northern plains.

Although this stopped the descent of attackers into the more populated regions of the state, the valleyites probably did not fight and die near their forts for any such altruistic reasons. In fact, they were acutely and angrily aware that other regions of the state obtained more help than they did. For instance, Thomas Urie, a member of the Executive Council and a resident of Bedford County, received the following letter from George Woods, a constituent and former representative:

> Dear Sir, . . . Our poor, Starving Contery, when they have Got Something on the Ground for Gethering, Dare not Go out to Save it. Our County Seems to be pointed for Distruction; every other frontier Settlement has Some Notice taken of them & assistance Sint them; in the name of wonder, if you are a member of Council for our County, will you never Get us taken Notice of or Git us a share of Relefe according to the rest of our Contery? . . . I am Certain you have a Gentleman [Joseph Reed] now at the head of your Board that would not Suffer us to be used in the mannor Did he but Knaw it. . . .[34]

The Roots of Resistance

Despite Lieutenant Ashman's remarks about moving his family, the recorded despair of the Bedford commissioners, and the anger of those such as George Woods, the majority of those in the valley simply stayed. While military help flowed to the east of the region and to the west, the people who lived in the valley took care of their own defenses. While admitting that the valley's soil is excellent, the water plentiful, and the vistas often pleasing, economics or aesthetics do not explain why the valleyites stood firm. The peak years for Indian attacks in the valley, 1779–82, forced some settlers out of the more exposed border regions,[35] but only the northwest corner lost more than half its settlers to attack or flight. In some areas, population retention neared 70 percent for the entire 1776–83 period.[36] Across the twelve townships that constituted the valley's northern and western borders, population retention exceeded 65 percent between 1776 and 1779, and 61 percent between 1779 and 1783.[37] When compared with the plight of the regions surrounding it, the Juniata Valley's resistance stands out. The county seat of Westmoreland County (immediately to the west of the Juniata) was burned to the ground, and the county largely emptied of whites. The West Branch Valley (immediately to the north of the Juniata) lost virtually all its settlers down to and past its junction with the main branch of the Susquehanna. The North Branch and Wyoming Valleys (to the northeast of the Juniata) were turned into smoldering masses of ruined lands, complete with massacres and mass flights.[38]

That the people of the Juniata Valley, depending almost entirely on their own resources, held on in the face of seven years of raids and warfare suggests that the culture of localism was the means of survival, not just a refusal to yield sovereignty. Certainly survival was not a matter of inspired resistance. If the despair of the oral histories and the official reports are representative, the morale of the people could scarcely have been lower.[39]

Instead, the stubborn resistance is best explained by reasons found in the oral traditions of the valley and in the history recorded by local historians. It sprang, at least in part, from cultural inheritance. The Scots-Irish and the Germans, so the stories go, came to be known for their resolute refusals to retreat from positions, whether theological, geographical, or political. The Scots-Irish, in particular, became famed within the valley for the pursuit of obduracy through other means—up to and into mass violence. In fact, as late as 1791, a successful armed rebellion against the Pennsylvania authorities was carried out by a Scots-Irish population living near Lewistown in the Lower Juniata Valley.[40] Yet an examination of the forts and those involved in the fighting indicates that residents with German and English surnames did not lag far behind the Scots-Irish in terms of mounting resolute defenses, and some Germans even appear to have been in front. For instance, Jacob Roller, a first- or second-generation German-American, and his family constructed one of the most exposed stockades in the valley and held on in it even after repeated attacks had forced the abandonment of nearby Fort Roberdeau. When the Rollers did finally evacuate, they moved less than ten miles, settling behind the second line of forts.[41] Much of the populace seems to have been predisposed toward self-initiated action and stern defense.

But this does not explain the efficacy of the defense. Stubbornness is one thing; effective stubbornness is something else. The settlers in the valley had become used to—maybe even preferred—operating without assistance or inter-ference from powers beyond themselves, a faculty for independent operation which had been honed by their experiences. Certainly, the townships (Bedford, Dublin,[42] and Huntingdon[43]) that had the greatest retention rates were those that had housed major forts in the years before the Revolution. These forts were no longer there, but they had earlier formed the anchors around which the populations of the valley swung. Since, all these forts had either fallen or been abandoned before the Revolution, however, there was no advantage in staying near their sites. But even without military structures, these original population centers became rallying points during the Revolution, suggesting that the popu-lations that had resided in the Juniata Valley for the longest time had accepted military risk and decided to resist doggedly any forces that sought to move them. These settlers were certainly not unaware of the Juniata watershed's risks. The valley's experiences before and during the Revolution could have left no reason-ably sentient person oblivious of the dangers. The evidence of persistence found in the tax lists and the reports from the time of the French and Indian War and Pontiac's Rebellion suggests that the settlers came into the Juniata Valley aware of the potential military risks and determined never to give up their land regard-less of outside pressure. Indeed, even during the worst periods of Pontiac's Re-bellion, many Juniata residents slipped back into the valley to harvest their crops during the peak of the fighting.[44] Those who survived then slipped out, return-ing to their status as refugees but intending to hold on to the farms they had created.

After two generations of military turmoil, such settlers did not simply scurry away in the face of threatened slaughter and rapine. That fact, in turn, points to another matter. The Upper Juniata Valley was the only part of Pennsylvania that was so consistently raked by military onslaughts. The Westmoreland region, to be sure, was devastated during the Revolution. The Wyoming and North Branch Valleys endured the Pennamite Wars between 1769 and 1775 and then suffered disaster in 1778 when Indians and their British/American allies scoured the region. The West Branch Valley, likewise, emptied out in the "Big Run-away" of 1778, following an unbroken string of defeats, the odd massacre, and the collapse of the West Branch's fort system. But only the Juniata watershed faced two generations—nearly forty years—of warfare and raid and survived. Just as during Pontiac's Rebellion, fighting between Indian groups and the set-tlers during the Revolution went on long after the war had stopped in other places, with raids occurring as late as August 1782.[45]

The list of those who led the Upper Juniata Valley between 1776 and 1782 indicates that power accrued to those who deserved it, not necessarily to "the better sort." While most of the leaders were either upper-or upper-middle class, there is no evidence that class was a prerequisite. But willingness and ability to lead was. Authority centered around a very small body of people. Of 79 known office-holdings (excluding the local justices of the peace, but counting each assumption of office as an office-holding even if it was due to reelection), 10 individuals held 41 offices. Of the top officers, John Burd, Samuel Davidson, Bernard Dougherty, David Espy, Robert Galbraith, John Piper, and Thomas Urie occupied the posts that conveyed military, political, and security leadership. John Cessna, Abraham Miley, and John Wilt occupied the offices concerned primarily with local affairs.[46] In addition, field military command devolved on Piper and Ashman (after November 21, 1780) as county lieutenants, and on Urie, Richard Brown, Abraham Cable, Hugh Davidson, Edward Coombs, James Martin, William Holliday, Thomas Holliday, and Robert Culbertson.

After 1776, elected officials came under even greater control of the electorate.[47] Indeed, as the Assembly walkout of 1777 indicates, the region's representatives were quite sensitive to any attempt to infringe on the autonomy of the region's voters. Hence, it is reasonable to suppose that these ten people were the valley's most trusted leaders during the crises that accompanied the Revolution. Given that the Upper Juniata had not only Indian raids to worry about, in the midst of a Revolution, but also bodies of loyalists to deal with, a scattered agrarian populace to protect, and an economy that can best be described as based on very small subsistence landholdings (and, though the documentation is slight, most likely weakened even more by the fighting), these ten apparently enjoyed considerable trust from their constituents.[48]

Confirming the persistence of long-established patterns, at least nine of the ten civil officials came from precisely the regions that had been settled longest. (John Wilt's residence has not been located.) This, of course, could be an argument for an oligarchy or for the domination by more populous regions of less populous regions. From a geographic perspective, however, such explanations seem tenuous. Burd, who was consistently elected to the Assembly, came from a region separated from the main valley of the Upper Juniata by virtually impenetrable mountains. Robert Galbraith, prothonotary, commissioner in charge of the personal effects of Tories, and judge of Common Pleas, lived near Burd, but in a location that was even more inaccessible. Thomas Urie, executive counselor, sub-lieutenant, commissioner in charge of the personal effects of Tories, sheriff, and prothonotary, was a lawyer whose landholdings were minimal and who came from west of the town of Bedford. Piper was, at best, a medium landholder (300 acres) living isolated near the top of the Raystown Branch. Dougherty may have been the richest man in the county, living in what would become the borough of Bedford. Beyond a commitment to the ongoing struggles, there seem to be few common denominators among the leadership.[49]

Similarly, the field commanders came from across the county and from across the socioeconomic spectrum. Brown and the Hollidays were from the northern and western borders. Like Piper, Brown owned 300 acres of land in a rather isolated location, while the Hollidays lived on a number of land tracts, and hence in aggregate were large landholders, although in the most exposed region of the upper valley. Coombs, in Bethel Township, far south of the most exposed regions, owned 50 acres of land. James Martin, who lived not far from Piper, was, like Piper, a medium landholder of 300 acres, while Robert Culbertson came from the same area and owned 150 acres. Hugh Davidson does not appear in any Revolutionary era tax records.[50]

It would be premature to attempt further generalizations about the region's Revolutionary leadership. Most did not have previous military experience, only a few (Dougherty, Espy, Galbraith, and Burd) had much experience in politics, and only Dougherty and Burd had taken part in the wider spectrum of Pennsylvania politics. Common denominators may be unearthed by more intensive research into a broader time period. As of now, however, it can be stated only that the leaders were varied in background, committed to the valley's struggle for survival over the long haul, and competent enough to win the trust of a widely scattered people during a most difficult passage toward an uncertain end.

Conclusion

The people and leaders of the Upper Juniata were organized to conduct war over the long haul without outside help or guidance. The settlers came from backgrounds that encouraged self-initiative, resolute defiance, independent responsibility, and military preparedness. Settlement patterns indicate a close relationship between population stability and military tenacity. The Juniata Valley's refusal to abandon even the most exposed positions during the Revolution—and to hold on in most places with little outside support—indicates military experience and ability not often displayed in other parts of Pennsylvania.

The last point is particularly important. By 1783, the Euro-American settlers of the Juniata Valley had evolved in a direction that was unique for Pennsylvania: they had become a good deal less European and a good deal more something else—perhaps something new. The durability of the valley during this period points to the valley residents' long experience with self-reliance, which had provided them with skills that rendered state and national government superfluous and created a society based on local autonomy.

The Revolutionary period in the Upper Juniata Valley was thus characterized by the emergence of a people and a leadership that had moved more and more steadily toward a strong preference for localism and self-reliance. Poor and left to shift for itself, the region had built three lines of forts, fought off repeated attacks, and put in power a group of leaders marked by a dogged commitment to local preservation. Having little reason to take part in governments that did not appear to take much interest in them, the valleyites turned their back on "formal" government.

On the other hand, there does not appear to have been much cooperation, beyond the acceptance of a few common leaders, within the upper valley itself. The fort systems were built with little coordination between areas. Accounts of the raids show that, with a few exceptions, each locality simply fought on its own, using as militia whoever could make it to the scene or the fort in time. Coordinated undertakings such as raiding parties and patrols were only occasionally carried out.[51] Even the few leaders who could command wide respect found that governing such a far-flung and exposed area was too much for them. As Bernard Dougherty and Charles Cessna wrote in 1781:

> The Only place in our county fit for storing Provisions in, is the Town of Bedford which is, in every direction, a considerable Distance from such places as are capable of making the necessary Defence.
>
> It is 55 Miles distant for the Lead Mine Gap [near Fort Roberdeau], 40 from the Gap of Frankstown [near Holliday's Fort], and also 40 from Conemaugh.
>
> These are the Common passes thro' which the Enemy penetrates into the Country;
>
> And sending Provisions to all or any of these Posts, will be attended with Expences, and which might be intirely out of our power to defray.[52]

Thus, the Upper Juniata may have taken the trends toward localism to their logical extreme due to tradition, skill, preference, and sheer necessity.

The Revolutionary period in the Juniata Valley entrenched the prevailing localism. Indeed, the Revolution and its immediate aftermath was the defining event in Juniata history. First, the valleyites did win their war. In the three previous wars, the attack by the Peters Expedition, the Delaware War of 1754–58, and Pontiac's Rebellion, the settlers lost. Moreover, they lost while outside governments either acted with hostility toward them or appeared indifferent to their pain and suffering. During the Revolution, outside authorities were no more helpful, but this time the settlers held on in their forts and threw back their Indian attackers. Second, the Revolution gave the valley its voice—whether recorded in the despair of a George Ashman or the growing defiance of delegations from the valley. Third, a joint leadership committed, however paradoxically, to localism did appear. And fourth, the Revolutionary experience strengthened any localistic traditions that did exist before the war, particularly in the populations of the upper valley, which had survived the previous assaults.

By the end of the war, the people of the Juniata would accept the authority only of those who worked and fought with them. Local governance became the accepted norm of this section of Pennsylvania for at least another century. As would be proven later on, state leaders did not want to risk the bloodshed necessary to combat entrenched localism and had to accept the valley's preference for home rule in almost all things.[53] The wars with the Indians may not have been a series of glorious victories for the whites, but they did go a long way toward establishing and empowering groups that did not write Declarations, or Appeals, or Bills of this or that, and that certainly did not levy excise taxes on people they had never seen. So, in the sense of establishing what already was, the Revolution became a true revolution in the Juniata Valley, legitimizing local sovereignty in a way that handfuls of earnest pronouncements and balanced constitutions could not. The Juniata Valley would, after the Revolution, continue on its own way, at least until the Civil War period.

9

Soldiers and Violence on the Pennsylvania Frontier

Gregory T. Knouff

The popular conception of the American Revolutionary War is of the conflict on the eastern seaboard. Most Americans imagine the birth of the United States as a battle between Patriot, Tory, and British forces, but scant attention is paid to the bloody events that took place on the frontier during the period 1775–83. For those who measure historical significance by great battles and campaigns, the hinterland war was a small-scale affair. In the state of Pennsylvania, military conflict slowly became general on the frontier between the local Indian groups and European-American settlers beginning in 1777. The Iroquois (except the

I wish to thank Peter Messer, Jacquelyn Miller, John Murrin, Thomas Slaughter, and participants in the Philadelphia Center for Early American Studies seminar for helpful criticisms and suggestions on earlier drafts for this chapter.

Oneida and Tuscarora), most Ohioan Indians, and later the Delaware were among the most important foes of Pennsylvanians.[1]

Both sides waged mostly guerrilla war, and only a few large-scale campaigns were mounted. In July 1778, a large force of Iroquois and Tories destroyed the settlement at Wyoming. In the following year, General John Sullivan launched his major punitive expedition into Iroquoia, while Colonel Daniel Brodhead led a supporting force into Indian lands in western Pennsylvania. Both resulted in a few victories for the Continentals and in the widespread destruction of Indian resources and villages. The final consequence, however, was an increase in Indian hostility toward the Revolutionaries. Bitter guerrilla war dragged on indecisively through the Treaty of Paris in 1783. The last significant action of the Revolution on the frontier by Pennsylvania troops occurred in 1782, when Colonel William Crawford's militia was routed by Indian warriors while invading the Ohio country.[2]

The intensity of military violence on the Revolutionary Pennsylvania frontier was no small affair to its participants. For hinterland Pennsylvanians, the backcountry war was the seat of the most important hostilities. Because the frontier conflict was fought predominantly among the region's residents, the stakes and animosity ran high. In contrast to supposedly prevailing eighteenth-century European notions of "limited war," both sides prosecuted what may be called "total war." Fighting was waged against entire peoples rather than military forces only. Prisoners were often refused quarter, mutilated, and tortured. Noncombatants, property, and food sources were seen as valid targets. Guerrilla raids struck at the enemy's social infrastructure. Pennsylvania soldiers developed these modes of warfare in common with their Indian foes. Racism among European-American combatants, however, further escalated military violence. Revolutionaries believed Indians to be inferior beings, and this concept had important implications for the prosecution of the war on the Pennsylvania frontier.[3]

This chapter argues that Revolutionary soldiers dehumanized their Indian enemies to justify their own conduct and military roles. Regional and class-based forms of racism were reinforced during the Revolution by an unprecedented collision of military cultures in the state's hinterland. Armed conflict served to bolster the historical construction of race. The Revolutionary soldiers' views of Indians allowed them to commit acts that were considered unacceptable against European or European Americans. In short, the racism of Pennsylvanians brutalized total war.[4]

The focus is on the dialectic between soldiers' preconceptions of Indians and the course of the war. The principal subject is backcountry enlisted men, who constituted the majority of the Revolutionaries who fought in the western part of the Pennsylvania. Many times, officers (especially lower-grade ones) tended to identify with the outlooks of their men in terms of the frontier war. The perceptions and actions of these officers are incorporated into the examination of the backwoods rank and file in such cases. Indians' war aims and conduct are analyzed primarily in terms of their effect on soldiers' perceptions. The first part of the chapter examines the coming of war to the Revolutionary frontier, as well as prewar attitudes toward Indians. The second section explores how racism was reaffirmed during hostilities and how it affected actions of backwoods soldiers. The chapter concludes with a discussion of eastern soldiers and elite officers who also served on the frontier. This comparison suggests the importance of local and class differences in the Revolutionaries' construction of race and the practice of total war.

My aim is to recover the perspectives of common men who fought in the Revolution. I hope to place two groups of scholars in conversation with each other: historians of the early American frontier, and social historians concentrating on Revolutionary military service. Recent scholarship on the cultural and diplomatic history of the frontier has enriched our knowledge, particularly about the Indian perspective. Yet there is little work on the perceptions of lower and lower-middling sort hinterland European Americans, particularly in the late-eighteenth century. Other historians have begun to explain the meaning of fighting in the Revolution but have virtually ignored the impact of the frontier war. This work intends to help fill these voids and to probe larger questions about race, violence, and the world-views of common people in early America.[5]

From the earliest phases of English colonization of North America, land-hungry settlers fought with the continent's original inhabitants. Although a few Britons believed briefly at the outset of contact that Indians were a different but not necessarily menacing culture, the majority forged an image of all Indians as "hostile savages." This degradation of another culture that was deemed a separate "race" served to rationalize mistreatment of Indians and seizure of Indian lands. More ominous was the generic belief that all Indians were incapable of becoming "civilized" and were antagonistic toward Europeans, and that created an expectation of military violence. By the 1620s, barely two decades after the first permanent English settlement, the stage was set for brutal warfare by colonists against an enemy they had already dehumanized.[6]

War did indeed follow. Indians and European American settlers often came to blows after individual scrapes. These, in turn, developed into general wars as each side misunderstood the military motives of the other. Precontact northeastern Indians practiced warfare that revolved around the concept of revenge. When an Indian was killed, his kin sought revenge against the offending party. Such incidents sparked wars between Indian groups that were limited in aims and violence. Conflict was on a small scale, characterized by ambushes, and resulted in few casualties. Captives were typically taken to assuage the need for vengeance and were either killed, ceremonially tortured, or adopted into the injured kin group to replace the dead. In contrast, Europeans of the seventeenth century carried out wars for political and economic reasons. Fighting usually took the form of engagement between two large armies. Although Europeans nominally sought to restrict war to battles between military forces, they also believed that if one side violated the norms of combat, the slaughter of civilians might well follow. Towns that refused to surrender during sieges were likely to be destroyed along with their inhabitants.[7]

Indian and European military cultures, then, differed sharply. A new hybrid type of war was born when the two clashed. Typically, Indians engaged in small-scale ambushes in retribution for deeds committed by the English settlers, such as murders or the occupation of lands. The colonists reacted by sending large bodies of soldiers to meet the enemy in battle. When Indian warriors refused to engage such imposing forces on the field, colonial militias believed that they were freed of the constraints of limited war and could justifiably wreak havoc on Indian homes and civilians. In turn, Indians, shocked at the brutality of these Europeans who burned entire villages and killed noncombatants, responded in kind, levying guerrilla attacks on English settlers' property and on civilians. During the seventeenth and early eighteenth century, such exchanges between northeastern Indians and British colonists resulted in a pattern of military conflict that targeted both the enemy's social infrastructure and their warriors. There developed a tradition of total war on the frontier that was more violent than either of its Indian or European predecessors. Even worse, the brutality of the colonists was fueled by their racist view of Indian opponents as subhuman "savages."[8]

Fortuitously, Pennsylvania enjoyed an unusually peaceful frontier in the early period of its colonial history. Pennsylvania, established in the late seventeenth century, did not exist when the bloody frontier conflicts earlier in that century embroiled New Englanders, Virginians, and Carolinians. Pennsylvanians also avoided full-scale involvement in the imperial wars of the early eighteenth century. Although the Quaker party, colonists, and proprietors acquired Indian lands through purchase, negotiation, deception, and squatting, no major wars broke out with Indians until the 1750s. The memory of William Penn's benign Indian policies, coupled with the colony's lack of an organized militia, prevented disagreements among settlers and Indians from turning into full-scale military confrontations.[9]

Moreover, the dominant pacifist Quakers in the colony helped to avoid war. The Society of Friends interacted with Indians differently than did other British-Americans. Quakers sought to deal with Indians through nonviolent negotiation rather than military repression. In addition, they transcended much of the predominant racialist discourse of the day to view Indians as fellow human beings with as much right to inhabit Pennsylvania as the property-oriented European American settlers. Although the Friends' ideals of how to treat Indians were not always met in reality, they did offer an important alternative discourse for frontier diplomacy. Those who lived most of their lives in the early colony never experienced firsthand the horrors of an American war. So while Indians were acclimating themselves to European ways of war, residents in William Penn's colony continued to live in peace.[10]

The mid-eighteenth-century showdown over the Ohio Valley drew unprecedented numbers of French, British, Indian, and European-Americans into a bloody hinterland war. During the Seven Years' War, Pontiac's War, and Dunmore's War, significant Indian raids racked the Pennsylvania backcountry for the first time. The majority of northeastern Indians (with the notable exception of most Iroquois) sided with the French against the aggressively expansionist British-Americans. In retaliation for murders of Indians and squatting on Indian lands, warriors devastated vulnerable Pennsylvania backwoods settlements. Both sides attacked noncombatants and destroyed property. Pennsylvanians managed one raid of consequence, surprising the Delawares at Kittanning and burning their town. Still, inhabitants of the colony were not able to practice all-out total war with Indians in the pre-Revolutionary conflicts. The strategic interests of the British Empire mediated the aims of the colonists. The crown cultivated Indian alliances and provided the main forces to defeat the French and their Indian allies. Furthermore, contrary to the wishes of most frontier inhabitants, in 1763 British authorities proclaimed the Alleghenies as the western limit of colonial settlement in order to avoid future frontier wars.[11]

These colonial wars did, nonetheless, allow a significant portion of backcountry Pennsylvanians to express their hatred of all Indians through some form of violence. A scalp bounty resulted in many hinterland residents attacking any Indians regardless of their wartime sympathies. Although the motive for such actions was primarily economic, indiscriminate scalping also reaffirmed the image of all Indians as "hostile savages." Moreover, the massacre of peaceful Conestoga Indians by the Paxton Boys in 1763 further demonstrated that many frontier inhabitants viewed Indians as a single race of enemies. Angry over raids by hostile warriors in Pontiac's War, the Paxton Boys believed the death of any Indian would serve their vengeance. Such murders of nonbelligerent Indians received widespread support from other backcountry settlers who came to see Indians as inferior and innately hostile. Conversely, Indians in the region found that Pennsylvanians could be as violent in war as any colonists. Indians' desires for revenge grew through the late 1760s and early 1770s, and such sentiments would have monumental consequences in the next war. As historian Alden Vaughan asserts, "The Paxton Boys' principal legacy was 'open season' on the Indian, friend or foe, a circumstance the Indians surely recalled when they chose sides in the American Revolution."[12]

When war with Britain came in 1775, an uneasy calm prevailed at first on the Pennsylvania frontier. Both Continental and British authorities actively cultivated alliances, or at least assurances of neutrality from eastern Indians. In terms of grand strategy, Revolutionary leaders knew that they could ill afford to fight powerful groups of Indians on the frontier when they were contending already with the British army and Tories. Previous local conflicts on the Pennsylvania frontier, however, continued in the early parts of the war. Some settlers initiated hostilities with their hated Indian neighbors by murdering Indians who were friendly to the Revolutionaries. George Morgan and John Neville related: "Many persons among ourselves wish to promote a war with the savages, not considering the distresses of our country on the sea coast." Indeed, these frontiersmen cared little for what happened between the regular armies in the eastern theaters. They instead single-mindedly pursued the violent extermination of all Indians in their locale and refused to differentiate among them.[13]

The insatiable land hunger of European Americans also drew them into conflict with Indians. Squatting by farmers on Indian land was long a source of irritation to all Indians in the hinterland. Whites continued to occupy Indian territory even when war threatened. In April 1777, word filtered back from Pittsburgh that many Indians were preparing to respond to Pennsylvanians' violence and appropriation of land. One newspaper reported: "The Indians killed one Andrew Simpson. . . . They scalped Simpson and left a tomahawk war belt on him." The victim, apparently a squatter, also had a notice attached to his corpse telling whites to get off Indian land on the Ohio and Susquehanna Rivers. The document was a copy of the resolves of a meeting of Mohawks, Onondaga, Cayugas, Tuscarora, Mingos, and Chippewa. War was again about to break out on the Pennsylvania frontier.[14]

Slowly but surely, it became apparent to most eastern Indians that their own interests were at stake in the Revolution. They realized that many frontiersmen coveted their land and were violently disposed toward them, and that the British were the last European power they could play off against their American enemies. Over the course of the war, Pennsylvania Revolutionaries could number most Iroquois (except most Oneida and Tuscarora), Wyandots, Mingos, Chippewa, Ottawa, Shawnee, and Delaware among their important enemies. Widespread Indian raids began to shake the Pennsylvania frontier by summer 1777. Indians took vengeance on their enemies by utilizing guerrilla tactics in a total war strategy, as they had in earlier wars. They struck settlements in small parties, killed civilians and soldiers, destroyed crops, took prisoners, and terrorized backcountry whites. Pennsylvania soldiers responded in kind against any or all Indians they could find, as they had in the 1750s and 1760s. Unlike previous conflicts, responsibility for conducting the war fell principally on the backcountry inhabitants. No one was much interested in diplomacy with Indians or restricting the war aims of the frontiersmen, other than the few high-ranking Continental officers and officials in the region. The war on the frontier would be unprecedented for Pennsylvania in its scale and brutality. Pennsylvanians prosecuted a total war, fueled by racism, in which they sought the destruction of entire Indian societies.[15]

Frontier soldiers drew on a prevalent hinterland image of Indians as "hostile savages." Some enlisted men had lived in the region long enough to have personal reasons for animosity toward Indians. Robert Scott, a volunteer in the Revolutionary frontier war, noted that his anger toward the enemy stemmed from the Seven Years' War, in which "his father and family were banished by the Indians" from their Northampton County farm. Similarly, Archibald Loudon, a Cumberland County soldier, formed his opinion of Indians as a young man who witnessed how "after Braddock's defeat by the Indians, they [the Indians] began to murder the inhabitants of Sherman's Valley where we lived." Henry Dugan was still brooding during the Revolution that his "wife and three children were killed by Indians" during Dunmore's War. It is important to note that these soldiers did not attribute these hostile deeds to a particular group of hostile Indians, but rather to "the Indians" as a single entity. William Jones made all Indians responsible for a single past act of military violence. Jones declared that he fought in the Revolution because his "father was killed by the Indians when he was a boy, after which time, he became their settled enemy." These men revitalized a tradition as old as the colonial wars by stressing a racialized stereotype of Indians as single group of hostile, warlike "savages."[16]

Many new immigrants to the frontier missed these earlier tumults and based their biases against Indians on hearsay and literary sources. The mid-eighteenth century's great influx of settlers to Pennsylvania's backcountry from Europe and the eastern regions of British America provided large numbers of new farmers who had little desire to associate with Indian neighbors but who did covet their lands. Unlike earlier traders who had compelling economic reasons for interaction with Indians, the immigrants saw Indians primarily as inferior people who were in the way of settlement. They were also exposed to a literary genre that colored their expectations about how to view Indians. Immigrants knew about stories of Indian actions in previous wars, particularly captivity narratives; if they did not read them, they undoubtedly heard them. These tales stressed the supposed brutality of Indian war, especially the treatment of women and children. In addition, by the mid-eighteenth century the narratives of frontier war justified land appropriation by killing Indians if necessary. Such moral messages assuaged the consciences of land-hungry farmers by positing Indians as a hostile race that deserved no quarter. It is not surprising that the new backwoods immigrants also justified their wartime attitude toward Indians by focusing on the latter's acts in war. Frontier soldiers constantly described Indians as terrorizing the inhabitants, killing and scalping noncombatants, torturing prisoners, and attempting to gain control over the settlers' land.[17]

Such images had some basis in fact. Indians did pursue these total war tactics in the Revolution, although they were careful to target only communities of active Revolutionaries or trespassers. War parties aimed to force settlers out of a specific area or to demoralize them, but frontier inhabitants in general interpreted Indian war aims as the removal of all whites from the backwoods. By the spring of 1778, militia officer James Potter believed that "the Indians are determined to clear the two branches of the Susquehanna this moon." The Pennsylvania government noted with alarm the flight of its frontier residents and asked for Continental help against "an enemy which with a small number of men may depopulate a greater country in a few days than a large British army would in a whole campaign." Other reports of hostile Indians putting

Pennsylvanians to panic poured in from throughout the state's frontier. Some Northumberland County residents believed they would "be obliged to evacuate this frontier." In the same year, farmers in Bedford Country were "preparing for a flight" in the face of Indian attacks. These Pennsylvanians saw Indian war aims as focused on terrorizing the inhabitants, destroying their livelihoods, and forcing them from the region. Their understanding of Indian objectives allowed frontier soldiers to rationalize the parallel goal of removing all Indians from the region.[18]

Backcountry troops, of course, viewed warfare against civilians as unfair and brutal when committed by Indian warriors. That these attacks were often in response to the deeds of the Revolutionaries themselves was not mentioned. Troops preferred to portray Indian actions as unprovoked acts of savagery. Anger over the deaths of friends, family, and neighbors ran deep. William Elliott of the Bedford militia recalled how the Indians "frequently came down upon the defenseless settlers and on one occasion killed nine out of one family." Andrew Dougherty of Westmoreland County enlisted after an Indian raid on his home left his father and brother dead. Thomas Black was shocked by attacks against his civilian neighbors. Nicholas Lyberger was outraged when Indians "burnt Ulrick's Mill and killed all Ulrick's family" in his Bedford County neighborhood. These soldiers all spoke of Indian attacks as unmanly butchery of "defenseless" civilians. The backwoodsmen were also angry that the guerrillas refused to meet them on the battlefield following attacks on civilian communities. Although the Revolutionaries would never think to stay around to fight warriors after their own raids on Indian communities, they were quick to decry their enemies' like behavior.[19]

Frontier soldiers skillfully utilized these condemnations of Indians' acts to vindicate their own total war. Backwoodsmen firmly believed that offensive operations against Indian societies would win the war. Archibald Lochry, for example, asked the state government to let a Westmoreland County militia raid and destroy the towns and crops of hostile Indians. Lochry argued: "The enemy are almost constantly in our country killing and captivating the inhabitants. I see no way we can have of defending ourselves other than by offensive operations." Such "offensive operations" were directed not against the enemies' war parties but at their societies. Like Indian raids, Revolutionary forays into the Indians' lands were terror campaigns that attacked noncombatants and disrupted Indian economies. Pennsylvania soldiers hoped that such blows would destroy Indian communities and open up a new supply of land.[20]

Backcountry enlisted men were always willing to go on campaigns against the homes of hostile Indians. They saw these attacks as honorable, even brave. David White of Washington County "volunteered three different times to go to the Shawnee towns." Northumberland County soldier Joseph Keefer proudly recalled how his unit "had a skirmish with the Indians and [the Revolutionaries] burnt and destroyed their town." George Reem of the same county accompanied John Sullivan's 1779 Continental expedition into Iroquois country. He admitted to "destroying the cornfields and burning the Indian villages" and went on: "I was at the burning of Chemung, Newtown, Catherine's Town, Gennesse Castle, and three other small villages." Westmoreland ranger Jacob Rudolf "assisted in taking the Muncy towns and destroying the corn of the Indians." Another Westmorelander, James Beer, volunteered in a "horse company . . . for the purpose of discovering an Indian town." In the eyes of these men, raids against the enemy homeland were both valid expressions of revenge and necessary strategy against a depraved culture.[21]

Such raids inevitably involved killing Indian noncombatants. Even though they denounced such actions by Indians as evidence of their brutal behavior, backcountry troops commonly killed civilians. This double standard contributed to a vicious circle of violence. Many times, soldiers avenged the deaths of comrades, kin, and neighbors who were, in turn, victims of Indian vengeance. Killing Indian women and children was not shameful to those who considered the victims "savages" and undeserving of respect given to white civilians. Only regular officers from the east found such frontier actions remarkable. For example, during the infamous "Squaw Campaign" of 1778 into Indian lands, Westmoreland County militia shocked their own leader, Edward Hand, the Continental commander of the Western Department from Lancaster County. To his "great mortification," the men eagerly killed women and children. When the militia encountered "only one man with some women and children," Hand noted: "The men were so impetuous that I could not prevent their killing the man and one of the women. Another woman was taken and with difficulty saved." At another Indian settlement, Hand was again unable to dissuade his men from killing all the Indians that they found. The troops found "four women with a boy, of these, one woman only was saved." On the same campaign, Samuel Murphy recalled how "a small Indian boy . . . was discovered and killed and several claimed the honor." Murphy also recounted how a militiaman scalped an elderly Indian woman.[22]

In battle, as in raids, frontier soldiers used tactics similar to the Indian tactics they decried as unfair. Ambushing Indian warriors gave frontiersmen the satis-faction of defeating the masters of this skill. Utilizing hit-and-run tactics as effectively as their foes, the Revolutionaries demonstrated that they too learned how to move stealthily through the backcountry. They displayed no scruples against killing sleeping or unwary Indians and then retreating before more enemy warriors arrived. They knew that their opponents, given the chance, would do the same. William Campbell of Westmoreland County, for example, explained how his patrol "discovered a light, three of us went to see what it was and found four Indians encamped. We fell on them and killed them all without firing a shot, they being asleep." Similarly, another Westmoreland militiaman, John Hutson recalled how he and his comrades "espied the Indians kindling a fire . . . then retired . . . and stayed there until they . . . would be in their first sleep." Hutson's company planned to "surround the Indians and tomahawk them without giving any alarm." A militiaman used his gun, and Hutson la-mented that "one [Indian] made his escape." Such acts were seen by these men as evidence of their superior skills as woodsmen and mastery over those believed to be a "savage" but cunning opponent.[23]

Scalping was another facet of total war on the Revolutionary frontier used by backwoods soldiers to portray their opponents as inhuman. To Indians, scalps were war trophies that demonstrated that vengeance against a foe had been carried out. On the other hand, backcountry accounts from throughout the war regarded the practice, when used by Indians, as an atrocity that proved Indian "savagery." In October 1777, word reached Fort Pitt that Indian warriors "killed one Smith and daughter and tomahawked his son, a boy about six years old and, after scalping him, left him." An officer reported from the frontier region of Cumberland County in 1778: "The Indians continue to murder men, women, and children on our frontiers. On last Friday, Jacob Stanford and his wife were inhumanly killed and scalped and his son, a lad of ten or eleven years of age, is yet missing." In 1779, the *Pennsylvania Evening Post* reported: "Three children were . . . killed and scalped by the Indians." In Westmoreland County, there was a report that "two children at Palmer's Fort [were] . . . killed and scalped." Although Pennsylvania frontiersmen themselves had been scalping In-dians since the 1750s, these accounts galvanized the frontier population against the Indians' supposedly violent "nature."[24]

Revolutionary soldiers of the region thus saw their own scalping as necessary revenge against a subhuman enemy. Far from considering their own war prizes as atrocities, troops considered them just retribution. Frontiersmen used this double standard to vindicate their idea of their own cultural superiority. As historian James Axtell points out of the European-American frontier inhabitants: "Rather than admitting that by adopting [scalping] they had been 'reduced to savagery' or had deviated seriously from 'civilized' Christian standards, they projected their guilt onto the Indians by insisting (mythically) 'unprovoked' assaults of savages demanded a savage response."[25]

Although scalp bounties again provided some measure of economic motivation, scalping's primary function was vengeance. As in Indian societies, the hair of a vanquished foe showed the community that retribution had been achieved. Pennsylvania soldiers avidly sought the gratification of taking a significant number of scalps from the very people who invented the convention. In 1779, Daniel Brodhead "sent out one scalping party toward the Mingo towns and [was] preparing another." A Captain Brady was recommended for promotion following a skirmish in which he "brought in an . . . Indian's scalp." In 1781, a Northampton militia made up of "spirited volunteers" reacted to an Indian attack by tracking down the perpetrators and taking "one Indian scalp." Baron Gustavus "John Rose" Rosenthal, who accompanied the Westmoreland County militia on Crawford's Expedition, remembered that the troops took "two scalps" in one minor action.[26]

Like scalping, Indians' treatment of prisoners in the war offered more propaganda for soldiers to solidify their racism. The killing or torturing of helpless soldiers by Indians was portrayed as both barbaric and craven. Following the attack on Wyoming, Captain Alexander Patterson reported his horror that the Indians and Tories had spared few lives after the soldiers surrendered. He claimed that "the enemy had treated such as fell into their hands with the greatest cruelties and that upwards of two hundred had been scalped." Ezekiel Lewis, captured while on a militia expedition, noted that the "Indians killed a great number of said prisoners."[27]

According to historian James Axtell, backcountry troops, unlike Indians, had little interest in adopting captives or receiving material rewards for their exchange. They apparently rationalized their refusal to grant quarter by invoking similar Indian behavior and by suggesting that Indians were not worthy of such conventions of war. When Indians were taken prisoner following skirmishes, some Revolutionaries hoped that they would provide information about enemy military strength. But it was difficult to restrain frontier whites from exacting vengeance on any hostile Indian, even if he could give intelligence. Such was the case in June 1780, when Colonel Matthew Smith recommended moving an

Indian prisoner from a frontier jail in Sunbury to a more settled region in Lancaster County. He explained, "It appeared not to be safe to leave him at Sunbury. The people are so exasperated there w[ere] several attempts made to shoot him while confined."[28]

It was, however, the torture of captives that drew the loudest cries of Indian barbarity from frontier soldiers. In fact, in cases such as the Indian attack on Wyoming in 1778, Revolutionaries actually invented atrocity stories of Indian torture and mistreatment of captives that were repeated throughout the backcountry. Backwoodsmen wanted to believe such tales because they confirmed prewar beliefs about Indian depravity. Other stories of ritual tortures that actually did occur were disseminated among backcountry soldiery, minus accounts of the Indians' motives. Torture was explained not in terms of vengeance but rather as a horror story about the innate violence of Indians.

When Lieutenant Boyd fell into the hands of vengeful Iroquois during General John Sullivan's 1779 expedition, his comrades were undoubtedly appalled to hear from their commander that the Indians "whipped him in the most cruel manner, pulled out Mr. Boyd's nails, cut off his nose, plucked out one of his eyes, cut out his tongue, stabbed him with spears in sundry places, and inflicted other torture which decency will not permit me to mention." No one mentioned that Boyd was undoubtedly tormented to avenge the sufferings of Iroquois who had lost family or had villages burned by Sullivan's troops. Another infamous incident of torture, that of Colonel William Crawford in 1782, reinforced backcountry soldiers' image of a brutal and honorless foe. Dr. John Knight, a military surgeon on Crawford's expedition, recounted his commander's treatment at the hands of a group of Delawares. Knight explained that the colonel was stripped naked and that seventy shots of powder were fired at his body. Indians then cut off his ears, prodded him with burning sticks, and tossed hot embers at him. Knight then described how Crawford

continued in the extremities of pain for an hour and three quarters or two hours longer, as near as I can judge, when at last, being almost totally exhausted, he laid down on his belly; they then scalped him and repeatedly threw the scalp in my face, telling me "that was my great captain." An old squaw . . . got a board, took a parcel of coals and ashes and laid them on his back and head, after he had been scalped, he then raised himself upon his feet and began to walk around the post; they next put a burning stick to him as usual, but he seemed more insensible of pain than before.

The *Pennsylvania Packet* reported that, upon hearing of Crawford's fate, the western Pennsylvania militia were "greatly enraged and determined to have ample satisfaction." The frontier soldiers glossed over the fact that Crawford was tortured in retribution for the Revolutionaries' slaughter of peaceful Delawares at Gnadenhutten earlier in the same year. In fact, the Delaware chief, Wingenund, explained to Crawford before the torture that he might have lived had not his expedition included Major David Williamson, who led the slaughter at Gnadenhutten. Even though these Delaware were practicing ritual torture in revenge for a specific act, the story of Crawford's torture among the backcountry soldiery was propagated as an act of unprovoked and unspeakable violence.[29]

The frontier troops' construction of Indian "otherness" was integrally related to wartime violence. The war in the Revolutionary backcountry consolidated the image of Indians as a bloodthirsty race that was hostile to European Americans and that vindicated the patriots' own brutality. It is not surprising that frontier soldiers' accounts of Indian actions feature prominently the terms "savage" and "barbarities."John Struthers, a Washington County soldier, described his "pursuit of the savages who had committed . . . barbarities." Troops from the Wyoming region angrily related how "the savages . . . made incursions and, in a most barbarous and inhuman manner, killed numbers of our parents and friends." Sergeant Theobald Coontz of the Pennsylvania Rangers also described Indians as "the savages." Lorentz Holben served on the frontier "for the protection of the inhabitants of that newborn land against the savage Indians." Some soldiers openly described Indians as subhuman. John Dougherty and his comrades sought to locate the Indians' "haunts," and "deflect their intended cruelties in any way they could." Dougherty implied that because he considered his foe less than human it would be perfectly acceptable to utilize "cruelties" himself. John Daley described how he and Daniel Bean served together in Washington County "with parties that were hunting the Indians." William Moore recalled that his unit helped ensure that the Indians would "not again infest" the frontiers.[30]

Furthermore, in the eyes of the Revolutionaries, Indians did not kill their adversaries, but rather "murdered" or "massacred" them. Christian Acker of Northampton County fought Indians who were "murdering the inhabitants." Peter Wolf accused Indians of "murdering." In battle, he noted, they "slaughtered a number of our troops." John Miller guarded "the citizens against the cruelties of the Indians who occasionally visited and committed murders and depredations." John Dean fought to "save the lives of the defenseless inhabitants from the cruelty of the savages." John Elder, a volunteer Northumberland County ranger, recalled how at the "Massacre of Wyoming . . . Captains Boon and Dougherty and nearly the whole of their command were put to death." George Vanzant of Bedford County served to "prevent the savages from murdering and plundering the inhabitants on the frontiers." Similarly, Andrew Myers of Washington County condemned Indian "outrages on the frontier inhabitants." Lawrence Konkle of Westmoreland County recalled that Indians committed "many murders and depredations." Thomas Rees of Northumberland County decried the "great number of murders by the Indians." That Indians' killing of civilians and soldiers was regarded as murder by frontier troops is significant. During the eighteenth century, popular narratives of murder in America were changing in important ways. No longer was the perpetrator's culpability derived from the human condition of original sin. Murderers came to be seen as "something other than human," as violent creatures lacking morals. The ominous dubbing of Indians as murderers, even during time of war, underscored the frontier soldiers' belief that Indians were subhuman brutes preying on "defenseless" inhabitants.[31]

Although frontiersmen reinforced their view of Indians as "others" primarily through anger over military actions, an additional element was needed to fully articulate their racism. It is surprising that enlisted men from the backcountry did not mention Indians' skin color. In fact, the few times backcountry troops discussed complexions, it was those of European Americans—for example, John Foster recalled that Indians "massacred the whites." Adam Wolfe of Westmoreland County was a guard "between the Indians and whites during the holding of a treaty at Pittsburgh." John Dougherty remarked on how "the Indians were killing the white people wherever they could find them." Andrew Myers recalled that "the Indians . . . [were] determined not to yield to the white people." Complexion was a source of common identity for an ethnically diverse European American frontier population. Indians were not "red," "black," or "yellow" to these soldiers, but rather they themselves were all white. "Whiteness" was a physical means of identifying the shared European heritage of hinterland residents. Using skin color to define themselves, frontier soldiers could racially distinguish Indians simply as "not white." Even if Indians took on European cultural traits, they could never look like their European American neighbors.

For instance, at Gnadenhutten, militiamen interpreted European goods used by the Europeanized Delawares not as evidence of cultural similarity but as obtained by Indians through raids on whites. The soldiers declared that these were "things as were made use of by white people and not by Indians." Thus, an equation was formed between "whiteness" and "civilization" among backcountry troops.[32]

The importance of skin color to frontier soldiers is further suggested by their treatment of Tories in the backcountry. European American opponents of the Revolution were particularly reviled by their pro-Revolutionary neighbors. Alienated by disputes with rival groups of settlers, many whites joined Indians to fight their old neighbors. Especially in the press, these Tories were portrayed as vicious traitors, not only to their communities but also to their race. James Dunlop of Cumberland County, for example, reported that a number of local men "left their habitations and [are] supposed to be joined to the savages." In 1778, the *Pennsylvania Packet* reported that word had arrived from Carlisle that "33 Tories lately formed the horrid design of joining the savages in murdering and scalping their neighbors." Later in the same year, the paper reported that the Tory John Snow, "one of those who had transformed themselves into savages," had been captured in New York.[33]

Yet it is significant that Tories were treated like white men in the war. European Americans who fought the Revolutionaries, even in conjunction with Indians, were dealt with as civil criminals. They were considered traitors, but their whiteness (that is, their European heritage) made it possible for them to receive the kind of treatment not granted to Indians. When captured, Tories were typically imprisoned and tried. Abner Mundell and his fellow soldiers "caught upwards of 100 Tories and lodged them in the jails." Richard Gunsalus "arrested two of the Tories who w[ere] engaged with the Indians in committing aggressions[?] on the Americans." David Barr, who was out on "several scouting parties against the Indians and Tories, . . . succeeded in capturing Shelly and conveyed him to Carlisle and lodged him in the jail." Occasionally Tories were put to death. William Dougherty "took a number of Tories and handcuffed them and confined them. . . . When one White and Isaac Boser[?] were hanged by our party, this declarant cut them down before they were dead and saved their lives." Hanging was not a procedure that soldiers would have inflicted on Indians, who commonly met with a more grisly end.[34]

This universalization of Indians as "savage," nonwhite enemies had important consequences even for Indian groups who were neutral or allied with the Revolutionaries. Frontier enlisted men whose families and property were endangered by hostile raids hated Indians in general. They often did not care whether vengeance was obtained against the responsible parties. The desire to make war against all Indians echoed the Paxton Boys' attitudes in the 1760s and escalated to total war. Many backwoods Revolutionaries saw the removal of all Indians from the region as an attractive possible outcome of the war. For example, a Northumberland County resident called on the Continental Army to send troops to help the local militia "extirpate [the Indians] from the face of the earth." Jacob Leatherman recalled that he served as a soldier to "conquer the savages." Racism, nurtured in war, found its fullest expression in indiscriminate military violence against hostile, neutral, and friendly Indians.[35]

Because frontiersmen viewed Indians as innately hostile, nonbelligerent or allied Indians could be suspected as clandestine foes. If settlers were attacked by Senecas, they felt justified in seeking retribution against the Delaware because they assumed that all Indians constituted a race of brutal enemies. For example, Captain Samuel Brady of the Eighth Pennsylvania Regiment swore vengeance for the deaths of his family members on all Indians. He vowed never "to be at peace with the Indians of any tribe." The animosity of many backcountry troops toward Indians was so intense that it made Continental officers in the region uneasy. In 1777, Edward Hand remarked: "The people here [Fort Pitt] are well-disposed, savage-like, to murder a defenseless unsuspecting Indian." John Gibson informed Hand that one of their Delaware allies, White Eyes, was "in danger of being killed" following a hostile Indian raid. A frustrated Colonel Daniel Brodhead was unable to procure supplies for his Indian allies because "so violent are the prejudices against the Indians . . . [among] the people in the back counties." Among the men of the Eighth Pennsylvania Regiment (raised primarily in the state's frontier counties), a soldier "fired a gun at one of the friendly Delawares." In 1783, when the Treaty of Paris formally ended hostilities between the Americans and the British, General William Irvine lamented that some Indians were still fighting and went on to assert: "I presume this conduct will give force to a temper already pretty prevalent among the back settlers, never to make peace with the Indians; and, indeed, I am almost persuaded it will be next to impossible to insure peace with them till the whole of the western tribes are driven over the Mississippi and lakes, entirely beyond American lines."[36]

The slaughter of neutral and friendly Indians continued throughout the war. In particular, large groups of Delawares who remained sympathetic to the

United States suffered at the hands of their supposed allies. As early as 1777, after a hostile Indian attack killed a militiaman, Edward Hand was informed it was "not safe for the [friendly] Delaware to pass unless you send a party down to escort them up [to Fort Pitt to treat]." A few weeks later, Hand reiterated to the Delaware that "it would be dangerous for any Indians to come near this place [Fort Pitt] owing to the foolish conduct of the Mingos and Wyandots." In 1780, a group of pro-American Delawares under Colonel Daniel Brodhead's protection at Fort Pitt was threatened by a large party of Westmoreland militia who "attempted to destroy" them. Brodhead added: "I suppose that the women and children were to suffer an equal carnage with the men."[37]

Perhaps the most infamous example of the indiscriminate racism and total war fought by Pennsylvania frontier soldiers was the 1782 attack on the neutral Delawares of Gnadenhutten. In response to hostile raids, a group of Washington County militia sought vengeance against these pacifist Moravian Indians, who were Christians and lived like European American farmers. Nevertheless, the militia held these Delaware responsible for assisting enemy warriors despite pro-testations of neutrality and friendliness to the Revolutionaries. The troops as-serted their "just right to revenge." The missionary John Heckewelder explained that the militia put men, women, and children (who did not resist) to death by beating them with mallets and then "taking off their scalps." One witness watched in horror as "the blood began to run a stream." The victims' bodies were then burned. Heckewelder noted: "The militia having in those parts no further opportunity of killing innocent people and no stomach to engage with warriors, set off [for] home with their horses and plunder they had taken and afterwards falling upon the peaceable Indians on the north side of the Allegheny River opposite Pittsburgh, killed several of those."

Clearly these frontier militiamen sought the blood of any Indian to assuage their anger. One of the few soldiers who recognized that not all Indians were responsible for the blood shed by others, John Struthers, had the courage to refuse to participate in the Gnadenhutten expedition, "at the risk of my popular-ity as a soldier." His unwillingness to take part in the raid was enough to cast aspersions on his membership in the brotherhood of frontier military men.[38]

The tendency of backcountry soldiers to fight against all Indians exacerbated the horrors of total war. They transformed a conflict among various local groups into a war between races. By 1783, the Pennsylvania backcountry had a sizeable population that had reaffirmed the colonial-era hatred of Indians in their own Revolutionary War experiences. Their deeds would on some level become identified with the cause of the new nation, because backcountry soldiers saw themselves as "patriot" forces. The views and actions of frontier troops were, however, the product of their local origins and social status. Other Revolutionaries who served in the west acted on their own class and region-specific perceptions of Indians.

Few soldiers from the settled parts of the state served on the Pennsylvania frontier. Those who did either were part of Sullivan's 1779 expedition or served in brief militia tours. Unfortunately, they left few impressions of their Indian foes. Like their frontier brethren, they were exposed to the popular image of Indians as "hostile savages" through war stories and captivity narratives. During the Paxton Boys' march on Philadelphia to present their grievances and kill neutral Indians, many common people of southeastern Pennsylvania had sympathized with the frontiersmen. Easterners from the social strata from which enlisted men would be drawn in the Revolution apparently identified with the common backcountry view of Indians as a race of cruel enemies, and went westward with views of Indians comparable to their frontier counterparts.[39]

The wartime racism of eastern soldiers, like that of their frontier counterparts, consolidated their prewar beliefs with their new military role. Although charged with total war tasks (attacking Indian societies as well as their military forces), they were typically more familiar with European-style military actions. Many had previous experience in engagements against the British. They centered their condemnation of Indian inferiority around the warriors' failure to meet them in open battle. Because the easterners' communities were not being raided, they did not focus as exclusively as the frontiersmen on attacks against white civilians. Instead, they reinforced their racism by decrying the strange "unfairness" of Indian war. Abraham Eschelman saw Indians as cowardly foes who "generally retreated before us." Similarly, John Swisshelm of Cumberland County volunteered to fight the Indians but was disappointed to find that his foes, "after having committed many depredations," had fled. George Espy, a veteran of the battle of Princeton, lamented that on his frontier service that he "saw no Indians," and continued: "They were often about and we heard their screams[?] sometimes and they sometimes killed some of the inhabitants."[40]

Elite officers left far more records of their impressions of Indians than did eastern enlisted men. During the war, commanders exhibited a view of Indians that differed from both the eastern and backcountry rank and file. High-ranking officers in the militia and the regular army tended to come from more socially prominent backgrounds than their soldiers. Their wartime accounts provide insight into how the upper sort viewed Indians. Furthermore, most of the high-ranking Continental officers in the Pennsylvania backcountry were from the settled parts of the state. Their perceptions of Indians resulted from an intersection of regional and class backgrounds. High-ranking officers from the frontier regions, who typically were also educated social elites, usually identified with their eastern counterparts' views of Indians. Class outlooks tended to be stronger than regional ones among these men.[41]

In almost all cases, upper-grade officers believed the Indians to be an inferior and mindless enemy spurred on by British to fight. This sneering image of frontier opponents connoted that Indians were unable to prosecute war on their own accord. George Morgan, a frontier diplomat, believed that Indians would fight only if manipulated by whites. Early in the Revolution, he wrote to a British official and warned of military action "should the savages be induced to strike our frontier settlements." Colonel Edward Hand, the Lancaster Countian who commanded the Continental Western Department from Fort Pitt, also revealed that he believed the Indian attacks were actuated by Europeans. He informed Jasper Yeates: "You will see how busy the British are to engage the savages to depopulate the frontiers." In this early stage of the backcountry war, Hand could not believe that Indians had their own reasons for striking European American settlements. Colonel Daniel Brodhead, another Eastern Pennsylvanian who commanded the Continental Western Department, informed the Pennsylvania government: "The Mingoes are again prevailed on by English goods and address to disturb our repose." Similarly, the Reverend William Rogers, a chaplain with the Pennsylvania troops on Sullivan's expedition against the Iroquois, believed that the British had "influenced the savage tribes to kill and wretchedly torture to death, persons of each sex and of every age." Such views also reflected a more cosmopolitan and nationalistic elite outlook on the Revolution. High-ranking officers believed that the main British army was the most important enemy and that hostile Indians were merely the Crown's pawns. Colonel Brodhead said as much when he lamented what he believed to be the secondary importance of his frontier command. He wrote to General Anthony Wayne in the east: "Damn my fortune for leaving the Grand Army and coming to serve where, if I do all I can, little of laurels or credit can be expected."[42]

Officers were also more likely than their soldiers to construct a view of racial difference based on the appearance of Indians. In contrast to frontier soldiers who emphasized their own complexions, officers remarked repeatedly on Indians' skin color. Typical of educated Anglo-American elites of the late eighteenth century, high-ranking officers were struck by perceived physical differences among what they considered to be another race of people. Daniel Brodhead referred to Indians variously as "yellow boys," "black rascals," and "black cai-tiffs." An intelligence report to General Edward Hand announced that a group of "whites and blacks" were moving out from Niagara. The Reverend William Rogers remarked on the Indians as "tawny." The more cosmopolitan among frontier officers also viewed Indians' complexions as their most outstanding characteristic. Michael Huffnagle, an officer from frontier Westmoreland County, referred to Indian warriors as "blacks."[43]

It is curious that some officers marked Indians' skin color as black. One possible explanation is that the easterners racialized the strange culture of Indians by likening them to African Americans, a group of racial others with whom they were more familiar. Because, by the mid-eighteenth century, racism toward African Americans was becoming centered around the idea of physical rather than cultural difference, it was natural to see Indians in similar terms. Officers constructed their wartime images of Indians from prewar conceptions about race. Their racism was paternalistic rather than violent, and rooted in assumptions about biology rather than anger from wartime deeds. They could not conceive of Indians acting independently of European or European-American machinations.

High-ranking officers were also more likely to differentiate among friendly, neutral, and hostile Indians. Their roles as frontier diplomats had convinced them that Indians could be won over by gifts. Continental commanders in the west took care to cultivate Indian allies. Although they might have had a condescending attitude toward Indians, these men did not necessarily want to destroy them. They realized that in the context of the grand strategy of the war Indian alliances or neutrality were of high importance. The commanders of the Continental Western Department, headquartered at Fort Pitt, all were charged with negotiating with Indians, in addition to coordinating the Revolutionary war effort in the backcountry. Some officers even displayed a grasp of the subtle differences within a single Indian nation in regard to their wartime sympathies. For example, Colonel Brodhead wrote in 1779: "The Wyandotts of Sandusky and the Mingoes of Tankhonnetick and the Peckawee and Chilacoffee tribes of the Shawanese nation continue their depredations . . . but the Delaware inform me that most of the other nations to the Westward and Southward are friendly to the United States."

Also, a Carlisle resident and commander at Fort Pitt, General William Irvine, was alarmed by a backcountry militia's slaughter of the Moravian Delawares and worried for the safety of his own Delaware scouts. These upper-grade officers were far more concerned than their backwoods troops with the delicate diplomacy of the frontier. Seeing the war primarily in terms of defeating the British, they sought to counter the diplomacy of the Crown in the west rather than to eliminate all Indians.[44]

Nevertheless, elite leaders also oversaw the prosecution of total war against hostile Indians. Sometimes commanding officers added their voices to calls for brutal measures to wipe out Indians who resisted the Revolutionaries. They retained their frontier diplomat mentality more often than not when planning attacks, and they confined their objectives to destroying hostile groups of Indians while sparing neutrals and allies. Colonel Daniel Brodhead, for example, in a moment of fury against his backcountry foes, revealed his plan for an expedition into Indian country in 1779. He declared: "The woods will soon swarm with men and I have every thing on the way for marking my route with the slaughter of villains. Mingoes die first and then our enemies at Detroit and Niagara. The scene will be closed with the remaining rascals that may be found in arms against us."[45]

At times, however, a few officers went beyond aiming to destroy enemy Indians and even alluded to genocide. Although elite eastern racism was paternalistic and based in biology, it remained predicated on the assumption that Indians constituted a race and were inferior to European Americans. Visions of the destruction of all Indians lurked ominously in some pronouncements by officers. New York officer Nicholas Fish declared before he went on Sullivan's expedition that, because it was "founded upon so general and extensive a plan as I imagine (an undistinguished destruction and carnage), I shall encounter every difficulty with cheerfulness." Other officers accompanying Sullivan drank a toast to "Civilization or death to all American Savages." The phrase makes clear that if Indians were not willing to accommodate themselves to the ways of European Americans, their complete destruction should be imminent.[46]

Clearly, the constructions of racism toward Indians varied among enlisted men and high-ranking officers. Frontier troops believed all Indians to be hostile "savages" who committed unspeakable atrocities on soldiers and civilians alike. This image of Indians, reaffirmed during the Revolution, allowed backcountry soldiers to justify their own acts. Furthermore, the frontiersmen's prosecution of armed conflict against all Indians escalated the violence of total war. Eastern soldiers went westward with similar notions of Indians as warlike and uncivilized. They consolidated their racism by condemning Indian military culture as cowardly. Elite officers viewed Indians merely as dark-skinned, childlike pawns of the British, who could be won over by gifts or threats. Thus, images of Indians as outsiders, as enemies or possible enemies, were solidified in the minds of soldiers and officers, who interpreted their wartime experiences in ways that were in accord with their prewar prejudices.

Although the manner in which the soldiers and officers from different regions and class backgrounds expressed their racism varied, all contributed to brutalization and total war on the frontier. Rank and file and elites believed Indians to be less than human and committed deeds against them that would have been considered unacceptable against European or European American opponents. Soldiers and officers alike saw nonwhite status as evidence of lack of "civilization." The Revolution in the backcountry was not a "glorious cause." Soldiers dehumanized their foes and then brutalized the conflict, using racism as their rationale. Such were the consequences of bloodshed between settlers and the original inhabitants of America that began in the colonial period and were reinforced in the American Revolution. Total war against Indians was integrally linked, especially among frontier soldiers, to the patriot cause and American national identity.

After the Revolution, border conflict with Indians continued. As Daniel Bean explained in 1783, "peace was signed with Great Britain but the war did not end with the Indians." The militiaman stated: "I continued to serve every season." The backcountry citizens of the United States proved insatiable in their desire to move onto western lands and as Indians continued bitterly to contest their neighbors' aggressiveness, war followed. Hostilities persisted in Western Pennsylvania and the Ohio Valley through the 1790s, until most of the Indians who had fought against the Revolutionaries were either defeated or forced to flee. In the nineteenth century, frontier wars moved farther west, involving Indian nations that had no role in the Revolution. But those Indians would suffer from the same dehumanization in military conflict that had spawned the horrors of total war on the Revolutionary frontier. [47]

Afterword:
Pennsylvania's Revolutions in Their Broader Contexts

William Pencak

While all generalizations are dangerous, not to link a particular case to wider trends threatens to reduce a subject to insignificance. Pennsylvania's major role in the American Revolution clearly requires some tentative effort to situate its experiences as part of the whole. Two broader contexts suggest themselves: back-country studies and studies of loyalism and Revolutionary allegiance.[1]

In the last decade, some of the most important work in early American history has dealt with the backcountry. Based on the pioneering theses in Carl Bridenbaugh's 1947 classic *Myths and Realities: Societies of the Colonial South,* and the more recent studies of geographer Robert D. Mitchell,[2] publications on the interrelated though by no means interchangeable topics of the frontier, the west, the backcountry, and Appalachia have revised our image of the region.[3] The stereotype of a wild and woolly west, populated primarily by poor subsistence farmers and cut off from the more cosmopolitan east, is simply false. Except for brief periods of initial settlement and unusually isolated places, the hinterland was from the beginning settled by people who retained strong ties with the east, who were interested in commercial development, and who quickly developed economic and political elites of their own.

For Pennsylvania, the poor, geographically isolated Juniata Valley was the exception to a commercially vibrant and politically maturing frontier. Studies by Stephanie Grauman Wolfe of Germantown and James Lemon of Chester County, Pennsylvania, have become models for studies of regions much farther removed from initial areas of settlement.[4] From the beginning, inhabitants outside of New England—and it is possible to argue about much of that region too[5]—were interested in commercial development, worked hard to earn not only a subsistence but a surplus, lived on individual farms, and were ready to form new communities if it suited their personal interests. If few individuals were capitalists by the extremely elevated standard of uncompromising and unlimited pursuit of profit at the expense of family, religious, and community ties, almost all were involved in the market to some extent.[6] Our "transition to capitalism" would not be very far along in 1998 if we could define only those who subordinated all other goals to the acquisition of wealth as capitalists.

Economic studies of the American Revolution and its aftermath suggest that the war devastated much of the economy.[7] The chapters in this volume demonstrate that, despite temporary hardship during and immediately after the war, much of Pennsylvania seems to have been less affected than the South, New England's coast and hinterland, and the region around New York City. Unlike Boston and New York, Philadelphia was not destroyed; unlike New York, Charleston, and Savannah, it did not endure a long British occupation. Inflation and demand for military supplies from Pennsylvania's patriotic central region stimulated industrial and agricultural production. The absence of so many men and of financial instability in the interior furthered the formation of an elite and a greater concentration of wealth. The Revolution thus paved the way for Pennsylvania to become the nation's industrial powerhouse in the nineteenth century.

Furthermore, guerrilla and Indian warfare affected only parts of Pennsylvania—Bucks and Chester Counties to a limited extent, the remote Juniata and Wyoming Valleys far more so. The Philadelphia region, largely because the British were there only in 1777 and 1778, was not the scene of endemic warfare that the areas around New York City and Charleston, occupied from 1776 to 1783 and 1779 to 1782, respectively, experienced. The frontier, on the other hand, both the Juniata and the Wyoming Valley regions, suffered destruction that was probably equal to any in the new nation.

In addition to developing a wider market for Pennsylvania products, the Revolution also undermined localism by involving more people in politics and the Revolutionary cause. Before the war, Pennsylvania Germans had little to do with politics; the Scots-Irish had protested on the frontier and in Philadelphia but did not have the experience of ruling. Following closely on the mid-century wars (1754–64), the Revolution increased the Quakers' withdrawal or ouster from political power; they devoted themselves increasingly to philanthropy, commerce, and antislavery causes.[8] Germans, the Scots-Irish, and people outside the three old counties were responsible for much formal and informal Revolutionary government.[9] In Philadelphia itself, Maurice Bric's work has shown that Irish immigrants, both Protestants and Catholics, broadened city politics and led to the beginnings of Republican organization there.[10]

Patterns of allegiance in revolutionary Pennsylvania reflect trends in other areas. Here, as in the four central colonies of Maryland, New York, Delaware, and New Jersey, the colonial Assembly retarded resistance to Britain and opposed independence. In all these states, loyalists were especially prominent in the capitals and in the prosperous and long-established commercial regions closely linked to them.[11] This generalization holds true even for New England and the Lower South. For instance, in Massachusetts there was little loyalist sentiment, but much of that came from well-to-do people and new immigrants in the area around Boston.[12]

In the hinterland, allegiance had much to do with whether the pre-Revolutionary elites had been responsive to popular demands for protection, religious freedom, equitable taxation, and a fair court system. It is no accident that loyalism was far more pronounced in the poor and hard-hit coastal region of Maine than in Massachusetts; the disgruntled towns there, which may be considered the state's second, northern frontier, ultimately seceded.[13] Vermont's dominant Green Mountain Boys flirted with the British to successfully establish their autonomy from New York's hated landlords.[14] Many of North Carolina's Regulators, defeated before the Revolution, in effect established their own state by going over the mountains to what became Tennessee. Others became loyalists.[15] In South Carolina and Virginia, elites responded fairly well to backcountry grievances, installing the court system that the Regulators demanded in the former case, and institutionalizing religious freedom and representation in the latter.[16]

In the Middle Colonies, however, it was easy for the disgruntled to become Revolutionaries because the provincial elites were not. Here the most pronounced internal revolutions occurred with new elements taking over state governments. Loyalism was not a backcountry phenomenon except in Upstate New York, where Whig landlords were the source of distress and the Johnson family powerfully influenced the Iroquois to side with the British.[17] In Pennsylvania's Wyoming Valley, Anne Ousterhout's term "disaffected" is more appropriate than "loyalist."[18] Pennsylvania settlers in that region had no real loyalty to Britain; they wanted land and accepted British support when the Continental Congress favored the more militant Connecticut settlers. After the Revolution, the Pennsylvanians did not emigrate, but instead pressed their land claims in the new nation and won. Nevertheless, the Pennsylvania frontier shared with the backcountry South and the region around New York City the dubious honor of hosting the Revolution's most bloody, irregular warfare.[19]

In studying the American Revolution, much is to be learned from new sociological studies of the "network analysis" school.[20] Social movements can rarely be accurately described in static categories as the work of a particular class, region, ethnic, or religious group. Rather, a crisis of authority creates a fluid situation in which groups and individuals combine and recombine according to their interests and proclivities. Such a theory not only has the attractive qualities of unpredictability and providing historical actors with a certain amount of freedom, it also explains a good deal that would otherwise be puzzling. Why would Massachusetts, so united in 1775, be the first state to suffer a serious internal rebellion? Why would Pennsylvania's central counties, so radical and pro-Revolutionary in 1776, give the Federalists far more support in 1787 than Upstate New York? How to explain Benjamin Franklin's political somersaults, or Thomas Paine's hostility to urban elites yet support for manufacturing? The answer lies in the pressure of fighting and consolidating a revolution, in different elite responses, and in their attitudes toward the lower orders and the more remote parts of their respective states.

History is a complex product of interacting personalities, interests, and institutions. Our book on Pennsylvania supports an interpretation of an American Revolution that varied greatly from place to place and re-created itself afresh as it went along. That it took more than two centuries for the Revolutionary history of Pennsylvania "beyond Philadelphia" to be told is proof that the historiography of the Revolution also requires an ongoing process of examination and readjustment.

Notes

Abbreviations

HSP Historical Society of Pennsylvania, Philadelphia
PA Samuel Hazard et al., eds., *Pennsylvania Archives,* ser. 1–9 (Philadelphia and Harrisburg, 1852–1935)
PCC Papers of the Continental Congress, microfilm, National Archives, Washington, D.C.
PMHB *Pennsylvania Magazine of History and Biography*
PRG Records of Pennsylvania's Revolutionary Governments, 1775–90, microfilm, Pennsylvania Museum and Historical Commission, Harrisburg, Pa.
RWPF Revolutionary War Pension and Bounty Land Warrant Files, National Archives, Washington, D.C.
SCP *The Susquehannah Company Papers,* vols. 1–4, ed. Julian P. Boyd; vols. 5–11, ed. Robert J. Taylor (Wilkes-Barre, Pa., Wyoming Historical and Geological Society, 1930–1971)
WHGS *Proceedings and Collections of the Wyoming Historical and Geological Society*
WMQ *William and Mary Quarterly*

Introduction

1. Steven Rosswurm, *Arms, Country, and Class: The Philadelphia Militia and the "Lower Sort" During the American Revolution, 1775–1783* (1961; reprint, New Brunswick, N.J.: Rutgers University Press, 1987); Thomas M. Doerflinger, *A Vigorous Spirit of Enterprise: Merchants and Economic Development in Revolutionary Philadelphia* (Chapel Hill: University of North Carolina Press, 1986); Richard A. Ryerson, *The Revolution Is Now Begun: The Radical Committees of Philadelphia, 1765–1776* (Philadelphia: University of Pennsylvania Press, 1978; Charles S. Olton, *Artisans for*

Independence: Philadelphia Mechanics and the American Revolution (Syracuse, N.Y.: Syracuse University Press, 1975).

2. Stella H. Sutherland, *Population Distribution in Colonial America* (New York: AMS Press, 1966), 128, 167, xii; Evarts B. Greene and Virginia D. Harrington, *American Population Before the Federal Census of 1790* (Baltimore: Genealogical Publishing Company, 1993), 116.

3. John Florin, "The Advance of Frontier Settlement in Pennsylvania, 1638–1850: A Geographic Interpretation," Papers in Geography, The Pennsylvania State University, no. 14, May 1977, 30. See also Paul A. W. Wallace, *Indians in Pennsylvania* (Harrisburg: Pennsylvania Historical and Museum Commission, 1961).

4. For a description of these early settlements, see Christopher Ward, *Dutch and Swedes on the Delaware, 1609–1664* (Philadelphia: University of Pennsylvania Press, 1930).

5. Wayland F. Dunaway, "The English in Pennsylvania," *PMHB* 52, (1928): 322–23.

6. Albert Cook Myers, ed., *Narratives of Early Pennsylvania, West New Jersey, and Delaware, 1630–1707* (New York: Barnes & Noble, 1912), 200–201.

7. Edwin B. Bronner, *William Penn's "Holy Experiment": The Founding of Pennsylvania, 1681–1701* (New York: Temple University Publications, 1962), 6–14.

8. Greene and Harrington, *American Population*, 114, 116.

9. Stevenson W. Fletcher, *Pennsylvania Agriculture and Country Life*, 2 vols. (Harrisburg: Pennsylvania Historical and Museum Commission, 1950–55), 1:18.

10. Arthur C. Bining, *Pennsylvania Iron Manufacture in the Eighteenth Century*, 2nd ed. (Harrisburg: Pennsylvania Historical and Museum Commission, 1973), 23; see also 19–38, 96–115.

11. See James T. Lemon, *The Best Poor Man's Country: A Geographical Study of Early Southeastern Pennsylvania* (Baltimore: John Hopkins University Press, 1972), xiii, 229 n. 1.

12. Sharon V. Salinger, *"To serve well and faithfully": Labor and Indentured Servants in Pennsylvania, 1682–1800* (Cambridge: Cambridge University Press, 1987), 30–96, 116–28.

13. Wayland F. Dunaway, *The Scotch-Irish of Colonial Pennsylvania* (Chapel Hill: University of North Carolina Press, 1944), 50–85.

14. *The Journals of Henry Melchior Muhlenberg*, trans. and ed. Theodore G. Tappert and John W. Doberstein, 3 vols. (Philadelphia: Muhlenberg Press, 1952), 1:261.

15. Carl Bridenbaugh, *The Colonial Craftsman* (New York: New York University Press, 1950), 67.

16. Carl Van Doren, *Benjamin Franklin* (New York: Viking Press, 1938), 69–124; Verner Crane, *Benjamin Franklin and a Rising People* (Boston: Little, Brown, 1952), 22–37.

17. Bronner, *William Penn's "Holy Experiment,"* 28.

18. Norman S. Cohen, "The Philadelphia Election Riot of 1742," *PMHB* 92 (July 1968): 310–14; William T. Parsons, "The Bloody Election of 1742," *Pennsylvania History* 36 (July 1969): 291–92, 305.

19. J. R. Pole, "Historians and the Problem of American Democracy," *American Historical Review* 67 (April 1962): 646; Gary B. Nash, *Quakers and Politics: Pennsylvania 1681–1726* (Princeton: Princeton University Press, 1968), 336–37.

20. Patricia U. Bonomi, *A Factious People: Politics and Society in Colonial New York* (New York: Columbia University Press, 1971).

21. Nash, *Quakers and Politics*, esp. 10–11, 77–80, 92–93, 97–114.

22. James H. Hutson, *Pennsylvania Politics, 1746–1770: The Movement for Royal Government and Its Consequences* (Princeton: Princeton University Press, 1972), 6–40.

23. For information on his career, see Paul A. W. Wallace, *Conrad Weiser, 1696–1760: Friend of Colonist and Mohawk* (Philadelphia: University of Pennsylvania Press, 1945).

24. Clarence S. Brigham, ed., *History and Bibliography of American Newspapers, 1690–1820* (Worcester, Mass.: American Antiquarian Society, 1947), 824–993, esp. 875.

25. Lawrence H. Gipson, "The American Revolution as an Aftermath of the Great War for Empire," *Political Science Quarterly* 65 (March 1950): 89–104.

26. Thomas P. Abernethy, *Western Lands and the American Revolution* (New York: Russell & Russell, 1959), 14–38.

27. Marc Egnal, *A Mighty Empire: The Origins of the American Revolution* (Ithaca, N.Y.: Cornell University Press, 1988), 11–12, 14–15.

28. J. Paul Selsam, *The Pennsylvania Constitution of 1776: A Study in Revolutionary Democracy* (Philadelphia: University of Pennsylvania Press, 1936), 46.

29. Edmund S. Morgan and Helen M. Morgan, *The Stamp Act Crisis: Prologue to Revolution* (Chapel Hill: University of North Carolina Press for the Institute of Early American History and Culture, 1953), 248–54.

30. Doerflinger, *Merchants,* 167–95.

31. See Ryerson, *Committees,* 39–116.

32. Gary B. Nash, *The Urban Crucible: Social Change, Political Consciousness, and the Origins of the American Revolution* (Cambridge: Harvard University Press, 1979), 374–82.

33. John Dickinson, *Letters from a Farmer in Pennsylvania* (Philadelphia: David Hall & William Sellers, 1768); Merrill Jensen, comp., *Tracts of the American Revolution, 1763–1776* (Indianapolis, Ind.: Bobbs-Merrill, 1967), 127–28.

34. Benjamin W. Labaree, *The Boston Tea Party* (New York: Oxford University Press, 1964), 196–216, 220.

35. David F. Hawke, *In the Midst of a Revolution* (Philadelphia: University of Pennsylvania Press, 1961), 165–79.

36. Rosswurm, *Arms, Country, and Class,* 92–108; Jackson T. Main, *Political Parties Before the Constitution* (Chapel Hill: University of North Carolina Press, 1973), 174, 177. For a detailed discussion, see Selsam, *Constitution of 1776,* esp. 169–204.

37. Robert L. Brunhouse, *The Counter-Revolution in Pennsylvania, 1776–1790* (Harrisburg: Pennsylvania Historical Commission, 1942), 27–227.

38. Greene, *American Population,* 117.

39. Julian P. Boyd, *The Susquehannah Company: Connecticut's Experiment in Expansion* (New Haven: Yale University Press for the Tercentenary Commission, 1935), 22–42.

40. For a summary of the grievances of residents of the interior, see Charles H. Lincoln, *The Revolutionary Movement in Pennsylvania, 1760–1776* (Philadelphia: For the University of Pennsylvania, 1901), 40–52.

41. Anne M. Ousterhout, *A State Divided: Opposition in Pennsylvania to the American Revolution* (Westport, Conn.: Greenwood Press, 1987), 104–5.

42. For the transition in British America, see Pauline Maier, *From Resistance to Revolution: Colonial Radicals and the Development of American Opposition to Britain, 1765–1776* (New York: Alfred A. Knopf, 1972), 228–70, and infra, chaps. 1, 8, and 5, 91.

43. Richard K. MacMaster, *Conscience in Crisis: Mennonites and Other Peace Churches in America, 1739–1789: Interpretation and Documents* (Scottdale: Herald Press, 1979), 354–406.

44. Ousterhout, *A State Divided,* 115–39.

45. Quoted in Clinton L. Rossiter, *The First American Revolution: The American Colonies on the Eve of Independence* (New York: Harcourt, Brace, 1956), frontispiece.

46. Bernard Bailyn, *The Ideological Origins of the American Revolution* (Cambridge: Belknap Press of Harvard University Press, 1967), esp. vi–vii.

47. Louis Hacker, "The First American Revolution," *Columbia University Quarterly* 27 (1935): 259–95, reprinted in Esmond Wright, ed., *Causes and Consequences of the American Revolution* (Chicago: Quadrangle Books, 1966), 115–42.

48. Carl L. Becker, "The History of Political Parties in the Province of New York, 1760–1776," *Bulletin of the University of Wisconsin*, History Series, no. 36, 2 (April 1909): 5.

49. Daniel J. Boorstin, *The Genius of American Politics* (Chicago: University of Chicago Press, 1953), 68–69.

50. Jack P. Greene, "Independence, Improvement, and Authority: Toward a Framework for Understanding the Histories of the Southern Backcountry in the Era of the American Revolution," in Ronald Hoffman, Thad W. Tate, and Peter J. Albert, eds., *An Uncivil War: The Southern Backcountry During the American Revolution* (Charlottesville: University Press of Virginia, 1985), 9.

51. Ibid., 4; Frederick Jackson Turner, *The Frontier in American History* (New York: Holt, Rinehart & Winston, 1947) (originally published as "The Old West" in *Proceedings of the State Historical Society of Wisconsin*, 1908), 99; Carl Bridenbaugh, *Myths and Realities: Societies of the Colonial South* (Baton Rouge: Louisiana State University Press, 1952), 127.

52. See, in addition to the chapters in this volume, Rosemary S. Warden, "James Fitzpatrick: Tory Bandit of Chester County," *Pennsylvania History* 62 (1995): 376–87.

53. A. G. Roeber, *Palatines, Liberty, and Property: German Lutherans in Colonial British America* (Baltimore: Johns Hopkins University Press, 1993).

54. Joseph Cope, "The Pamphlet Response to the Paxton Boys," paper delivered at the Pennsylvania Historical Association Annual Meeting, State College, Pa., October 1996.

55. For Oakboys and Steelboys, along with a cogent argument that the Scots-Irish were as industrious as their German neighbors but in the habit of hiding their wealth from English tax collectors by appearing slovenly, see Maldwyn A. Jones, "The Scots-Irish in America," in Bernard Bailyn and Philip D. Morgan, eds., *Strangers Within the Realm: Cultural Margins of the First British Empire* (Chapel Hill: University of North Carolina Press, 1991), 300, 309. For general connections among British and American radicals, see John Brewer, *Party Ideology and Popular Politics at the Accession of George III* (Cambridge: Cambridge University Press, 1976), 201–16; for the Irish, both Catholic and Protestant, see Dennis Clark, *The Irish in Philadelphia: Ten Generations of Urban Experience* (Philadelphia: Temple University Press, 1973), 10–12; for Brissot de Warville, William Pencak, "Brissot de Warville and America," *Proceedings of the Annual Meeting of the Western Society for French History* (Auburn: Western Society for French History, 1990), vol. 17, 187–93.

56. For historians who see a "democratic" constitution, see Brunhouse, *Counter-Revolution in Pennsylvania*; Elisha P. Douglass, *Rebels and Democrats: The Struggle for Equal Political Rights and Majority Rule During the American Revolution* (Chapel Hill: University of North Carolina Press, 1955); and Sally Schwartz, "Religious Pluralism in Colonial Pennsylvania," 57–67, in Robert D. Mitchell, ed., *Appalachian Frontiers: Settlement, Society, and Development in the Preindustrial Era* (Lexington: University Press of Kentucky, 1991).

57. Charles Royster, *A Revolutionary People at War: The Continental Army and American Character, 1775–1783* (Chapel Hill: University of North Carolina Press, 1979). The best general study of the extralegal organizations of the Revolution is still Agnes Hunt, *The Provincial Committees of Safety of the American Revolution* (Cleveland, Ohio: Winn & Judson, 1904).

58. Lancaster County, not covered in this volume, has been thoroughly discussed in Jerome H. Wood Jr., *Conestoga Crossroads, Lancaster, Pennsylvania, 1730–1790* (Harrisburg: Pennsylvania Historical and Museum Commission, 1979). Although primarily dealing with the city, Wood shows how trends described for the surrounding counties—the coming together of ethnic and religious groups against a small number of loyalists; economic growth through munitions manufacture, agricultural productivity, and the influx of cash from a government-in-exile; and dissension

among a populace suffering from scarcity, inflation, and the uneven burdens of the war—held true for Lancaster. See also H. M. J. Klein, ed., *Lancaster County, Pennsylvania: A History* (Chicago: Lewis Historical Publishing Company, 1924), esp. 325–50, 523–28, 573–90; and Frederic Shriver Klein, *Old Lancaster: Historic Pennsylvania Community from Its Beginnings to 1865* (Lancaster, Pa.: Early America Series, 1964).

59. R. Eugene Harper, *The Transformation of Western Pennsylvania, 1770–1800* (Pittsburgh: University of Pittsburgh Press, 1991).

60. Anne M. Ousterhout, "Frontier Vengeance: Connecticut Yankees vs. Pennamites in the Wyoming Valley," *Pennsylvania History* 62 (1995): 330–63; and idem, *A State Divided.* The articles in the special issue of *Pennsylvania History* 62 (1995) on Pennsylvania loyalists show considerable genuine loyalty to the British in and around Philadelphia, and only there: J. Walter High, "Thomas Coombe, Loyalist," 276–92, and Kevin J. Dellape, "Jacob Duché, Whig Loyalist?" 293–305, for Anglican clergy; Judith Van Buskirk, "They Didn't Join the Band: Disaffected Women in Revolutionary Philadelphia," 306–29, for the colonial elite; James Farley, "The Ill-Fated Voyage of the *Providentia*: Robert Vaux, Loyalist Merchant, and the Trans-Atlantic Mercantile World in the Late-Eighteenth Century," 364–75; and Rosemary S. Warden, "James Fitzpatrick," 376–87, for partisan warfare.

61. Peter C. Mancall, *Valley of Opportunity: Economic Culture Along the Upper Susquehanna* (Ithaca, N.Y.: Cornell University Press, 1991).

62. The words *nations, groups, peoples,* and *societies* are used in this book to denote groups of Indians rather than "tribes." Besides suggesting a primitive form of social organization, the word connotes a coherent, long-standing group with its own customs. The mixing of peoples in North America following the arrival of Europeans meant that groups of Indians encountered by settlers were, for the most part, recent combinations of peoples. The word "Indian" is used in preference to "Native American" because the latter creates confusion with the concept of people born in the western hemisphere.

63. Alden T. Vaughan, *Roots of American Racism: Essays on the Colonial Experience* (New York: Oxford University Press, 1995); Richard White, *The Middle Ground: Indians, Empires, and Republics in the Great Lakes Region, 1660–1815* (Cambridge: Cambridge University Press, 1991).

64. Edward Countryman, "Indians, the Colonial Social Order, and the Social Significance of the American Revolution," and comments by Philip J. Deloria, Sylvia R. Frey, and Michael Zuckerman, *WMQ,* 3rd ser., 53 (1996): 342–62.

65. Ryerson, *Committees;* Rosswurm, *Arms, Country, and Class;* Brunhouse, *The Counter-Revolution in Pennsylvania.*

66. Owen S. Ireland, *Religion, Ethnicity, and Politics: Ratifying the Constitution in Pennsylvania* (University Park, Pa. : The Pennsylvania State University Press, 1995).

67. John S. Morrill, *The Nature of the English Revolution: Essays* (New York: Longman, 1993); Richard Cust and Ann Hughes, eds., *Conflict in Early Stuart England: Studies in Religion and Politics, 1603–1642* (New York: Longman, 1989); David Underdown, *Fire from Heaven: Life in an English Town in the Seventeenth Century* (New Haven: Yale University Press, 1992); idem, *Revel, Riot, and Rebellion: Popular Politics and Culture in England, 1603–1660* (New York: Oxford University Press, 1985).

Chapter 1. Chester County

1. James T. Lemon, *The Best Poor Man's Country: A Geographical Study of Early Southeastern Pennsylvania* (Baltimore: Johns Hopkins University Press, 1972), 194–97, 200–203.

2. Ibid., 114–16, 194–97, 200–203; Arthur C. Bining, *Pennsylvania Iron Manufacture in the Eighteenth Century* (Harrisburg: Pennsylvania Historical Commission, 1938), 49–61, 158; John H. Martin, *Chester (and Its Vicinity), Delaware County, Pa.* (Philadelphia: William H. Pile & Son, 1877).

3. *Pennsylvania Packet,* June 30, 1781. In her advertisement to rent the tavern, Sarah Kennedy described its capacious facilities, including a ballroom and bathhouses. She sought a tenant who would restore the tavern to a better condition after its use as an army hospital. Sarah was the widow of Dr. Samuel Kennedy, who served as director of the Yellow Springs Hospital. Kennedy had started the hospital in the fall of 1777 for the Continental Army wounded from the campaign in Pennsylvania and the sick from the Valley Forge encampment. Kennedy died early in 1778 from exhaustion and illness caught treating the soldiers.

4. *Pennsylvania Gazette,* June 24, 1774; September 27, 1775; February 28, 1776; May 1, 1776; May 30, 1776; June 26, 1776; June 23, 1779. The Court of Quarter Sessions recommended ninety-eight people as tavernkeepers in Chester County in 1772, about one for every 300 inhabitants. "A List of Persons Recommended as Public House Keepers in Chester County, 25th August, 1772," Chester County Collections no. 159, Historical Society of Pennsylvania, Philadelphia; Joseph J. Harris, "Robert Smith," *PMHB* 4 (1880): 79–88; *Dilworth Families in America,* comp. Virginia W. Bushman (Philadelphia: Dilworth Descendants, printed by Virginia W. Bushman, 1970), 33–39; J. Smith Futhey and Gilbert Cope, *History of Chester County, Pa.* (Philadelphia: Louis H. Everts, 1881), 374.

5. Lemon, *The Best Poor Man's Country,* 79, 116; Frederick Sheeder, "East Vincent Township: Chester County, Pennsylvania," *PMHB* 34 (1910): 74–98, 194–212, 361–80; *The History of Old St. David's Church, Radnor, in Delaware County, Pa.* (Philadelphia: John C. Winston Company, 1907), 75; John T. Faris, *Old Churches and Meeting Houses In and Around Philadelphia* (Philadelphia: J. B. Lippincott Company, 1926), 131–34; William S. Hanna, *Benjamin Franklin and Pennsylvania Politics* (Stanford, Calif.: Stanford University Press, 1964), 69; J. Lewis Fluck, *A History of the Reformed Churches in Chester County* (Norristown, Pa.: Herald Printing Company, 1892), chapters on Brownback's Reformed Church (East County Township), East Vincent Reformed Church, and St. Peter's Lutheran Church (Pikeland Township); *The Story of St. Paul's "on Delaware," 1703–1903* (n.d.), Delaware County Church Pamphlets, vol. 1, HSP; A. Wayne Morris, *The Octoraro Family of Churches* (Honeybrook, Pa.: Herald Publishing Company, 1969); James McClune, *History of the Presbyterian Church in the Forks of the Brandywine* (Philadelphia: J. B. Lippincott Company, 1855).

6. Lemon, *The Best Poor Man's Country,* 17, 50–56, 63, 71, 82–83, 188–89.

7. The average length of Assembly service of the eight Chester County members in 1765 was sixteen years. The average would have been longer except for Nathaniel Pennock's refusal on conscientious grounds to serve for four years of the French and Indian War, and for Charles Humphreys's and Isaac Pearson's conscientious withdrawal from politics in 1776. The single term of John Fairlamb, who died in office in 1765, was omitted from the calculation of this average. *PA,* ser. 2, 3:732, 737; David H. Fisher, *Albion's Seed: Four British Folkways in America* (New York: Oxford University Press, 1989), 462–67. Theodore Thayer advanced the notion that the proprietors sought to offset the power of the Quaker party by establishing a Proprietary-Presbyterian party, using appointive local offices and particularly judicial appointments as a "magnet which had long held the Proprietary party together when it was possible to elect only a few gentlemen to the Assembly." Theodore Thayer, *Pennsylvania Politics and the Growth of Democracy, 1740–1776* (Harrisburg: Pennsylvania Historical and Museum Commission, 1953), 91–92. Three of the seventeen justices of the peace for Chester County listed in the 1765 commission were western town-

ship Scots-Irish Presbyterians: William Boyd, John Culbertson, and William Clingham. Of the twelve new members of the Commission of the Peace of 1770, only one, Thomas Hockley, was definitely a proprietary supporter. Two others—James Moore, a Presbyterian, and Evan Evans, a Baptist—may have supported proprietary interests. These justices or their families (Boyd and Culbertson died in 1767) were firm supporters of the Revolution, tending to support James Hutson's thesis that the Proprietary-Presbyterian party formed the core of later Revolution resistance to England. James H. Hutson, *Pennsylvania Politics, 1746–1770: The Movement for Royal Government and Its Consequences* (Princeton: Princeton University Press, 1972). In Chester County, however, the numbers of possible Proprietary party justices was so small that the necessity of spreading appointments of justices of the peace throughout the townships, rather than an attempt to counter Quaker party influence, accounts for these appointments. It could provide only a small seed of Revolutionary resistance in Chester County.

8. *Pennsylvania Gazette,* November 25, 1771; December 28, 1773; Charles Palmer, *A History of Delaware County, Pa.,* vol. 1 (Harrisburg, Pa.: National Historical Association, 1932), 62–63; Henry G. Ashmead, *History of Delaware County, Pa.* (Philadelphia: L. H. Everts & Company, 1884), 37–39.

9. Futhey and Cope, *History of Chester County,* 60. The Philadelphia Committee "had first been an instrument of one occupational class (1765), and then a traditionally elitist representative of the whole community (June 1774)." Not until the Philadelphia Committee election of November 1774 did this committee become a "new aggressive advocate drawn from and speaking for, the middle classes that would soon politically dominate the whole community," younger, less wealthy, and more ethnically diverse. More than a year later, radicals among the members of the Philadelphia Committee advocated only a "strong, vocal support of the First Continental Congress and strict enforcement of the nonimportation Association." Even in January 1775, not all radicals on the Philadelphia Committee supported mobilizing a militia in Pennsylvania. Richard A. Ryerson, *The Revolution Is Now Begun: The Radical Committees of Philadelphia, 1765–1776* (Philadelphia: University of Pennsylvania Press, 1978), 89 n. 2, 179.

10. *Pennsylvania Gazette,* July 20, 1774. James T. Lemon states that nonimportation disrupted the economy of southeastern Pennsylvania, particularly the export of foodstuffs to the British Isles, which was well-established in the pre-Revolutionary period. Exports did not recover to pre-Revolutionary levels until 1789. However, Lemon points out that merchants suffered much more than farmers, who predominated in Chester County. He finds that "the more successful farmers" in southeastern Pennsylvania flourished during the Revolution, based on a comparison of prewar and postwar inventories and tax assessments. Lemon, *The Best Poor Man's Country,* 224–25. According to Thomas M. Doerflinger, not all merchants suffered. He points to the "extremely diverse" experiences of Philadelphia merchants during the war, with new extremes of wealth, increased bankruptcies, and a larger and more heterogeneous merchant community. Doerflinger, *A Vigorous Spirit of Enterprise: Merchants and Economic Development in Revolutionary Philadelphia* (Chapel Hill: University of North Carolina Press, 1986), 250.

11. "Votes of Assembly," *PA,* ser. 8, 8:7098–100. Although an Anglican, Morton, a farmer and lawyer from Ridley, near Philadelphia, was a twenty-year assemblyman. A moderate with friends on all sides of the political debate, he became Speaker of the Assembly in 1775. He signed the Declaration of Independence before his premature death early in 1777. Charles Humphreys of Haverford, also in the east, was descended from a wealthy and politically prominent Welsh Quaker family. He was a longtime assemblyman and collector of excise. Humphreys voted against the Declaration of Independence in the Pennsylvania delegation to Congress in 1776 and withdrew from politics until after the Revolution, when he was again elected to the Assembly. Futhey and Cope, *History of Chester County,* 758–59.

12. "Votes of Assembly," 7158–62; *Pennsylvania Packet,* December 26, 1774. Anglicans, with nine members, were underrepresented on this committee, while Lutherans and Baptists had only two members each. One-third of the committee members were from western townships. The new committee membership showed little change in economic status.

13. *Pennsylvania Gazette,* February 22, 1775. The Meeting for Sufferings was the ongoing administrative meeting of the Philadelphia Yearly Meeting, which met only once a year. The Philadelphia Yearly Meeting represented Meetings for all of Pennsylvania, central and southern New Jersey, Delaware, and parts of Maryland. In the early days of the Society of Friends in England, the Meeting for Sufferings served to record religious persecution of Friends. This remained among its functions in Pennsylvania during the Revolution. Arthur J. Mekeel, *The Relation of the Quakers to the American Revolution* (Washington, D.C.: University Press of America, 1979), 335.

14. Darby Meeting Records and Chester Monthly Meeting Records, Swarthmore College Friends Library. From the few committee delegates disowned, such as Samuel Fairlamb of Chester, Hugh Lloyd of Darby, and Joseph Musgrave of Concord, the numbers of Quakers disowned for Revolutionary activities grew rapidly in 1775 and 1776, when most disownments occurred. Most disownments were for military service. The Radnor Meeting had the most such disownments (27 members, or 13.6 percent), followed by Springfield (15 members, or 7.6 percent), Birmingham (14 members, or 7.1 percent), Concord (11 members, or 5.5 percent); most other meetings in the county had a much smaller proportion of members disowned. Kenneth A. Radbill, "Socioeconomic Background of Nonpacifist Quakers During the America Revolution" (Ph.D. diss., University of Arizona, 1971), 1–2, 89.

15. The Chester County Committee left no record of specific methods it used to enforce non-importation. Futhey and Cope, *History of Chester County,* 61.

16. In 1775, the Pennsylvania Assembly had 41 members: 15 from the underrepresented western counties, 2 from the city of Philadelphia, and 24 from the conservative eastern counties—Philadelphia County, Bucks County and Chester County—which formed the core of Quaker party support in the Assembly. If assemblymen from these eastern counties stood firmly against the Radicals, Radical proposals would be defeated by a margin of at least seven votes (24–17). J. Paul Selsam, *The Pennsylvania Constitution of 1776: A Study of Revolutionary Democracy* (Philadelphia: University of Pennsylvania Press, 1936), 32–39. Two important issues show these Chester County Assembly members' fluctuations between conservative and Radical positions. In March 1775, Assembly Speaker Joseph Galloway, later a loyalist, sponsored a separate petition to the King from the Pennsylvania Assembly. The Assembly did not know the fate of a similar petition sent by the Congress. A separate petition by the Assembly would be a blow to the unity of the protest movement. Galloway succeeded in deferring a final vote, which he feared would go against him, with the help of several Chester County votes, but in the end, of the Chester County delegation, only Joseph Pennock voted for a separate Assembly petition. On another issue, the increasingly radical Philadelphia Committee offered a resolution to admit some of the "reputable inhabitants of the city" to observe Assembly meetings from the gallery. Of the Chester County members, only Anthony Wayne voted for the resolution. The other four Chester County members voting—John Jacobs, Isaac Pearson, Charles Humphreys, and John Morton—stood with other Quaker party members to defeat the radical resolution. John Morton's election as Speaker of the Assembly, after Joseph Galloway's resignation, enhanced the power of this swing group. "Votes of Assembly," 7202, 7209, 7211–13, 7217.

17. "Votes of Assembly," 7245–49; "Minutes of the Committee of Safety," *Colonial Records* 10:571–73; Futhey and Cope, *History of Chester County,* 62; Christopher Ward, *The War of the Revolution* (New York: Macmillan, 1952), 372–77.

18. "Minutes of the Committee of Safety," *Colonial Records* 10:279, 282, 346, 459. Other examples of the Chester County Committee's role in outfitting the militia (and later Continentals) may be found in *Colonial Records* 10, esp. 527–741. Eventually the Pennsylvania Council of Safety (formerly the Committee of Safety) erected earth-walled forts on both sides of the Delaware River just below Philadelphia. Chester Countian Robert Smith designed and erected two rows of che-vaux-de-frise, sunken boxes constructed of logs, filled with rocks and with spikes attached to the top pointing downriver, on the Delaware between the town of Chester and Philadelphia. These fortifications did not protect Chester from the British fleet. The British may have been deflected from invading Pennsylvania via the Delaware River partly because of mistaken respect for these fortifications, but they quickly cleared the river after occupying Philadelphia.

19. "Votes of Assembly," 7352–53. Joseph Pyle alone of the Chester County members stopped attending meetings of the Assembly when independence was imminent. He became a member of the Meeting for Sufferings, which recorded Quakers' tribulations during the war.

20. Although no record of a roll-call vote on the militia act remains, certainly at least three Chester County assemblymen—James Gibbons, Joseph Pennock, and Joseph Pyle—as Quakers in good standing, could not have voted for the militia bill. Some of Chester County's "swing votes" almost certainly did, along with the radical Bartholomew, or the bill could not have passed. "Votes of Assembly," 7351–52, 7365; *Pennsylvania Gazette,* October 23, 1775. The Chester County Committee movement took a different course than that Ryerson described for the Philadelphia Committee, which became larger, younger, less wealthy, more ethnically diverse, and more radical during this period. Ryerson, *The Revolution Is Now Begun.* The Chester County Committee of October 1775 was not noticeably younger or less wealthy than the larger county committee of 1774, and it was less diverse because Quakers in good standing could not be members. As applied to Chester County politics, "radical" had a rapidly changing connotation between 1774 and 1776. In 1774, a radical might seek no more than to organize the nonviolent Continental Association; by mid-1775, a radical also supported military organization; early in 1776, a radical favored inde-pendence; by late summer 1776, he strongly supported the new Pennsylvania constitution. By early 1776, some Chester County Committee members, while actively supporting military organi-zation, lagged behind the more radical Philadelphia Committee's rapidly evolving support for independence, as Francis Johnston's letter of March 2, 1776, to Anthony Wayne (below) indicates. "Votes of Assembly," 7351–52, 7365.

21. McClune, *Presbyterian Church in the Forks of the Brandywine,* 70–72, 106–7, 114–15; Morris, *Octoraro Family of Churches;* Faris, *Old Churches and Meeting Houses;* Futhey and Cope, *History of Chester County,* 365–88, 485, 639–40, 661–62; "Clinghan Family Notes," HSP; Lewis R. Culberson, *Genealogy of the Culberson and Culbertson Families* (Zanesville, Ohio: Courier Com-pany, 1922); "Interments in Brandywine Manor Grave Yard," MS, Chester County Historical Society; W. S. Long, "Judge James Moore and Major James Moore, of Chester County, Pennsylva-nia," *PMHB* 12 (1880): 304–9, 465–74; *Ancestors and Descendants of Thomas Montgomery,* comp. Ella Montgomery Allison and Henry T. Montgomery (n.p., 1963), 2; J. W. Jordan, *A History of Delaware County, Pa.* (New York: Lewis Historical Publishing Company, 1914), 204–9; Harris, "Robert Smith," 79–88; "Boyd Family Notes," HSP.

22. Until 1780, all militia officers were elected; after 1780, all lower than colonels. William C. Clarke, *Official History of the Militia and the National Guard of the State of Pennsylvania,* 3 vols. (Philadelphia: Charles J. Hendler, 1901), vol. 1, chap. 2; *PA,* ser. 2, 14:68–131 and 3:636; Ash-mead, *History of Delaware County,* 65. Chester County's militia operated along different political fault lines than the Philadelphia militia, which Rosswurm argues became an instrument of class warfare for the "lower sort" in Philadelphia. Steven Rosswurm, *Arms, Country, and Class: The*

Philadelphia Militia and the "Lower Sort" During the American Revolution, 1775–1783 (New Brunswick, N.J.: Rutgers University Press, 1987).

23. Francis Johnston to Anthony Wayne, March 2, 1776, Wayne Papers, HSP. The delegates who informed Johnston were very likely Charles Humphreys, a conservative, and John Morton, a moderate, both of Chester County. Wayne was in Philadelphia serving on the provincial Committee of Safety. Similar concerns were voiced in a petition to the Assembly dated June 7, 1776, by "A Number of the Inhabitants of Chester County." "Votes of Assembly," 7538–39.

24. "Provincial Conference of 1776," *PA,* ser. 2, 3:648–52. The "test oath" was only one factor lowering voting in Chester County, so it is difficult to weigh its effect precisely. Selsam and Brunhouse agree that voting statewide in 1776 was extremely light, partly because of opposition to the constitution and the "test oath." Selsam, *Constitution of 1776,* 221–30; Robert L. Brunhouse, *The Counter-Revolution in Pennsylvania, 1776–1790* (1942; reprint, Harrisburg: Pennsylvania Historical and Museum Commission, 1971), 21. Although results for the election of 1776 in Chester County are no longer available, the results for the next two years suggest how light the vote must have been. In 1777 the highest vote-getter in Chester County received 284 votes, and in 1778 the highest was 375 votes; both figures are small fractions of the normal vote before the Revolution or in the 1780s. *PA,* ser. 6, 11:121–49. Some Chester Countians ignored the Constitutional Convention's election decree and held a separate election, "apparently with a view of supporting the late Government of the King of Great Britain." County Sheriff Nathaniel Vernon, an avowed loyalist who later bore arms for the British and was proscribed as a traitor, certified the returns of this election. "Minutes of the Council of Safety," *Colonial Records* 10:742, 775; *PA,* ser. 2, 1:652.

25. Wayne's troops mustered at his home, Waynesboro, in Easttown Township. Many officers serving under him had close personal ties to Wayne. They included Thomas Robinson, his brother-in-law; James Hunter, whose family were vestrymen with the Waynes at St. David's in Radnor; and neighbors the Reverend David Jones of Great Valley Baptist Church, who became his chaplain, and Benjamin Bartholomew, John Bull, and Persifor Frazer. Wayne Papers, HSP, 1:13; *PA,* ser. 2, 10:119, 530. In later years Wayne was assiduous in "promoting the interest of the gentlemen of the Army upon all Occasions" in local political contests, but he was often absent from the political scene in the early years of the war. Anthony Wayne to Francis Johnston, September 17, 1783, Wayne Papers, HSP. The lack of militia muster rolls makes it impossible to assign a number to Chester County troops in the Long Island campaign. Futhey and Cope, *History of Chester County,* 65–66.

26. The Presbyterian convention delegates were Robert Smith, John Mackey, John Fleming, Thomas Strawbridge, and Samuel Cunningham. Cunningham, Joseph Gardner, and John Fulton were the Presbyterian assemblymen; the other three assemblymen were disowned Quakers. Owen S. Ireland accurately points to ethnic and religious identity as the crucial indicator of support for the constitution of 1776 in Chester County and in Pennsylvania as a whole in "The Ethnic-Religious Dimension of Pennsylvania Politics, 1778–1779," *WMQ,* 3rd ser., 30 (1973): 423–48, esp. 440–44. The appearance of new western township Scots-Irish assemblymen largely bears out Jackson Turner Main's thesis in "Government by the People: The American Revolution and the Democratization of Legislatures," *WMQ,* 3rd ser., 23 (1966): 391–407, that the Revolution brought about much greater representation of poorer western areas in state legislatures. However, contrary to Main's findings in other states, county tax lists show that Revolutionary Chester County assemblymen were not, on the whole, less affluent than their pre-Revolutionary counterparts. Furthermore, despite statewide expansion of suffrage, the "test oath" reduced suffrage in Chester County for several years below pre-Revolutionary levels.

27. Thomas Bull to Anthony Wayne at Ticonderoga, March 19, 1777, Wayne Papers, HSP.

28. Persifor Frazer to Mary Worrall Taylor Frazer, October 2, 1776, *PMHB* 31 (1907): 315.

29. Francis Johnston to the Council of Safety, October 1776, *PA,* ser. 1, 5:100. Quakers were not alone in refusing to accept the rapidly inflating Congressional paper money. Colonel Matlack to Justices of Philadelphia, Bucks, Chester, and Bedford Counties, *PA,* ser. 2, 3:240–41; *History of Old St. David's Church,* 75–85.

30. Radbill, "Nonpacifist Quakers," 2, 77–78; Carlos E. Godfrey, "Muster Rolls of Three Troops of Loyalist Light Dragoons, Raised in Pennsylvania 1777–1778," *PMHB* 34 (1910): 2; Futhey and Cope, *History of Chester County,* 754; Chester Friends Meetings Records, Swarthmore College Friends Library; Francis B. Heitman, *Historical Register of the Officers of the Continental Army During the American Revolution, April 1775 to December 1783* (1914; reprint, Baltimore: Genealogical Publishing Company, 1967), 560; Futhey and Cope, *History of Chester County,* 115. John A. Munroe describes a similar minority of active loyalists in Delaware, a state contiguous to southeastern Chester County, where most believed "life had been good under the old empire" and "few had peculiar reasons for dissatisfaction with their status," yet only a minority went as far as open loyalism. John A. Munroe, "Reflections on Delaware and the American Revolution," *Delaware History* 17 (1976): 1–11, and *History of Delaware,* 2nd ed. (Newark: University of Delaware, 1979, 1984), 62, 76.

31. Harris, "Robert Smith," 79–88.

32. Ashmead, *History of Delaware County,* 49; Ward, *The War of the Revolution,* 328–35.

33. Ward, *The War of the Revolution,* 336–40; Edward A. Gifford, *The American Revolution in the Delaware Valley* (Philadelphia: Pennsylvania Sons of the Revolution, 1976), 55–65; Jordan, *History of Delaware County,* 266.

34. Joseph Townsend, "Some Account of the British Army and the Battle of Brandywine," *Bulletin of the Historical Society of Pennsylvania* 1 (September 1846): 1–7; Edward P. Cheney, "Thomas Cheney, A Chester County Squire . . . ," *PMHB* 40 (1936): 209–28.

35. Ward, *War of the Revolution,* 352–54; Townsend, "Some Account of the British Army," 5; "Before and After the Battle of Brandywine. Extracts from the Journal of Sergeant Thomas Sullivan of H.M. Forty-ninth Regiment of Foot," *PMHB* 31 (1907): 412–17; Howard Peckham puts British casualties at Brandywine at 90 killed, 448 wounded, and 6 missing, and American casualties at 200 killed, 500 wounded, and 400 captured. Howard H. Peckham, ed., *The Toll of Independence: Engagement and Battle Casualties of the American Revolution* (Chicago: University of Chicago Press, 1974), 40.

36. "Representation of Colonel Cheyney," June 2, 1778, *PA,* ser. 2, 3:201; William W. Polk, "History of Kennett Square," Chester County Collections 1–8 (West Chester, Pa.: Anderson & Darlington, n.d.), 231–34.

37. Ward, *War of the Revolution,* 543–55. Benjamin H. Newcomb attributes Washington's choice of Valley Forge mainly to "military necessity," citing concerns over competition with refugees for scarce resources if a site farther west were chosen, as well as the importance of countering British marauders from Philadelphia, though Newcomb also acknowledges political pressure on Washington to camp as near to Philadelphia as possible. Benjamin H. Newcomb, "Washington's Generals and the Decision to Quarter at Valley Forge," *PMHB* 117 (1993): 309–29. Wayne Bodle judges that Washington's encampment at Valley Forge was dictated more by concern to protect the Revolution in southeastern Pennsylvania than by military considerations, which might have led to a withdrawal to what Washington calls "the Reading-Lancaster line" farther west. Bodle finds that supporters of Washington's encampment closer to Philadelphia included Pennsylvania Revolutionary supporters without regard for faction, as well as Pennsylvanians among Washing-

ton's officers and military advisers. Wayne Bodle, "Generals and 'Gentlemen': Pennsylvania Politics and the Decision for Valley Forge," *Pennsylvania History* 62 (1995): 59–89.

38. John Armstrong to the President of the Council, December 22, 1777, in "Letters of Two Distinguished Pennsylvania Officers," *PMHB* 63 (1939): 306–7.

39. *The Journals of Henry Melchior Muhlenberg,* trans. Theodore S. Tappert and John W. Doberstein (Philadelphia: Muhlenberg Press, 1942, 1958), 1:763 and 2:31, 74, 79, 160, 377; "Minutes of the Supreme Executive Council," *Colonial Records* 11:298, 360, 402, 535; Ashmead, *History of Delaware County,* 68; *Pennsylvania Evening Post,* January 2, 1778.

40. *Dilworth Families in America,* 33–39; Martin, *Chester,* 175; Ashmead, *History of Delaware County,* 72.

41. *Pennsylvania Evening Post,* January 2, 1778.

42. *PA,* ser. 1, 5:476; Ashmead, *History of Delaware County,* 67; *Colonial Records* 11:339.

43. Muhlenberg, *Journals,* 2:81–82, 625.

44. Anthony Wayne to General Washington, December 26, 1777; George Washington to Anthony Wayne, December 27, 1777; Anthony Wayne to Joseph Ellis, February 21, 1778, Wayne Papers, HSP; Ward, *War of the Revolution,* 358–59.

45. William Montgomery, James McDowell, and John Mackey to the Pennsylvania Committee of Safety, February 12, 1776, Wayne Papers, HSP; "Testimony Concerning a Riot in Chester County," *Colonial Records* 11:553–54; Council Secretary Matlack to the Speaker of the Assembly, December 5, 1781, *PA,* ser. 1, 9:459; Supreme Executive Council to Colonel Hannum, May 12, 1780, *PA,* ser. 1, 8:244; "Proclamation of Reward for the Murderers of William Boyd," May 13, 1780, *PA,* ser. 4, 3:760–61.

46. Futhey and Cope, *History of Chester County,* 499; Polk, "History of Kennett Square," 306–9; Ashmead, *History of Delaware County,* 166–71; "Minutes of the Supreme Executive Council," *Colonial Records* 11:582–83, 616–17. Fitzpatrick's trial and execution in just over a month following his capture in August 1778 reflected the constitutionalists' desire to punish those who had attacked the Revolutionary government during its weakest period, their political strength and cohesion, and their concern over continued loyalist activity in the county. This may be contrasted with the treatment of the loyalist Doan gang of Bucks County, several of whom were captured in the early to mid-1780s. G. S. Rowe emphasizes the opposition to such harsh sentences after threats to the Revolution had dissipated, as well as constitutional and legal issues involved. G. S. Rowe, *Thomas McKean: The Shaping of an American Republicanism* (Boulder: Colorado Associated University Press, 1978), 202–26.

47. Council of Safety to Committee of Chester, February 1777, *PA,* ser. 2, 1:699–700; Mekeel, *The Relation of the Quakers to the American Revolution,* 189–93; Godfrey, "Muster Rolls of Loyalist Light Dragoons," 5; George Evans to Thomas McKean, n.d., and "Affidavit of Samuel Ramsey," April 20, 1781, McKean Papers, HSP; Rev. John Carmichael to the President of the Supreme Executive Council, January 27, 1780, *PA,* ser. 2, 3:385–86.

48. President Thomas Wharton to Colonels Cheyney and Grunow, *PA,* ser. 1, 5:732–33.

49. "Minutes of the Supreme Executive Council," October 7, 1778, *Colonial Records* 11:596; James R. Aldrich, "The Revolutionary Legislature in Pennsylvania: A Roll Call Analysis" (Ph.D. diss., University of Maine, 1969). Extant voting returns are listed in *PA,* ser. 2, vol. 6. Owen S. Ireland emphasizes Presbyterianism as a continuing primary characteristic of constitutionalists throughout the state in the late 1770s in "The Crux of Politics: Religion and Party in Pennsylvania, 1778–1789," *WMQ,* 3rd ser., 42 (October 1985): 453–75.

50. Aldrich, "The Revolutionary Legislature in Pennsylvania"; *PA,* ser. 2, vol. 6.

51. Brunhouse, *Counter-Revolution,* 197; Richard Riley, "Record of Proceedings as Justice of

the Peace, 1765, 1774–76," HSP; Anthony Wayne to Francis Johnston, September 17, 1783, Wayne Papers, HSP; Futhey and Cope, *History of Chester County*, 380–82.

52. Brunhouse, *Counter-Revolution*, 45.

53. Harris, "Robert Smith," 86–87.

54. Lemon, *The Best Poor Man's Country*, 24, 73, 225–30.

Chapter 2. Bucks County

1. For similar treatment of the impact of the war, see Sung Bok Kim, "The Limits of Politicization in the American Revolution: The Experience of Westchester County, New York," *Journal of American History* 80 (December 1993): 868–89. The phrases describing war are from Abraham Lincoln, "Second Inaugural Address," March 1865; and Stephen Crane, *Red Badge of Courage* (1895), chap. 3, cited in John Bartlett, *Familiar Quotations*, 16th ed., ed. Justin Kaplan (Boston, 1992).

2. Alexander Graydon, *Memoirs of His Own Time*, ed. John Stockton Littell (1846; reprint, New York, 1969), 22.

3. John Lacey, "Memoirs of Brigadier-General John Lacey of Pennsylvania," *PMHB* 25 (1901): 3; William Smith to the Society for the Propagation of the Gospel in Foreign Parts, October 14, 1772, in Horace W. Smith, *Life and Correspondence of the Reverend William Smith, D.D.* (Philadelphia, 1880), 1:478.

4. J. H. Battle, ed., *History of Bucks County, Pennsylvania* (1887; reprint, Spartansburg, S.C., 1985), 28–85.

5. Most of the material describing the settlement patterns in Bucks County relies on William W. H. Davis, *The History of Bucks County, Pennsylvania* (Doylestown, Pa., 1876), and materials *in Bucks County Historical Society Papers*, vols. 1–8.

6. Graydon, *Memoirs*, 16–17.

7. Population figures for Bristol and Newtown from Edward K. Muller, ed., *A Concise Historical Atlas of Pennsylvania* (Philadelphia, 1989).

8. Thomas Doerflinger, "Farmers and Dry Goods in the Philadelphia Market Area, 1750–1800," in Ronald Hoffman, John McCusker, Russell Menard, and Peter Albert, eds., *The Economy of Early America: The Revolutionary Period, 1763–1790* (Charlottesville, Va., 1988), 176, 187. Lucy Simler's detailed research on Chester County has led her to conclude that the "evidence of the penetration of the consumer revolution into the Philadelphia hinterland by 1775 indicates the deep market involvement of the farm population and implies diversity in production as well as an appropriate labor force and access to markets." Lucy Simler, "The Landless Worker: An Index of Economic and Social Change in Chester County, Pennsylvania, 1750–1820," *PMHB* 114 (April 1990): 171 n. 23. For a dispute over the commercial use of the Neshaminy Creek on the eve of the Revolution that suggests the commercial development of Bucks County, see "Votes of the Assembly," January 30, 1770, *PA*, ser. 8, 7:6488–89. Both David Haugaard, associate editor, and Robert Wright, assistant editor, of the *Biographical Directory of Early Pennsylvania Legislators*, have read and commented on an earlier draft of this chapter. I wish to thank them for their efforts to keep me from egregious error and to absolve them of responsibility for the errors that remain. Haugaard agrees that Bucks County was prosperous; Wright agrees that Bucks was a commercial farming area. Private correspondence, Wright/Haugaard to Ireland, October 30, 1996.

9. Before the war, Joseph Galloway's father-in-law had been the major stockholder in the firm. Galloway himself had apparently inherited the firm and was active in supervising its operation in 1775. During the early years of the war, while most of Pennsylvania's eastern furnaces cast cannon for the patriot cause, Durham's principal contribution was shot. It is not known whether technical/ strategic considerations or the political proclivities of the owners led the Durham Works to produce shot rather than cannon. For details on Pennsylvania's production of cannon, see Daniel K. Perry, "The Origins, Procurement, and Production of Iron Cannon in Pennsylvania During the American Revolution" (M.A. thesis, The Pennsylvania State University, 1986). For Galloway's father-in-law and the Durham Iron works, see Joseph Illick, *Colonial Pennsylvania: A History* (New York, 1976), 242. Galloway's defection to the British in December 1776 opened the way for confiscation of his property, including that in Durham. James B. Nolan, *Southeastern Pennsylvania* (1943), 1:378–79; John Bishop, *A History of American Manufacturing from 1608 to 1860* (1860; reprint, New York, 1966), 1:559; Victor S. Clark, *History of Manufacturing in the United States* (Washington, D.C., 1916), 1:497. Muller, *Concise Historical Atlas of Pennsylvania,* 102, indicates a far greater number of charcoal furnaces in Chester and Berks than in Bucks, and substantially more in Philadelphia, Montgomery, Lancaster, Dauphin, and Cumberland.

10. See *PA,* ser. 3, 13:13–146 for tax lists for 1779 and 1781. Estimates of relative wealth based on landholding data from printed township tax lists in the *Pennsylvania Archives* present numerous difficulties. We lack data on the relative value of the land listed; the quantities listed for any given individual vary considerably from year to year, suggesting the operation of such hidden factors as assessor error or the presence of unstated criteria. Land is only one source of wealth; we cannot always be sure we are distinguishing among owners, tenants, and inmates. And historians have recently discovered a number of discrepancies between the printed tax lists and the originals. Reliance on landholding lists within a single county compounds the difficulties, because some individuals held land in more than one township and in more than one county. Nonetheless, as Lemon and Nash have noted, "land composed the largest part of assessable wealth in rural areas," and despite all its limitations, land distribution data in the printed tax lists provide a rough, if crude, measure of relative degrees of economic status. Furthermore, assuming the absence of any systematic bias in the records (that is, assuming that all the printed tax records are equally likely to reflect the same kinds of error or bias), landholding patterns provide a basis for comparisons between townships within one county and between counties. See James T. Lemon and Gary B. Nash, "The Distribution of Wealth in Eighteenth-Century America: A Century of Change in Chester County, Pennsylvania, 1693–1802," *Journal of Social History* 2 (1968): 24; and Jackson T. Main, *Society and Economy in Colonial Connecticut* (Princeton, 1985), for more detailed discussion of these problems. Lucy Simler, David Haugaard, and Robert Wright have all warned me about the unreliable nature of the data printed in *Pennsylvania Archives.* I accept their admonitions and offer these figures as tentative and suggestive only.

11. Main has argued that in pre-Revolutionary Connecticut a young family without children could get by on 24 to 40 acres but that a "young married farm couple needed at least forty acres" while "eighty acres was adequate for a yeoman and his family." Main, *Connecticut,* 30. Lemon has estimated that a family of five could support itself on 75 acres in eighteenth-century Chester County. See James T. Lemon, *Best Poor Man's Country: A Geographical Study of Early Southeastern Pennsylvania* (Baltimore: Johns Hopkins University Press, 1972), 88–89. Simler has demonstrated that in Chester County a surprising number of households combined farming and some other form of income-producing labor such as skilled crafts or dairying. Consequently, households holding relatively small amounts of land might achieve a substantial degree of economic autonomy. On the other hand, Simler has also argued persuasively that many small holders were in fact

"cottagers," maintaining a separate household on small plots they did not own, and heavily dependent on wages for survival. The tax lists for Bucks County printed in *Pennsylvania Archives* do not provide sufficient information to distinguish between these two types of small holders. See Simler, "The 'Best Poor Man's Country' in 1783: The Population Structure of Rural Society in Late Eighteenth-Century Southeastern Pennsylvania," *Proceedings of the American Philosophical Society* 113 (1989): 234–61; Simler, "Landless Worker," 163–99; and Simler and Paul Clemens, "Rural Labor and the Farm Household in Chester County, Pennsylvania, 1750–1820," in Stephen Innes, ed., *Work and Labor in Early America* (Chapel Hill, N.C., 1988), 106–44.

12. Daniel Vickers, "Competency and Competition: Economic Culture in Early America," *WMQ*, 3rd ser., 48 (January 1990): 3–29; and Main, *Connecticut*, 30.

13. Simler and Clemens, "Rural Labor," 108.

14. See Main, *Connecticut*, 137. Differences in context, data, and criteria make comparisons with Main's findings in Connecticut difficult and tentative but important. He estimates that colony-wide in Connecticut about 25 percent were landless in the mid-eighteenth century, and possibly 20 percent in 1774 (125), and that the young and the old made up the overwhelming majority of those without land (Appendix 4H, 161, 123, 137). Quotations from Main, *Connecticut*, 382, 151.

15. Sally Schwartz, *"A Mixed Multitude": The Struggle for Toleration in Colonial Pennsylvania* (New York, 1988), 302, 290, 292, 295.

16. Alan Tully, "Ethnicity, Religion, and Politics in Early America," *PMHB* 107 (October 1983): 493, 528, 532; Alan Tully, *William Penn's Legacy: Politics and Social Structure in Provincial Pennsylvania, 1726–1755* (Baltimore, 1977), xvi, xvii, 59–62, 83, 141–52.

17. Tully, *William Penn's Legacy*, 177–78. Between 1729 and 1754, for example, Quakers made up about 75–80 percent of the men annually elected to the eight-man Bucks County Assembly delegation.

18. Tully, *William Penn's Legacy*, 83. At mid-century, John Kinsey Jr., clerk of the Quaker Yearly Meeting, also served as the Speaker of the Assembly. Ibid., 92–98. In spite of the impressive work by Schwartz and Tully, I suspect that a fair amount of ethnic-religious-based hostility permeated Pennsylvania politics on the eve of the Revolution. John B. Frantz, "The Awakening of Religion Among the German Settlers in the Middle Colonies," *WMQ*, 3rd ser., 33 (April 1976): 266–88, has argued that the Great Awakening heightened denominational consciousness among Germans in Pennsylvania. Henry M. Muhlenberg, especially in the 1770s, reveals his mounting resentment of the Presbyterians. See Henry M. Muhlenberg, *The Journals of Henry M. Muhlenberg*, trans. Theodore G. Tappert and John W. Doberstein (Philadelphia, 1942–45), 3:26, 551, 625–26. Marianne Wokeck, "A Tide of Alien Tongues: The Flow and Ebb of German Immigrants to Pennsylvania, 1683–1776" (Ph.D. diss., Temple University, 1983), esp. 271–83, 285, and fig. 11, has documented a flood of Scots-Irish immigration into Pennsylvania on the eve of the Revolution that may well have heightened awareness of differences and exacerbated tensions. Much of the scholarship published before Tully highlighted the ethnic-religious dimension of pre-Revolutionary politics in Pennsylvania. See especially James Hutson, *Pennsylvania Politics, 1746–1770: The Movement for Royal Government and Its Consequences* (Princeton, 1972); and Arthur D. Graeff, *The Relations Between the Pennsylvania Germans and the British Authorities, 1750–1776* (Norristown, Pa., 1939). According to Graeff, "from the beginning of the province until 1730 the Germans were invited, even coaxed, to settle in Pennsylvania. From 1730 to 1750 they were tolerated. After the middle of the century welcome waned and suspicion took its place" (31–32).

19. Theodore Thayer, *Pennsylvania Politics and the Growth of Democracy, 1740–1776* (Harrisburg, Pa., 1953), 119; and James Hutson, *Pennsylvania Politics*, 155.

20. Terry McNealy, librarian of the Spruance Library of the Bucks County Historical Society, Doylestown, Pa., has concluded that "there is no evidence that there were any committees organized in Bucks County before 1774, although many Bucks Countians must have been well aware of events in the city." Terry A. McNealy, "Justices in Revolt: Bucks County Political Leaders, 1774–1776," *Mercer Mosaic* 2 (May–June 1985): 7–18. See also Battle, *History of Bucks County,* 301.

21. Committee of Safety, "Minutes," *PMHB* 15 (1891): 257–59.

22. Ibid., 258–59.

23. Ibid., 259–60.

24. John Adams, *Diary and Autobiography of John Adams,* ed. L. H. Butterfield (Cambridge, Mass.: Belknap Press of Harvard University Press, 1961), 2:164.

25. Ethnic and religious identifications here and in following paragraphs are based on data made available to me by Wayne Bockelman; on McNealy, "Justices in Revolt," 7–18; and on my own gleanings (graciously facilitated by Frances Waite, library assistant) in the rich collection of primary and secondary materials at the Bucks County Historical Society.

26. Committee of Safety, "Minutes," 259–60.

27. Ibid., 260.

28. Anne M. Ousterhout, *A State Divided: Opposition in Pennsylvania to the American Revolution* (Westport, Conn., 1987), 87, 103; "Proceedings of the Convention, . . . January 23–25, 1775," *PA,* ser. 2, 3:549–54. *Pennsylvania Gazette,* April 26, 1775.

29. Ousterhout, *A State Divided,* 106; June 23–24 and 30, 1775, *PA,* ser. 8, 8:7237–41, 7245–49.

30. Richard Bauman, *For the Reputation of Truth: Politics, Religion, and Conflict Among the Pennsylvania Quakers, 1750–1800* (Baltimore, 1971), 147–48; "General Epistle" of January 5, 1775; Ousterhout, *A State Divided,* 91–93.

31. Bauman, *For the Reputation of Truth,* 148, 147, 161.

32. Bucks Quarterly Meeting at Middletown, November 28, 1776; Bucks County Historical Society, MS 303. The Falls Monthly Meeting in 1779 and apparently in 1780 also appointed visiting committees to "Excite, Encourage and Strengthen Each other to a Steady watchful care . . . [and] Forceably to Admonish our Brethren." These documents also suggest the "feminist" orientation of late-eighteenth-century Quakers. The key phrase was later revised to read "Brethren and Sisters." The Falls Monthly Meeting of Women Friends, informed of the action of the "men friends," declared their support and added seven women to the men's visiting committee. See MS 303, Bucks County Historical Society

33. Committee of Safety, "Minutes," 261.

34. Ibid., 263.

35. Ibid., 265.

36. Ibid., 263, 266, 267.

37. Ibid., 267, 276, 280. See Louis Ely Thompson, "An Introduction to the Loyalists of Bucks County," *Papers of the Bucks County Historical Society* 2(1937): esp. 204–5.

38. See above, notes 10 and 11.

39. For sources of information on these and other officeholders, see above, note 25.

40. Bucks County held eight seats in the pre-Revolutionary legislature. In the early 1770s, Quakers regularly controlled at least five of these; minorities, at least two others. I cannot at this time classify the eighth and last seat, but I presume that it was a Quaker seat. Three different men held it at one time or another in the pre-Revolutionary period. One was a Quaker; the religion of the other two remains unknown. Thus, the Quakers probably controlled six of the eight seats.

With respect to the German and Dutch seats, there is no direct evidence that Quakers deliberately set aside two minority seats. Such a policy would, however, have been consistent with the inclusive and accommodating political strategy attributed to them by Alan Tully (see above, note 16). In addition, the literature contains scattered references to the Shepherd-Heany seat as the "German" seat, and it seems improbable that a non-Quaker could have consistently won county-wide election in Bucks without the tacit approval of the dominant Quakers. Joseph Hart, one of the most well-to-do and politically active men in the county, illustrates the point. Although descended from the original English Quaker settlers in the County, his family had early broken with the Meeting and become Baptists. After that, despite their social and economic prominence and their innumerable judicial appointments, neither Hart nor his father won election to the legislature.

41. For details of the October 1776 election in Bucks, see "Pennsylvania's Revolutionary Government, 1775–1790," microfilm reel 44, frames 0966–0995-B, Pennsylvania Historical and Museum Commission, Harrisburg.

42. Not only did turnout in November compare poorly with turnout in October, it also paled into insignificance when compared with popular participation both before and immediately after the Revolution. In prewar Bucks County, hotly contested elections could bring 1,000 to 1,500 men to the polls. In post-Revolutionary Bucks County in the late 1780s, turnout averaged about 1,500, and in 1789 it exceeded 1,700.

43. George Washington, *The Writings of George Washington from the Original Manuscript Sources, 1745–1799,* ed. John C. FitzPatrick (Washington, D.C., 1932), 6:397, 369, 418, 366–67, 369, 418; 7:274.

44. Ibid., 426–27, 372, 376, 399, 400, 386.

45. Ibid., 505, 421, 409, 505.

46. John B. B. Trussell Jr., *The Pennsylvania Line: Regimental Organization and Operations, 1776–1783* (Harrisburg, Pa., 1977), 237–41. Bucks County's 3,500–4,000 adult males represented about 7 percent of the adult males in the state. If Bucks had contributed its fair share to the Continental Army, it would have manned ten or eleven companies—that is, a 100 to 120 percent increase over its actual contribution.

47. About 2,000 men signed up, and about the same number refused, but the failure of some townships to enumerate their non-Associators skews the totals. A closer look at selected townships suggests a higher proportion of non-Associators than of Associators. Hilltown and Falls, two widely separated and different kinds of towns, both reported more non-Associators than Associators, and 11 of the 21 townships that published the names of Associators and non-Associators did the same. Hilltown, with 148 households, listed 65 Associators and 89 non-Associators, or 58 percent non-Associators; Falls, with 135 households, had 56 Associators and 102 non-Associators (65 percent). A few towns reported minuscule levels of non-Association. Nockamixon, for example, listed 95 Associators and 9 non-Associators (8.5 percent). Such, however, were clear exceptions and may represent missing documents or possible errors [intentional or accidental] by the original recorders. See *PA*, ser. 2, 14:145–251.

48. Reed to Wharton, December 15, 1777, in William B. Reed, *The Life and Correspondence of Joseph Reed* (Philadelphia, 1847), 1:355; Lacey, "Memoirs," 26:267.

49. Lacey, "Memoirs," 26:101; Joseph Reed to President Wharton, October 30, 1777. in Reed, *Reed,* 1:333; Lacey, "Memoirs," 26:267. Congressional Resolution of February 27, 1778 as printed in Reed, *Reed,* 1:359.

50. Reed, *Reed,* 1:359.

51. Wayne Bodle, "This Tory Labyrinth: Community, Conflict, and Military Strategy During the Valley Forge Winter," in Michael Zuckerman, ed., *Friends and Neighbors: Group Life in America's First Plural Society* (Philadelphia, 1982), 231, 234. Lacey, "Memoirs," 26:267.

52. February 1, 1778, in Reed, *Reed,* 1:358.

53. Reed to Wharton, ibid.; Washington's proclamation, December 20, 1777, in ibid., 355; Washington to Stewart, January 22, 1778, in ibid., 358; Bodle, "This Tory Labyrinth," 229; David F. Hawke, *The Colonial Experience* (Indianapolis, Ind., 1966), 620.

54. Lacey to Van Horn, March 19, 1778, "Battle of Crooked Billet," typescript in Manuscript Collection 39, folder 5, Bucks County Historical Society.

55. John Brook, January 5, 1778, quoted in Bodle, "Tory Labyrinth," 225; Anne Bezanson, *Prices and Inflation During the American Revolution, 1770–1790* (Philadelphia, 1951), 30; Reed, *Reed,* 1:331; Reed to Wharton, December 13, 1777, in ibid., 355; Lacey "Memoirs," 26:267.

56. Lacey, "Memoirs," 26:267.

57. Sessions Docket, Court of Quarter Sessions, Bucks County Historical Society.

58. John J. McCusker and Russell R. Menard, *The Economy of British America, 1607–1789* (Chapel Hill, N.C., 1985), 373–74, 358–59, 366–67, 374–75.

59. Anne Bezanson, *Prices and Inflation,* 339, 340–41. For a discussion of the degree to which the market economy had penetrated the region around Philadelphia, see Doerflinger, "Farmers and Dry Goods," 166–96. Robert Wright convincingly argues that "a truly . . . compelling analysis would use all major socioeconomic sources including: tax records, probate records, deeds, account books, Bank of North America ledgers, price indices, transportation cost indices, land office accounts . . . [and] mortgage books, among others. . . . It would take a massive effort of data collection, record-linkage, and analysis." Private correspondence, Wright/Haugaard to Ireland, October 30, 1996.

60. Battle, *History of Bucks County,* 650–54.

61. Ireland, "Germans Against Abolition: A Minority's View of Slavery in Revolutionary Pennsylvania," *Journal of Interdisciplinary History* 3 (Spring 1973): 685–706. See tax lists for 1775 in Terry A. McNealy and Frances Wise Waite, comp., *Bucks County Tax Records, 1693–1778* (Doylestown, Pa., 1982), 51–82; U.S. Census, *Heads of Families at the First Census of the United States . . . 1790 . . .* (Washington, D.C., reissued in microfilm, 1960), reel 3. The estimate of 245 to 250 for 1775 is interpolated for the county as a whole based on the extant evidence for 15 of 28 political subdivisions.

62. McNealy and Waite, *Bucks County Tax Records,* 51–82.

63. My calculations from the data in U.S. Census, *Return of the Whole Number of Inhabitants Within Several Districts of the United States* (Philadelphia, 1791), 45; and John Nicholson, *State of the Finances of the Commonwealth of Pennsylvania* (Philadelphia, November 1787), in Clifford K. Shipton, ed., *Early American Imprints: Reproduction on Readex Microprint of the Works Listed in Charles Evans, American Bibliography* (Worcester, Mass.: American Antiquarian Society, 1955–69), Evans no. 45137. The legislature generally distributed the tax burden proportionally. For petitions for tax and debt relief see, "Assembly Minutes," March 27, 1788, March 25, 1788, 169, 161–62; and *Pennsylvania Packet,* March 29, 1788, and March 15, 1788.

64. Ralph K. Turp, "General John Lacey: People and Progress," printed essay in the genealogy file at St. Andrew's Episcopal Church, 121 High Street, Mount Holly, N.J. Turp cites as his source "The Life and Services of . . . John Lacey," in *Graham's Magazine,* 1854, 186, 187. I wish to thank Mrs. Thomas Bryant, at the St. Andrew's rectory, for her assistance in obtaining this document. I found no evidence that Lacey was charged with this death. It may have been a duel, or the story might be apocryphal.

65. Battle, *History of Bucks County,* 296, 300, 605. For an interesting analysis of some of the constitutional issues involved in the efforts of the courts to deal with the Doans, see G. S. Rowe,

Thomas McKean: The Shaping of an American Republicanism (Boulder: Colorado Associated University Press, 1978), 202–26.

66. Nolan, *Southeastern Pennsylvania*, 1:375–80; and Battle, *History of Bucks County*, 295–300; Rowe, *McKean*, 203, 207.

67. Battle, *History of Bucks County*, 296–99; Pauline Cassell, *History of Bedminster, Bucks County, Pennsylvania* (1976; reprint, Bedminster, Pa., 1983), 12; Rowe, *McKean*, 207, 225.

68. Battle, *History of Bucks County*, 570–71, 605; Cassell, *History of Bedminster*, 108–9; Rowe, *McKean*, 202.

69. Robert L. Brunhouse, *The Counter-Revolution in Pennsylvania, 1776–1790* (Harrisburg: Pennsylvania Historical Commission, 1942), 455, 446, 449. The Act of October 1, 1779, set varying final dates, depending primarily on distance from Philadelphia. December 1, 1779, was the latest. James T. Mitchell and Henry Flanders, *The Statutes at Large of Pennsylvania* (Harrisburg, Pa., 1903), chap. 852, 9:405–7; Owen S. Ireland, "The Ethnic-Religious Dimension of Pennsylvania Politics, 1778–1779," *WMQ*, 3rd ser., 30 (July 1973): 423–48.

70. I cannot define precisely the number of adult males in Bucks County who voluntarily or involuntarily withdrew from political participation during the war. A number of indirect indicators suggest, however, that the proportion was large. The county militia muster lists 3,205 officers and men. The U.S. Census for 1790 lists 6,575 men ages sixteen and over in Bucks. The militia lists therefore account for about half the men at risk (*PA*, ser. 2, 114:243–51). About 1,570 Quakers lived in Bucks in 1760, or 700–800 men, none of whom could remain in the Meeting and vote or hold public office after September 1776. The Bucks Meeting disciplined about 50 for war-related offenses. Kenneth Radbill, "The Socioeconomic Background of Nonpacifist Quakers During the American Revolution" (Ph.D. diss., University of Arizona, 1971), 89–95. More than 600 men braved the patriot fury by voting in the election of October 1, 1776. Few if any of these would have remained politically active under the new government (see above). Finally, the tax lists for 1779 identify about 400 men who were paying a double tax. This may represent the approximate number of nonjurors in the county at this time, because the Test Acts imposed double taxes on nonjurors. *PA*, ser. 3, 13:3–111. An item in the *Freeman's Journal* of November 10, 1784, reflecting Bucks County's support for continued exclusion of nonjurors from the political community, estimated the number of nonjurors at two-fifths of the otherwise eligible voters in the County. Brunhouse, *Counter-Revolution*, 165. However, the number of nonjurors may not reflect the number of true political dissidents in the county. Some evidence suggests that large Quaker families may have transferred their property to one adult male, who himself took the Test Oath, and incurred the religious sanction of the Meeting but thereby protected the family property from the Revolutionary government. Two kinds of evidence are consistent with such a pattern. The tax lists indicate that some Quaker dissidents who had been well-to-do before the war held little or no property by 1779. In addition, a small number of prominent Quakers took the Test Oath and suffered formal excommunication, but continued to hold office and exercise leadership in the Meeting. Further research is needed here.

71. See especially "Uniform," in *Freeman's Journal*, September 12, 1781; "A Constitutionalist," in ibid., September 28, 1781; "Comus," in ibid., January 30, 1782.

72. *Freeman's Journal*, June 4, 1783; June 18, 1783; July 9, 1783.

73. Ibid., July 2, 1783; August 13, 1783.

74. *Pennsylvania Gazette*, November 10, 1784.

75. "Minutes," Pennsylvania General Assembly, September 29, 1784; *Pennsylvania Gazette*, November 10, 1784. James Allen, "Diary of James Allen, Esq., of Philadelphia, Counsellor-at-Law, 1770–1778," *PMHB* 9 (1885): 176–97 (quotation from 196).

Chapter 3. The Lehigh Valley

1. William Allen owned more than 3,000 acres in Northampton County and made approximately 700 acres available to establish Allentown. See Mahlon H. Hellerich, ed., *Allentown, 1762–1987: A 225-Year History* (Allentown, Pa.: Lehigh County Historical Society, 1987), 6, 12.

2. E. Gordon Alderfer, *Northampton Heritage: The Story of an American County* (Easton, Pa.: Northampton County Historical and Genealogical Society, 1953), 134; W. Ross Yates, *The History of the Lehigh Valley Region* (Bethlehem, Pa.: Joint Planning Commission of Lehigh and Northampton Counties, 1962), 36.

3. Yates, *History of the Lehigh Valley*, 2–30.

4. Ibid., 35–36.

5. Ibid., 27–28, 36. Today, of course, interstates, local roads, and bridges make such travel inconsequential. In actual miles, from historic area to historic area, Easton is 11 miles from Bethlehem and 17 miles from Allentown through Bethlehem; Bethlehem is 5 miles from Allentown, 7 miles from Emmaus, and 9 miles from Nazareth; Allentown is 5 miles from Emmaus.

6. Alderfer, *Northampton Heritage*, 134. Northampton County had been created in part to add proprietary strength in an area that was coming more and more under Quaker influence in Bucks County and under German influence farther north, with the Moravian communitarian settlements in 1740–42 and the many individual German farm families scattered throughout the valley. Mostly Scots-Irish Presbyterians occupied areas farther north from Catasauqua, north of Allentown to Bath, north of Bethlehem. The largest concentrations were the Craig settlement in Allen Township and the Hunter settlement in Mount Bethel. To avoid the potential impact of the Moravians and the Germans, the county seat was located at the forks of the Delaware and Lehigh Rivers, just across from New Jersey. Proprietary control of the town's lots put Easton under English dominance. The Provincial Council appointed the key county government officials, justices of the peace, and other administrators. The county still remained about 85 percent German, but there were also families of Welsh, Swiss, Dutch, and French Huguenot origin, as well as a significant minority of Scots-Irish, although the largest landowners initially were the English. See Yates, *History of the Lehigh Valley*, 18–23; Alderfer, *Northampton Heritage*, 98–99; and Karyl Lee Kibler Hall and Peter Dobkin Hall, *Lehigh Valley: An Illustrated History* (Woodland Hills, Calif.: Windsor Publications, 1982), 223.

7. Hellerich, *Allentown*, 13–14.

8. Ibid., 14.

9. Alderfer, *Northampton Heritage*, 134.

10. Ibid., 135; Hellerich, *Allentown*, 14.

11. The Northampton County Battalion of the Flying Camp suffered heavy casualties in the battle of Long Island in 1776. Four companies totaling 328 men engaged the enemy. Richard E. Myers, *Northampton County in the American Revolution* (Easton, Pa.: Northampton County Historical and Genealogical Society, 1976), 21.

12. Alderfer, *Northampton Heritage*, 135–36; Hellerich, *Allentown*, 14–15; Myers, *Northampton County*, 18–19; William J. Heller, *History of Northampton County and the Grand Valley of the Lehigh*, vol. 1 (New York: American Historical Society, 1920), 134. Myers sets the total number of Associators at 2,357.

13. At a mass meeting of some 900 men from the Second Battalion of Associators of Northampton County on May 27, 1776, the group, mostly from the western end of the county (present Lehigh County), adopted resolutions calling for a Provincial Conference of Committees (as requested by Philadelphia radicals on May 20) to prepare for a state constitutional convention be-

cause the Pennsylvania Assembly was no longer "competent to the exigencies of our affairs." See Mahlon H. Hellerich, "Political Leadership in Lehigh County During the Revolutionary War," *Proceedings of the Lehigh County Historical Society,* vol. 38 (Allentown, Pa., 1984), 20; Charles Rhoades Roberts et al., *History of Lehigh County, Pennsylvania,* vol. 1 (Allentown, Pa.: Lehigh Valley Publishing Company, 1914), 124–25; Hellerich, *Allentown,* 15.

14. Alderfer, *Northampton Heritage,* 136; *PA,* ser. 2, 14 (1888), 599–600; Northampton County Bicentennial Commission, *Two Hundred Years of Life in Northampton County,* vol. 4 (Easton, Pa., 1976), 7, 54; Hellerich, *Allentown,* 15. Local merchant Rhoads maintained an active role in the Revolutionary effort, serving as a member of the Pennsylvania Committee of Safety in July 1776 and representing the county in the Pennsylvania Assembly from 1777 to 1780. Burkhalter won election to the Assembly in 1776 and 1777. See Hellerich, *Allentown,* 22.

15. Alderfer, *Northampton Heritage,* 137.

16. Ibid.

17. Ibid., 144–45.

18. Ibid., 104, 146–48.

19. William Allen Benton, *Whig-Loyalism: An Aspect of Political Ideology in the American Revolutionary Era* (Teaneck, N.J.: Fairleigh Dickinson University Press, 1969), 76.

20. Heyl, "James Allen and Trout Hall," *Proceedings of Lehigh County Historical Society* 24 (1962): 73.

21. Because of his political neutrality and social well-being, Allen and his family were frequently harassed by local patriots. Diary entries from November 1777 demonstrate his concerns: "My situation continues as before living in perpetual fear of being robbed, plundered and insulted. . . . Every species of oppression and waste of property continues as before." See ibid., 84.

22. Allen's diary entry of July 26, 1775 (ibid., 72), clearly sets forth his views on the crisis at hand: "Many thinking people believe America has seen its best days, and should it even be victorious, peace and order will with difficulty be restored. My profession is visibly on the decline. . . . We however keep up our spirits and, gloomy as things appear, prefer our situation to a mean acquiescence. It is a great and glorious cause. The eyes of Europe are upon us; if we fail, Liberty no longer continues as inhabitant of this globe: for England is running fast to slavery. The King is as despotic as any prince in Europe; the only difference is the mode; and a venal parliament are as bad as a standing army.

23. Ibid., 82; Richmond E. Myers, *Lehigh Valley: The Unsuspected* (Easton, Pa.: Northampton County Historical and Genealogical Society, 1972), 76–79.

24. Alderfer, *Northampton Heritage,* 148–49.

25. Ibid., 149.

26. Raymond Walters, *Bethlehem Long Ago and Today* (Bethlehem, Pa.: Carey Printing Company, 1922), 47; W. Ross Yates, ed., *Bethlehem of Pennsylvania: The First 100 Years* (Bethlehem, Pa.: Bethlehem Chamber of Commerce 1968), 111–12; John W. Jordan, "Bethlehem During the Revolution," *PMHB* 13 (1889): 72–73.

27. Yates, *Bethlehem of Pennsylvania,* 110.

28. Alderfer, *Northampton Heritage,* 150; Heller, *History of Northampton County,* 134. In 1779, Easton was the scene of a heavy troop concentration because the town served as a base for General Sullivan's campaign against the Indians in the Wyoming Valley and southern New York. After the Wyoming massacre, a bloody battle between British-Indian allied forces and a smaller American detachment in Pennsylvania's northeastern frontier, Washington proposed a major expedition into Iroquois country to destroy the heart of the Six Nations and to capture Fort Niagara, the source

of British supplies. Beginning May 26, 1779, troops began to assemble in Easton. By the time they left on June 18 on their mission, some 5,000 men had mobilized under Sullivan's command. See Yates, *Lehigh Valley*, 37; Heller, *History of Northampton County*, 138; and Philip Klein and Ari Hoogenboom, *A History of Pennsylvania*, 2nd ed. (University Park, Pa.: The Pennsylvania State University Press, 1980), 100–101.

29. George M. Shultz, "Historic Nazareth, 1740–1856," in *Two Centuries of Nazareth, 1740–1940* (Nazareth, Pa.: Nazareth, Pa., Bicentennial, 1940), 50–54.

30. Alderfer, *Northampton Heritage*, 150.

31. Ibid.

32. Ibid., 138, 151. David Deshler, a leading businessman in Allentown and a politically active patriot, began storing powder and arms in Allentown in August 1776. In February 1778, he became commissioner of purchases, and Allentown became a center for the storage of military provisions. See Hellerich, *Allentown*, 20–21.

33. Alderfer, *Northampton Heritage*, 151; Heller, *History of Northampton County*, 139–41.

34. Alderfer, *Northampton Heritage*, 138; *A Book of Appreciation and Accomplishment*, 7.

35. Alderfer, *Northampton Heritage*, 137.

36. Taylor had leased a sizeable portion of the Durham Iron Works property. Unfortunately for him, the property was owned by Joseph Galloway, prominent Pennsylvania loyalist, who had his property confiscated in 1778 under the Pennsylvania Test Act. Because his personal investment in the iron works had been rather extensive, Taylor never recovered from his losses. Earlier in 1776, he had sold his Catasauqua property to devote his time and energy to producing military products for the war effort and remaining closer to the action in the Easton area. See Mildred Rome Trexler, "George Taylor, Esquire," *Proceedings of the Lehigh County Historical Society* 27 (Allentown, Pa.: Lehigh County Historical Society, 1968), 21, 57–59.

37. Ibid., 32–33. In the two recorded positive votes on October 26, 1764, and October 15, 1765, to send Benjamin Franklin to join Richard Jackson as province's agents to England, Taylor dissented, openly upset at Franklin's quarrels with the Proprietors. Taylor opposed converting the province to a royal colony. See ibid., 31, 33.

38. On January 24, 1777, Taylor and George Walton were awarded $1,000 by the Continental Congress to represent it at the Easton Conference with the Indian nations. The money was for presents to be offered to the Indian representative in attendance. At the conference, the Indians pledged their neutrality in the war between England and the colonies. Heller, *History of Northampton County*, 135; Trexler, "George Taylor, Esquire," 40.

39. Alderfer, *Northampton Heritage*, 139–41; Myers, *Northampton County*, 209–11; Trexler, "George Taylor, Esquire," 37–38. No records remain to explain his financial status at his death. The only thing that is clear is that in February 1781, when he died, there remained insufficient property to pay off his debts. By then, he had lost or sold most of his real estate, including his summer residence. See Heller, *History of Northampton County*, 133.

40. John B. B. Trussell Jr., ed., *Pennsylvania Landmarks of the Revolution* (Harrisburg, Pa., 1976), 48.

41. Alderfer, *Northampton Heritage*, 151–52; Yates, *Bethlehem of Pennsylvania*, 109–10; Walters, *Bethlehem Long Ago*, 47.

42. Yates, *Bethlehem of Pennsylvania*, 113–14; Worthington C. Ford, ed., *Journals of the Continental Congress, 1774–1789* (Washington, D.C.: U.S. Government Printing Office, 1907), 8:748. Briefly, General Johan deKalb and the corps of engineers gave consideration to using the Bethlehem area as potential headquarters for the Continental Army that eventually set up camp at Valley Forge. In fact, George Washington's baggage was brought to Bethlehem and kept there until

Christmas. See Yates, *Bethlehem of Pennsylvania*, 116. Moravians themselves urged those in charge of such planning not to locate their headquarters in Bethlehem, fearing the strain such an intrusion would have on the church and its community. See Jordan, "Bethlehem During the Revolution," 72–73. When a cartridge factory was set up in Bethlehem in September 1777, the Moravians objected and Continental authorities moved it to Allentown, which became a supply center for military provisions and a wagon depot during this stage of the war. The townspeople also engaged in arms repair and the manufacturing of saddles and bayonet scabbards. See Hellerich, *Allentown*, 20–21.

43. *Two Hundred Years*, 58; Hellerich, *Allentown*, 21.

44. Preston A. Barba, *They Came to Emmaus: A History* (Allentown, Pa.: Holben Printing, 1960), 118–19, 122; Alderfer, *Northampton Heritage*, 144.

45. Yates, *Bethlehem of Pennsylvania*, 110, 115, 117–18.

46. Ibid., 115.

47. Alderfer, *Northampton Heritage*, 154. According to one local historian, Lafayette "was attentively nursed by Boeckel's wife Barbara and daughter Liesel, and pretty little stories with variations connected with his sojourn under that roof were current among the local traditions many years afterward." See Joseph M. Levering, *A History of Bethlehem, Pennsylvania, 1741–1892* (Bethlehem, Pa.: Times Publishing Company, 1903), 465.

48. Yates, *Bethlehem of Pennsylvania*, 112–15; Jordan, "Bethlehem During the Revolution," 71–72. In the Moravian settlement, single men and women lived in segregated buildings.

49. Trussell, *Pennsylvania Landmarks*, 49.

50. Yates, *Bethlehem of Pennsylvania*, 110, 117, 118, 120; Alderfer, *Northampton Heritage*, 152.

51. Walters, *Bethlehem Long Ago*, 52.

52. Myers, *Lehigh Valley*, 37; Robert Secor, ed., *Pennsylvania, 1776* (University Park, Pa.: The Pennsylvania State University Press, 1975), 339; Robert K. Mentzell, *The Liberty Bell's Interlude in Allentown* (Sellersville, Pa.: Sellersville Historical and Achievement Authority, 1974), 4–5; Hellerich, *Allentown*, 19. The Liberty Bell Shrine located beneath the very same Zion's Reformed Church today in Allentown proudly proclaims itself as the safe hiding place for the Liberty Bell and the bells of Christ Church during the uncertain months in the fall of 1777 and the winter of 1778. See Roberts, *History of Lehigh County*, 1:137–38.

53. Yates, *Bethlehem of Pennsylvania*, 112, 116; Barba, *They Came to Emmaus*, 121–23. Moravians were displeased also by the numbers of "low women and thieves" who wandered into town. See Jordan, "Bethlehem During the Revolution," 74.

54. Yates, *Bethelem of Pennsylvania*, 110, 119.

55. Among those who visited Bethlehem during the war were some distinguished members of various countries' military or government. John Hancock stayed there in September 1777 and again in 1778. Henry Laurens arrived in the town in November 1777 before being elected president of the Continental Congress. Richard Henry Lee journeyed there, and Gouverneur Morris, who earlier had considered the Moravians loyalists, paid a visit in 1778. Numerous military personalities enjoyed some rest and relaxation in Bethlehem: General Henry Knox in August 1777, and Baron Frederick William Augustus von Steuben later in 1778. The Baron Frederick A. Riedesel, major general in the British army, a paroled prisoner, visited with the baroness and their three children in early 1779 and returned several other times; paroled British army officer General William Phillips stayed there also. General Pulaski, Count Casimir, visited Lafayette during his recuperation and actually stood sentinel to protect the Sisters House from rowdy troops. Pulaski proved to be a town favorite. In 1778, General Horatio Gates and Mrs. Gates and his army inspector, Chevalier de La Neuville, Colonel Ethan Allen, the wife of General Nathanael Greene,

Samuel Adams, the first Minister Plenipotentiary from France to the United States, Chevalier Conrad Alexander Gerard, and the unofficial representative from Spain to the United States, Don Juan de Miralles all visited the town. Later in 1782, the Marquis François Jean de Chastellux, under the services of Rochambeau, journeyed to Bethlehem. In the summer of 1783, with the war over, Philadelphia merchant Samuel Wharton accompanied John Paul Jones to Bethlehem. Martha Washington stayed overnight and attended Moravian services on her visit in mid-June 1779. And in July 1782, General George Washington himself arrived "quite unexpectedly and very quietly" with just two aides-de-camp. He inspected the Moravian main buildings with Bishop John Ettwein and attended a service that evening. The following morning, he left for Easton. See Yates, *Bethlehem of Pennsylvania,* 117–27. Nazareth too hosted an impressive array of military and political leaders, both domestic and foreign, over the course of the war. See Shultz, "Historic Nazareth," 60–61.

56. Yates, *Bethelem of Pennsylvania,* 119.

57. Beverly Prior Smaby, *The Transformation of Moravian Bethlehem: From Communal Mission to Family Economy* (Philadelphia: University of Pennsylvania Press, 1988), 39.

58. Alderfer, *Northampton Heritage,* 141.

59. Ibid., 141–42; Yates, *Bethlehem of Pennsylvania,* 117.

60. Alderfer, *Northampton Heritage,* 142; Yates, *Bethlehem of Pennsylvania,* 107.

61. Hall and Hall, *Lehigh Valley,* 30.

62. Hellerich, *Allentown,* 18.

63. Alderfer, *Northampton Heritage,* 143.

64. Ibid., 143–44.

65. Ibid., 143.

66. Yates, *Bethlehem of Pennsylvania,* 107. Indeed, at Nazareth the fines became so unbearable, and the sacrifices so severe, that "some of the younger brethren secretly joined the militia, to the extent at least of attending the drill day exercises." See Shultz, "Historic Nazareth," 52.

67. Smaby, *Moravian Bethlehem,* 39.

68. Ibid.; Yates, *Bethlehem of Pennsylvania,* 108.

69. Yates, *Bethlehem of Pennsylvania,* 122.

70. Smaby, *Moravian Bethlehem,* 39–40.

71. Yates, *Bethlehem of Pennsylvania,* 123.

72. Ibid., 131.

73. Hall and Hall, *Lehigh Valley,* 22.

74. Damage to the community was extensive. Among the losses for which the Moravians requested compensation were 22 acres of buckwheat that were destroyed, the 15,500 fence rails used by troops while encamped in those fields, and an additional 11 acres of Indian corn, turnips, and cabbage, the entire flax crop, and 600 cords of wood. See Jordan, "Bethlehem During the Revolution," 73.

75. Yates, *Bethlehem of Pennsylvania,* 120; Levering, *History of Bethlehem,* 500–503.

76. Barba, *They Came to Emmaus,* 124; Shultz, "Historic Nazareth," 50–54. Andreas Giering, a leading Emmaus Moravian, was a particular target of local authorities. Accused of being a Tory, he was arrested and fined in August 1776; he was attacked in December 1777, and in April 1778 along with a dozen fellow Emmaus brethren he was arrested for refusing to take the Test Oath and hauled off to Easton to serve seven weeks in prison. Eventually, he took the oath. John Wetzel, the county lieutenant had a special zeal for seeking out Moravians, who he adamantly believed to be the enemy and deserving of no leniency. Ironically, Wetzel's mother and father were charter members of the Emmaus Moravian Church and John was baptized at age seventeen but later left the church. See Hellerich, *Allentown,* 17–18; Barba, *They Came to Emmaus,* 115, 119–21, 123–24.

77. Smaby, *Moravian Bethlehem,* 41–42. In the smaller Moravian settlement at Emmaus, of thirty-two male adults, twelve enlisted in the Revolutionary cause. See Barba, *They Came to Emmaus,* 128–33.

78. Shultz, "Historic Nazareth," 54–55, 67.

79. Roberts et al., *History of Lehigh County,* 1:148.

80. Hellerich, *Allentown,* 24–25.

81. In January 1777, the value of $100 in specie in Continental money was $105; by January 1781, the Continental had depreciated to $7,400. See Roberts, et al., *History of Lehigh County,* 1:148.

82. Hellerich, *Allentown,* 27.

83. Ibid., 25.

84. Wilbur Henry Seibert, *Loyalists of Pennsylvania* (Boston: Gregg Press, 1972), 58–59. In fact, only one property was confiscated and auctioned by order of the Supreme Executive Council. See Seibert, *Loyalists,* 92.

85. Yates, *Lehigh Valley,* 38; Alderfer, *Northampton Heritage,* 158; Hellerich, *Allentown,* 31.

86. Jackson Turner Main, *The Anti-Federalists: Critics of the Constitution, 1781–1788* (Chicago: Quadrangle Books, 1964), 21–22. As Jackson T. Main observed more than three decades ago, "no leaders emerged to arouse opposition" to a unified nation or a conservative state government on the shores of the Delaware River. Dependent in part on the river and on Philadelphia for commerce, Northampton County solidly supported both the national Federalist cause and the state Republican/Federalist cause.

87. Hellerich, *Allentown,* 15, 32–34.

88. Yates, *Lehigh Valley,* 39–40.

Chapter 4. Berks County

1. *Votes and Proceedings of the House of Representatives of the Province of Pennsylvania,* vol. 5 (Philadelphia: Henry Miller, 1775), February 10, 1764, 313; February 15, 1764, 313–14; Charles H. Lincoln, *The Revolutionary Movement in Pennsylvania, 1760–1776* (1901; reprint, Cos Cob, Conn.: John E. Edwards, 1968), 46; Henry Melchior Muhlenberg Richards, "The Pennsylvania German in the Revolutionary War, 1775–1783," *Proceedings of the Pennsylvania German Society,* vol. 17 (1908; reprint, Baltimore: Genealogical Publishing Company, 1978), 17. See also, for a text of the petition, "A Remonstrance from the Pennsylvania Frontier," February 13, 1764, in *Sources and Documents Illustrating the American Revolution, 1764–1788, and the Formation of the Federal Constitution,* ed. Samuel Eliot Morison, 2nd ed. (New York: Oxford University Press, 1965), 9–10.

2. Philip Pendleton, "The Origin of the Swedish Settlement at Old Morlatton," *Historical Review of Berks County* 53 (1988): 129–33, 141, 143; Louis Richards, "Swedish Settlement at Morlatton," *Transactions of the Historical Society of Berks County* 3 (1910–16): 125–33; Amon Stapleton, "The Huguenot Element in the Settlement of Berks County," *Transactions of the Historical Society of Berks County* 2 (1905–10): 386–401. For more information on the settlement of the Oley Valley, see Peter G. Bertolet, *Fragments of the Past: Historical Sketches of Oley and Vicinity* (Oley: Women's Club of the Oley Valley, 1980), 1–2; P. C. Croll, *Annals of the Oley Valley in Berks County, Pa.: Over Two Hundred Years of Local History of an American Canaan* (Reading, Pa.:

Reading Eagle Press, 1926), 7–16; Philip E. Pendleton, *Oley Valley Heritage: The Colonial Years, 1700–1775* (Birdsboro: Pennsylvania German Society; Oley, Pa.: Oley Valley Heritage Association, 1994). The religious diversity of early Berks County is examined in Karen Guenther, "A 'Garden for the Friends of God': Religious Diversity in the Oley Valley to 1750," *Pennsylvania Folklife* 33 (1984): 138–44; Guenther, "The Religious Environment of Eighteenth-Century Berks County, Pennsylvania," in "A Quaker Community on the Pennsylvania Frontier: Exeter Monthly Meeting, 1737–1789" (Ph.D. diss., University of Houston, 1994), 30–75; and William W. Hummel, "Religion on a Moving Frontier: The Berks County Area, 1700–1748," *Pennsylvania Heritage* 4 (March 1978): 22–26.

3. Frank E. Lichtenthaeler, "Storm Blown Seeds of Schoharie," *Pennsylvania German Folklife Society* 9 (1941): 3–105; Morton L. Montgomery, *School History of Berks County in Pennsylvania* (Philadelphia: J. B. Rodgers Printing Company, 1889), 27–31; Commissioners of Berks County, *Berks County, Pennsylvania: Its History and Government,* 3rd ed. (Kutztown, Pa.: Kutztown Publishing Company, 1980), 5–6.

4. John E. Eshelman, "Anthony and Mary Lee: Pioneer Quakers of Oley," *Historical Review of Berks County* 17 (1952): 115; Guenther, "Exeter Monthly Meeting," passim; John J. McKenna Jr., "Early Irish in Berks County," *Historical Review of Berks County* 17 (1951): 20–21, 25; McKenna, "Early Welsh in Berks County," *Historical Review of Berks County* 15 (1950): 179–86; *The Goshenhoppen Registers, 1741–1819* (Baltimore: Genealogical Publishing Company, 1984), passim; Warrantee Township Maps, Berks County, Pa., at the Historical Society of Berks County.

5. Pendleton, *Oley Valley Heritage,* 29–31, 34–36; James T. Lemon, *The Best Poor Man's Country: A Geographical Study of Early Southeastern Pennsylvania* (New York: W. W. Norton & Company, 1972), 150–83; Stevenson Whitcomb Fletcher, *Pennsylvania Agriculture and Country Life, 1640–1840,* 2nd ed. (Harrisburg: Pennsylvania Historical and Museum Commission, 1971), 123–228; Montgomery, *School History of Berks County,* 96–100.

6. Pendleton, *Oley Valley Heritage,* 37–47; Guenther, "Quaker Community," 196–97; "Proprietary Return for the County of Berks for the Year 1767," *Pennsylvania Archives (PA),* ser. 3, 18:3–86; "Register of the Property of the Inhabitants of Berks County," *PA,* ser. 3, 18:177–301 (hereafter 1779 Tax List); Montgomery, *School History of Berks County,* 100–102; Laura Leff Becker, "The American Revolution as a Community Experience: A Case Study of Reading, Pennsylvania" (Ph.D. diss., University of Pennsylvania, 1978), 108–47.

7. Pendleton, *Oley Valley Heritage,* 42–43; Arthur Cecil Bining, *Pennsylvania Iron Manufacture in the Eighteenth Century,* 2nd ed. (Harrisburg: Pennsylvania Historical and Museum Commission, 1973), 40, 171–76; Gerald G. Eggert, *The Iron Industry in Pennsylvania,* Pennsylvania Historical Studies no. 25 (Harrisburg: Pennsylvania Historical Association, 1994), 16–19, 21–26.

8. On the requirements for naturalization and voting, see William T. Parsons, *The Pennsylvania Dutch: A Persistent Minority* (Boston: G. K. Hall & Company, 1976), 59; and Theodore Thayer, *Pennsylvania Politics and the Growth of Democracy, 1740–1776* (Harrisburg: Pennsylvania Historical and Museum Commission, 1953), 6. For more information on the settlement of the Pennsylvania hinterland, see Lemon, *Best Poor Man's Country,* 42–97, 118–49; and Russell Sage Nelson, "Backcountry Pennsylvania (1709 to 1774): The Ideals of William Penn in Practice" (Ph.D. diss., University of Wisconsin, 1968), 27–222, 253–99.

9. Kenneth Gertney, "The Formation of Berks County," *Historical Review of Berks County* 37 (1972): 88–89, 101–9; "Petition of the Inhabitants," Draper MSS 2 C 8.2–8.3 (microfilm) (Handwritten, Draper Manuscript Collection, State Historical Society of Wisconsin, Madison, Wis.). See also Earl J. Heydinger, "The Schuylkill, Lifeline to Valley Forge," *Historical Review of Berks County* 41 (1976): 104, 106–8, 126–27.

10. Gertney, "Formation of Berks County," 88–89, 101–9; Raymond W. Albright, *Two Centuries of Reading, Pa., 1748–1948: A History of the County Seat of Berks County* (Reading, Pa.: Historical Society of Berks County, 1948), 1–17; Morton L. Montgomery, *History of Berks County, Pennsylvania* (Philadelphia: Everts, Peck & Richards, 1886), 23–45; J. Bennett Nolan, *The Foundation of the Town of Reading in Pennsylvania* (Reading, Pa.: Edward Pengelly & Bro., 1929), 13–66; I. Daniel Rupp, *History of the Counties of Berks and Lebanon . . .* (Lancaster: Gilbert Hills, 1844), 3–22.

11. Minutes of the Supreme Executive Council, February 5, 1770, *Colonial Records* 9:650; Morton L. Montgomery, *Political Hand-Book of Berks County, Pennsylvania, 1753–1883* (Reading, Pa.: B. F. Owen, 1883), 10–12, 15–17, 19–20, 23, 26–27, 29–32; Laura Leff Becker, "Diversity and Its Significance in an Eighteenth-Century Pennsylvania Town," in *Friends and Neighbors: Group Life in America's First Plural Society,* ed. Michael Zuckerman (Philadelphia: Temple University Press, 1982), 201–2; Becker, "The American Revolution as a Community Experience," 269–74. For more on Berks County politics during this era, see William W. Hummel, "The Emergence of a Ruling Elite in Berks County," *Historical Review of Berks County* 49 (1984): 101–6, 115–20.

12. *Votes,* vol. 5, March 29, 1763, 255–56; February 15, 1764, 313–14; May 16, 1764, 340; *Votes and Proceedings of the House of Representatives of the Province of Pennsylvania,* vol. 6 (Philadelphia: Henry Miller, 1777), January 20, 1768, 21; January 27, 1768, 29; Lincoln, *Revolutionary Movement,* 46–49. There is no evidence that laws passed by Parliament during the 1760s, such as the Stamp Act, aroused much passion in Berks County, although county economic and political leaders undoubtedly had access to the arguments presented in the Philadelphia press. See A. G. Roeber, *Palatines, Liberty, and Property: German Lutherans in Colonial British America* (Baltimore: Johns Hopkins University Press, 1993), 283–310.

13. *Votes,* vol. 6, February 10, 1773, 442–43; January 11, 1774, 501–2 (source for quote); February 25, 1775, 567; February 28, 1776, 676; March 5, 1776, 684.

14. Minutes of the Supreme Executive Council, *Colonial Records* 9, January 30, 1768, 9:440 (source for first quote); January 19, 1769, 556; January 19, 1769, 561 (source for last quote).

15. "Berks County Resolves, 1774," *PA,* ser. 2, 14: 321–22.

16. Ibid., 321–22 (quote from 321); Morton L. Montgomery, *History of Berks County, Pennsylvania, in the Revolution, from 1774 to 1783* (Reading, Pa.: Charles F. Haage, 1894), 23–29.

17. Craig Biddle, "Edward Biddle," *PMHB* 1 (1879): 100–103; Montgomery, *Berks in Revolution,* 209–12; and Minutes of the Supreme Executive Council, *Colonial Records,* October 15, 1774, 10:213; March 15, 1775, 10:241.

18. Montgomery, *Berks in Revolution,* 28, 138, 194; Becker, "American Revolution as a Community Experience," 413–15.

19. "Proceedings of the Standing Committee," *PA,* ser. 2, 14:322–23 (quote from 322); Albright, *Two Centuries of Reading,* 65.

20. Montgomery, *Berks in Revolution,* 32–33, 75–144; Albright, *Two Centuries of Reading,* 82.

21. "Extract of a Letter from Reading, Pennsylvania, Dated April 26, 1775," *American Archives,* ser. 4, 2:400.

22. Albright, *Two Centuries of Reading,* 69–70; Richards, *Pennsylvania-German in Revolutionary War,* 17–20, 22; *The Papers of George Washington,* Revolutionary War Series, ed. W. W. Abbot, vol. 1 (Charlottesville: University Press of Virginia, 1985), 445–46. That September, one member of Nagel's company, Private John Lehman, was fined 20s. and sentenced to six days imprisonment for "disobedient and mutinous Behaviour." "General Orders," September 13, 1775, in ibid., 454–55 (quote from 455).

23. Albright, *Two Centuries of Reading,* 82; Montgomery, *Berks in Revolution,* 32–33, 75–144;

Becker, "American Revolution as a Community Experience," 332, 335. Montgomery's volume includes lists of members of Berks County companies and regiments in specific battles on 75–144.

24. Albright, *Two Centuries of Reading*, 71; John B. Frantz, " 'Prepare Thyself . . . to Meet the Lord Thy God!': Religion in Pennsylvania During the Revolution," *Pennsylvania Heritage* 2 (June 1976): 29; Charles H. Glatfelter, *Pastors and People: German Lutheran and Reformed Churches in the Pennsylvania Field, 1717–1793*, vol. 1: *Pastors and Congregations* (Breinigsville, Pa.: Pennsylvania German Society, 1980), 89–90; Montgomery, *Berks in Revolution*, 208; Philip E. Pendleton, " 'Dutch Buggers': The Anglican Elite of Berks County, Pennsylvania, in the American Revolution" (M.A. thesis, University of North Carolina at Chapel Hill, 1981), 142; Morton L. Montgomery, comp., *1748–1898 History of Reading, Pennsylvania, and the Anniversary Proceedings of the Sesqui-Centennial, June 5–12, 1898* (Reading, Pa.: Times Book Print, 1898), 17–18; Becker, "American Revolution as a Community Experience," 334.

25. "Minutes of Committee of Berks County, 1775," *PA*, ser. 1, 4:649 (source for quote); William Reeser to Committee of Safety, September 11, 1775, *PA*, ser. 1, 4:653; Albright, *Two Centuries of Reading*, 66; Montgomery, *Berks in Revolution*, 37.

26. Lincoln, *Revolutionary Movement*, 277; J. Paul Selsam, *The Pennsylvania Constitution of 1776: A Study in Revolutionary Democracy* (1936; reprint, New York: Octagon Books, 1971); Robert L. Brunhouse, *The Counter-Revolution in Pennsylvania, 1776–1790* (1942; reprint, Harrisburg: Pennsylvania Historical and Museum Commission, 1971), 19–20.

27. William Henry Egle, "The Constitutional Convention of 1776: Biographical Sketches of Its Members," *PMHB* 3 (1879): 323–24, 441, 443–44; 4 (1880): 89, 98, 233, 367.

28. Selsam, *Constitution of 1776*, 164; Brunhouse, *Counter-Revolution*, 19–20.

29. Brunhouse, *Counter-Revolution*, 34, 55–56, 90.

30. Pendleton, " 'Dutch Buggers,' " 142; Montgomery, *Berks in Revolution*, 174–81; Bining, *Pennsylvania Iron Manufacture*, 133–45; Albright, *Two Centuries of Reading*, 75; Heydinger, "Schuylkill," 106–7.

31. Bining, *Pennsylvania Iron Manufacture*, 124–25, 133–45; Daniel K. Perry, "The Origins, Procurement, and Production of Iron Cannon in Pennsylvania During the American Revolution" (M.A. thesis, The Pennsylvania State University, 1986), 22, 45, 59, 82; Joseph E. Walker, *Hopewell Village: A Social and Economic History of an Iron-Making Community* (Philadelphia: University of Pennsylvania Press, 1966), 24–27.

32. Albright, *Two Centuries of Reading*, 75–76; Minutes of the Council of Safety, *Colonial Records*, November 16, 1776, 9:7; December 4, 1776, 9:30 (source for quote); January 12, 1777, 9:86.

33. Montgomery, *Berks in Revolution*, 174, 198; Albright, *Two Centuries of Reading*, 75; "Resolutions of Congress, 1778," January 17, 1778, *PA*, ser. 1, 6:177; March 19, 1778, 6:374; George Washington to President Thomas Wharton, February 10, 1778, *PA*, ser. 1, 6:250 (source for first quote); Minutes of the Supreme Executive Council, March 24, 1778, *Colonial Records* 11:446 (source for last quote). For more information on the selection of Valley Forge as the site for the encampment, see Wayne Bodle, "Generals and 'Gentlemen': Pennsylvania Politics and the Decision for Valley Forge," *Pennsylvania History* 62 (1995): 59–89.

34. Albright, *Two Centuries of Reading*, 77; *Minutes and Letters of the Coetus of the German Reformed Congregations in Pennsylvania, 1747–1792, Together with Three Preliminary Reports of the Rev. John Philip Boehm, 1734–1744*, ed. James I. Good and William J. Hinke (Philadelphia: Reformed Church Publication Board, 1903), 364–65.

35. Alexander Graydon, *Memoirs of His Own Time, with Reminiscences of the Men and Events of the Revolution*, ed. John Stockton Littell (Philadelphia: Lindsay & Blakiston, 1846), 298.

36. James Sproat Journal, 30–31 (Handwritten, General Manuscript Collection, MS 98, HSP).

37. Colonel I. Melcher to President Thomas Wharton, October 8, 1777, *PA,* ser. 1, 5:653 (source for quote); Albright, *Two Centuries of Reading,* 80; Jacob Fry, *The History of Trinity Lutheran Church, Reading, Pa., 1751–1894* (Reading, Pa.: By the Congregation, 1894), 89; Daniel Miller, *History of the Reformed Church in Reading, Pa.* (Reading, Pa.: Daniel Miller, 1905), 169; John E. Eshelman, "The Society of Friends, and Their Meeting Houses, in Berks County," *Historical Review of Berks County* 19 (1954): 108; "Exeter Monthly Meeting Book B," Minutes of Exeter Monthly Meeting, 1765–85, 26th day, 11th month, 1777 (Handwritten, Friends Historical Library, Swarthmore College, Swarthmore, Pa.).

38. Montgomery, *Berks in Revolution,* 151–59; Bining, *Pennsylvania Iron Manufacture,* 99; "Records of Trinity Evangelical Lutheran Church, Reading, Berks County, Pennsylvania, 1751–1812," copied by J. W. Early, Baptisms (Handwritten, Historical Society of Berks County, Reading, Pa.); Raymond W. Ford Jr., "Germans and Other Foreign Stock: Their Part in the Evolution of Reading, Pennsylvania" (Ph.D. diss., University of Pennsylvania, 1963), 60–62. For further information on Hessian prisoners, see Andrew Shaaber, "The Hessian Camp of Reading, Pa., 1781–1783," *Transactions of the Historical Society of Berks County* 3 (1910–16): 24–29; and Larry Wildemuth, "Hessians and the Citizens of Reading," *Historical Review of Berks County* 35 (1970): 46–49, 66–68, 70–75.

39. Wildemuth, "Hessians," 46–48; Montgomery, *History of Berks,* 152.

40. Minutes of the Council of Safety, *Colonial Records,* July 8, 1776, 10:636; September 10, 1776, 10:714; "Proceedings of the Committee of Berks Company, 1776," September 3–5, 1776, September 1776, *PA,* ser. 1, 5:19–20; Wildemuth, "Hessians," 48.

41. Colonel Jacob Morgan to President Thomas Wharton, September 18, 1777, *PA,* ser. 1, 5:632.

42. Captain P. Pitcairn to John Jay, President of Congress, May 5, 1779, *PA,* ser. 1, 7:374 (source for quote); President Joseph Reed to the Board of War, May 31, 1779, *PA,* ser. 1, 7:450; Richard Peters to President Joseph Reed, June 11, 1779, *PA,* ser. 1, 7:480; Wildemuth, "Hessians," 68.

43. President Joseph Reed to Valentine Eckert, June 27, 1781, *PA,* ser. 1, 9:230–31 (source for first quote); Valentine Eckert to President Joseph Reed, June 24, 1781, *PA,* ser. 1, 9:225–26 (second quote from 226); Lieutenant Colonel R. P. Mentges to President Joseph Reed, June 20, 1781, *PA,* ser. 1, 9:299; Wildemuth, "Hessians," 70–71.

44. James Read to Timothy Matlack, February 7, 1778, *PA,* ser. 1, 6:245.

45. "Proceedings of the Committee [of Observation]," January 30, 1776, *PA,* ser. 2, 14:323–25 (quotes from 324); 1779 Tax List.

46. Henry Haller to the Council of Safety, *PA,* ser. 1, 5:144 (source for first quote); Israel Putnam to the Council of Safety, January 21, 1777, *PA,* ser. 1, 5:196 (source for last two quotes); Montgomery, *Berks in Revolution,* 110–13.

47. Pendleton, " 'Dutch Buggers,' " 147–48, 150; Edgar Legaré Pennington, "The Anglican Clergy of Pennsylvania in the American Revolution," *PMHB* 63 (October 1939): 404–5; Great Britain, Public Records Office, Audit Office 12, "Proceedings of the Commissioners of American Claims Under the Acts of the 23rd, 25th, 26th, 27th, 28th, & 29th George III containing the Reports and Statement of the Said Commissioners," 42:2–4 (quote from 4) (microfilm) (Handwritten, Library of Congress Manuscript Division, Washington, D.C.); Minutes of the Supreme Executive Council, August 31, 1778, *Colonial Records,* 11:564–65; *Journal of the House of Representatives of the Commonwealth of Pennsylvania . . . 1776–1781* (Philadelphia, 1782), 166. For more information on Murray's experiences during the Revolution, see Karen Guenther, " 'A Faithful

Soldier of Christ': The Career of the Reverend Dr. Alexander Murray, Missionary to Berks County, Pa., 1762–1778," *Historical Magazine of the Protestant Episcopal Church* 55 (1986): 12–15. The Continental Congress issued a reprimand that fall to the Berks County Committee of Observation for acts of violence against individuals suspected of being loyalists. Anne M. Ousterhout, *A State Divided: Opposition in Pennsylvania to the American Revolution* (Westport, Conn.: Greenwood Press, 1987), 120, 128. For more information on opposition to the Revolution, see Richard K. MacMaster, *Conscience in Crisis: Mennonites and Other Peace Churches in America, 1739–1789: Interpretation and Documents* (Scottdale, Pa.: Herald Press, 1979), chaps. 3–7.

48. Albright, *Two Centuries of Reading,* 69; Brunhouse, *Counter-Revolution,* 40–41; MacMaster, *Conscience in Crisis,* chaps. 3–7; and *The Statutes at Large of Pennsylvania, from 1682 to 1801,* comp. James T. Mitchell and Henry Flanders (Harrisburg, Pa.: William Stanley Ray, State Printer, 1902), 9:110–14.

49. Miscellaneous Papers, Philadelphia Yearly Meeting, Meeting for Sufferings, 15, 30, 48, 49 (source for quote), 83 (Handwritten, Friends Historical Library).

50. 1779 Tax List; Jacob Morgan to President Thomas Wharton, April 27, 1777, *PA,* ser. 1, 5:322–23; MacMaster, *Conscience in Crisis,* 364.

51. Minutes of the Supreme Executive Council, December 13, 1780, *Colonial Records,* 12:568 (source for quote); MacMaster, *Conscience in Crisis,* 363–64, 384–85.

52. MacMaster, *Conscience in Crisis,* 385–86; Joseph S. Foster, *In Pursuit of Equal Liberty: George Bryan and the Revolution in Pennsylvania* (University Park: The Pennsylvania State University Press, 1994), 154–55 (quote from George Bryan to Joseph Reed, November 7, 1780, Reed Papers, New York Historical Society, cited by Foster). By 1780, Pennsylvania currency was greatly inflated.

53. "Document 233," Petition of Inhabitants of Tulpehocken and Bethel Townships to President Joseph Reed, January 11, 1781, in MacMaster, *Conscience in Crisis,* 387–88 (quote from 388); Minutes of the Supreme Executive Council, *Colonial Records,* January 17, 1781, 12:601–2; January 26, 1781, 12:608.

54. "Exeter Monthly Meeting Book B," 3rd day, 4th month, 1782; "A Record of Manumission," Exeter Monthly Meeting, 1–6 (Handwritten, Friends Historical Society); *1779 Tax List;* "Act for the Gradual Abolition of Slavery," in *Unity from Diversity: Extracts from Selected Pennsylvania Colonial Documents, 1681–1780, in Commemoration of the Tercentenary of the Commonwealth,* comp. and ed. Louis M. Waddell (Harrisburg: Pennsylvania Historical and Museum Commission, 1980), 87–88; *Journal of the House of Representatives,* 325, 392, 398–99, 402, 410, 424, 435, 455; Gary B. Nash and Jean R. Soderlund, *Freedom by Degrees: Emancipation in Pennsylvania and Its Aftermath* (New York: Oxford University Press, 1991), 105.

55. Journal of the House of Representatives, 325, 392, 398–99, 402, 410, 424, 435, 455; *1779 Tax List;* "Return and Assessment for the County of Berks for the Year 1780" (hereafter 1780 Tax List), *PA,* ser. 3, 18:305–430; "Return and Assessment for the County of Berks for the Year 1781," *PA,* ser. 3, 18:433–555; U.S. Census, *Heads of Families at the First Census of the United States Taken in the Year 1790: Pennsylvania,* "Berks County" (Washington, D.C.: U.S. U.S. Government Printing Office, 1908), 26–45.

56. Nash and Soderlund, *Freedom by Degrees,* 104–8; Owen S. Ireland, "Germans Against Abolition: A Minority's View of Slavery in Revolutionary Pennsylvania," *Journal of Interdisciplinary History* 4 (1973): 685–706; *1780 Tax List;* Paul N. Schaeffer, "Slavery in Berks County," *Historical Review of Berks County* 6 (1941): 112; Bining, *Pennsylvania Iron Manufacture,* 171–76. See also Richard Johnson, "Slavery and Indentured Blacks in Berks County Before 1800," *Historical Review of Berks County* 37 (Winter 1971–72): 8–14.

57. Ireland, "Germans Against Abolition," 689–706; *Journal of the House of Representatives*, 435–36; "Act for the Gradual Abolition of Slavery," 87–88; Ira V. Brown, *The Negro in Pennsylvania History*, Pennsylvania History Studies 11 (University Park: Pennsylvania Historical Association, 1970), 6–8; Nash and Soderlund, *Freedom by Degrees*, 99–113.

58. Minutes of the Supreme Executive Council, *Colonial Records*, May 9, 1781, 12:721–22; *Colonial Records*, August 15, 1781, 13:350; September 14, 1782, 13:368–69.

59. Montgomery, *Berks in Revolution*, 194–97; Becker, "American Revolution as a Community Experience," 417–26.

60. Bining, *Pennsylvania Iron Manufacture*, 127–29; Walker, *Hopewell Village*, 28–32; Brunhouse, *Counter-Revolution*, 328; Montgomery, *Berks in Revolution*, 194–97.

Chapter 5. York County

1. John Gibson, ed., *History of York County* (Chicago: F. A. Battey Publishing Company, 1886); George Prowell, *History of York County, Pennsylvania* (Chicago: J. H. Beers & Company, 1908), 2 vols. Much of the general information comes from Gibson and Prowell. Other sources used included County Deed Books, Wills, Estate Records, and Orphans' Court Records in the York County Courthouse and *Pennsylvania Archives (PA)* and *Colonial Records* in Harrisburg, Pa.

2. Estimates concerning the percentages of Germans in the county have been determined by tallying various land records, tax records and church records.

3. A. G. Roeber, *Palatines, Liberty, and Property: German Lutherans in Colonial British America* (Baltimore: Johns Hopkins University Press, 1993); Sally Schwartz, *A Mixed Multitude: The Struggle for Toleration in Colonial Pennsylvania* (New York: New York University Press, 1987). The cultural evolution of York County Germans was consistent with the patterns described by Roeber. Likewise, Schwartz provides a good general description of German habitation in Pennsylvania.

4. Although not a sect by most standards, Moravians were referred to as such by many Lutheran and Reformed York County Germans because of the authority held by Count Zinzendorf. Some York Countians were convinced that Zinzendorf was plotting to consolidate all German churches under his authority.

5. *Dictionary of American Biography* (New York: Scribner & Sons, 1928–36), 2:283–84; Edward Spangler, *Annals of the Families of Caspar, Henry, Baltzer, and George Spengler* (York, Pa., 1896), 2:390–92 (hereafter *Spengler Annals*); John Jordan, "Biographical Sketch of Colonel Thomas Hartley," *PMHB* 25 (1908): 306–9. (Spengler later became Spangler.)

6. *PA*, ser. 2, 14:545–61. The other members were George Eichelberger, Michael Doudel, David Grier, Michael Swope, Peter Reel, Thomas Hartley, George Irwin, James Donaldson, Michael Smyers, Baltzer Spengler Jr., and John Hay.

7. *PA*, ser. 2, 14:545–61; *Spengler Annals*, 2:402.

8. *Spengler Annals*, 2:402.

9. Hay Papers, Historical Society of York County, York, Pa., February 14, 1775; A. W. Eichelberger, *Eichelberger Family Record* (Hanover, Pa.: Hanover Herald Publishing, 1901), 21.

10. *PA*, ser. 5, 10:3, 22–23; John Heisey, *York County in the American Revolution* (York, Pa.: Historical Society of York County, 1971), 4–5; Philip Schlegel, *Recruits to Continentals: A History of the York County Rifle Company, June 1775–January 1777* (York, Pa.: Historical Society of York County, 1979), 9–10.

11. *PA*, ser. 5, 10:22–24; Schlegel, *Recruits to Continentals*, 10–11.

12. Hay Papers, July 1, 1775; George Neisser, trans., "Moravian Diaries from the Congregation at York," May 31, 1775 (unpublished, Historical Society of York County).

13. *PA*, ser. 1, 4:642; Schlegel, *Recruits to Continentals*, 10–11.

14. Platt file (M804), Historical Society of York County; Peter Tritt file (M804, reel 2414), Historical Society of York County; *Pennsylvania Evening Post*, August 31, 1775; *The Pennsylvania Journal*, July 25, 1775; *Boston News-Letter*, August 31, 1775. William Thompson was a surveyor from Carlisle. His battalion was comprised of riflemen from both York and Cumberland counties. Legend has it that Thompson's unit became the first from west of the Hudson River to join Washington's Continental Army. Thompson's battalion fought in many of the engagements between July 1775 and July 1776. The unit later became part of the America expedition into Canada.

15. This conclusion was reached by comparing the roster from Doudel's unit with church records, land records, and available tax records.

16. *Pennsylvania Packet*, December 29, 1785. Determining an exact number of men in York County during the war years is impossible. However, tax records and deeds indicate that there were about 4,500 men between the ages of 15 and 55 within the county. The *Packet* estimated that there were 6,281 taxables in the county in 1785.

17. *PA*, ser. 1, 4:688.

18. File 291, "Revolutionary Papers," Historical Society of York County.

19. Hay Papers, February 5, 1776.

20. Neisser, trans., *Moravian Diaries*, May 28, 31, 1776; Hay Papers, March 30, 1776; *Spengler Annals*, 2:349.

21. *PA*, ser. 1, 4:641; Eichelberger, *The Eichelberger Family*, 20.

22. Neisser, trans., *Moravian Diaries*, July 17 and September 19, 1776.

23. *Spengler Annals*, 2:463; George Prowell, *History of York County* (Chicago: J. H. Beers, 1907), 2:651. The Yorktown response was to the Continental Congress's approval of Richard Henry Lee's July 2 resolution endorsing independence.

24. Neisser, trans., *Moravian Diaries*, July 17, 1776.

25. Ibid., July 31 and August 18, 1776.

26. Schlegel, *Recruits to Continentals*, 29–34; Heisey, *York County in the American Revolution*, 8–9.

27. *Journals of the Continental Congress, 1774–1789* (Washington, D.C.: U.S. U.S. Government Printing Office, 1904–9), 8:742, 751–52, 755; L. H. Butterfield and K. Friedlander, eds., *The Adams Family Correspondences* (Cambridge: Harvard University Press, 1973), 2:342.

28. John Adlum, "Memoirs," 12–20, Historical Society of York County.

29. Butterfield and Friedlander, eds., *Adams Correspondences*, 2:342, 352, 361–62.

30. William Eddis, *Letters from America* (London, 1792), 145–48.

31. Ibid.

32. Neisser, trans., *Moravian Diaries*, February 2 and March 21, 1778.

33. Heisey, *York County in the American Revolution*, 14–17.

34. John C. Miller, *The Triumph of Freedom, 1775–1783* (Boston: Little, Brown & Company, 1948), 248–55, 257, 260–61; James L. Stokesbury, *A Short History of the American Revolution* (New York: William Morrow & Company, 1991), 178–79.

35. Estate Inventories, Wills Office, York County Courthouse. This web of credit relationships was obtained by examining sixty-one wills and estate records of York Countians who died between 1749 and 1775. The credit methods that evolved in Yorktown and County were not unusual in colonial America.

36. Ibid.; Leslie V. Brock, *The Currency of the American Colonies, 1700–1764: A Study in Colonial Finance and Imperial Relations* (New York: Arno Press, 1975). The three-tier currency system that evolved in York County was not unique in colonial America. As Brock describes, many communities devised local systems that enabled them to generate vigorous commerce despite the absence of specie.

37. Ibid.

38. Ibid.; York County Commissioners Books, book 1, Historical Society of York County; Book of Wills, York County Courthouse, Books A–M. For two specific examples of early estates, see Daniel Dinkle (Book A: 119–20) and John Meirs (Book B: 12). Two examples of later estates are those of Martin Frey (Book E: 101) and George Irwin (Book M: 394).

39. "Baker Report," Historical Society of York County.

40. Ibid.

41. Book of Wills, York County Courthouse; Estate Records, York County Courthouse; Orphan's Court Books, York County Courthouse, books 1–5.

42. *Spengler Annals,* 1:452–54, 521–22, 533.

43. *PA,* ser. 8, 5:189; ser. 1, 6:53; ser. 1, 5:536–37, 558–60.

44. Ibid., 5:536–37.

45. Ibid., 514–20.

46. Ibid., 775–76.

47. Ibid., 661–62.

48. Ibid., 662, 682–83, 704–5.

49. Ibid., 1:606.; *Pennsylvania Packet,* July 3, 20, and 22 and September 14, 1779; William Duane, ed., *Diary of Christopher Marshall* (Albany, N.Y., 1877), June 14, 16, 18, and 28 and July 6, 15, and 21, 1779.

50. *Spengler Annals,* 2:306–7.

51. *Pennsylvania Packet,* September 10, 1779.

52. *PA,* ser. 1, 6:775–76.

53. Ibid., 196, 426, 497; 7:367–68,

54. Ibid., 6:775–76; 7:110.

55. Ibid., 496–97, 498–99, 500, 520.

56. Ibid., 5:788; *Journals of the Continental Congress,* 9:1018; File 743.2, Historical Society of York County; Charlotte J. Epping, trans., *The Journal of DuRoi the Elder* (New York City: Appleton & Company, 1911), 143; Robert Lamb, *Journal of the Occurrences During the American War for Its Commencement to the Year 1783* (Dublin, Ireland, 1809), 202.

57. *Spengler Annals,* 2:569–71; John C. Jordan, "York, Pennsylvania, in the Revolution," *PMHB* 32 (1915): 492–93.

Chapter 6. Cumberland County

1. J. Paul Selsam, *The Pennsylvania Constitution of 1776* (Philadelphia: University of Pennsylvania Press, 1936), 4.

2. William Steven Perry, ed., *Historical Collections Relating to the American Colonial Church* (n.p., n.d.), 351, as cited in D. W. Thompson et al., eds., *Two Hundred Years in Cumberland County* (Carlisle, Pa.: Hamilton Library, 1951), 41.

3. I. D. Rupp, *History and Topography of Dauphin, Cumberland, Franklin, Bedford, Adams, and Perry Counties* (Lancaster, Pa.: Gilbert Hills, 1846), 49.

4. Shippen to Morris, June 13, 1755, in Samuel Hazard, ed., *Pennsylvania Archives (PA)*, ser. 1, 3:359 as printed in William A. Hunter, *Forts on the Pennsylvania Frontier, 1753–1758* (Harrisburg: Pennsylvania Historical and Museum Commission, 1960), 171.

5. Morris to Braddock, July 3, 1755, *PA*, ser. 1, 2:372, as printed in Hunter, *Forts*, 71.

6. Burd to Morris, July 25, 1755, in *PA*, ser. 1, 2:171.

7. For descriptions of the forts and activities associated with them, see Hunter, *Forts*, and Hunter, *The Provincial Fort at Carlisle, 1755–1758* (Carlisle, Pa.: Cumberland County Historical Society, 1956).

8. For the accounts of military units, see Donald Kent et al., eds., *The Bouquet Papers* (Harrisburg: Pennsylvania Historical and Museum Commission, 1951–), which is invaluable.

9. Thomas G. Tousey, *Military History of the Carlisle Barracks* (Richmond, Va.: Dietz, 1919), 48 (hereafter Tousey, *History*.)

10. Bouquet to Hamilton, July 13, 1763, in Louis M. Waddell, ed., *The Papers of Henry Bouquet*, vol. 6 (Harrisburg: Pennsylvania Historical Commission, 1994), 307–8.

11. Croghan to Bouquet, June 11, 1763, in Waddell, ed., 218–19.

12. Pennsylvania Gazette, July 28, 1763, as printed in H. H. Hain, *History of Perry County* (Harrisburg, Pa.: Hain-Moore, 1922), 87.

13. Croghan to Hamilton, July 2, 1763, as printed in Nicholas Wainwright, *George Croghan: Wilderness Diplomat* (Chapel Hill: University of North Carolina Press, 1959).

14. Wilbur S. Nye, *James Smith: Early Cumberland Valley Patriot* (Carlisle, Pa.: Cumberland County Historical Society, 1969).

15. Theodore Thayer, *Pennsylvania Politics and the Growth of Democracy, 1740–1776* (Harrisburg: Pennsylvania Historical and Museum Commission, 1953), 72.

16. Ibid., 95.

17. Charles H. Lincoln, *The Revolutionary Movement in Pennsylvania, 1760–1776* (1901; reprint, Philadelphia: University of Pennsylvania Press, 1953).

18. Rhea S. Klenovich, "James Smith and the Black Boys: Rebellion on the Pennsylvania Frontier, 1763–1769," *Cumberland County History* 8 (Summer 1991): 24.

19. Nye, *Smith*, 17.

20. James Smith, *An Account of the Remarkable Occurrences in the Life and Travels of Col. James Smith* (Lexington, Ky.: John Bradford, 1799) (hereafter Smith Autobiography), printed in Nye, *Smith*, 21.

21. Samuel Hazard, ed., *Colonial Records* (Harrisburg: Commonwealth of Pennsylvania, 1838–53), 9:443, as printed in Linda Reis, "The Rage of Opposing Government: The Stump Affair of 1768," *Cumberland County History* 1 (Summer 1984): 28.

22. Hazard, *Colonial Records*, 9:446.

23. Alden T. Vaughan, "Frontier Banditti and the Indians: The Paxton Boys' Legacy, 1763–1775," *Pennsylvania History* 51 (1984): 1–29; Shippen to James Tilghman, February 2, 1766, Shippen Papers, HSP, 6:196.

24. Smith Autobiography, 119–20.

25. Pennsylvania Gazette, November 2, 1769.

26. G. S. Rowe, "Crime and Its Resolution in Eighteenth-Century Cumberland County," *Cumberland County History* 3 (Summer 1986): 23.

27. W. S. Powell, James K. Huhta, and Thomas J. Farnham, eds., *The Regulators in North Carolina: A Documentary History, 1759–1776* (Raleigh: North Carolina Archives, 1971), xv.

28. Charles H. Glatfelter, "The German Lutheran and Reformed Churches in Cumberland County, 1763–1793," *Cumberland County History* 1 (Winter 1984): 21.

29. William T. Swaim, "The Evolution of the Ten Pre-1745 Presbyterian Societies in the Cumberland Valley," *Cumberland County History* 2 (Summer 1985): 3.

30. See Milton E. Flower, *John Armstrong: First Citizen of Carlisle* (Carlisle, Pa.: Cumberland County Historical Society, 1971); and Robert G. Crist, "John Armstrong: Proprietors' Man" (Ph.D. diss., The Pennsylvania State University, 1981).

31. For these individuals, see Conway P. Wing, *History of Cumberland County, Pennsylvania* (Philadelphia: James Scott, 1879), 80–81, 85–88; Robert G. Crist, *William Thompson: A Shooting Star* (Carlisle, Pa.: Cumberland County Historical Society, 1976); Anna A. Hays, *Col. Ephraim Blaine: Commissary General of the Revolutionary Army* (Carlisle, Pa.: Cumberland County Historical Society, 1935); Charles F. Hime, *Col. Robert Magaw: The Defender of Fort Washington* (Carlisle, Pa.: Cumberland County Historical Society, 1915); and Aumine Nixon Hart, "General James Potter," *PMHB* 1 (1877): 34.

32. Lincoln, *Revolutionary Movement*, 52.

33. Ibid., 47.

34. Selsam, *Constitution of 1776*, 99.

35. See Guy S. Klett, *Presbyterians in Colonial Pennsylvania* (Philadelphia: University of Pennsylvania Press, 1937), 231–34.

36. Wing, *History*, 76.

37. Henry J. Young, "The Spirit of 1775," *John and Mary's Journal* 1 (Summer 1975): 38.

38. Selsam, *Constitution of 1776*, 70.

39. See Robert G. Crist, *Robert Whitehill and the Struggle for Civil Rights* (Carlisle, Pa.: Cumberland County Historical Society, 1958); and Thayer, *Pennsylvania Politics*, 188.

40. Selsam, *Constitution of 1776*, 96.

41. Charles Hoban, ed., *PA*, ser. 8 (Harrisburg: Commonwealth of Pennsylvania, 1935), 6:730.

42. Penn Manuscripts, Official Correspondence 2, HSP, 238, as printed in Thayer, *Growth of Democracy*, 88.

43. Wing, *History*, 78.

44. Samuel Bates, *History of Cumberland and Adams County, Pennsylvania*, vol. 1 (Chicago: Warner & Beers, 1886), 80.

45. Wing, *History*, 79.

46. Ibid., 86.

47. Pennsylvania Gazette, August 14, 1776.

48. See Robert G. Crist, *William Hendricks and the March to Quebec* (Carlisle, Pa.: Cumberland County Historical Society, 1960).

49. Fred Anderson Berg, *Encyclopedia of Continental Army Units* (Harrisburg, Pa.: Stackpole, 1972), 99.

50. Ibid., 95.

51. Ibid., 96.

52. Bates, *History*, 1:88.

53. Berg, *Encyclopedia*, 97.

54. Ibid.

55. Ibid.

56. Ibid., 98.

57. Ibid.

58. Ibid., 26.

59. H. H. Hain, *History of Perry County, Pennsylvania* (Harrisburg, Pa.: Hain Moore Company, 1922), 172.

60. Lamberton Scotch-Irish Collection, HSP, no. 19, as cited in *Pennsylvania Constitution,* 212.

61. Ibid.

62. Ibid.

63. *Pennsylvania Evening Post,* March 15, 1777.

64. Samuel Hazard, ed., *Register of Pennsylvania* (Philadelphia: Hazard, 1828–35), 6: 35.

65. Robert L. Brunhouse, *Counter-Revolution in Pennsylvania, 1776–1790* (Harrisburg: Pennsylvania Historical Commission, 1942), 34.

66. Montgomery to Wilson, April 21, 1777, Gratz Collection, Members of Congress, HSP as cited in Brunhouse, *Counter-Revolution,* 36.

67. Declaration of People of Cumberland County, March 1777, Lamberton Collection, HSP, 2:19, as quoted in Brunhouse, *Counter-Revolution,* 38, 238 n. 42.

68. Brunhouse, *Counter-Revolution,* 33.

69. Irvine to Wayne, July 6, 1781, HSP, Irvine MSS, 71, cited in Brunhouse, *Counter-Revolution,* 94.

70. Roland M. Baumann, *George Stevenson, 1718–1783: Conservative as Revolutionary* (Carlisle, Pa.: Cumberland County Historical Society, 1978).

71. Samuel Hazard, ed., *PA,* ser. 1, 11: 624, 634, 635, 639, as printed in Tousey, *History,* 95.

72. Baumann, *Stevenson,* 36.

73. John C. Fitzpatrick, ed., *Writings of George Washington* (Washington, D.C.: 1931–44), 9:74, as quoted in Tousey, *History,* 94.

74. Carl Van Doren, *The Secret History of the American Revolution* (New York: Viking, 1941), 129ff.

75. Ibid., 133.

76. Tousey, *History,* 154.

77. Ibid., 90.

78. Ibid., 74.

79. Ibid., 240.

80. Ibid., 74.

81. Ibid., 154.

82. D. W. Thompson and Merri Lou Schaumann, "Goodbye Mollie Pitcher," *Cumberland County History* 6 (Summer 1989): 3–27.

Chapter 7. The Wyoming Valley

1. Report of John Penn and Richard Peters, August 5, 1754; Robert Hunter Morris to Conrad Weiser, March 1, 1755, both in *The Susquehannah Company Papers,* vol. 1, ed. Julian P. Boyd (Wilkes-Barre, Pa.: Wyoming Historical and Geological Society, 1930), 123–27, 234–35; C. A. Weslager, *The Delaware Indians: A History* (New Brunswick, N.J.: Rutgers University Press, 1972), 215–18; Paul A. W. Wallace, *Indians in Pennsylvania,* rev. ed. (Harrisburg: Pennsylvania Historical and Museum Commission, 1986), 155–59.

2. Throughout the Revolutionary War, the Wyoming Valley backcountry was embroiled in a bitter land struggle among the Susquehannah Company claimants from Connecticut, Pennsylva-

nia's claimants, and the Iroquois League. The Iroquois League signed the Treaty of Fort Stanwix (1768), seeking the political stability of the Wyoming Valley under Pennsylvania's control as a last-chance buffer against an invasion of its homeland through its southern gate at Tioga by the Susquehannah Company settlers' insatiable greed for land. Ironically, just as the Iroquois had feared, their lush homeland was torn asunder by the political instability brought on by the interne-cine dispute over Wyoming lands between Susquehannah Company claimants and Pennsylvania claimants (the Yankee-Pennamite Wars, 1769–84). The "gathering storm" of the American Revo-lution also contributed to the political and cultural demise of the Iroquois and ensured for Anglo-American civilization its final battle against Indian civilization on the New York and Pennsylvania frontiers. This study shows that the Wyoming Valley between 1763 and 1784 was a frontier region preoccupied with dispute over soil rights between Pennsylvania and Connecticut and far too turbulent during the revolutionary period to send delegates to the Continental Congress. A German traveler to the area, Johann David Schoepf, found in 1783 that even though the valley was devastated by the joint British Ranger and Indian invasion of July 3, 1778, the civil dispute begun at the Albany Conference in 1754 between the Susquehannah Company and the colony of Pennsylvania raged on. He wrote: "Wyoming, according to the New England claim, lies in Westmoreland County; but in Pennsylvania it forms a part of Northumberland County." And in a footnote to the 1788 edition of his book Schoepf noted: "There have been of late [1787] other bloody proceedings in Wyoming, and the disquiets among the colonists of both states have only very recently been brought to a peaceable conclusion." Johann David Schoepf, *Travels in the Con-federation, 1783–1784*, trans. and ed. Alfred J. Morrison (Philadelphia: William J. Campbell, 1911), 172. As for the Iroquois League, the American Revolution brought an end to its tribal existence. At the start of the Anglo-American invasion of Wyoming lands, John Penn and Richard Peters reported to the governor of Pennsylvania, August 5, 1754, on their mission at the Albany Congress to purchase Wyoming lands from the Iroquois. Agents from the Susquehannah Company were there, also fraudulently trying to do the very same thing. Report of John Penn and Richard Peters, August 5, 1754, *SCP*, 1:123–27. The Iroquois were represented at Albany by the Mohawk Chief Hendrick, who sent the following pointed and ironic message to the governor of Pennsylva-nia: "We desire You to give Ear to what We are now going to say. Land is grown very dear You know, and is become very valuable. We desire You would content yourself with what we shall now grant you. We will never part with Land at Shamokin and Wyoming. Our Bones are scattered there, and on this Land there has always been a Great Council Fire. We desire You will not take it amiss that we will not part with it, for We reserve it to settle such of our Nations upon as shall come to us from Ohio, or any others who shall deserve to be in our Alliance. Abundance of Indians are moving up and down, and We shall invite all such to come and live here, that so We may strengthen ourselves," Ibid., 125. Moreover, after Susquehannah Company schemes in 1773 and again in 1775 failed to plant towns on the West Branch of the Susquehanna on lands already settled by Pennsylvania claimants, the company's leadership looked to expand upriver around Wyalusing, Sheshequin, and Tioga—again on lands primarily occupied by Pennsylvania claimants and still existing Indian towns. After an aborted raid against the Wyoming settlement by a large posse financed by Pennsylvania in December 1775, the company's principal agents, large and influential landowners like Zebulon Butler, Nathan Denison, and the Reverend Jacob Johnson planned to use the emotional fervor wrought by the start of the Revolutionary War to eventually seize the property of Pennsylvania claimants settled upriver. The means was to brand them as Tories—a self-fulfilling prophecy in the end. Thus, what preoccupied the Susquehannah Company settlers throughout the revolutionary period, was their land hunger for the lush upriver property of Pennsylvania claimants and their numerous Indian neighbors, not independence from the

Crown. The best collection of primary source material on the dispute between Connecticut and Pennsylvania over Wyoming Valley lands is *The Susquehannah Company Papers* (hereafter *SCP*), vols. 1–4, ed. Julian P. Boyd (Wilkes-Barre, Pa.: Wyoming Historical and Geological Society, 1933), and vols. 5–11, ed. Robert J. Taylor (Ithaca, N.Y.: Cornell University Press, 1968–71). Both Boyd and Taylor provide a thorough and balanced introduction to the complex political struggle for Wyoming lands.

3. Minutes of an Indian Conference, September 28, 1771, *SCP,* 4:269–70; Francis Jennings, *Empire of Fortune* (New York: W. W. Norton & Company, 1988), 98–108; Georgiana C. Nammack, *Fraud, Politics, and the Dispossession of the Indians: The Iroquois Land Frontier in the Colonial Period* (Norman: University of Oklahoma Press, 1969), 42–47.

4. Sir William Johnson to John Bradstreet, March 2, 1764; Sir William Johnson to Cadwallader Colden, March 2, 1764; and Sir William Johnson to Thomas Gage, March 2, 1764, *The Papers of Sir William Johnson* (hereafter *Johnson Papers*), vol. 6, ed. Alexander C. Flick (Albany: State University of New York, 1928), 349–52; Anthony F. C. Wallace, *King of the Delawares: Teedyuscung 1700–1763* (Syracuse, N.Y.: Syracuse University Press, 1990), chap. 29; Weslager, *The Delaware Indians,* 246–52; extract from *Pennsylvania Gazette,* October 27, 1763, *SCP,* 2:277.

5. Oscar Jewell Harvey, *A History of Wilkes-Barre, Luzerne County, Pennsylvania,* vol. 2 (Wilkes-Barre, Pa.: By the author, 1909), 866–71; David Craft, *History of Bradford County, Pennsylvania* (Philadelphia: L. H. Everts & Company, 1878) (micropublished as publication no. 54 on reel of "Pennsylvania County and Regional Histories" [New Haven, Conn., Research Publications, 1973]), 52–62; Anne M. Ousterhout, *A State Divided: Opposition in Pennsylvania to the American Revolution* (Westport, Conn.: Greenwood Press, 1987), chap. 7, "Frontier Allies: Indians and Tories," 229–47; Oscar Jewell Harvey's comprehensive *History of Wilkes-Barre,* vols. 1 and 2, is filled with valuable primary source materials. Harvey painstakingly collected letters, documents, and reminiscences from valley residents, and sometimes includes them in their entirety in his life's work. He published the first two volumes at great expense to himself. Although Harvey's book has all the defects of a nineteenth-century Anglo-Saxon historical interpretation (racism, provincialism, and Social Darwinism, and a pro-Connecticut stance), it remains, apart from *The Susquehannah Company Papers,* the best single sourcebook of Wyoming Valley history. Harvey is still used by local historians to cement their images of the eighteenth- and nineteenth-century history of the Wyoming Valley.

6. For example, on July 30, only twenty-seven days after the Wyoming Valley was left deserted, the bodies of their fallen comrades still rotting on the battlefield, Nathan Denison, a large Susquehannah Company landowner, wrote from Fort Penn (Stroudsburg) to Zebulon Butler, the primary agent for the Susquehannah Company, then in the safety of Easton, that he had received word that there was a "scheem" afoot for "The Pennsilvany People to git in Possession of our settlement." *WHGS* 7 (1901): 132. See also Charles Miner, *History of Wyoming* (Philadelphia: J. Crissy, 1845), chaps. 22–27; William E. Price, "A Study of a Frontier Community in Transition: The History of Wilkes-Barre, Pennsylvania, 1750–1800" (Ph.D. diss., Kent State University, 1979), chap. 2, 82–98. Charles Miner's *History of Wyoming* (1845) is filled with valuable knowledge gleaned from contemporary letters and remembrances collected in the valley from still living eyewitnesses. It is a history intentionally slanted toward the Connecticut claims of Miner's ancestors. Miner's history was an important source for Harvey and is also gospel to many local historians.

7. Sir William Johnson to Richard Peters, January 8, 1768, *Johnson Papers,* 6:71–73; see also preface, ix–x, and Joseph Chew to Sir William Johnson, May 29, 1769, 782–84.

8. Sir William Johnson to Daniel Butler, December 10, 1768; Thomas Penn to John Penn, January 31, 1769, *SCP,* 3:41–42, 64–65. See also Sir William Johnson to Thomas Gage, August

9, 1769, 162–63; Sir William Johnson to Richard Peters, October 15, 1769, 168–69; Ray A. Billington, "The Fort Stanwix Treaty of 1768," *New York History* 25 (1944): 182–88; and Peter Marshall, "Sir William Johnson and the Treaty of Fort Stanwix," *Journal of American Studies* 1 (1967): 178–79.

    9. John Heckewelder, *A Narrative of the Mission of the United Brethren Among the Delaware and Mohegan Indians, from Its Commencement, in the Year 1740, to the Close of the Year 1808* (reprint, New York: Arno Press, 1971), 108, 114–20. Heckewelder and his Moravian brethren realized that Friedenshütten was in a precarious position between the Southern gateway to the Iroquois League at Tioga and the Yankee settlement at Wyoming. Two years earlier, on June 14, 1768, he wrote: "Two Mohawks arrived at [Friedenshütten], sent by the Six Nations to the Yankees: 'That if They did not leave Wyomick, they would come down and STRIKE THEIR HEADS.' " *The Annals of Friedenshütten on the Susquehanna, 1765–1772,* in *Now and Then,* vol. 5, ed. T. Kenneth Wood (Williamsport, Pa.: Williamsport Printing & Binding Company, 1936), 62.

    10. Harvey, *History of Wilkes-Barre,* 1:456. See John Penn to Thomas Penn, Philadelphia, November 6, 1768; and Minutes of the Susquehannah Company, December 28, 1768, *SCP,* 3:43–47.

    11. Minutes of a Meeting of the Susquehannah Company, December 28, 1768, *SCP,* 3:40; Harvey, *History of Wilkes-Barre,* 1:465–66.

    12. James Tilghman to Sir William Johnson, January 22, 1769, *SCP,* 3:58–59; Miner, *History of Wyoming,* 107–8.

    13. Depositions of John Jennings and Joseph Morris, June 1, 1769, *SCP,* 3:130–35; Harvey, *History of Wilkes-Barre,* 1:473–75.

    14. John Penn to William Pitkin, Philadelphia, February 13, 1769; and William Pitkin to John Penn, Hartford, June 26, 1769, *SCP,* 3:73–75, 140–41.

    15. Depositions of John Jennings and Joseph Morris, Philadelphia, June 1, 1769, *SCP,* 3:133–34. See also Introduction, *SCP,* 3:xxvi–xxvii.

    16. Oscar Zeichner, *Connecticut's Years of Controversy, 1750–1776* (Chapel Hill: University of North Carolina Press, 1949), 223. See also Harvey, *History of Wilkes-Barre,* 2:480–88.

    17. John Penn to Turbutt Francis, Philadelphia, May 16, 1769, *SCP,* 3:127–28. See also Frederick C. Johnson, "Count Zinzendorf and the Moravian and Indian Occupancy of the Wyoming Valley, 1742–1763," *WHGS* 8 (1904): 119–47.

    18. Agreement Between Connecticut and Pennsylvania Settlers at Wyoming, November 14, 1769, *SCP,* 3:200–203; extract from *Pennsylvania Gazette,* December 21, 1769, *SCP,* 3:216–18; Articles of Agreement at Wyoming, 1769, *Pennsylvania Archives (PA),* ser. 1, vol. 4, ed. Samuel Hazard (Philadelphia: Joseph Severns & Company, 1853), 352–54.

    19. Executive Committee to John Montgomery and Lazarus Young, Windham, January 15, 1770, *SCP,* 4:5–6; Minutes of the Pennsylvania Council, July 16, 1771, *SCP,* 4:223–25; Zeichner, *Connecticut's Years of Controversy,* 104–5; Brooke Hindle, "The March of the Paxton Boys," *WMQ* 3 (October 1946): 461–86; Alden T. Vaughan, "Frontier Banditti and the Indians: The Paxton Boys' Legacy, 1763–1775," *Pennsylvania History* 51 (1984): 1–22.

    20. John Penn to Thomas Penn, Philadelphia, March 10, 1770, *SCP,* 4:42–43.

    21. Miner, *History of Wyoming,* see letter X, 114–24, and letter XI, 125–34; see also *SCP,* vol. 4, Introduction, i–xxv; Provincial Council Meetings, July 16, 1771, August 3, 5, 13, and 19, 1771; *Minutes of the Provincial Council of Pennsylvania, [Colonial Records],* vol. 9 (Harrisburg, Pa.: Theo. Fenn & Company, 1852), 749–59.

    22. Charles Stewart to James Tilghman, August 16, 1779; Minutes of the Pennsylvania Council, August 19, 1771, *SCP,* 7:243–44, 245–46. See also William L. Stone, *The Poetry and History*

of Wyoming (Albany: J. Munsell, 1864), 167–80; J. P. Boyd, "Connecticut's Experiment in Expansion: The Susquehannah Company, 1753–1803," *Journal of Economic and Business History* 4 (1931): 49–50.

23. Minutes of the Pennsylvania Council, September 24, 1771, *SCP*, 4:267–68.

24. Heckewelder, *A Narrative of the Missions of the United Brethren*, 117–21; Weslager, *The Delaware Indians*, 252–55; Wood, *Now and Then*, 5:62; Nammack, *Fraud, Politics, and Dispossession of the Indians*, 93–96.

25. Harvey, *History of Wilkes-Barre*, 2:765–69; Price, "A Study of a Frontier Community in Transition," 123–25.

26. William Plunket and others to the Governor and Council of Pennsylvania, Fort Augusta, June 11, 1773, *SCP*, 5:148–49.

27. The Petition of Divers of the Inhabitants of Northumberland, December 9, 1773, *Colonial Records*, 10:111–13.

28. Jonathan Trumbull to John Penn, January 31, 1774; John Penn to Jonathan Trumbull, February 24, 1774; John Penn Proclamation, February 28, 1774; *Colonial Records*, 10:151–55.

29. John Penn Proclamation, February 28, 1774, *Colonial Records*, 10:153–55.

30. Minutes of a Meeting of the Proprietors and Settlers in Wilkes-Barre, November 22, 1774, and Resolution of the Continental Congress, December 10, 1775, *SCP*, 6:292–93, 420–21. See also Introduction to vol. 5, xlvi–lii.

31. Harvey, *History of Wilkes-Barre*, 2:828–29; "Had a late conference here with the Indians, August 20, 1775," Zebulon Butler Papers, Wyoming Historical and Geological Society, Folder 18–326.

32. Harvey, *History of Wilkes-Barre*, 2:828–29. See also Minutes of an Indian Conference Held at Wyoming, Westmoreland, August 20, 1775, *SCP*, 6:342–45.

33. Extract from the Record of a Conference with the Six Nations at Albany, August 31, 1775; Oliver Wolcott to the Connecticut Delegates to the Continental Congress, *SCP*, 6:348–49. See also Barbara Graymont, *The Iroquois in the American Revolution* (Syracuse, N.Y.: Syracuse University Press, 1972), 70–74.

34. Isabel Thompson Kelsay, *Joseph Brant, 1743–1807: Man of Two Worlds* (Syracuse, N.Y.: Syracuse University Press, 1984), chap. 10, "The Divided Longhouse"; Graymont, *The Iroquois*, chap. 6, "The Tree Uprooted."

35. William Maclay to Joseph Shippen Jr., September 22, 1775, *SCP*, 6:352–53.

36. John Montgomery to Colonel James Wilson, October 9, 1775, *SCP*, 6:367. See also Extracts from the Votes of Assembly, October 27, 1775, *PA*, ser. 1, 4:677–78; and E. Dyer to Zebulon Butler, October 1, 1775, Zebulon Butler Papers, Folder 18.

37. Memorial of a Committee of Northumberland and Northampton Counties, October 12, 1775, *SCP*, 6:369–70.

38. Extract from the Minutes of the Pennsylvania Assembly, November 23, 1775, *SCP*, 6:391–92.

39. Governor Penn to William Plunket and others, Philadelphia, November 25, 1775; William Scull, Sheriff, and others to Governor Penn, Sunbury, December 30, 1775, *SCP*, 6:392, 425–26.

40. Extract from the *Connecticut Courant*, January 19, 1776, *SCP*, 6:422–23. See James Edward Brady, "Wyoming: A Study of John Franklin and the Connecticut Settlement into Pennsylvania" (Ph.D. diss., Syracuse University, 1972), 79–85; Harvey, *History of Wilkes-Barre*, 863, 870.

41. Resolution of the Continental Congress, December 20, 1775, *SCP*, 6:420–21; Brady, "Wyoming," 80.

42. Extract from the Journals of the Continental Congress, December 23, 1775, *SCP*, 6:422.

43. Alexander Patterson, *A Petition to the Legislature of Pennsylvania* (Lancaster, Pa.: Robert Bailey, 1804), 14–15; Wood, *Now and Then,* 63–65; H. L. Bourdin and S. T. Williams, "Crevecoeur on the Susquehanna: 1774–1776," *Yale Review* 14 (1925): 583; Craft, *History of Bradford County,* 51–53, 69–70; Harvey, *History of Wilkes-Barre,* 813–14; Ousterhout, *A State Divided,* 239–41.

44. Meeting of Inhabitants of Westmoreland, January 6, 1776; Committee of Inspection to Adonijah Stanburrough and others, January 1, 1777, *SCP,* 7:1, 33; Miner, *History of Wyoming,* 190, 198; Harvey, *History of Wilkes-Barre,* 2:867–68, 912; Ousterhout, *A State Divided,* 240.

45. Miner, *History of Wyoming,* 186; Harvey, *History of Wilkes-Barre,* 2:889–91.

46. Harvey, *History of Wilkes-Barre,* 2:890.

47. Patterson, *Petition to the Legislature,* 15.

48. Wilbur H. Siebert, "The Loyalists and Six Nation Indians in the Niagara Peninsula," *Proceedings and Transactions of the Royal Society of Canada* 9:81, May 1915; Ernest Cruikshank, *The Story of Butler's Rangers and the Settlement of Niagara* (1893; reprint, Owen Sound, Ont.: Richardson, Bond & Wright, 1975), 34, 39, 40; Wilbur Henry Siebert, *The Loyalists of Pennsylvania* (Boston: Gregg Press, 1972), chap. 2.

49. Siebert, *The Loyalists of Pennsylvania,* 19–20.

50. Cruikshank, *The Story of Butler's Rangers,* 34–40; Harvey, *History of Wilkes-Barre,* 2:939; Craft, *History of Bradford County,* 65.

51. Nathan Denison to Oliver Wolcott Sr., September 20, 1777, *SCP,* 7:36–37; Siebert, *The Loyalists of Pennsylvania,* 20; Wood, *Now and Then,* 30–31; Cruikshank, *The Story of Butler's Rangers,* 39, 41; Alexander Fraser, ed., *Second Report of the Bureau of Archives of the Province of Ontario, Parts 1 and 2, 1904* (Toronto: L. K. Cameron, 1905), 139–40, 331, 477–78, 963, 973–74, 997, 1001, 1263.

52. Officials of Westmoreland to Connecticut Delegates in the Continental Congress, August 6, 1776; Roger Sherman to Zebulon Butler, August 20, 1776, *SCP,* 6:18–21; Harvey, *History of Wilkes-Barre,* 2:876–99.

53. Cruikshank, *The Story of Butler's Rangers,* 40; Harvey, *History of Wilkes-Barre,* 937–38.

54. Cruikshank, *The Story of Butler's Rangers,* 45–46.

55. Petition of the Inhabitants of Westmoreland to the Continental Congress, March 12, 1778, *SCP,* 7:38–39; William Stone, *Life of Joseph Brant-Thayendanega,* vol. 1 (New York: George Dearborn & Company, 1838), 330–31.

56. Thomas R. Pastore, "The Board of Commissioners for Indian Affairs in the Northern Department and the Iroquois Indians, 1775–1778" (Ph.D. diss., University of Notre Dame, 1972), 205; Graymont, *The Iroquois in the American Revolution,* 167–68.

57. Major John Butler to Lieutenant Colonel Mason Bolton, July 8, 1778, ed. K. G. Davies, *Documents of the American Revolution, 1770–1783,* Colonial Office Series 15, Transcripts, 1778 (Irish University Press, 1976), 165. See also Carl F. Klinck and James J. Talman, eds., *The Journal of Major John Norton, 1816* (Toronto: Champlain Society, 1970), 275–76.

58. Captain Walter Butler to Lieutenant Colonel Mason Bolton, November 17, 1778, in Davies, *Documents,* 262; Graymont, *The Iroquois in the American Revolution,* 171–74, 184.

59. Major John Butler to Lieutenant Colonel Mason Bolton, July 8, 1778, in Davies, *Documents,* 166; Colonel John Franklin, Narrative (hereafter Franklin Narrative), n.d., 3, Lackawanna Historical Society Collection, Scranton, Pa.

60. Orderly Book of Colonel Zebulon Butler, October 21, 1778, *WHGS,* vol. 7, 1902, 124.

61. Major John Butler to Lieutenant Colonel Mason Bolton, July 8, 1778, in Davies, *Documents,* 166. See also Walter Butler to James Clinton, February 11, 1779, in Maryly B. Penrose,

Indian Affairs Papers: American Revolution (Franklin Park, N.J.: Liberty Bell Associates, 1981), 185. The fact that none of the noncombatants were harmed was confirmed by the eyewitness account of Lieutenant John Jenkins: ". . . The 6, 7, 8 [July] the enemy plundered, burned, and destroyed all before them. The remainder of the inhabitants were waived off. . . ." Journal of Lieutenant John Jenkins, Revolutionary War, 3, Lackawanna Historical Society; Franklin Narrative, 3; C. E. Cartwright, *Life and Letters of the Late Hon. Richard Cartwright* (Toronto: Belford Brothers, 1876), 31; Jack M. Sosin, "The Use of Indians in the War of the American Revolution: A Re-Assessment of Responsibility," *Canadian Historical Review* 46 (June 1965): 101–3, 118–21.

62. C. Hale Sipe, *The Indian Wars of Pennsylvania* (Harrisburg, Pa.: Telegraph Press, 1929), 558–61. See also Matthew Smith to V. P. Bryan, July 12, 1778; Peter De Haven to Colonel T. Matlack, July 12, 1778; Bartrem Galbraith to Vice President George Bryan, July 14, 1778, *PA*, ser 1. 6:632–33, 642.

63. Thomas Hartley to Council, September 1, 1778; John Hambright to Vice President Bryan, October 1, 1778; Lieutenant Samuel Hunter to Vice President Bryan, October 7, 1778, all in *PA*, ser. 1, 6:729–30, 770, 773–74. See also Thomas S. Abler, ed., *Chainbreaker: The Revolutionary War Memories of Governor Blacksmoke* (Lincoln: University of Nebraska Press, 1989), 101–3, 135–39.

64. Instructions to Major General John Sullivan, Middlebrook, May 31, 1779, in John C. Fitzpatrick, ed., *Writings of George Washington*, vol. 15 (Washington, D.C.: U.S. U.S. Government Printing Office, 1936), 190.

65. Division of Archives and History, *The Sullivan-Clinton Campaign in 1779, Chronology and Selected Documents* (Albany: University of the State of New York, 1929), 9–48; Jeptha R. Simms, *History of Schoharie County and Border Wars of New York* (Albany, N.Y.: Munsell & Tanner, 1845), 304–6; Joseph R. Fischer, *A Well-Executed Failure: The Sullivan Campaign Against the Iroquois, July–September 1779* (Columbia: University of South Carolina Press, 1997), chaps. 3–6.

66. Frederick Cook, ed., *Journals of the Military Expedition of Major General John Sullivan Against the Six Nations of Indians in 1779* (1885 ed.; reprint, New York: Books for Libraries Press, 1972) (note especially the Journal of Lieutenant Eukuries Beatty, 16–38); Arthur C. Parker, "The Indian Interpretation of the Sullivan-Clinton Campaign," *Rochester Historical Society Publication Fund Series*, vol. 8 (Rochester, N.Y.: Rochester Historical Society, 1929), 45–59.

67. General Sullivan to John Jay, September 30, 1779, in Otis G. Hammond, ed., *Letters and Papers of Major General John Sullivan, 1779–1795*, vol. 3 (Concord: New Hampshire Historical Society, 1939), 134.

68. James E. Seaver, *A Narrative of the Life of Mrs. Mary Jemison* (Syracuse, N.Y.: Syracuse University Press, 1990), 59

69. "Christopher Yates Draws a Gloomy Picture of Life on the Frontier, March 17, 1780," in Hugh Hastings, ed., *Public Papers of George Clinton, First Governor of New York*, vol. 5 (Albany: State of New York, 1901), 548–49; Donald R. McAdams, "The Sullivan Expedition: Success or Failure," *New York Historical Society Quarterly* 64 (1970): 80–81; Mary Elaine Fleming Mathur, "The Iroquois in Time and Space: A Native American Nationalistic Movement" (Ph.D. diss., University of Wisconsin 1971), 119–21; William Brewster, *The Pennsylvania and New York Frontier* (Philadelphia: George S. McManus Company, 1954), 202–4, 210–12; Kelsay, *Joseph Brant*, chap. 14; Miner, *History of Wyoming*, chap. 20; Peter C. Mancall, *Valley of Opportunity: The Economic Culture Along the Upper Susquehanna, 1700–1800* (Ithaca, N.Y.: Cornell University Press, 1991), 139–40, 144, 149–52.

70. *Journals of the Military Expedition of Major General John Sullivan*, 35.

71. Ernest Gray Smith and Oscar Jewell Harvey, *A History of Wilkes-Barre, Luzerne County, Pennsylvania*, vol. 3 (Wilkes-Barre, Pa.: By the authors, 1927), 1239–58, 1271–72.

72. Joseph Reed to the Board of War, Philadelphia, November 20, 1780, *SCP*, 7:68.

73. George Washington to Zebulon Butler, New Windsor, December 29, 1780, *SCP*, 7:77–78.

74. Act of the Connecticut Legislature Appointing Agents, January 10, 1782, *SCP*, 7:84–96 and xx–xxi. See also the Connecticut-Pennsylvania Territorial Dispute, 1782–1784, in Julian Boyd, *The Papers of Thomas Jefferson*, vol. 6 (Princeton: Princeton University Press, 1952), 474–507; Robert J. Taylor, "Trial of Trenton," *WMQ*, 3rd ser., 26 (1969): 521, 523–24, 526.

75. *SCP*, 7:245 (the full Trenton Trial Proceeding and documents are in 144–246); *Journals of the Continental Congress, 1774–1789*, vol. 24: *1783* (Washington D.C.: U.S. Government Printing Office, 1922), 6–32; Robert L. Brunhouse, *The Counter-Revolution in Pennsylvania, 1776–1790* (Harrisburg: Pennsylvania Historical Commission, 1942), 129–31.

76. George Washington to President John Dickinson, Newburgh, January 12, 1783, in *The Writings of George Washington*, 26:33–34; Captain Thomas Robinson to President Dickinson, March 26, 1783; Captain Philip Shrawder to President Dickinson, Wyoming, March 29, 1783, *PA*, ser. 1, 10:14–15, 23.

77. An Act to Prevent and Stay Suits Against Inhabitants of Wyoming During the Time Therein Mentioned, 1783; Resolution of General Assembly, 1783, *PA*, ser. 1, 10:5, 21; Report of Commissioners to Wyoming, 1783, *PA*, ser. 1 , vol. 12, Appendix, 73–74.

78. Pennsylvania Commissioners to the Connecticut Claimants, Wyoming, April 19, 1783, *SCP*, 7:277–78.

79. Report of Wyoming Commissioners to the Pennsylvania General Assembly, August 25, 1783; Resolution of the Pennsylvania General Assembly, September 2, 1783, *SCP*, 7:99–302.

80. Repeal of the Act Staying Suits of Ejectment Against Connecticut Settlers, September 9, 1783, *SCP*, 7:304–5.

81. Schoepf, *Travels in the Confederation, 1783–1784*, 1:178.

82. Brady, "Wyoming," 167–75. See also Petition and Remonstrance of Connecticut Settlers to the Pennsylvania General Assembly, November 18, 1783; Obadiah Gore to William Judd, November 21, 1783, *SCP*, 7:328–34; and Edwin MacMinn, *On the Frontier with Colonel Antes* (Camden: S. Chew & Sons, 1900), 426–32.

83. *The John Franklin Papers*, Wyoming Historical and Geological Society, MS-9, Colonel Franklin Letters of January 8, 1806, 60; Leroy E. Bugbee, "John Franklin and the Wild Yankees," *WHGS* 23 (1970): 49–52; Miner, *History of Wyoming*, 344–48.

84. Smith and Harvey, *History of Wilkes-Barre*, 3:1389–92.

85. John Dickinson to the Judges of the Pennsylvania Supreme Court, Philadelphia, May 25, 1784; Thomas McKean, William Atlee, and Jacob Rush to John Dickinson, Reading, June 7, 1784, *SCP*, 7:423–24, 431–32. See also John Dickinson's Proclamation, October 5, 1784, *Colonial Records*, 14:220–24.

86. Miner, *History of Wyoming*, 368; Brady, "Wyoming," 204–5; Bugbee, "John Franklin and the Wild Yankees," 52–64.

87. Extracts from Timothy Pickering's Journal, August and September 1786, *SCP*, 8:384.

88. Confirming Act, April 12, 1787, *SCP*, 9:82–86; Compromise Act of 1799, April 4, 1799, *SCP*, 10:468–74; Amendments to the Compromise Act, April 9, 1807, *SCP*, 11:519–21; Julian P. Boyd, "Attempts to Form New States in New York and Pennsylvania, 1786–1796," *New York Historical Society Quarterly* 12 (1931): 258–63; William Brewster, *A History of the Certified Township of Kingston, Pennsylvania, 1769–1929* (Wilkes-Barre, Pa.: Smith Bennett Company, 1930), chap. 10, "The Fourteenth Commonwealth, 1782–1788," and chap. 11, "Settlement of Disputed Titles, 1787–1808"; Henry M. Hoyt, *Brief of a Title in the Seventeen Townships in the County of Luzerne: A Syllabus of the Controversy Between Connecticut and Pennsylvania* (Harrisburg, Pa.: Lane S. Holt, 1879), chap. 6, "The Confirming Act."

89. Anthony F. C. Wallace, *The Death and Rebirth of the Seneca* (New York: Alfred A. Knopf, 1972), chap. 6, "The Collapse of the Confederacy"; Henry S. Manley, *The Treaty of Fort Stanwix, 1784* (Rome, N.Y.: Rome Sentinel Company, 1932); Stephen Howard Coe, "Indian Affairs in Pennsylvania and New York, 1785–1794" (Ph.D. diss., American University, 1968), 1–16; Abler, *Chainbreaker,* chap. 4, "Negotiating Peace"; Graymont, *The Iroquois in the American Revolution,* chap. 10, "Peace Comes to the Longhouse"; Kelsay, *Joseph Brant,* chap. 17, "Outrageous Fortune"; Anthony F. C. Wallace, "Origins of the Longhouse Religion"; Elisabeth Tooker, "Iroquois Since 1820," in Bruce G. Trigger, ed., *Northeast,* vol. 15 (Washington, D.C.: Smithsonian Institution, 1978), 442–65.

Chapter 8. The Upper Juniata Valley

1. It would be wrong, and elitist, to see the residents of the Upper Juniata Valley as "inarticulate." The people of the valley were quite able to articulate their preferences, which in many instances meant that they asked to be left alone by those whom later generations would perceive as being "articulate."

2. J. Simpson Africa, *History of Huntingdon and Blair Counties, Pennsylvania* (Philadelphia: Louis H. Everts, 1883), 8–9.

3. Richard Peters to James Hamilton, Esq., Lieutenant Governor and Commander-in-Chief, Province of Pennsylvania and Counties of New Castle, Kent, and Sussex on Delaware, July 2, 1750, HSP. See also Paul A. Wallace, *Conrad Weiser: Friend of Colonist and Mohawk* (Philadelphia: University of Pennsylvania Press, 1945), 294–97; Hubertis Cummings, *Richard Peters: Provincial Secretary and Cleric, 1704–1776* (Philadelphia: University of Pennsylvania Press, 1944), 150–55; Joseph J. Kelley, *Pennsylvania: The Colonial Years, 1681–1776* (Garden City, N.Y.: Doubleday & Company, 1980), 272–75.

4. Paul A. Wallace, *Indians in Pennsylvania,* rev. ed. (Harrisburg: Pennsylvania Historical and Museum Commission, 1986), 136, 137; Solon J. Buck and Elizabeth Hawthorne Buck, *The Planting of Civilization in Western Pennsylvania* (Pittsburgh: University of Pittsburgh Press, 1939), 137.

5. For a thorough treatment of the impact of these attacks, see Frederick Warren Hawthorne, "The Delaware Indian War on the Pennsylvania Frontier, 1755–1759" (M.A. thesis, The Pennsylvania State University, 1980), 32–33. See also Chester H. Sipe, *Indian Wars of Pennsylvania* (Harrisburg, Pa.: Telegraph Press, 1929), 216; idem, *The Indian Chiefs of Pennsylvania* (Butler, Pa.: Ziegler Printing Company, 1927), 292–94; William A. Hunter, *Forts on the Pennsylvania Frontier, 1753–1758* (Harrisburg: Pennsylvania Historical and Museum Commission, 1960), 210–11.

6. By the first weeks of July 1763, the valley had been nearly emptied of its people. The "houses, barns, corn, wheat and rye, hay" had been torched once more until "the whole country seemed to be one blaze." Letters to the *Pennsylvania Gazette* indicated that the towns below the valley had become refugee centers; on July 30, 1763, Shippensburg, a substantial village twenty miles south of the valley, held 1,384 "back inhabitants" housed "in barns, stables, cellars, and old, leaky sheds, the dwelling houses being all crowded." An observer in Carlisle—a town thirty miles to the east of Shippensburg—noted that by the middle of July Carlisle had "become the barrier, not a single inhabitant being beyond it." For the third time in thirteen years, the people of the valley had been burned out. *Pennsylvania Gazette,* July 28, 1763; see also August 21, 1763. U. J. Jones suggests that the dangers of Native American raids prevented the settlement of the northwest

corner of the valley until nearly 1770. See U. J. Jones, *History of the Early Settlement of the Juniata Valley, Embracing an Account of the Early Pioneers* (Philadelphia: H. B. Ashmead, 1856), in publication no. 144, reel 62, *Pennsylvania County and Regional Histories* (New Haven, Conn.: Research Publications, 1973), 54.

7. Charles Beatty, *Journals of Charles Beatty, 1762–1769,* ed. Guy Soulliard Klett (University Park, Pa.: The Pennsylvania State University Press, 1962), 51, states that settlement in 1765 had passed no farther than the eastern border of present-day Huntingdon County, at the very edge of the upper valley.

8. See, for instance, Paul A. W. Wallace, *Pennsylvania: Seed of a Nation* (New York: Harper & Row, 1962), 63–64. Any estimate of the area's population before 1790 would be simply guesswork. There are no even remotely reliable records before the Revolution, and, as indicated below, the war so disturbed the functioning of the government that not even tax records can be regarded as adequate.

9. The use of three separate tax records seemed prudent because, as indicated below, the gathering of taxes in the Upper Juniata was episodic at best.

10. Thanks are extended to the Huntingdon and Blair County historical societies, which have graciously allowed the author to use their facilities and their staff in search of the appropriate genealogies, as well as to the workers at the Pennsylvania State Library, Capitol Complex, Harrisburg, who repeatedly came up with the answers to the most demanding questions. I have also used the American Council of Learned Societies' *Surnames in the United States Census of 1790* (Baltimore: Genealogical Publishing Company, 1971), and Patrick Hanks and Flavia Hodges, *A Dictionary of Surnames* (New York: Oxford University Press, 1989).

11. See note 7, above.

12. Most reports of loyalist activity indicate that it emerged as a powerful phenomenon in the region near and around the northernmost plains of the central valley and the regions immediately west and north of those plains. These regions were the last settled in the Juniata Valley and may have contained few settlers who had been associated with the region long. More research on this is clearly indicated. See Jones, *Early Settlement,* 248–49, 259–65.

13. Anonymous, *History of Bedford, Somerset, and Fulton Counties, Pennsylvania* (Chicago: Waterman, Watkins & Company, 1884), 81, 217.

14. Jones, *History of the Early Settlers,* 252–57.

15. *Pennsylvania Journal and Weekly Advertiser,* March 19, 1777.

16. If Robert Brunhouse is correct in his calculation that only 2,000 of 50,000 eligible voters were allowed to vote, the delegates from the upper valley knew whereof they spoke. Robert L. Brunhouse, *The Counter-Revolution in Pennsylvania, 1776–1790* (Harrisburg: Pennsylvania Historical Commission, 1942), 21.

17. See note 16.

18. Jones, *History of the Early Settlers,* 253–57.

19. Ibid.

20. Arell Morgan Gibson, *The American Indian: Prehistory to the Present* (New York: D. C. Heath & Company, 1980), 256.

21. This is not to impute a lack of interest in supporting the valley. The Executive Council must have operated for long periods without any means to put its decisions into effect. In many cases, the strain must have approached the intolerable—which could account for the testiness of some of the letters that issued from the Executive Council. Similarly, with attackers striking without warning and without apparent letup, the people of the valley certainly could be testy in their own turn, not only toward the State of Pennsylvania, but also toward each other. See, for instance,

Pres[ident] Reed to Col[onel] John Piper, [May 9] 1780, [State of Pennsylvania] *Pennsylvania Archives (PA)*, ed. Samuel Hazard (Philadelphia: Joseph Severns & Company, 1853), ser. 1, 8:235–36. As for local feeling, see Jones, *Early Settlement*, 191.

22. Jay Gilfallan Weiser, "The Frontier Forts in the Cumberland and Juniata Valleys," *Report of the Commission to Locate the Sites of the Frontier Forts of Pennsylvania*, vol. 1 (Harrisburg, Pa.: Clarence M. Busch, state printer, 1896), 467–627.

23. The heart of the Cove was held by Dunkers, who refused protection. Jones, *Early Settlement*, 208–9.

24. Darwin H. Stapleton, "General Daniel Roberdeau and the Lead Mine Expedition, 1778–1779," *Pennsylvania History* 38 (1971): 361–71.

25. Weiser, *Frontier Forts*, 499–504. See also Roberdeau's remarks in his letter to Jasper Yeats: Daniel Roberdeau to Jasper Yeats, April 19, 1782, Dreer Collection, HSP.

26. Weiser, *Frontier Forts*, 499–504.

27. Potter's Fort guarded the northern access to what is now the Mifflin County region. The last mountains suitable for defense are found in this region north of Harrisburg. A breakthrough here would have meant that raiding columns could have traveled fifty or more miles closer to the Lancaster–York–Carlisle heartland or cut off the forts along the northern plains of the Juniata. A "massacre" like the one that occurred in the Wyoming Valley could easily have ensued if Potter's Fort had not anchored the eastern corner of the Juniata defenses.

28. In one instance, a defensive patrol of at least ten people was annihilated, perhaps after being tortured. The spot was reasonably close to two of the forts, and the patrol seems simply to have been in the wrong place as an Indian force slipped between the forts. Col[onel] John Piper to Pres[ident] Reed, [August 6,] 1780, *PA*, ser. 1, 8:488–89.

29. *PA*, ser. 1, 7:418–19, 534, 624, 696–97, 702; 8:278–79, 297, 488–89, 530, 567; 9:152–153, 202–3, 467, 522, 529, 539, 543, 546–47, 553–54, 619–20, 628. See also Jones, *Early Settlement*; J. Simpson Africa, *History of Huntingdon and Blair Counties* (Philadelphia: Louis H. Everts, 1883); and Anonymous, *History of Bedford, Somerset, and Fulton Counties* (Chicago, Waterman, Watkins & Company, 1884).

30. Bedford County (Pa.) Commissioners, "Minutes of the Bedford County Commissioners," June 5, 1780. (Held in basement vault of Bedford County Courthouse, Bedford, Pa.)

31. George Ashman to President Reed, Bedford County, June 12, 1781, *PA*, ser. 1, 9:202–3.

32. See the letters from Bernard Dougherty to President William Moore, *PA*, ser. 1, 9:553, 543, 546–47, 619–20. Note that these letters were written nine months or more after Cornwallis's surrender.

33. [Executive] Council [of Pennsylvania] to Lieutenants, Circular, [July 16] 1778, *PA*, ser. 1, 6:650.

34. George Woods to Thomas Urie, [July 4] 1779, *PA*, ser. 1, 7:534.

35. Photocopies of the 1776, 1779, and 1783 tax lists for the Bedford County Townships were secured through the Church of the Latter-Day Saints, Salt Lake City, Utah, and its library resources in Reading, Pennsylvania.

36. In Dublin and Bedford Townships, retention rates topped 70 percent. See tax lists for Bedford County townships as cited in note 35.

37. Ibid.

38. Jones, *Early Settlement*.

39. A good discussion of the Scots-Irish/German/English culture of Central Pennsylvania at this time can be found in George Dugan Wolf, "The Fair Play Settlers of the West Branch, 1769–1784: A Study of Frontier Ethnography" (Ph.D. diss., University of Pennsylvania, 1964).

40. See Tim H. Blessing, "The Lewistown Riots of 1791: A Study in Conflicting Sovereignties," manuscript, available from the author, Alvernia College, Reading, Pa. 19607.

41. There is a story that Jacob Roller Jr., son of the Jacob Roller who built Roller's Fort, died near his father's fort during an attack. This story is in U. J. Jones's *Early Settlement,* 241–45. Jones tended to be careful about using his collection of oral histories, and the loss of his eldest son may have been the blow that caused Jacob Roller Sr. to move south near to present-day Huntingdon. He appears in the Bedford County tax lists of 1783.

42. Dublin Township was divided into Dublin and Shirley Townships between 1779 and 1783.

43. Huntingdon Township was separated from Barree Township before 1783.

44. *Pennsylvania Gazette,* July 28, 1763; August 4, 1763.

45. B[ernard] Dougherty to Pres[ident] Moore, [August 19] 1782, *PA,* ser. 1, 9:619.

46. Officeholders are listed in *PA,* ser. 2, 3:671–75. For property holdings, see note 35 above.

47. Owen Ireland, "The People's Triumph: the Federalist Majority in Pennsylvania, 1787–1788," *Pennsylvania History* 56 (April 1989): 94.

48. The median landholding of those living in the upper valley was less than 300 acres. See note 35 for the 1779 tax list of Bedford County. The nature of landholding and rental in this area is unclear, however. The raw data indicates that most occupants owned their land, but more information needs to be developed.

49. See note 35, above.

50. See note 35, above.

51. Jones, *History of the Early Settlement.*

52. B[ernard] Dougherty and C[harles] Cessna to V. P. Potter, December 17, 1781, *PA,* ser. 1, 9:467.

53. See Tim H. Blessing, "The Lewistown Riots of 1791: A Study in Conflicting Sovereignties," manuscript, available from the author at Alvernia College, Reading, Pa., 19607.

Chapter 9. Soldiers and Violence on the Frontier

1. The spelling and punctuation of the original sources have been modernized. The frontier region of Pennsylvania in the Revolution is here defined as north and west of the Blue Mountain. During the Revolution, this area comprised Bedford, Westmoreland, Washington, and Northumberland Counties entirely, as well as parts of Berks, Northampton, Lancaster, and Cumberland. Although historians are paying more attention to the Revolutionary War on the frontier, college survey textbooks portray the conflict in a cursory manner. Even two of the newer social history texts that demonstrate a consideration for the importance of Indians and frontier contact—Paul S. Boyer et al., *The Enduring Vision: A History of the American People* (Lexington, Mass., 1990), and James Henretta et al., *America's History* (New York, 1993)—little space to the frontier war in their chapter on the Revolution and portray the backcountry conflict as a minor sideshow to main events in the east. Several early American historians have recently suggested the importance of Indians and the frontier to the course of the American Revolution, and they link events in the American West to constructions of race and gender, patterns of conquest, and American identity. See Edward Countryman, Philip J. Deloria, Sylvia R. Frey, and Michael Zuckerman, "Forum: Rethinking the American Revolution," *WMQ,* 3rd ser., 53 (1996): 341–86. In order to examine how cultural and military conflict on the Pennsylvania frontier forces us to reappraise our assump-

tions about the nature of the American Revolution, this chapter builds on some of the theoretical insights of these roundtable participants.

2. On the major campaigns in northeast Pennsylvania, see Fon W. Boardman, *Against the Iroquois: The Sullivan Campaign of 1779 in New York State* (New York, 1978); Joseph R. Fischer, *A Well-Executed Failure: The Sullivan Campaign Against the Iroquois July–September, 1779* (Columbia, S.C., 1997); and Barbara Graymont, *The Iroquois in the American Revolution* (Syracuse, N.Y., 1976). On the war in western Pennsylvania, see Randolph C. Downes, *Council Fires on the Upper Ohio* (Pittsburgh, 1989), 179–276; and Solon J. and Elizabeth Hawthorn Buck, *The Planting of Civilization in Western Pennsylvania* (Pittsburgh, 1939), 175–203.

3. On eighteenth-century European and European American attempts to limit the destructiveness of war by confining it to contending military forces, see M. S. Anderson, *War and Society in Europe of the Old Regime, 1618–1789* (London, 1988).

4. On the cultural construction of race, see Barbara Fields, "Slavery, Race, and Ideology in the United States," *New Left Review*, no. 181 (May–June 1990): 95–118; Franklin G. Pease G.Y. [*sic*], "Spanish and Andean Perceptions of the Other in the Conquest of the Andes," in William B. Taylor and Franklin Pease G.Y., eds., *Violence, Resistance, and Survival in the Americas* (Washington, D.C., 1994), 15–39; and Audrey Smedley, *Race in North America: Evolution of a Worldview* (Boulder, Colo., 1993).

5. The ranks of the Continental Army and the militia were predominantly made up of what may be termed the lower and lower middling orders of early American society: less affluent artisans, small farmers, laborers, apprentices, etc., according to Mark E. Lender, "The Enlisted Line: The Continental Soldiers of New Jersey" (Ph.D. diss., Rutgers University, 1975), 110–39; Charles Royster, *A Revolutionary People at War: The Continental Army and American Character, 1775–1783* (New York, 1979), 373; Steven Rosswurm, *Arms, Country, and Class: The Philadelphia Militia and the "Lower Sort" During the American Revolution* (New Brunswick, N.J., 1987), 49–77. Among the more important recent works on the early American frontier are Gregory Evans Dowd, *A Spirited Resistance: The North American Indian Struggle for Unity, 1745–1812* (Baltimore, 1992); Francis Jennings, *Empire of Fortune: Crowns, Colonies, and Tribes in the Seven Years War in America* (New York, 1988); Michael McConnell, *A Country Between: The Upper Ohio Valley and Its Peoples, 1724–1774* (Lincoln, Nebr., 1992); James H. Merrell, *The Indians' New World: Catawbas and Their Neighbors from European Contact Through the Era of Removal* (New York, 1989); Daniel K. Richter, *The Ordeal of the Longhouse: The Peoples of the Iroquois League in the Era of European Colonization* (Chapel Hill, N.C., 1992); and Richard White, *The Middle Ground: Indians, Empires, and Republics in the Great Lakes Region, 1650–1815* (New York, 1992). Among the most important recent works on the social aspects of Revolutionary War military service are Lender, "The Enlisted Line"; and John W. Shy, *A People Numerous and Armed: Reflections on the Military Struggle for American Independence* (Ann Arbor, Mich., 1989). I was influenced early in graduate school by James H. Merrell's plea to integrate Indians into early American history: "Some Thoughts on Colonial Historians and Indians," *WMQ*, 3rd ser., 46 (1989): 94–119.

6. On the early beliefs that Indians were not a race of enemies, but rather a unique culture that could be friendly toward the English, see Edmund S. Morgan, *American Slavery-American Freedom: The Ordeal of Colonial Virginia* (New York, 1975), 3–24; and Alden T. Vaughan, "From White Man to Redskin: Changing Anglo-American Perceptions of the American Indian," *American Historical Review* 87 (1982): 917–53. On the congealing English view of Indians as "hostile savages" once the colonists' desire for Indian land made military conflict inevitable, see Gary B. Nash, "Red, White, and Black: The Origins of Racism in Colonial America," in Gary B. Nash and Richard Weiss, eds., *The Great Fear: Race in the Mind of America* (New York, 1970), 4–5.

7. On the respective precontact European and Indian military cultures, see Adam Hirsch, "The Collision of Military Cultures in Seventeenth-Century New England," *Journal of American History* 74 (March 1988): 1187–212. Hirsch obviously focuses on New England, but his provocative model for how British and Indian cultures clashed in a military arena is applicable for other areas of early colonial North America as well. On the precontact military culture of the Iroquois in particular, see Richter, *The Ordeal of the Longhouse*, 30–49. On sixteenth- and seventeenth-century European military culture, see J. R. Hale, *War and Society in Renaissance Europe, 1450– 1620* (Baltimore, 1986); and Anderson, *War and Society*. Obviously, the total war of the Thirty Years' War was much on the minds of English settlers with regard to what could happen if a side did not follow the "rules" of war. The excesses of the English Civil War, such as the destruction of towns that refused to surrender and the murder of civilians in "hot blood," were also well-known to British colonists who fought Indians. On these instances of total war in the English Civil War, see Barbara Donagan, "Atrocity, War Crime, and Treason in the English Civil War," *American Historical Review* 99 (1994): 1137–66.

8. Hirsch, "The Collision of Military Cultures," 1195–212. Also on the development of a tradition of total war among British colonists coming out of frontier clashes with Indians, see John Ferling, *A Wilderness of Miseries: War and Warriors in Early America* (Westport, Conn., 1980), 44; and Patrick Malone, *The Skulking Way of War: Technology and Tactics Among the New England Indians* (Baltimore, 1993), 88–125.

9. On the brutality of the Pequot War and King Philip's War in late-seventeenth-century New England, see Francis Jennings, *The Invasion of America: Indians, Colonialism, and the Cant of Conquest* (New York, 1976), 177–326. On the frontier war related to "Bacon's Rebellion" in 1676, see Stephen Saunders Webb, *The Governors-General: The English Army and the Definition of the Empire, 1569–1681* (Chapel Hill, N.C., 1979), 341–49. On the Yamasee war that racked the southern British North American colonies in 1715, see Merrell, *The Indians' New World*, 68–75. On early Pennsylvania relations with Indian residents, see Downes, *Council Fires*, 18; and Richter, *Ordeal of the Longhouse*, 273–76. For an account of colonial Pennsylvania's dealings with Indians that reveals the duplicity of European Americans, even though they were not forced to wage war to attain their goals, see Jennings, *Empire of Fortune*, 3–45.

10. On the Quakers' use of a peaceful language of diplomacy toward Indians, see Robert Daiutolo, "The Early Quaker Perception of the Indian," *Quaker History* 72 (1983): 103–19; Wilbur R. Jacobs, *Dispossessing the American Indian: Indians and Whites on the Colonial Frontier* (New York, 1972), 2, 109; and Jennings, *Empire of Fortune*, 266, 270–71.

11. Downes, *Council Fires*, 80–120; Jennings, *Empire of Fortune*, 200–202, 371–404, 439–53. On Dunmore's War, see Downes, *Council Fires*, 168–69; McConnell, *A Country Between*, 274–79; and White, *The Middle Ground*, 361–65. On the conflicting goals of British-American settlers and the Imperial authorities, see Jennings, *Empire of Fortune*, 459–73; and White, *The Middle Ground*, 364–65.

12. See McConnell, *A Country Between*, 124, on Pennsylvania's scalp bounty and how it encouraged the killing of both friendly and hostile Indians. Alden Vaughan, "Frontier Banditti and the Indians: The Paxton Boys' Legacy," *Pennsylvania History* 51 (1984): 1–29, quotation from 2.

13. On British and American attempts to keep Indians neutral or to enlist their help early in the Revolution, see Downes, *Council Fires*, 179–211; and Barbara Graymont, *The Iroquois in the American Revolution* (Syracuse, N.Y., 1976), 26–103. For more on how frontier soldiers' motives for fighting grew out of their local situation, and particularly their desire for Indians' lands, see Gregory T. Knouff, " 'An Arduous Service': The Pennsylvania Backcountry Soldiers' Revolution," *Pennsylvania History* 61 (1994): 45–74; and George Morgan and John Nevill[e], Fort Pitt, to Governor Patrick Henry, April 1, 1777, PRG.

14. *Pennsylvania Packet,* April 8, 1777.

15. On Indians' reasons for fighting the Revolutionaries, Dowd, *A Spirited Resistance,* 47–64, gives an account of how the Revolution provided the opportunity for pro-British and nativist Indians to cooperate against a common enemy, frontier whites. See also Francis Jennings, "The Indians' Revolution," in Alfred F. Young, ed., *The American Revolution: Explorations in the History of American Radicalism* (DeKalb, Ill., 1976), 321–48. On the Indian enemies of backcountry Pennsylvanians, see Buck and Buck, *The Planting of Civilization,* 175–203. On Indian activities and the commencement of war on the frontier, see Downes, *Council Fires,* 179–211. It is also important to note, as Russel Lawrence Barsh finds in "Indian Loyalists and Patriots: Reflections on the American Revolution in Indian History," *Indian Historian* 10 (1977): 9–19, that, in contrast to the western Indians, Indians in the settled eastern seaboard area of the colonies tended to side with the Revolutionaries. With little military strength, diminishing numbers, and European Americans in uncontested control of the region, the decisions of these eastern Indians were not surprising.

16. RWPF, M804, files W3305 and S4573. Auditor General, Revolutionary War Pension File, 1809–93, Record Group 2, microfilm, Pennsylvania State Archives, Harrisburg, reel 155, frame 78; RWPF file W2124. On the link between a racialized view of Indians and anger over Indian deeds in military conflict, see Vaughan, "From White Man to Redskin," 939.

17. On migration to the Pennsylvania frontier, see David Hackett Fischer, *Albion's Seed: Four British Folkways in America* (New York, 1989), 633–39; R. Eugene Harper, *The Transformation of Western Pennsylvania, 1770–1800* (Pittsburgh, Pa., 1991), 17–57; Mark Haberlien, "German Migrants in Colonial Pennsylvania: Resources, Opportunities, and Experience," *WMQ,* 3rd ser., 50 (July 1993): 555–74; and Marianne S. Wokeck, "A Tide of Alien Tongues: The Flow and Ebb of German Immigration to Pennsylvania, 1683–1775" (Ph.D. diss., Temple University, 1983), 110, 245, 314–15. On the decline of cultural contact as the new farmers superseded earlier Indian traders, see Peter C. Mancall, *Valley of Opportunity: Economic Culture Along the Upper Susquehanna, 1700–1800* (Ithaca, N.Y., 1991), 69–93. For the movement of new settlers to the Pennsylvania backcountry from the settled regions of the colony following Pontiac's War, see Theodore Thayer, *Pennsylvania Politics and the Growth of Democracy, 1740–1776* (Harrisburg, Pa., 1953), 127. On how captivity narratives emphasized Indian misdeeds toward civilians, particularly women, see Annette Kolodny, *The Land Before Her: Fantasy and Experience of the American Frontiers, 1630–1860* (Chapel Hill, N.C., 1984), 28–34. For an example of the captivity narrative genre, see Mary Rowlandson, *The Narrative of the Captivity and Restoration of Mrs. Mary Rowlandson* (Boston, 1930). Rowlandson's tale was among the most popular and, significantly for the Revolutionary War generation, was republished twice in 1773. On the "Land Imperative" narrative of the mid-eighteenth century, see James Levernier and Hennig Cohen, eds., *The Indians and Their Captives* (Westport, Conn., 1977), xii.

18. On the continuity of Indian war aims to remove land-hungry settlers from the Trans-Allegheny West beginning in the Seven Years' War and Pontiac's War, see Stephen F. Auth, *The Ten Years' War: Indian-White Relations in Pennsylvania, 1755–1765* (New York, 1989); James Potter to Major General John Armstrong, May 7, 1778, PCC reel 83, vol. 1, item I, 69, 537; Petition of Northumberland County Inhabitants, PRG, reel 14, frame 304; David Espy to Edward Hand, February 27, 1778, Draper Manuscript Collection, microfilm, State Historical Society of Wisconsin, 2 U 5.

19. RWPF files S16378, W2078, S22651, W8075.

20. Archibald Lochry to Joseph Reed, July 4, 1781, PRG, reel 18, frame 547.

21. RWPF files S22586, R5815, R8633, S4164, S2064.

22. Edward Hand to Jasper Ewing, March 7, 1778, in Reuben Gold Thwaites and Louise

Phelps Kellogg, *Frontier Defense on the Upper Ohio, 1777–1778* (Madison, Wis., 1912), 215–16; "Recollections of Samuel Murphy," ibid., 219–20.

23. RWPF file R1638; John C. Dann, *The Revolution Remembered: Eyewitness Accounts of the War for Independence* (Chicago, 1980), 266–67.

24. Colonel John Gibson to Edward Hand, October 22, 1777, Thwaites and Kellogg, *Frontier Defense,* 142; Colonel Arthur Buchanan to John Carrothers, May 11, 1778, PRG, reel 13, frame 1335; *Pennsylvania Evening Post,* May 11, 1779; Thomas Galbraith to President Wharton, PCC, reel 83, vol., 1, item I, 69, 439.

25. James Axtell, "Scalping: The Ethnohistory of a Moral Question," in *The European and the Indian: Essays in the Ethnohistory of Colonial North America* (New York, 1981), 209.

26. On the vengeance function of scalping among frontier whites, see ibid., 229; Daniel Brodhead to General Washington, June 5, 1779, Samuel Hazard et al., eds., *PA,* ser. 1, vol. 12, 127; Brodhead to Washington, June 29, 1780, in *ibid.,* 243; *Pennsylvania Packet,* June 31, 1781; Baron Rosenthal ("John Rose"), *Journal of a Volunteer Expedition to Sandusky* (n.p., 1969), 142.

27. In practice, Indian warriors were far more likely than European Americans to take captives for adoption into their communities; see James Axtell, "The White Indians of Colonial America," in Stanley N. Katz and John Murrin, eds., *Colonial America: Essays in Politics and Social Development* (New York, 1983), 16–47. On the Indian tradition of killing prisoners of war, especially the wounded and the weak, who were not candidates for adoption, see Graymont, *The Iroquois in the American Revolution,* 232. Deposition of Captain Alexander Patterson, 12th Pennsylvania Regiment, July 6, 1778, PCC, reel 55, item I, 53, 59; RWPF file S4631.

28. Axtell, "White Indians," 16–47; Colonel Matthew Smith to Joseph Reed, June 26, 1780, PCC, reel 83, vol. 2, item I, 69, 252.

29. On the fabrication of atrocity stories from the Wyoming attack, see Boardman, *Against the Iroquois,* 15; *Pennsylvania Packet,* October 9, 1779; "Narrative of Dr. Knight," *PA,* ser. 2, 14:714–15; *Pennsylvania Packet,* July 27, 1782. On the motives of Indians in Crawford's torture, see C. Sipe Hale, *Fort Ligonier and Its Times* (n.p., 1971), 560.

30. Dann, *The Revolution Remembered,* 254; Robert J. Taylor, ed., *The Susquehannah Company Papers* (Ithaca, N.Y., 1969), 7:79; Petition of Sergeant Theobald Coontz, December 20, 1782, PRG, reel 19, frame 1282; RWPF files S22309, S12779, W8124, W25718.

31. RWPF files S22073, S7963, R7207, S12751, W24117, S23042, W5155, S22341, S7377. On the changing image of murderers in popular early American stories, see Karen Halttunnen, "Early American Murder Narratives: The Birth of Horror," in Richard Wrightman Fox and Jackson Lears, eds., *The Power of Culture: Critical Essays in American History* (Chicago, 1993), 67–101, quotation from 85.

32. RWPF files S23637, S4731, S12779, W5155; Paul A. W. Wallace, ed., *Thirty Thousand Miles with John Heckewelder* (Pittsburgh, 1958), 193. The omission of mention of the skin color of Indians is even more glaring among the soldiers quoted here. The pension applications were given in the 1820s and 1830s, a period in which, according to Alden Vaughan in "From White Man to Redskin," 918, red had become the "universally accepted color label" for Indians. Apparently the veterans preferred to continue to infer that Indians were nonwhite rather than any specific color of their own.

33. For more on the motivations and images of Pennsylvania frontier Tories, see Knouff, " 'An Arduous Service,' " 61–62, 68–69; James Dunlop to Jonathan Hoge, June 22, 1778, PRG, reel 14, frame 309; *Pennsylvania Packet,* May 6, 1778, and August 13, 1778.

34. RWPF files S22395, S23246, S6564, W4182.

35. The English experience in the conquest of Ireland in the sixteenth and seventeenth centuries

was a similar situation. Like frontier soldiers, the English forces came to see their opponents as a savage race, deserving of no quarter. The desolation of Ireland in the period was a direct outgrowth of the conquerors' racism as a rationalization for total war against the entire Irish people. See Nicholas P. Canny, "The Ideology of English Colonization: From Ireland to America," in Katz and Murrin, *Colonial America*, 47–68. *Pennsylvania Packet*, August 27, 1782; RWPF file R6231.

36. The quotation attributed to Brady is in Sipe, *Fort Ligonier and Its Times*, 468; Edward Hand to Jasper Yeates, October 2, 1777, in Thwaites and Kellogg, *Frontier Defense*, 119; Colonel John Gibson to General Edward Hand, August 1, 1777, in ibid., 35; Colonel Brodhead quoted in Downes, *Council Fires*, 250; Orders: July 29, 1779, Orderly Book of the Eighth Pennsylvania Regiment, Draper Manuscript Collection 2, ser. NN 108; William Irvine to George Washington, April 16, 1783, in C. W. Butterfield, ed., *Washington-Irvine Correspondence* (Madison, Wis., 1882), 149.

37. John Gibson to Edward Hand, August 1, 1777, Edward Hand Correspondence, 1777–85, Darlington Memorial Library, University of Pittsburgh; Edward Hand to the Delawares, September 17, 1777, Thwaites and Kellogg, *Frontier Defense*, 86; Daniel Brodhead to Joseph Reed, November 2, 1780, PRG, reel 16, frame 1273.

38. Wallace, *Thirty Thousand Miles*, 189–99; quotes on 195 and 197; Dann, *The Revolution Remembered*, 256.

39. Vaughan, "Frontier Banditti," 4–5.

40. RWPF files S22757, W8300, S23621.

41. On the generally higher social status of officers than their men, see Royster, *A Revolutionary People at War*, 86–89. On the nationalist outlook of Pennsylvania officers, especially those who had served out of state at some point, see William A. Benton, "Pennsylvania Revolutionary Officers and the Federal Constitution," *Pennsylvania History* 31 (1964): 419–35.

42. George Morgan to Governor Hamilton, May 31, 1776, Ferdinand J. Dreer Autograph Collection, Soldiers of the Revolution, HSP; Edward Hand to Jasper Yeates, July 12, 1777, in Thwaites and Kellogg, *Frontier Defense*, 19. Colonel Brodhead to President Reed, May 13, 1780, PRG, reel 16, frame 122; Journal of Reverend William Rogers, *PA*, ser. 2, 15:265–66; Daniel Brodhead to Anthony Wayne, October 19, 1778, Anthony Wayne Papers 5:22, HSP.

43. Daniel Brodhead to Captain Samuel Morehead, May 8, 1779, Order Book of Daniel Brodhead, Darlington Memorial Library, University of Pittsburgh; Brodhead to Lieutenant Nielly, April 30, 1779, ibid.; Daniel Brodhead to Nathanael Greene, September 6, 1780, Woods Collection of Western Pennsylvania Documents, Historical Society of Western Pennsylvania. Intelligence from James Deane enclosed in General Sullivan to [Edward Hand?], May 31, 1779, Hand Papers, 1:85, HSP. Journal of the Reverend William Rogers, 278; Michael Huffnagle to President Moore, July [?], 1782, PRG, reel 19, frame 930. On the formulation by European Americans of racial difference based on complexion and other perceived biological factors, see Winthrop Jordan, *White over Black: American Attitudes Toward the Negro, 1550–1812* (New York, 1977), 216–65. On the late eighteenth-century North American tendency to define Indians and African Americans in terms of "physical characteristics," see Audrey Smedley, *Race in North America*, 178–79. Alden Vaughan points out in "From White Man to Redskin," 921, that the perception of Indians as "red" was not as prevalent even among eighteenth-century elites as it would be in the following century. Vaughan finds other early American descriptions of Indians as "olive," "tawny," "yellow," and "brown." All these characterizations of Indian skin color were consistent with Revolutionary officers' perceptions.

44. Daniel Brodhead to Timothy Pickering, November 3, 1779, *PA*, ser. 1, 12:179–80; William Irvine to George Washington, April 20, 1782, *Washington-Irvine Correspondence*, 99–106.

45. Daniel Brodhead to Major Nesnon[?], April 28, 1779, Order Book of Daniel Brodhead, manuscript, Darlington Memorial Library, University of Pittsburgh.

46. Nicholas Fish to Richard Varick, May 21, 1779, Feinstone Collection, David Library of the American Revolution, Washington Crossing, Pennsylvania, item 1870; Officers' toast on Sullivan's expedition quoted in James H. Merrell, "Declarations of Independence: Indian-White Relations in the New Nation," in Jack P. Greene, ed., *The American Revolution: Its Character and Limits* (New York, 1987), 198.

47. On the continuation of war in the "old Northwest" after the cessation of hostilities against the British, see Downes, *Council Fires,* 284–310; RWPF file W8124.

Afterword

1. Although this volume discusses the Revolution in both the general hinterland of Pennsylvania and its frontier, or backcountry (Cumberland County and the Juniata and Wyoming Valleys), insights from the burgeoning field of backcountry history raise questions relevant for much of the state.

2. Robert D. Mitchell, *Commercialism and Frontier: Perspectives on the Early Shenandoah Valley* (Charlottesville: University Press of Virginia, 1977); Robert D. Mitchell, ed., *Appalachian Frontiers: Settlement, Society, and Development in the Preindustrial Era* (Lexington: University Press of Kentucky, 1991).

3. See, for example, Stephen Aron, *How the West Was Lost: The Transformation of Kentucky from Daniel Boone to Henry Clay* (Baltimore: Johns Hopkins University Press, 1996); Alan Taylor, *William Cooper's Town: Power and Persuasion on the Frontier of the Early American Republic* (New York: Knopf, 1995); Michael Puglisi, ed., *Diversity and Accommodation: Essays on the Cultural Composition of the Virginia Frontier* (Knoxville: University of Tennessee Press, 1997); Warren R. Hofstra, ed., *George Washington and the Virginia Backcountry* (Charlottesville: University of Virginia Press, 1997); Kenneth E. Koons and Warren R. Hofstra, eds., "After the Backcountry: Rural Life and Society in the Nineteenth-Century Valley of Virginia," proceedings of a conference held at the Virginia Military Institute, March 1995, publication forthcoming.

4. James T. Lemon, *The Best Poor Man's Country: A Geographical Study of Early Southeastern Pennsylvania* (Baltimore: Johns Hopkins University Press, 1972); Stephanie Grauman Wolf, *Urban Village: Population, Community, and Family Structure in Germantown, Pennsylvania, 1683–1800* (Princeton: Princeton University Press, 1976).

5. See, for example, Darrett B. Rutman, *Winthrop's Boston: Portrait of a Puritan Town, 1630–1649* (Chapel Hill: University of North Carolina Press, 1965); Edward Byers, *The Nation of Nantucket: Society and Politics in an Early American Commercial Center, 1660–1820* (Boston: Northeastern University Press, 1987); Christine Leigh Heyrman, *Commerce and Culture: The Maritime Communities of Colonial Massachusetts, 1690–1750* (New York: W. W. Norton, 1984).

6. The debate over whether early American society was capitalist or precapitalist seems endless. For extensive bibliographical references and a different interpretation, see Michael Merrill, "Putting 'Capitalism' in Its Place: A Review of Recent Literature," *WMQ,* 3rd ser., 52 (1995): 315–26.

7. For a succinct summary, see Stuart Bruchey, "Social and Economic Developments After the Revolution," in Jack P. Greene and J. R. Pole, eds., *The Blackwell Encyclopedia of the American Revolution* (Cambridge: Blackwell, 1991), 555–68.

8. Jack Marietta, *The Reformation of American Quakerism, 1748–1783* (Philadelphia: University of Pennsylvania Press, 1984).

9. A. G. Roeber, *Palatines, Liberty, and Property: German Lutherans in British Colonial America* (Baltimore: Johns Hopkins University Press, 1993), esp. 329. For a parallel situation, see Klaus Wust, *The Virginia Germans* (Charlottesville: University Press of Virginia, 1969), chaps. 5, 6, 8, 10.

10. Maurice Bric, "Ireland, Irishmen, and the Broadening of the Late-Eighteenth Century Philadelphia Polity" (Ph.D. diss., Johns Hopkins University, 1991).

11. See especially John Monroe, *Federalist Delaware, 1775–1815* (New Brunswick, N.J.: Rutgers University Press, 1954); Ronald Hoffman, *A Spirit of Dissension: Economics, Politics, and the Revolution in Maryland* (Baltimore: Johns Hopkins University Press, 1973); Edward Countryman, *A People in Revolution: The American Revolution and Political Society in New York, 1760–1790* (Baltimore: Johns Hopkins University Press, 1981), 120–50. See also appropriate sections in works by Calhoon in note 12 below.

12. See sections on these states in Robert M. Calhoon, *The Loyalists in Revolutionary America, 1763–1783* (New York: Harcourt, Brace, Jovanovich, 1973); idem, *The Loyalist Perception and Other Essays* (Columbia: University of South Carolina Press, 1988); and William Pencak and Ralph J. Crandall, "Metropolitan Boston Before the American Revolution: An Urban Interpretation of the Imperial Crisis," *Bostonian Society Proceedings* (1977–85), 51–77.

13. James S. Leamon, *Revolution Downeast: The War for American Independence in Maine* (Amherst: University of Massachusetts Press, 1993).

14. Michael Bellisles, *Revolutionary Outlaws: Ethan Allan and the Struggle for Independence on the Early American Frontier* (Charlottesville: University Press of Virginia, 1993).

15. A. Roger Ekirch, *"Poor Carolina": Politics and Society in Colonial North Carolina* (Chapel Hill: University of North Carolina Press, 1981), chaps. 6 and 7; James P. Whittenburg, "Planters, Merchants, and Lawyers: Social Change and the Origins of the North Carolina Regulation," *WMQ*, 3rd ser., 34 (1977): 215–38; Albert H. Tillotson Jr., "The Southern Backcountry: A Survey of Current Research," *Virginia Magazine of History and Biography* 98 (1990): 387–422.

16. Tillotson, "Southern Backcountry"; Rachel N. Klein, *Unification of a Slave State: The Rise of the Planter Class in the South Carolina Backcountry, 1760–1808* (Chapel Hill: University of North Carolina Press, 1990); Rhys Isaac, *The Transformation of Virginia, 1740–1790* (Chapel Hill: University of North Carolina Press, 1982).

17. Edward Countryman, *A People in Revolution: The American Revolution in New York, 1760–1790* (Baltimore: Johns Hopkins University Press, 1981); Isabel Thompson Kelsay, *Joseph Brant, 1743–1807: Man of Two Worlds* (Syracuse, N.Y.: Syracuse University Press, 1984), 272; Harley L. Gibb, "Colonel Guy Johnson, Superintendent General of Indian Affairs, 1774–1782," *Papers of the Michigan Academy of Science, Arts, and Letters* 27 (1941): 595–613.

18. Anne M. Ousterhout, "Frontier Vengeance: Yankees vs. Pennamites in the Wyoming Valley," *Pennsylvania History* 62 (1995): 330–63.

19. John S. Pancake, *This Destructive War: The British Campaign in the Carolinas, 1780–1782* (Tuscaloosa: University of Alabama Press, 1982).

20. Mustafa Emirbayer and Jeff Goodwin, "Network Analysis, Culture, and the Problem of Agency," *American Journal of Sociology* 99 (1984): 1411–54; Jeff Goodwin, "Toward a New Sociology of Revolutions," *Theory and Society* 23 (1994): 731–66.

Contributors

TIM H. BLESSING (Ph.D., Penn State University) is Professor and Chairman of the Social Science Department at Alvernia College in Reading, Pennsylvania.

ROBERT G. CRIST (1924–1995) (Ph.D., Penn State University) was former President of the Pennsylvania Historical Association and Instructor in History at the York and Harrisburg Campuses of Penn State University.

PAUL E. DOUTRICH (Ph.D., University of Kentucky) is Associate Professor of History at York College of Pennsylvania.

JOHN B. FRANTZ (Ph.D., University of Pennsylvania) is Associate Professor of History at Penn State University and former President of the Pennsylvania Historical Association.

KAREN GUENTHER (Ph.D., University of Houston) is Assistant Professor of History at Mansfield State University, Mansfield, Pennsylvania.

OWEN S. IRELAND (Ph.D., University of Pittsburgh) is Professor of History at the State University of New York at Brockport.

GREGORY T. KNOUFF (Ph.D., Rutgers University) is Assistant Professor of History at Keene State College, Keene, New Hampshire.

WILLIAM PENCAK (Ph.D., Columbia University) is Professor of History at Penn State University and the editor of *Pennsylvania History*.

EUGENE R. SLASKI (Ph.D., Florida State University) is Campus Executive Officer, Academic Officer, and Associate Professor of History at the Berks–Lehigh Valley College Campus of Penn State University.

FREDERICK J. STEFON (D.Ed., Penn State University) is Assistant Professor of History at the Wilkes-Barre Campus in the Commonwealth College of Penn State University.

ROSEMARY S. WARDEN (Ph.D., Syracuse University) is Instructor in History at Abington College of Penn State University.

Index